Gender and Politics

Series Editors
Johanna Kantola
University of Tampere
Tampere, Finland

Sarah Childs
Birkbeck, University of London
London, UK

The Gender and Politics series celebrated its 7th anniversary at the 5th European Conference on Politics and Gender (ECPG) in June 2017 in Lausanne, Switzerland having published more than 35 volumes to date. The original idea for the book series was envisioned by the series editors Johanna Kantola and Judith Squires at the first ECPG in Belfast in 2009, and the series was officially launched at the Conference in Budapest in 2011. In 2014, Sarah Childs became the co-editor of the series, together with Johanna Kantola. Gender and Politics showcases the very best international writing. It publishes world class monographs and edited collections from scholars - junior and well established - working in politics, international relations and public policy, with specific reference to questions of gender. The titles that have come out over the past years make key contributions to debates on intersectionality and diversity, gender equality, social movements, Europeanization and institutionalism, governance and norms, policies, and political institutions. Set in European, US and Latin American contexts, these books provide rich new empirical findings and push forward boundaries of feminist and politics conceptual and theoretical research. The editors welcome the highest quality international research on these topics and beyond, and look for proposals on feminist political theory; on recent political transformations such as the economic crisis or the rise of the populist right; as well as proposals on continuing feminist dilemmas around participation and representation, specific gendered policy fields, and policy making mechanisms. The series can also include books published as a Palgrave pivot.

More information about this series at
http://www.palgrave.com/gp/series/14998

Hanane Darhour · Drude Dahlerup
Editors

Double-Edged Politics on Women's Rights in the MENA Region

Editors
Hanane Darhour
Faculty of Languages, Arts
and Human Sciences
Ibn Zohr University
Ait Melloul, Morocco

Drude Dahlerup
Department of Political Science
Stockholm University
Stockholm, Sweden

ISE
Roskilde University
Roskilde, Denmark

ISSN 2662-5814 ISSN 2662-5822 (electronic)
Gender and Politics
ISBN 978-3-030-27734-5 ISBN 978-3-030-27735-2 (eBook)
https://doi.org/10.1007/978-3-030-27735-2

© The Editor(s) (if applicable) and The Author(s), under exclusive license to Springer Nature Switzerland AG 2020
This work is subject to copyright. All rights are solely and exclusively licensed by the Publisher, whether the whole or part of the material is concerned, specifically the rights of translation, reprinting, reuse of illustrations, recitation, broadcasting, reproduction on microfilms or in any other physical way, and transmission or information storage and retrieval, electronic adaptation, computer software, or by similar or dissimilar methodology now known or hereafter developed.
The use of general descriptive names, registered names, trademarks, service marks, etc. in this publication does not imply, even in the absence of a specific statement, that such names are exempt from the relevant protective laws and regulations and therefore free for general use.
The publisher, the authors and the editors are safe to assume that the advice and information in this book are believed to be true and accurate at the date of publication. Neither the publisher nor the authors or the editors give a warranty, expressed or implied, with respect to the material contained herein or for any errors or omissions that may have been made. The publisher remains neutral with regard to jurisdictional claims in published maps and institutional affiliations.

Cover credit: dancingfishes/Getty Images

This Palgrave Macmillan imprint is published by the registered company Springer Nature Switzerland AG
The registered company address is: Gewerbestrasse 11, 6330 Cham, Switzerland

Preface

The Post-Arab Spring has become an age of uncertainty for women's rights. The Uprising opened a window of new opportunities for women in public life in the MENA region, yet, it also increased the risks of reactions against women's rights. It is a time of empowering *and* sidelining of women in the region. This book includes chapters on individual countries and chapters that compare several MENA countries. We explore how recent mobilizations and regime changes in the region have altered the opportunity structures and allowed for an increase in women's activism and women's political representation, partly through the adoption of gender quotas, but at the same time remained resistant to change with respect to several pernicious forms of discrimination as well as prejudices against women in public and private life.

The contribution to the book is based on a selection of papers presented at the International Conference on Gender and Politics (ICGP), "Women in Politics in an Age of Uncertainty: The Road to Sustainable Democracy and Democratization," which was co-convened by Hanane Darhour and Aili Mari Tripp and organized by the Polydisciplinary Faculty of Ouarzazate, Ibn Zohr University, in collaboration with Wisconsin-Madison University in November 2017.

The book is written by experienced scholars in the field, but it also includes several younger scholars. It presents new research, theoretically framed and based on empirical investigations, including new survey data and data on changes in states' support of women's rights and women's political activism and representation in the MENA countries.

It is relevant to graduate and postgraduate students, researchers and development professionals with an interest in sociology, political science, and gender studies more broadly. We hope it will also be of interest to a broader audience, who takes an interest in the development of women's rights in transition periods in the MENA region and beyond.

This edited volume does not present one unified position on these historical changes. Optimistic as well as more pessimistic views for the future are represented; however, all gathered under the position that this is a period of uncertainty for women in the MENA region, and that the support by part of the ruling elites to women's rights is ambiguous and double-edged.

Finally, this work would not have been possible without the academic collaboration and unconditional support of Professor Aili Mari TRIPP from the University of Wisconsin Madison during the organization process of the 2017 ICGP conference and after. We also want to pay tribute to all the contributing authors for their time, expertise and dedicated work during the preparation for this collected volume. Thanks are also due to Annette Bruun Andersen, who offered professional help with the formatting of the manuscript. We trust that our readers will find the contents of this book both interesting and useful for their future studies of the region.

Ouarzazate, Agadir, Morocco   Hanane Darhour
Stockholm, Sweden; Copenhagen, Denmark   Drude Dahlerup
June 2019

Contents

1 Introduction: The Arab Uprisings and the Rights of Women 1
Drude Dahlerup and Hanane Darhour

Part I Women's Rights, Feminism and Islamism

2 The Center: A Theoretical Framework for Understanding Women's Rights in Pre- and Post-Arab Spring North Africa 49
Fatima Sadiqi

3 Whose Gender Equality? On the Boundaries of Islam and Feminism in the MENA Region 71
Ilyass Bouzghaia

Part II Post-Spring Dynamics and Feminist Norm Diffusion

4 Cultural Change in North Africa: The Interaction Effect of Women's Empowerment and Democratization 97
Ginger Feather

5 Changing Tides? On How Popular Support
   for Feminism Increased After the Arab Spring   131
   Saskia Glas and Niels Spierings

Part III Women's Activism and the Reconfigured State

6 Women's Activism in North Africa: A Historical
   and Socio-Political Approach   157
   Moha Ennaji

7 Political Opportunities for Islamist Women
   in Morocco and Egypt: Structure or Agency?   179
   Anwar Mhajne

8 Contrasting Women's Rights in the Maghreb
   and the Middle East Constitutions   205
   Aili Mari Tripp

Part IV Empowered or Sidelined? On Women's
         Political Representation and Influence

9 Examining Female Membership and Leadership
   of Legislative Committees in Jordan   231
   Marwa Shalaby and Laila Elimam

10 Empowering Young Women? Gender
   and Youth Quotas in Tunisia   257
   Jana Belschner

11 Whose Empowerment? Gender Quota Reform
   Mechanisms and De-democratization in Morocco   279
   Hanane Darhour

Index   303

Notes on Contributors

Jana Belschner is a Ph.D. candidate at the Department of Comparative Politics at the University of Bergen, Norway. Her research interests cover the fields of gender and diversity in politics, the institutional dynamics of democratization processes, and political parties in European and North African countries. Her Ph.D. project explores the adoption and implementation of gender and youth quotas by focusing on the impact of quota regulations on political parties' recruitment and nomination practices. e-mail: jana.belschner@uib.no

Ilyass Bouzghaia is a Researcher at the Center for Women's Studies in Islam, affiliated to the Rabita Mohammadia of Ulema (www.annisae.ma). He is a Doctoral Researcher at Sidi Mohamed ben Abdellah University, Fes, Morocco. He holds a degree from the Women's and Gender Studies Master Program (2011), and he has published his M.A. thesis titled *The Feminist Movement and Social Change in Morocco: Trends and Impacts*. His research focuses on women's rights, gender studies, feminism, Islamic feminism, decolonial studies, social values, and transformation. He has written several articles in English and Arabic and has participated at many national and international events. e-mail: ilyass-academics@hotmail.com

Drude Dahlerup is Professor of Political Science at Stockholm University, Sweden, and Honorary Professor at Roskilde University, Denmark. Her research focuses on gender and politics, gender quota systems, the history of women's movements, and theories of feminism. She has worked as a global advisor for the UN, the Inter-Parliamentary

Union, and other international organizations on how to empower women in politics, including by introducing electoral gender quotas. Her most recent publications in English include: *Has Democracy Failed Women?* (2018); a special section of the journal *Teorija et Practice* on "The Legitimacy and Effectiveness of Gender Quotas in Politics in Central East Europe" (co-edited with Milica Antic Gaber, 2/2017); *Breaking Male Dominance in Old Democracies* (co-edited with Monique Leyenaar, 2013); *Women, Quotas and Politics* (2006). She has written on women in politics in the Arab region in *Al-Raida* (issue 126–127, Summer/Fall 2009) and in *Women's Studies International Forum* (with Hanane Darhour, vol. 43 (2), 2013). e-mail: drude.dahlerup@statsvet.su.se

Hanane Darhour is Associate Professor in the Faculty of Languages, Arts and Human Sciences of Ait Melloul at Ibn Zohr University, Agadir, Morocco. She has published on gender and politics, gender quotas, and political empowerment of women. She is a co-leader of the 2019 APSA MENA workshops in Abu Dhabi (June 2019) and Rabat (October 2019). In October 2017, she co-organized the International Conference on Gender and Politics on the theme of "Women and Politics in Age of Uncertainty: The Road to Sustainable Democracy and Democratization." She authored an article on "Islamic Women's Political Activism: A Bulwark Against Islamist" in a volume edited by Fatima Sadiqi et al. She co-authored an article entitled "Sustainable representation of women through gender quotas: A decades experience in Morocco" in *Women's Studies International Forum*, and published the book *Implementation of Electoral Gender Quotas: Evidence from the 2002 Moroccan Elections* in 2012. She participated in many international projects, most recently in 2013 when she served as a consultant and Morocco national researcher with the London School of Economics and Political Science. e-mail: h.darhour@uiz.ac.ma

Laila Elimam is a Political Science Researcher. She was previously a Research Associate at the Women's Rights in the Middle East program at Rice University's Baker Institute for Public Policy, Houston, TX, USA. Her research areas are authoritarian politics and legislatures in non-democracies. Her work has appeared in the *Journal of Comparative Politics, Carnegie Sada and Rice University's Baker Institute for Public Policy*. She holds a master's degree in Public Policy from the University of California, Los Angeles. e-mail: lailaelimam@gmail.com

Moha Ennaji is Professor of Social and Cultural Studies. In addition to his academic career at the University of Fes, Morocco, he is the founding president of the International Institute for Languages and Cultures, and a founding member of the South North Center for Intercultural Dialogue and Migration Studies. He previously held Visiting Professor positions at Rutgers University (2006–2009), at the University of Pennsylvania (2003), and the University of Arizona (1990). His research areas cover migration, language, gender, and ethnicity in North Africa. His most recent publications include: *New Horizons of Muslim Diaspora in North America and Europe* (2016); *Minorities, Women, and the State in North Africa* (2015); *Moroccan Feminisms: New Perspectives* (with Fatima Sadiqi and Karen Vitges, 2016); *Muslim Moroccan Migrants in Europe* (2014); and *Multiculturalism and Democracy in North Africa* (2014). e-mail: mennaji2002@yahoo.fr

Ginger Feather has a Ph.D. in Political Science and master's degree in Arabic/Islamic Studies from the University of Kansas and a master's degree in International Affairs from George Washington University, USA. Her primary research focuses on the impact of discriminatory legal codes on violence against women in Morocco and Tunisia. She further conducts cross-sectional time-series analysis across the 49 Muslim-majority countries analyzing the interaction of women's empowerment and democratization, good governance, and reduced corruption. She has presented her research in the USA, UK, Sweden, Germany, Canada, Lebanon, and Morocco and has published in the *Journal of Women and Human Rights in the Middle East*, the *Journal of Applied Language and Cultural Studies*, the *Journal of North African Studies*, and the *Review of Middle East Studies* as well as several edited volumes. Her first book project entitled *Torn Between Bad Choices: Moroccan and Tunisian Women's Battle Against Discrimination and Violence* takes an intersectional approach to analyze the impact of legal discrimination on women who fall outside the traditional marital framework, specifically single mothers, divorcees, widows, and prostitutes—often conflated—and their children. e-mail: grfeather@issuespace.org

Saskia Glas, M.A., M.Sc. is a Ph.D. candidate in Sociology at Radboud Social and Cultural Research, Radboud University, the Netherlands. The Ph.D. project is funded by the NWO. Her main research interests include (attitudes regarding) women's equality, (attitudes regarding) politics, and religiosity, in particular in the Arab Middle East and North Africa. e-mail: s.glas@ru.nl

Anwar Mhajne is a Postdoctoral Teaching Fellow at Stonehill College, Massachusetts, USA. She is a political scientist specializing in international relations and comparative politics with a focus on gender and politics. Her current research lies at the intersection of gender, religion, and Middle Eastern politics with a focus on how Islamic beliefs and institutions in the Middle East structure Muslim women's political understandings, agencies, and opportunities at local, national, and international levels. Due to her political science and interdisciplinary training in gender politics, international relations, and comparative politics, her research strengths lie in the following areas: feminist international relations and security studies; democratization; governance and institutions; civil society and activism; political Islam; Middle East; gender politics; social movements; and regime change. Her work has been featured in *The International Feminist Journal of Politics, Political Research Quarterly, The Conversation, Times of Israel, Haaretz, Middle East Eye, +972 Magazine, Quartz,* and *Carnegie Endowment for International Peace*. e-mail: anwar.mhajne@gmail.com

Fatima Sadiqi is Professor of Linguistics and Gender Studies at the University of Fes, Morocco. Her work focuses on women's issues in modern North Africa, the Middle East, and the Mediterranean world. In June 2018, she was elected President of the Association for Middle East Women's Studies—AMEWS, the first non-American to be elected to this post. In 2017, she was invited to serve on the Editorial Board of the *Oxford Encyclopedia of African Women's History*. Sadiqi is author and editor of numerous volumes and journal issues, including *Women, Gender and Language* (2003), "Women's Activism and the Public Sphere: Local/Global Linkages" (*Journal of Middle East Women's Studies*, 2006), *Women and Knowledge in the Mediterranean* (2013), *Moroccan Feminist Discourses* (2014), and *Women's Movements in the Post-"Arab Spring" North Africa* (2016). Her work has been supported by numerous prestigious awards and fellowships from Harvard University, the Woodrow Wilson Center, the Rockefeller Foundation's Bellagio Center, and Fulbright. e-mail: sadiqi_fatima@yahoo.fr

Marwa Shalaby is Anna Julia Cooper Fellow and Assistant Professor of Political Science and Gender and Women's Studies at the University of Wisconsin, Madison, USA. Her research areas are comparative politics, democratization, and research methodology. Her work focuses primarily on the intersection of the politics of authoritarianism and women in politics. Her work has appeared in *the Journal of Comparative Politics, Political Research Quarterly, Parliamentary Affairs*, and *the Middle East Journal*. She has co-authored an edited volume, *The Evolving Role of Women after the Arab Spring* (with Valentine Moghadam, 2016). e-mail: marwa.shalaby97@gmail.com

Niels Spierings is Assistant Professor in Sociology at Radboud Social and Cultural Research, Radboud University, the Netherlands. Among his main research interests are women's societal and economic position, religion, migration, and political behavior and sociopolitical attitudes. Two of his current projects are funded by the NWO and focus on Islam and social attitudes in the Middle East and North Africa. e-mail: n.spierings@ru.nl

Aili Mari Tripp is Wangari Maathai Professor of Political Science and Gender and Women's Studies at the University of Wisconsin-Madison, USA. Her research has focused in recent years on women and politics in Africa, the gendered nature of peacebuilding, women's movements in Africa, and transnational feminism. Her current research involves a comparative study of women and legal reform in North Africa. She has a forthcoming book on *Seeking Legitimacy: Why Arab Autocracies Adopt Women's Rights*. She is author of several award-winning books, including *Women and Power in Postconflict Africa* (2015), *Museveni's Uganda: Paradoxes of Power in a Hybrid Regime* (2010), *African Women's Movements: Transforming Political Landscapes* (with Isabel Casimiro, Joy Kwesiga, and Alice Mungwa, 2009), and *Women and Politics in Uganda* (2000). She has also co-edited *Women's Activism in Africa* (with Balghis Badri, 2017), *Gender, Violence, and Human Security: Critical Feminist Perspectives* (with Myra Marx Ferree and Christina Ewig, 2013), *Global Feminism: Transnational Women's Activism, Organizing, and Human Rights* (with Myra Marx Ferree, 2006), and *The Women's Movement in Uganda: History, Challenges and Prospects* (with Joy Kwesiga, 2002) in addition to publishing numerous other books, articles, and publications. e-mail: atripp@wisc.edu

List of Figures

Fig. 1.1	Level of Democracy and women's parliamentary representation worldwide, in percent	6
Fig. 1.2	Women elected to parliaments worldwide and regional averages, 1995 and 2019	25
Fig. 4.1	Income tax rate across North Africa	119
Fig. 5.1	Trends in support for feminism in countries with steeper increases after the Arab Spring	142
Fig. 5.2	Trends in support for feminism in countries without steeper increases after the Arab Spring	143
Fig. 9.1	Percent female committee leadership positions compared to total leadership (average across terms)	246
Fig. 10.1	The interrelation between electoral quotas and democratization	261
Fig. 10.2	Shares of gender and age groups of Tunisian elected MPs, 2011 and 2014 elections (%)	267
Fig. 10.3	Number of MPs after gender and age group in the PRA (2014)	268

List of Tables

Table 1.1	Level of democracy by region in 2017	5
Table 1.2	MENA countries ratifications and reservations to the CEDAW	15
Table 1.3	National women's machineries in the Arab world (selected countries)	18
Table 1.4	Post-spring national gender equality strategies	19
Table 1.5	Major legal reforms in the Maghreb and Egypt	23
Table 1.6	Three selected regions. Women in parliament (%)	25
Table 1.7	Six dimensions of male dominance in politics	30
Table 1.8	Women's representation and national quota systems in the MENA region	34
Table 4.1	Cultural change toward women's personal-legal empowerment (i.e., rejecting domestic violence) cross-sectional, time-series, by gender, and generation	110
Table 4.2	Cultural change toward women's social empowerment (i.e., rejecting a man's greater right to a university education) cross-sectional, time-series, by gender, and by generation	112
Table 4.3	Cultural change toward women's economic empowerment (i.e., agreeing men have a greater right to employment) cross-sectional, time-series, by gender, and by generation	115
Table 4.4	Cultural change toward women's political empowerment (i.e., agreeing men make better political leaders) cross-sectional, time-series, by gender, and by generation	117

xviii   LIST OF TABLES

Table 4.5	Cultural change toward social democracy (i.e., "agreeing" that a government's ability to tax the rich and subsidize the poor is an essential element of a democracy) cross-sectional, time-series, by gender, and by generation	120
Table 5.1	Items on feminism and religiosity	140
Table 5.2	Per-country trends in support for feminism after Arab Spring	144
Table 5.3	Overview of clusters of feminism results	145
Table 5.4	Overview of clusters of Muslim and secularist feminism results	148
Table 8.1	Unified courts and laws in MENA Region, 2018	211
Table 8.2	Convergence of gender-related provisions in Maghreb constitutions	213
Table 8.3	Constitutional provisions regarding women's rights (Maghreb countries highlighted)	214
Table 8.4	Gender equality provisions in Tunisia's 2014 constitution	220
Table 8.5	Gender equality provisions in Morocco's 2011 constitution	222
Table 8.6	Gender equality provisions in Algeria's 2016 constitution	224
Table 9.1	Female representation in Jordan (2003–2018)	239
Table 9.2	Women in committees in Jordan (2003–2018)	243
Table 9.3	Female committee memberships in Jordan House of Representatives (2003–2018)	244
Table 9.4	Summary of female committee leadership positions in Jordan's House of Representatives	245
Table 10.1	Conditional probabilities for positioning on electoral lists after MPs' gender and age	269
Table 10.2	Electoral lists of Nidâa Tounès and Ennahdha in the districts of Jendouba and Sfax 2 with placement, gender and age of candidates in 2014 elections	269
Table 10.3	Median participation rates (in %) and median number of committee memberships of Tunisian MPs after gender and age groups	272
Table 10.4	Distribution of committee presidencies and vice-presidencies after gender and age groups	272
Table 11.1	Women's representation in *Maijliss-annouwab* (1997–2016)	285
Table 11.2	Women elected to the parliament via NLs and DLs across parties, 2016	286
Table 11.3	Gender quota design and reform mechanisms (2002–2016)	289
Table 11.4	Women elected and re-elected to district seats (2002–2016)	294

CHAPTER 1

Introduction: The Arab Uprisings and the Rights of Women

Drude Dahlerup and Hanane Darhour

Gender equality and women's empowerment are broadly addressed as core democratic and development concerns. Research on how democracy intersects with gender equality has centered around three theories. The first prominent position is that democratic states tend to strengthen gender equality through increasing civic space for women's activism and expanding women's engagement in the political process through voting (Paxton 1997; Beer 2009). The second view, however, reverses the link, regarding gender equality as a driver of democratization through increased economic and political empowerment (Balaev 2014). The third explanation posits that the most important explanatory factor of

---

Authors have contributed equally to this introduction.

D. Dahlerup (✉)
Stockholm University, Stockholm, Sweden

Institute of Social Sciences and Business, Roskilde University, Roskilde, Denmark

H. Darhour
Faculty of Languages, Arts and Human Sciences, Ibn Zohr University, Ait Melloul, Morocco

© The Author(s) 2020
H. Darhour and D. Dahlerup (eds.), *Double-Edged Politics on Women's Rights in the MENA Region*, Gender and Politics, https://doi.org/10.1007/978-3-030-27735-2_1

the relationship is modernization, which in turn drives cultural change toward progressive liberal values, including democracy and gender equality (Inglehart et al. 2002).

The path-breaking events in the MENA region often named the Arab Spring or, less expectant, the Arab Uprisings created openings for women's agency and raised great expectations, which, however, in many cases were not followed by substantive changes. The post-spring period has been a time of empowering and, at the same time, sidelining of women. Many patriarchal structures have remained intact or reemerged in new forms; yet, many traditional norms have changed. The Middle East and North Africa is still the least free region of the world, and instability continues to threaten possibilities for democratization in many of its countries and uncertainty looms especially on the future of women's rights. However, seeing so many women in protests and demonstrations, raised in Marwa Shalaby's words "the hopes that Arab women were finally breaking their silence, defying the status quo and fighting for their own rights" (Shalaby and Moghadam 2016: 1). Yet, the question remains how women in this predominantly Muslim region can gain greater control, through their mobilization and contestation, over the circumstances that influence their lives and contribute to processes of democratization

THE AIM OF THE BOOK

The purpose of this book is to analyze changes in women's position in public life, including the changing discourses on gender in the periods just before, during and after the uprisings. It presents new research, theoretically framed and based on empirical investigations, including analyses of development of women's activism, women's political representation and position in political life in the MENA countries. The analyses of the discursive development focus especially on secular and Islamic feminism, and changes in popular opinions on women's position in society. The book includes chapters on individual countries, and chapters, which compare several MENA countries. The focus is North Africa and the Middle East (the MENA region), but some chapters widen the perspective to encompass all Arab countries.

The book considers frequently less studied issues, including how the recent mobilizations and regime changes in MENA countries have altered the opportunity structures and allowed for an increase in women's political representation and activism, partly through the adoption of gender quotas, but at the same time remained resistant to change with respect to several pernicious forms of discrimination against women in public and private life. Addressing the lacuna in the literature on this issue, this book opens new avenues of thought and research on the status of women's rights in the MENA region with a special focus on the mobilization and contestation aspects around the *political arena* that followed the Arab Spring Uprisings. This edited volume does not present one unified position on these historical changes. Optimistic as well as more pessimistic views for the future are represented; however, all gathered under the position that this is a period of *uncertainty* for women in the MENA region, and that the support by part of the ruling elites toward women's rights and empowerment of women is ambiguous and double-edged.

This introduction will present and discuss some of the key issues of this book around recent development in the MENA region. It offers an overview over women's position in the public sphere in the MENA region seen in a global perspective as well as over recent law reforms and national machineries for women/gender equality. The significant issue of the relation between feminism and Islam, a subject of several chapters of the book, will be introduced. At the end of this introduction, the reader will find a summary of the individual chapters of the book.

DEMOCRATIZATION IN THE MENA REGION

The link between the inclusion of women and processes of democratization is of special importance to the MENA region. Caldwell (1982) has identified the region as part of the "patriarchal belt" and Kandiyoti (1988) named it as the world of "classic patriarchy". Sharabi (1988) rather talked about MENA "neopatriarchy" which referred to the entrenched traditional hierarchical relations in a modernizing context. In 2002, the Arab Human Development Report drew a gloomy picture of a region lagging behind the rest of the world because of major deficits in freedom, women's empowerment and education, and called for the inclusions of women in all spheres of life.

When the UN Arab Human Development Report from 2002 stated, that the three deficits of "freedom, empowerment of women, and knowledge" represent the key challenge to the development in the Arab region, it was the first time that women's widespread illiteracy, lack of bodily freedom and exclusion from public life were described so distinctively in a UN report as one of the main disabling factors to the development process: "Society as a whole suffers when half of its productive potential is stifled. These deficits must be addressed in every field: economic, political, and social" (UNDP 2002: 4–5). Ironically, this knowledge of the crucial importance of including women as active partners in all spheres of society has only to a limited extent reached the textbooks of economic history and is still not part of the general understanding in most parts of the world. In Chapter 4, Ginger Feather suggests, "turning the causal arrow around", by studying the co-constitution of women's empowerment and democracy—more specific 'social democracy'.

The Arab Uprisings have vitalized this discussion of the importance of the empowerment of women—for women as individuals and citizens, and for the whole society. Women took an active part in the mobilization during the uprisings, but were only to a limited extent included in the subsequent reconstruction of public life, however, with large variation between the MENA countries (Tripp 2015; Karshenas et al. 2016). Historical lessons from backlash in women's rights following revolutionary periods were intensively discussed within the women's movements, and there was a strong will to prevent history from repeating itself.

One late night during the popular occupation of the parliament building in Moscow in 1993, male activists suddenly began to tell the participating women that they should return home at midnight, since this was too dangerous for women! Surprisingly, this way of constructing the uprising as a male business was heard in Tahrir Square twenty years later, but also in this case the women activists refused (Dahlerup 2018).

Authoritarian Regimes and the Inclusion of Women

Sometimes it is asked, whether it is worth working for women's access to political decision-making in semi- or even non-democratic political systems of the MENA region and elsewhere? Nevertheless, in all regimes, there are women's movements and groups, who fight for the inclusion of women in actual political decision-making. In the book *Political Institutions Under Dictatorship* (2008), Jennifer Gandhi shows that legislatures, parties and social movements can very well have an influence on politics in non-democratic states, and that under pressure political leaderships might give concessions in order to neutralize threats and to further cooperation.

In Chapter 8, Aili Mari Tripp, who has written extensively on post-conflict development in Africa (Tripp 2015), discusses and rejects the argument heard among right-wing parties in the West that Islam should be incompatible with democratization. The variety of developmental paths within the MENA countries is evidence to the contrary.

The promotion of women's rights in the region seems to depend on a number of factors, which are all subjects to discussion in this book, such as the legal system, electoral laws, political party strategies, including different strategies among leading Islamist parties—and the strength of women's movements and feminists of all genders as well as changes in public opinion about women's position in society. Consequently, it is important to move away from sweeping generalizations about women's position to geographically focused and empirically based analyses of women's inclusion in political decision-making and actual influence, as it is done in this book. However, many themes are still left for future research.

Democracy in the MENA Region

According to Freedom House, democracy is in a retreat across the globe. "The values it embodies, particularly the right to choose leaders in free and fair elections, freedom of the press, and the rule of law, are under assault and in retreat globally" (Freedom House 2018 report). The MENA region ranks at the bottom of all regions, see Table 1.1 with a rate of 67% of the countries being categorized as 'not free', which indicates that the region is dominated by autocratic regimes. There is a general agreement that the Maghreb countries are more open regimes than the Middle East countries.

Another major global democracy index, *The Economist Intelligence Unit's Democracy Index* (EIU), has a slightly different conclusion: "The retreat of global democracy has stopped", adding "or has it just paused?". The EIU index is based on broader and more demanding criteria than Freedom House: electoral process and pluralism, the functioning of government, political participation, political culture and civil

Table 1.1 Level of democracy by region in 2017

Regions	Total no. of countries	Free (%)	Partly free (%)	Not free (%)
Americas	35	66	28	6
Asia Pacific	39	46	33	21
Eurasia	12	–	42	58
Europe	42	86	12	2
MENA	18	11	22	67
Sub-Saharan Africa	49	18	43	39

Source Freedom House (2018). This index is based on the aggregate scores for countries based on 10 political rights and 15 civil liberties

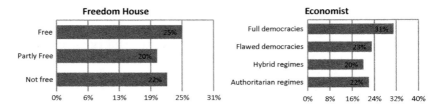

Fig. 1.1 Level of Democracy and women's parliamentary representation worldwide, in percent (*Source* Freedom House 2016 [on 2015] and The Economist: Democracy Index 2015. From Dahlerup 2018: 53 [Own calculations, based on IPU's figures])

liberties. Consequently, we can conclude that political participation through protests and anger have grown, but trust in the institutions decreased. "The most striking advance has been in the participation of women – in the past decade the indicator has improved more than any other single indicator in our model.

This improvement takes place amid a deterioration of trust in democracy, evident in the worsening of most categories in this year's Index" (2018-report).

In a global perspective, following the widespread adoption of electoral gender quotas, the differences in women's parliamentary representation according to level of democracy have levelled down, see Fig. 1.1, even if women's representation is still the highest in democratic states. However, recent developments have invalidated the old theory that the richer a country, the higher women's political representation (Dahlerup 2018: 53). The variations between the two indexes can be explained by differences in the construction of the indexes, and EIU index having four, Freedom House only three levels.[1]

Women's Rights in an Age of Uncertainty

The Arab Uprisings, or what we call hereafter an age of uncertainty, brought clear evidence of crisis and uncertainty in MENA region countries, which resembles the post-independence era of the 1950s (Sadiki et al. 2013). Age of uncertainty is not synonymous to the Arab Spring Uprisings, but it is a defining aspect of it. The uprisings created unprecedented possibilities for political openings seen in the emergence of new forms of political mobilization from below. It also reconfigured the regional political landscape (Dabashi 2012; Salime 2015) and imposed new state–society relations. The displacement of entrenched incumbents initiated transitions represented mainly in expanding the scope of political participation, organizing multi-party elections and reforming constitutions. Political parties and activists that had previously been oppressed, Islamist parties in particular, entered the political arena, and newly formed Civil society organizations (CSOs) with various conceptual frameworks proliferated.

Like much of the early transition literature, the term transformation/change captures the fluidity and unpredictability of transitional settings (Heydemann 2016). Transition periods provide considerable scope for *contingency* and *agency*. O'Donnell and Schmitter maintain that transition periods, characterized with a "high degree of indeterminacy embedded in situations where unexpected events … insufficient information, hurried and audacious choices, confusion about motives and interests, plasticity, and even indefinition of political identities, as well as the talents of specific individuals", shape political outcomes and directions (1986: 5).

The framework of this book is this atmosphere of uncertainty and irresolution, which on the one hand opens up for new opportunities, but on the other hand also may involve repressive constraints of choice, agency and contingency. Inspired by Ruth Lister's understanding of citizenship as both inclusionary and exclusionary (1997), we use in this book the concept of 'double-edged' gender policies and attitudes to refer to the ambiguity and uncertainty of MENA politics and policies with regard to women's empowerment and rights during and after the uprisings. Both mobilizations and contestations from the top (state feminism) and from below (feminist activism and population attitudes) are contextually conditioned to both/either empower and/or sideline women. From old as well as from some of the new elites comes a wish to either destabilize or keep firm control of the status quo. Hence, one of the objectives of this book is to answer these questions: How do the protests, the civil society activists and the people negotiate the new power dynamics? How do states respond to calls for more gender equality and justice for women? And finally how do post-transition dynamics affects state–society relations?

Scholarship on MENA region uprisings makes a distinction between the "political society" and the "civil society" (Bellin 2011; Stepan 2012) and how each affects and is affected by the other. In Bayat's (2013) terms, *political society* refers to actors within political institutions and processes that represent the structure of the state (i.e., parliament, parties, government), while *civil society* refers to the expression of *politics* outside the restricted spaces of political institutions (i.e., civil society organizations, social movements). CSOs are important actors, putting pressure on the political institutions, in democracies as well as in more or less authoritarian regimes. The state of flux that followed the upsurge of the popular protests and social/political unrest that convulsed the MENA in 2011 has considerably transformed or reconfigured the state–society relations. According to Colombo (2018: 2), even in countries that were not affected by the Arab Uprisings and didn't have massive protests, state–society relations "have been the object of a constant, more or less visible process of contestation and reshaping" because of regional and international pressures. Importantly, the issue of women's empowerment and gender equality garnered a central position during this process of political reshaping and intensified controversies between the religious and the secular paradigms.

Although it is generally acknowledged that democracy is good for women's rights, stakeholders, academics, development practitioners and grassroots constituencies still question how Muslim women can gain greater control over the circumstances that influence their lives and contribute to processes of democratization and modernization (Pratt and Richter-Devroe 2013), especially at a time when ideological paradigms fluctuate within the dualistic nature of policies and social values in Muslim-majority countries. This book explores how the underlying double-edged post-spring dynamics of the Islamic secular feminist discourses regarding women's empowerment in the MENA region considerably affect MENA state politics and policies.

Women's Rights, Feminism and Islamism

Modern debates on women and gender in relation to Islam shows how the *woman question* was constructed during the colonial period and depicted *Muslim woman oppression* as caused by an archaic *Muslim culture* that stood in opposition to the colonisers' modern Western culture (Ahmed 1992). After the colonization era, women activists faced the dilemma of defending principles of gender equality, often associated with "Westernized demands" (Ahmed 1982). Alternative modes of contestation of these Western paradigms came with the rise of Islamism. Sharabi (1988) describes Islamism as a movement of political emancipation and cultural revival that opposed Westernization and criticized nationalism's, communism's and socialism's inability to oppose imperialism. Zubaida (1989) contextualizes Islamism within the framework of nation-state formation and the process of modernization imposed by colonization. After 2011, the rise of political Islam into power (especially in Tunisia, Egypt and Morocco) paved the way for new modes of women's activism, i.e., *Islamist feminism*. The movement conceives itself as being pragmatic, rooted in local values and invokes the centrality of religion in its premise. The changing opportunity structure opened the political space for new women organizations ideologically closer to Islamist governments and to some extent pushed back secular feminist movements. This development may be conceptualized as a development of many feminisms in plural between two extremes on the same continuum, secular feminism and Islamist feminism, not any longer seen at totally separate entities, see the discussion in this book, chapter 2, 5 and 7.

The women's movement in MENA region is not a monolithic block as it is premised by the binary thinking about the East and the West. Kandiyoti (1988) states that Western bias previously made researchers unable to see the internal heterogeneity of Middle Eastern women. Kandiyoti shows how women strategize within a concrete set of constraints, which she termed "patriarchal bargains". Kandiyoti highlights the various forms of patriarchy, as well as the contexts in which they are deployed, which present women with distinct "rules of the game" and strategies to "maximize security and optimize life options" with varying potentials for active or passive resistance. From this perspective, we believe that the evolution of different strands of the women's movement in the MENA region reveals several divergences springing from the context under which they were born, ideological foundations, as well as strategies and choices of each strand.

Most importantly the *socio-political context* in which various women activists/groups are involved makes their conception of the ways and strategies leading to women's empowerment so diverse and polyvocal. In times of political uncertainty, when state institutions are being reconfigured, women's movements also undertake a pragmatic reshaping of their ideological positioning, with regard to Islamist or feminist frameworks (see Chapter 7). *Ideological positioning* refers to situating oneself within a specific ideological framework or what Jost et al. (2009) define ideological self-placements in explaining political behavior.

In this book, the Chapters 2 and 3 discuss, to what extend the emergence of Islamist feminism has created new opportunities for intersections between Islamist values and modern values and thereby for destruction of dichotomies between Islamism/feminism and traditionalism/modernity. Chapter 3 talks about processes of 'Feminizing Islam' and 'Islamizing feminism', which has allowed for renegotiation of meaning incited by interaction with the secular and modern values and the creation of a religious-based conception of emancipation. Chapter 7 studies how the activities of Islamist women impact political elites' backing for the movement's agenda and vice versa. Overall, most women's rights activists use the language of women's rights and renegotiate political and religious boundaries to reinvent women's rights at times of uncertainty.

STUDYING THE IMPACT OF WOMEN'S ACTIVISM

In most of this book's chapters, references are made to the impact of women's activism and women's rights advocates in the MENA region, both before, during and after the uprisings. It is evident that most reforms of women's position have been initiated by women's groups and implemented through pressure from women's movements. Even if many feminists disagree on the ability of the state to change fundamentally women's position in society, the Arab Spring has furthered a widespread aspiration among active women to be included in political institutions and from there participate in the political decision-making and in the reorganization of the polity. This resembles the spirit of the UN Worlds Conference on Women, Beijing 1995, of which Devaki Jain wrote: "There was an almost universal or palpable desire to be in power, to be in leadership, to change the terms of the relationship with the great globe" (2005: 145).

The opportunity structure framing women's activism varies between the countries of the MENA region. In some countries, women activists have been actively involved in reform processes, including in powerful circles, while in others, women's rights advocates have to fight hard to be heard, sometimes in vain, as discussed in Chapters 7 and 8. Yet, the Arab Uprisings take place in a period of strong international support for women's political empowerment and extensive international communication among feminists. During the last two decades, transnational feminist movements have had a considerable *discursive influence* in our increasingly global world, not least through United Nations (Baksh and Harcourt 2015; Dahlerup 2018). However, the new international discourses on women's empowerment only become forceful, when local, national and regional women's movement makes use of them, 'squeezing' political decision-makers between local and international pressure. Attempts by opponents of women's rights to dismiss feminist claims as a purely Western invention have been turned down with reference to the strength of local mobilizations.

The Internet and social media have dramatically improved women's movements' capacity to connect at all level of society and around the globe. In location or in periods, when threats to women's bodily integrity are mounting, social media makes it possible to organize, form coalitions and challenge the establishment without placing your body in the public room. Unfortunately, social media also produce numerous sites for hate-speech against women and virtual sexual harassment. We need more research on social media's impact on women's rights movements, for good and for worse (Ferree and Pudrovska 2006; Maddison and Sawer 2013).

It is well known that not all women are feminist, and that not all feminists are women! However, everywhere women are in the lead of feminist mobilizations and demands, yet, at the same time inviting feminist men to participate in the struggle. Consequently, researchers should study, when, where and how—and on what issues—it has been possible to form new coalitions among feminist groups across religious, social and geographical cleavages. When women activists and feminists of all genders across all their internal divisions have been able to work together, for instance on combatting violence against women, improving girls' education, or introducing gender quotas to break male dominance in politics, the chances of success increase. As social movements, one branch of women's activism is directed toward *social-cultural change* in civil society, including in changing norms and practices in everyday life. Other parts of women's activism target the political institutions and work as *political pressure groups* in order to make political decision-making more inclusive to women and in order to change legislation. There might be tension between these different types of movements; however, both are needed to make sustainable changes in relation to the empowerment of women and promotion of gender equality.

State response to the demands by feminist and women activists follows different patterns. We need more research on what determines state response under different circumstances. In this endeavor, inspiration is offered by William Gamson's classic analysis of possible outcomes of protest movements, and his four categories of response (Gamson 1990):

First, the response can be ridicule, pure *rejection*, or even legal persecution, as we have seen in Egypt, where Mozn Hassan, founder and executive director of the young organization, *Nazra for Feminist Studies*, has been charged in the case known as the NGO Foreign Funding Case (https://nazra.org/en/2018/06/feminist-activist-mozn-hassan-released-bail-amounting-egp-30000). Second, more fundamental demands by women's movements may be *pre-empted* by just symbolic concessions, as in the Saudi Arabian case of allowing women to acquire a drivers' license. Third, the response may be an attempt of *cooptation*, i.e., giving limited positions to a few women, while at the same time rejecting the movement's demand of empowerment of all women (may be the Moroccan case of the Women's List may fall in this category, see Chapter 11). Fourth, *partial or full response* to the new ideas of the protest movement. The chapters of this book reflect the variety of response to women's activism in the MENA region, but more research is needed, including research on simply lack of response and silent rejection. In the MENA region during this period, many reforms have been accepted, especially in the Maghreb region, but there are endless examples of pre-empting of feminist demands or cooptation of some leaders, which may silence the protest or, at best, only represent an opening on long terms. Full response to feminist claims remains a dream in the MENA region as everywhere else in the world.

Why Parity? International Norms of Full Inclusion of Women in Public Decision-Making

Today, an all-male political assembly has lost its democratic legitimacy and will be met with protests all over the world. Previous demands for 'more women in politics' have been replaced by international quests for *parity* as expressed in the UN Sustainable Development Goals, SDG, which should be reached by 2030.

> Ensure women's full and effective participation and equal opportunities for leadership at all levels of decision-making in politics, economics and public life. (SDG 2015: Art. 5:5)

Equal and effective representation of women in all public decision-making is a key demand of national and transnational women's organizations. The full inclusion of women was also a central request from women's organizations during the Arab Uprisings, and the change of regimes gave hope for changing the patriarchal structure of politics.

The goal of parity is of key importance for several reasons. Firstly, women's full and equal representation is an important symbol of women's full citizenship; and conversely, the de facto exclusion of women from important sites of political power is a sign, that women are seen as second-class citizens, whose voice is of no significance. This is the *rights/ justice argument*, according to which full participation and representation of women can thus been seen as a right and a goal in itself. This implies that elected assemblies should reflect the social composition of the population in terms of women and men, majorities and minorities. However, and secondly, the feminist movements have always seen full political participation and representation, as means to have *women's experiences* represented, included those of specific groups of women, following the fact that women and men have so different life conditions, inducing within most subgroups such as immigrants and minorities. Thirdly, *the conflict of interest* argument rests on the assumption that on certain political issues, for instance marriage laws, equal pay regulations and redistribution of power, men and women do not have identical interests, and consequently, women need an equal share in the power of decision-making. The two latter arguments, according to which full inclusion of women is seen as a means, are subject of continuous discussions within feminist movements and in Feminist Theory about what constitutes 'women's interests' (Escobar-Lemmon and Taylor-Robinson 2014).

With the famous UN document *Platform for Action*, adopted at the World Conference on Women, held in Beijing 1995, and signed by most countries of the world, some, however, with reservations, a fourth argument, have paved its way into the global discourse: The *democracy argument* widens the argument from what is good for women to what is necessary for making democracy real.

> Achieving the goal of equal participation of women and men in decision-making will provide a balance that more accurately reflects the composition of society and is needed in order to strengthen democracy and promote its proper functioning. (Platform for Action, Art. 183)

The Declaration of the African Union, adopted in 2002 in Durban, South Africa, contains a similar argument, yet AU was among the very first to promote the principle of 'parity':

We reaffirm, in particular, the pivotal role of women in all levels of society and recognize that the objectives of the African Union cannot be achieved without the full involvement and participation of women at all levels and structures of the Union.

There is, however, a fifth argument for full inclusion of women, *the utility argument*, featuring prominently in contemporary neo-liberal discussion, e.g., around gender quotas in order to increase the number of women on company boards. 'It is a waste not to use all talents in society in advance by excluding half the population'. Some advocates even argue that the economic result of the companies with many women on the board will tend to be better than those of companies with only few women, even if researchers do not agree on the direction of causality. The utility argument may turn out to be in conflict with the justice/right argument; specifically, what will happen to the claim for parity, if the inclusion of women does not improve the results of the firm? In contrast, the quest for gender parity, based on a pure justice argument, does not depend on 'women making a difference' and, consequently, can foster the broadest coalitions of women's organizations across class and ideological cleavages.

Status of MENA Countries' Compliance with International Norms

Most MENA countries have ratified the Committee on the Elimination of Discrimination against Women (CEDAW) which is considered a global pact for women's rights. Signatory states are required to align all national legislation with constitutional principles with international conventions and human rights principles. The mechanism of the CEDAW process is important. Every fourth year the individual countries are up for scrutiny at the CEDAW Committee, and the government report on progress in gender equality in the country will often be supplemented by a critical report from women's NGOs in the country.

Table 1.2 reveals that of all Arab countries only Somalia and Sudan did not ratify the convention. The level of MENA countries commitment to international standards varies from one country to another depending on the reservations it expressed about several provisions of CEDAW due to religious and cultural constraints. It must be noted that significant domestic pressure alone is unlikely to be decisive if it does not align with international pressure. However, overt International efforts to champion

Table 1.2 MENA countries ratifications and reservations to the CEDAW

Country	Date of ratification	Reservations	Withdrawal of reservations	Optional protocol
Algeria	22 May 1996	Articles 2, 9(2), 15(4), 16, 29		
Bahrain	18 June 2002	Articles 2, 9(2), 15(4), 16, 29(1)		
Egypt	18 September 1981	Articles 2, 9(2), 16, 29		
Kuwait	2 September 1994	Articles 9(2), 16(f), 29(1)		
Lybia	16 May 1989	Articles 2 and 16(c), (d)		June 2004
Iraq	13 August 1986	Articles 2(f), (g), 9(1), (2), 16, 29(1)		
Jordan	1 July 1992	Articles 9(2), 15 (4), 16(1c), (1d) and (1g)		
Lebanon	21 April 1997	Articles 9(2), 16(1c), (1d), (1f, 1g), 29(1)		
Morocco	21 June 1993	Articles 2, 9(2), 15(4), 16 and 29	Lifted its reservations on Articles 9(2) and 16 in 2011	Declared accession in March 2006
Oman	7 February 2006	Articles 9(2), 15(4), 16(1a), (1c), (1f), 29(1)		
Palestinian Authority	2 April 2014	–		Ratification without any reservation as a non-member state
Qatar	26 April 2009	Articles 2(a), 9(2), 15(1), (4), 16(1a), (1c), (1f), 29(1)		
Saudi Arabia	7 September 2000	Articles 9(2), 29(1)		
South Sudan	30 April 2015			
Tunisia	20 September 1985	9(2), 15(4), 16(c), (d), (f), (g), (h) and 29(1)	Lifted all reservations in 2014	2008
United Arab Emirates	6 October 2004	Articles 2(f), 9, 15(2), 16, 29(1)		
Yemen	30 May 1984	Article 29(1)		

Source CEDAW, https://tbinternet.ohchr.org/_layouts/TreatyBodyExternal/Treaty.aspx?CountryID=117&Lang=EN, accessed 1 April 2019

Notes Article 2 deals with discrimination against women in all its forms. Article 11 deals with equality in employment. Article 9 ensures equality of nationality and citizenship rights, including the transmission of citizenship from mother to child. Article 15(4) ensures equality to choose residence. Article 16 deals with equal rights in marriage and family issues, including the obligation to ensure women and men equal rights to marry; to exercise free and full consent; to dissolve marriage; to make parental decisions; to decide on the number and spacing of children; to act as guardian to their children; to choose a profession; and to own and manage property rights might be ineffective or incur a reactive local resistance (Adler-Nissen 2014; Bush and Jamal 2015). In 2011, following the *Jasmin Revolution*, Morocco and Tunisia lifted reservations, see Table 1.2. Chapter 3 of this book examines the different ways gender equality is perceived in CEDAW and in the Islamic *Sharia*, which led to these reservations, and discusses ways out of this schism.

Tools of 'State Feminism'

The concept of 'state feminism' seems to be a contradiction in terms. Feminism is the ideology of the women's movements, which often challenge the state, so how can state policies be 'feminist'? Nevertheless, the concept of 'state feminism' soon started to be used in Feminist research all over the world, following the expansion of gender equality policies and the development of gender equality institutions and departments affiliated to the state.

After the adoption by consensus of the Beijing Declaration and Platform for Action in 1995, gender issues have gained significant momentum in the Arab countries.

This section will focus mainly on the following: (1) national women's machineries, i.e., specialized governmental institutions, (2) national strategies for the advancement of women and (3) the major constitutional and legal reforms promoting women's rights.

Constitutional Provisions

In the past fifty years, constitutions in more than half of the countries in the world have been redrafted, and feminists have seized these opportunities to write an equal protection provision that includes gender as a prohibited category of discrimination. Currently, 139 states have enshrined equal protection provisions in their constitutions. In the last decade, MENA region transitions provided a window of opportunity to transform institutions and to reform the rules as the state is rebuilt, leading to progressive new constitutions and legal reforms (see Chapter 8). As the supreme source of law, the new constitutions in the region have become vital national references in defining and determining the status of women in the region in accordance with the International norms of human rights. Chapter 8 shows how the many new or rewritten constitutions in recent years in Africa, especially in postconflict countries, have included principles of women's rights in ways not seen in the past. These reforms are particularly evident in clauses pertaining to gender equality, gender discrimination, political participation and labor. It is added that only a handful of constitutions in the world use both male and female pronouns and three of these countries are Tunisia, Algeria and Morocco.

Even with the widespread rhetorical commitments and seeming progress in women's empowerment, there is still concern with why *substantive* gains remain uneven, incomplete and sometimes double-edged in the region—as in the rest of the world. No country in the world has ever obtained full gender equality, and gender inequalities or 'gender gaps' continue to exist, although to a variety of degrees, as depicted in the *Gender Gap Index* issued by the World Economic Forum every year.

National Women Machineries

The term national women machineries, NWMs, refers to formal government institutions delegated to promote systematically gender equality and the status of women's rights. Using Beijing Platform for Action terms, NWMs are assigned to *mainstream gender* in government policies. Paragraph 57 of the Beijing Platform (1995) notes that "the success of policies and measures aimed at supporting or strengthening the promotion of gender equality and the improvement in the status of women should be based on the integration of a gender perspective in general policies relating to all spheres of society".

NWM can take different forms: specialized department within the executive branch of government, inter-ministerial commissions, advisory groups and councils, gender observatories, parliamentary committees and/or gender units within various public institutions. Research has shown that NWMs might be considered more autonomous, or less influential, depending on many factors. Most important of all is their location at the highest levels of government (Goetz 2003), the clarity of their mission and mandate, and the quality of their links with women's organizations and NGOs representing women's interests (Beijing Platform for Action 1995[2]; Lycklama et al. 1998; Tripp et al. 2009; McBride and Mazur 2010).

Examining these structures in the Maghreb and Egypt shows that the machineries take a wide variety of forms, from formal ministries to a unit

Table 1.3 National women's machineries in the Arab world (selected countries)

	Type	National women's machineries
Algeria	Combined ministry	Ministry of National Solidarity, Family and Women's Affairs
Egypt	Council under the authority of the President	National Council for Women
Iraq	Full-fledged ministry	Ministry of State for Women's Affairs
Morocco	Combined ministry	Ministry of Solidarity, Women, Family and Social Development
Palestine	Full-fledged ministry	Ministry of Women's Affairs
Tunisia	Combined ministry	Ministry of Women, Family and Childhood

Source ESCWA compilation (2015)

or a department within a ministry with a broader portfolio (Table 1.3). In Palestine and Somalia, full-fledged ministries solely dedicated to women's affairs have been set up, signaling a strong commitment to gender equality. Egypt comes second in terms of the location of NWM at the highest level of government compared to Tunisia, Morocco and Algeria where gender institutions are located in a combined ministry, related to family, childhood and social development ministries.

NWMs have contributed to the development of both strategic and sectoral plans for the advancement of women (see Table 1.4) covering a range of themes, such as violence against women, women's health, women's political empowerment, women's education and linkages between gender and the environment. Other institutional tools used by NWMs include gender mainstreaming, systematic gender analysis of government policies, the collection of data disaggregated by sex and the adoption of gender-sensitive budgets. An other important function of NWMs is to ensure coordination between governmental and non-governmental institutions, religious and secular stakeholders.

National Gender Equality Strategies

Important institutional tools adopted by NWMs to promote gender equality include the development of national strategies and action plans for gender equality (NGES). Over the past decade, many countries in the MENA region have developed national gender equality strategies

Table 1.4 Post-spring national gender equality strategies

Country/year of adoption	National strategy	National strategy short name	Partners	References
Algeria 2013	Programme pour l'Égalité entre les genres et l'autonomisation de la femme en Algérie (Program for Gender Equality and the Empowerment of Women in Algeria AL INSAF)	AL INSAF	Joint project 12 ministerial sectors, civil society organizations, and 7 UN organizations (UNDP, UNFPA, UNICEF, UNAIDS, ILO, UNIDO and UNIFEM)	MDGs
Egypt 2015	National Strategy for the Empowerment of Egyptian Women 2017–2020	–	12 governmental institutions, NGOs and Religious institutions (i.e. Wakfs (Endowment), the Grand Azhar and the Orthodox Coptic Church)	Egyptian constitution 2014, National Strategy 2030, and SDGs adopted in 2015
Morocco 2018	l'Agenda gouvernemental pour l'égalité Icram 2 (governmental plan for equality ICRAM 2) 2017–2021	ICRAM 2	Ministries, civil society, private sector, universities, development agencies, and local authorities	Constitution, the 2030 Agenda for Sustainable for Development, and CEDAW
Tunisia 2017	Programme de promotion de l'égalité centre les femmes et les hommes en Tunisie MOUSSAWAT (Program for the Promotion of Equality between Women and Men) (MOUSSAWAT)	MOUSSAWAT	Joint project between Ministry of Women's Issues and Family and EU in consultation with national governmental institutions and representatives of civil society	NA

Source Authors' compilation based on: OECD (2014), Algerian Ministry of National Solidarity, Family and Women's Status (2013), Egyptian National Council for Women (2015), Moroccan Ministry of Women's Issues and Family and Children (2018) and Tunisian Ministry of Women, Family, Children and the Elderly Semester Report (2018)

(Table 1.4), reflecting a political commitment to empowering women across the region (CAWTAR/OECD 2014).[3] NGES are of paramount importance as they convey a country's vision of gender relations and serve as benchmarks for measuring progress and upholding women's rights in post-spring contexts yet as always, the crucial (McBride and Mazur 2010). The Action Plans are drawn up by state countries' NWMs working together with all political and social stakeholders (GOs and NGOs) and are based on international conventions.

The CAWTAR/OECD (2014) survey showed that most MENA states's institutional frameworks for promoting gender equality tend to focus primarily on women's roles in traditional areas (i.e., education, health and social protection) and very few explicitly integrate international standards regarding women's rights as the supreme reference in their national strategies, i.e., Egypt (P. 60).

Algeria
The Algerian program AL INSAF is a joint project realized by the Algerian Government and the United Nations in 2013 and funded by the Government of Spain through the UNDP administered MDG Fund. Its development and implementation involves twelve ministerial sectors including the Ministry of National Solidarity, Family and Women's Affairs as the key partner, as well as CSOs, and the support of seven UN organizations (see Table 1.4). The purpose of AL INSALF program is to support national efforts for gender equality and women's empowerment to contribute to accelerating the process of the implementation of the Millennium Development Goals. The program is thematically structured around the following strategic objectives: capacity building of national institutions in terms of undertaking gender analysis, increasing women's employability and access to decent work and finally conducting awareness-raising campaigns around the values of equity and equality in cooperation with NGOs (Algerian Ministry of National Solidarity, Family and Women's Status 2013: 10).

Egypt
The NWM called National Council for Women (NCW) in Egypt has adopted a strategy of networking and coordination with governmental and non-governmental agencies. Cooperation in the drafting, preparation and execution of Egypt National Strategy for Combating all forms of Violence against Women have been ensured by the signing of 12

memoranda of understanding and protocols of cooperation with ministries as well as the participation of representatives of non-governmental organizations, youth organizations, the Ministry of Wakfs (Endowment), the Grand Azhar and the Orthodox Coptic Church (Egyptian National Council for Women 2015: 8).

Morocco
Morocco's second governmental plan ICRAM 2 came as a result of a long concerted effort of all stakeholders, i.e., ministries, civil society, private sector, universities, trade unions, development agencies and local authorities. It aims to promote gender equality and empower women and girls, based on a human right-based approach. It also applies the constitutional provisions, stipulating gender equality, and aligns with the international benchmarks, namely the 2030 Agenda of Sustainable Development Goals, SDG and CEDAW. The focal points of the plan include strengthening women's social, economic, legal and political empowerment and fighting all forms of discrimination against women with a specific regard to multiplying gender mainstreaming efforts in the different regions of the country (Moroccan Ministry of Women's Issues and Family and Children 2018).

Tunisia
The MOUSSAWAT program[4] contributes to the achievement of equality between women and men in Tunisia by reducing inequalities at national, regional and local levels through the following axes: strengthening the capacity of the Ministry of Women's Issues and Family and Children and its partners—state and non-state—in integrating the gender approach; improving the participation of women in economic and public life; and reducing gender-based discrimination and violence. The program aims to work toward a better coordination and coherence of actions in favor of women and to anchor the principles of equality within the framework of the emerging new democracy, particularly at regional level, as well as with the governmental and non-government stakeholders. It is also a question of favoring the emergence of a new indispensable partnership, for the question of gender. It aims to strengthen tools such as planning, statistics, budgeting, evaluation, dialogue and consultation with equality stakeholders (Tunisian Ministry of Women, Family, Children and the Elderly Semester Report 2018).

Legal Reforms Promoting Women's Rights

Significant legal progress in the status of women's rights in the MENA region started since 2000s. Yet, several countries have taken steps to respond more positively and remarkably to the demands for justice and equality after the 2011 revolutions. Women of all kinds, secularists and political Islamic activists, veiled and unveiled, conservatives and liberals, and professionals and mothers have all fueled the revolutions and deconstructed the myth of a monolithic, stereotypical notion of a Muslim woman. The uprisings have elucidated the diversity and plurality in women's concerns and objectives across the region, but also many common causes. In many cases, legal reforms have become remarkably prioritized policy issues in some post-spring transitional states, although calls for such reforms have been ongoing for many decades.

Pre-Spring Legal Reforms

The years 2003–2011 conveyed continued progress in promoting gender equality in the legal systems of the Arab region. One of the main demands of the women's rights groups across the region was the *family law*. Tunisia amended its personal status code in 1993 and gave more rights to Tunisian women. Beside others, the most progressive amendments in the MENA region has been the parental authority of the mother, the banning of polygamy and extrajudicial divorce and the guardianship of children to the mother. Egyptian, Moroccan and Algerian family laws have also amended some of their provisions to promote women's empowerment and adapt to the changing social realities of their societies.

Egypt's pioneering reform of the *nationality law* in 2004[5] encouraged regional emulation from other countries to follow (see Table 1.5). The issue of women's nationality garnered the interest of national and regional women's rights NGOs across the MENA region and impelled them to start the Collective for Research and Training on Development-Action (CRTD.A).[6]

The coalition identified the unequal treatment of women in their countries' nationality laws as the heart of women's social disadvantage in the region. The coalition has been an active agent in the process for change by adopting multiple strategies: sharing information on the challenges faced in each country, developing country-specific legal reform initiatives, promoting coalition building with national parliamentarians, unions and lawyers and finally exerting pressure by submitting shadow reports to the CEDAW Committee highlighting legal inequality.[7]

Table 1.5 Major legal reforms in the Maghreb and Egypt

Period	Laws	Algeria	Egypt	Morocco	Tunisia
Post-spring reforms	Removing "Marry your rapist" law	Article 326 (NA)	Article 291 (1999)	Article 475 (2014)	Article 227 (2017)
	Violence against women law (independent law)	–	–	Law 103-13 (September 2018)	Law 2017-58 (August 2017)
	Women allowed to marry non-muslims	–	–	NI	Repeal marriage restriction of 1973 in 2014
	Equal Inheritance Law	–	–	–	November 2018 (Bill approved not yet enacted)
Pre-spring reforms	Criminalizing sexual harassment (Penal code)	Law 04-15 (2004)	May 2014	Code of criminal procedure (2003)	Law 2004-73 (2004)
	Family Law	Law 084-11 (2005)	Law 4 (2000, 2005)	Law 70.03 (2004)	Law 93-74 (1993)
	Nationality Law	Law 1970-86 (2005)	Law 26 of 1975 (2004)	Law 1-07-80 Reformed in 2007 consolidated in 2011	Law 63-6 Reformed in 2010 consolidated in 2011

Sources Authors' compilation based on www.refworld.org, the Global Database on Violence Against Women; Reunite International: http://www.reunite.org
Notes Not available (NA); Not yet implemented (NI)

Post-Spring Legal Reforms

The Arab Spring has expedited constitutional reform in addition to other legislative amendments. Activism from women's movements and CSOs have impelled transitioning states to promote legal reforms promoting women's rights. Following the efforts taken by Egypt in 1999, Morocco amended the law that allowed rapists and kidnappers to escape prosecution by marrying their victims in 2014. Tunisia followed suit and removed this provision from the penal code in 2017.

Very recently, pressured by strong feminist movement mobilizations, Tunisia and Morocco have enacted a long awaited independent violence against women law (VAW) in July 2017 and September 2018, respectively. Another controversial issue hindering states to reform clauses in personal status laws is the inheritance equal law, which is considered incompatible to Sharia, see Chapter 3. A groundbreaking process has been instigated by Tunisia (November 2018) when the Bill for equal inheritance was approved. Clearly, there is momentum for significant regional reform where Tunisia takes the lead in addressing of gender inequality in legislation despite various cultural and religious constraints.

DEVELOPMENT IN WOMEN'S DESCRIPTIVE REPRESENTATION

Women's political representation in elected assemblies has increased remarkably in the post-transition MENA countries, especially in the Maghreb countries. This has created high expectations, yet everywhere women only constitute a minority in the assemblies and in governments. Figure 1.2 shows that the Arab region elects the second lowest share of women in a global perspective, but also, that this region in statistical terms has experienced the highest increase during the last twenty years, from 4.3 to 19%. The Americas ranks the highest, not because of the countries in North America, but because of the widespread use of gender quotas in Latin America, see later. Sub-Saharan Africa has experienced a rapid increase and is at the level of the world average.

Disintegrating the figures in Fig. 1.2, Table 1.6 shows the specific development over the last twenty years in three selected regions. The five small Nordic countries were for long the forerunners in terms of women's representation together with the Netherlands and were the first to pass the 30% threshold in the 1990s. Lately, however, the six countries

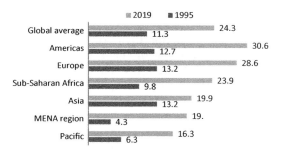

Fig. 1.2 Women elected to parliaments worldwide and regional averages, 1995 and 2019 (*Source* www.ipu.org, single or lower chambers. Election-day figures)

Table 1.6 Three selected regions. Women in parliament (%)

	1997	*2019*
Nordic countries	36	41
East Africa (EAC)	13	36
Maghreb countries	4	26

Source www.ipu.org, 1 January 2019. Single or lower chambers

of the East African Community have taken a large leap forward in including women in parliamentary decision-making. Today, they almost match the Nordic countries, and number one in the world is an EAC-country, Rwanda, with 61.3% women, and the first country in the world to pass the 50% threshold. The three Maghreb countries also show a remarkable development and are today a little above the world average.

The local level represents an interesting area for future research. Local and regional councils are arenas of decision-making of great importance for everyday life in terms of water, schools, health, housing, roads—and with the newest development, for such important issues as combatting domestic violence. By the use of effective gender quotas, remarkable increases have taken place recently at the local level in Tunisia and Morocco, where women now occupy seats at the local decision-making tables at a higher level than at the national level: 44 and 38%. The new 25% quota law in Egypt is yet to be tested in election.

Why Are Women Under-Represented?

For long, women were blamed for their low representation. Even in research, we found explanations with focus on women's alleged lack of knowledge, lack of political interest, or lack of time because of family obligations. Newer research, including this book, turns the question around asking *why men are over-represented?* (Bjarnegaard 2013). To come to term with the continuous bias against women in the political system, feminist institutionalism studies the *lack of inclusiveness of political institutions*. In most countries, the *gatekeepers* to elected positions are the political parties or in many Arab countries the clans, because they control the selected and nomination of candidates for election. More empirical research is needed on how candidates are selected in various countries in the MENA region, the priority given to incumbent (male) candidates and the power of what has been named 'old boy's network'. No doubt, it is favorable to be of the male sex, if you seek nomination and election—an informal quota for men. The problem is not lack of qualified and competent women in society, the main problem is a lack of demand for women by those who control the recruitment to political assemblies.

When the voters enter the polling stations, the candidates have usually already been nominated. In most Arab countries with proportional representation electoral systems or in the PR part of mixed electoral systems, the names of the candidates are not even to be found written on the ballot, and consequently, the voters can only choose between political parties. Even in the Moroccan case, where 60 seats for women and 30 seats for youth of both genders below 35 years of age are reserved for women on a special National List, the voters cannot mark a preference for anyone of the female or young candidates, only for their party, see Chapter 11. In majority/plurality systems, or the majoritarian part of a mixed system, even individual candidates are often associated with a political party or clan, even if some countries such as Egypt does give room for truly independent, individual candidates. Consequently, as several chapters of this book show, pressure from independent women's organizations and, not least, pressure from women and feminists within parties or clans are key to changing the over-representation of men, seen in relation to their share of the population.

Many MENA countries have in relation to the uprisings changed electoral system. It should be noticed that electoral systems are never gender neutral. It is a general conclusion from research that an electoral system based on proportional representation (PR), i.e., multimember constituencies, where each political party nominate several candidates for their list, is more favorable for the election of women than plurality/majority systems, under which each party usually only present one candidate—most often a man.

Descriptive, Substantive and Symbolic Representation

In contemporary studies of women's political representation, a distinction is made between *descriptive, substantive and symbolic representation.* While descriptive representation refers to the numerical gender composition of elected assemblies, i.e., the number or share of women, substantive representation—inspired by Hannah Pitkin's concepts (1967)—refers to the policy content of representation, e.g., to what extent women representatives stand for or act in the interest of the female voters, minority MPs for minority voters etc. Symbolic representation is about the meaning attached to being a representative, for instance voters' perceptions of women as politicians or the importance of, e.g., the first woman prime minister or president in a country, who break the norm that only men can be head of state or a P.M. Substantive representation is far the most contentious concepts of the three. What is substantive representation, if there is no agreement about what women's interests are?

In an early criticism of the feminist movement, *Judith Butler* stated: "For the most part, feminist theory has assumed that there is some existing identity, understood through the category of women, who not only initiate feminist interests and goals within discourse, but constitute the subject for whom political representation is sought" (Butler 1990: 3). On the one hand, Judith Butler is right that there is not unified women's identity. Yet, on the other hand she seems wrong, when she criticizes feminist movements for seeking political representation for some assumed 'essentialist' common identity of women. Historical studies of the feminist movements show clearly that most feminist movements have been well aware of the fact that making and diverse groups of women's organizations cooperate around a common cause in spite of social and political cleavages is not a given, but requires hard work and organizational skills.

Consequently, it is interesting to study empirically which political issues have gathered women from different walks of life, different sexual orientations, age and different ideologies, e.g., secular versus Islamist feminist organizations. Suffrage for women, empowering women in political decision-making, girls' education and combatting sexual violence against women constitute some issues, which have formed the broadest coalitions of women and/or feminists of all genders. Judith Butler later modified her critique of women acting as a group (Butler 1999: Preface), but her initial strong criticism of what she and contemporary critiques call 'identity politics' has become highly influential in the present individualistic era (Dahlerup 2014). Changing identities has always been key to feminist movements, yet the feminist movement should be seen as a *political* movement, combatting discrimination and exclusion of women (Dahlerup 2018: 12).

Karen Beckwith has tried to solve these theoretical controversies about 'women's interests' by introducing the distinction between interests, issues and preferences. Women's *interests* are according to Beckwith the most fundamental and derived from similar, shared experiences, which differ from those of men. Women's interests are constructed in specific instances by political, economic and social arrangements. Intersectional disputes predominantly among women indicate actually, Beckwith argues, that women's interests are at stake. In contrast, *issues* are more specific, immediate and limited, while *preferences* are strategic alternatives. Karen Beckwith (2014) applies the case of freedom from violence against women as an example of a fundamental 'interest', under which the prioritized 'issues' may be spousal assault or rape or sexual harassment, whereas there can be an endless range of 'preferences'. From her deliberative point of view, *Iris Marion Young* (2000) moved the discussion in the direction of the dynamic interaction between the represented and the representatives. It is not a question of representing some fixed and static ('essentialist') notion of women and women's interests, since representation should be seen as *speaking for*, not *speaking as*.

In empirical research, the complex relation between descriptive and substantive representation—will more women in politics change the political culture and policies? —can be studied using a variety of approaches, which do not require a priori theoretical definition of women's interests. The focus of investigations could be the ideology and actual claims of various *women's organizations* in their interaction with changing political institutions. A second approach is to study the actual interventions and strategies used by *women politicians* themselves, while a third approach is the study of formal and informal norms and practices of *political institutions*, and to what extent they tend to include or exclude women or minorities.

All three approaches are represented in this book (see especially Chapters 3, 6, 7, 8 and 11).

Patriarchal Structures of Political Life

Electing women to parliament, regional and local councils is important, but not a sufficient measure. Everywhere we do find inequalities embedded in the walls of political institutions, of which many were established before women had access. Identifying the patriarchal or male-dominated structures of political institutions is an important field for gender and politics studies. It is important to move beyond the sweeping generalizations such as 'women have no political power at all' or 'women have an equal share of power in politics and in society'. It is often heard that Rwandan women MPs in spite of being a majority in parliament (61.3%) have 'no power', or that women politicians have no power because they are all unqualified (how qualified are the male politicians?) or dependent on their family ties and their party (so are the male politicians!). There is a need for empirical analyses of changing discourses as well as formal and informal norms and practices in political institutions, and for analyzing under what conditions women's groups have been successful in pressing for change. This book intends to move this research field forward, based on clarifications of key concepts and empirical analysis of specific fields or issues.

The model shown in Table 1.7 shows six key areas of male dominance/patriarchal structures in politics, many of which are analyzed by individual chapters of this book. To what extent do we find change, following the Arab Uprisings, and when and where were male-dominated structures left unchanged? When does transformation of one dimension lead to changes in other dimensions? Table 1.6 starts with the numerical dimension, i.e., the social composition of elected assemblies, already depicted in Fig. 1.2. Most of the chapters in this book touch upon the questions of changes in women's representation in elected assemblies, and Chapters 8, 10 and 11 deal specifically with this dimension. Politics as a workplace, with its written and unwritten rules, forms the second area. Today, female politicians all over the world complain that inequalities seem to be embedded in the walls of their workplace: from the harsh tone in political debates to exclusion from informal meetings and problems with family obligations, when meetings last long into the night. The #MeToo movement revealed that sexual harassment also takes place within the political institutions and during electoral campaigns.

The third dimension of importance is women's access to positions of power within parliaments and municipal assemblies, such as committee chair, leader of party group or speaker, seen in relation to their share of the assembly, of course. Is Robert Putman's "law of increasing disproportion" still valid, in the sense of "the higher up, the fewer", with regard to women? To what extent is the *glass ceiling*, a metaphor for this "iron law", being broken? The fourth dimension, horizontal gender segregation, points to the traditional division between men and women in committee work and portfolios, even in governments. We all know that there are many female ministers of social and educational affairs (mistakenly often labeled 'soft areas' in spite of large budgets). However,

Table 1.7 Six dimensions of male dominance in politics

1. Representation	Women's numerical underrepresentation in elected assemblies because of biased recruitment
2. Politics as a workplace	Male-coded norms and practices in elected assemblies
3. Vertical gender segregation	The higher up in political hierarchies, the fewer women
4. Horizontal gender segregation	Limited access for women to a range of portfolios and committees
5. Public policy	Policies biased in favor of men Limited concern for gender equality
6. Discourses and framing	Demeaning of women politicians and sidelining gender equality policies

Source Based on Dahlerup and Leyenaar (2013: 8)

is this the result of exclusion of women politicians from other policy areas or of their own preference, based on their education and occupational experiences? Chapter 9 shows how an analysis of both the vertical and the horizontal gender segregation can be scrutinized, here with the Jordanian parliament as a case.

The fifth dimension refers to policy-making. Which issues reach the political agenda and which are being excluded? To what extent can public policy still be interpreted as biased in favor of men or groups of men, as was so unmistakably the case when the French Civil Code (Cope Napoleon) forbade the search for the father of a child born out of wedlock? Two questions are debated all over the world today following the #MeToo movement. First, why do all political regimes fail to give women full protection from sexual assaults, crimes which severely restrict women's citizenship rights? And secondly, why are anti-discrimination regulations still so relatively ineffective for women who are still paid less on the labor market than men, meet glass ceilings when seeking promotion, get lower pensions etc.? The sixth dimension concerns the gendered perceptions of politicians, especially how women politicians are depicted in the media, and how party leaders—when looking for candidates—tend to frame women within a traditional discourse of how a "strong" politician looks like. The greatest barrier against change is the conception that the existing political structures are the natural order of things. May be gender quotas are so controversial, because they display, not least to the younger generations, that male dominance can be changed, and is not a product of some natural order. It is being told that a 4-year-old boy asked during Bro Harlem Brundtland's long prime ministership as the first women in Norway's history: "Mammy, can a man become a prime minister?"

Gender Quotas: A Trend in the MENA Region and in the World

The MENA region has a long tradition for reserving seats for certain groups. Gender quotas are *not* a Western invention. On the contrary, the old democracies in the West have until recently been reluctant to adopt quotas, which has been considered a violence of liberal democracy. Quotas for women in politics existed in various forms in most communist countries, and in Pakistan since 1956, Bangladesh since 1972 with some interruptions and in Egypt in 1979–1984 (Abou-Zeid 2006). In none of these countries were the woman quota popular among the citizens. It is, however, difficult to know if the resistance derived from the specific format of the quota regulation, or rather from a general disgust at women in public life. In addition, Egypt has since Nasser and until recently upheld a radical class quota system, demanding that not only 50% of the candidates shall be workers or farmers, but even 50% of those elected, if necessary corrected after the election. Yet, quotas for women have been the main target of quota opponents.

In the 1970s and 1980s, green, left socialist and social-democratic parties in the Nordic countries started using gender quotas for their own internal organization and their lists for elections, the so-called *voluntary party quotas*. The recent trend in quota adoption by law, the so-called *legislated candidate quotas*, started with Argentina's quota law of 1991, which requires a minimum of 30% candidates of each gender on the electoral lists, mandatory for all political parties (Htun and Jones 2002). India was also among the first, although with a different quota method, the so-called *reserved seat quotas*, since through the constitution amendment of 1993–1994, one third of the seats in the local councils, the Panchayats, are reserved for women in advance of the election, and only women can compete for these seats, distributed among the wards on the basis of rotation (Rai et al. 2006). As of 2019, around 90 countries in the world have adopted some type of electoral gender quotas by constitution and/or law (legislated quotas or reserved seats quotas). In addition, around 30 countries some individual parties, most often Green and Left parties, incl. Social-Democrats have adopted their own voluntary party quota rules. Well-known are ANCs party statues, which today demand 'no less than 50% women' on the party's lists for elections in South Africa. All these imply that more than half the countries of the world now have adopted gender quotas in politics.

The CEDAW convention from 1979 paved the way for gender quotas by stating that the adoption by State Partners of "temporary special measures aimed at accelerating de facto equality between men and women shall not be considered discrimination" (Art. 4.1).[8] Later, *The Platform for Action Declaration*, adopted in 1995 by the UN World Congress on Women in Beijing linked an equal participation of women and men in decision-making to the strengthening of democracy, and recommended that this should be achieved "if necessary through Positive Action" (Art. 183, 190.a). Transnational women's movements were instrumental to the adoption of these seminal declarations, and national women's movements to their implementation, also in the MENA region, see Chapters 6 and 7.

From its start, The African Union was in the forefront in terms of manifesting gender equality. In the text of the seminal *Solemn Declaration on Gender Equality in Africa*, adopted in Addis Ababa 2004, it is noted *"with satisfaction that our Decision on gender parity is a historic achievement that does not yet exist in any other continent or regional organizations"*. A reference is here made to the decision of AU that at least half of the 10 commissioners of the African Commission should be women, a measure which was and is unique for regional unions globally. The African Union member states decided in this 2004 declaration to further "expand and promote the gender parity that we have adopted regarding the Commission of the African Union to all other organs of the African Union, including its NEPAD programme, to the Regional Economic Communities, and to the national and local levels in collaboration with political parties and the National parliaments in our countries"(Art. 5).

Variation in the Use of Gender Quotas in the MENA Region

Table 1.8 brings an overview over women's parliamentary representation (last election) and the present use of gender quotas in elections in the MENA region. It is remarkable that all countries have adopted some kind of gender quota regulation, with the exception of Lebanon, which also has the lowest representation of women. All included countries operate electoral systems with party competition.

Table 1.8 demonstrates that two of the three main gender quota types are in use in the MENA countries, namely candidate quotas by law and reserved seat quotas. *Candidate quotas by* law, known from Tunisia, Palestine and France, regulate the gender composition, and in PR systems often also the rank order of candidates presented at the ballot. Because it is a legally mandated system, binding for all parties in the election, legal sanctions for non-compliance are possible. The most effective sanction is that the Electoral Authorities reject lists, which do not follow the quota regulations, while financial penalties use to be less effective.

Table 1.8 Women's representation and national quota systems in the MENA region

Country	Women in parliament %	Women in parliament in numbers	Electoral system	Regime type	Gender quotas
Tunisia	31.3 (2014)	68/217	PR	Flawed democracy	Cand.Q. Law: alternating women and men: 'zipper-system'
South Sudan	28.5 (2018)	109/383	In transition	NA	RS: National List for women, 25%
Sudan	30.5 (2015)[a]	130/426	Mixed	Authoritarian	RS: National List for women
Algeria	25.8 (2017)	119/462	PR	Authoritarian	Cand Q Law: varied 20–50%
Iraq	25 (2018)	83/329	PR	Hybrid regime	RS for women, 25%
Morocco	20.5 ((2016)	81/395	PR	Hybrid regime	RS: National List for Women: 60 seats and 30 for youth
Libya	16.0 (2014)	30/188	Mixed	Authoritarian	Cand.Q. Law: 80 seats elected by PR, alternating men and women: 'zipper-system'
Palestine O.T.	12.9 (2006)	17/132	Mixed	NA	Candidate Quota Law
Jordan	15.4 (2016)	20/130	PR	Authoritarian	RS: 13 reserved seats—best loser system
Egypt	14.9 (2015)	TRS and PBV 89/596	Mixed	Authoritarian	Cand. Q. Law for PBV (1/5): About 50–50%, but no rank order
Lebanon	4.7 (2018)	6/128	PR	Hybrid regime	No quotas

Source www.ipu.org and www.quotaproject.org. Single or lower houses. Election-day figures

[a]Incl. those elected in South Sudan, who later withdrew

Notes: *Electoral systems*: PR: proportional representation (Party-list system); Mixed: a combination of PR and plurality/majority elections, here also including 'parallel systems'). TRS: Two Round system. PBV: Party block vote (see www.idea.int—electoral system design)

Regime types: Full democracies, flawed democracies, hybrid regimes or authoritarian regimes. Economist Intelligent Unit's Democracy Index, 2018. Based on a broad set of factors: electoral process and pluralism, functioning of government, political participation, political culture and civil liberties

Quota systems: Cand.Q.Law: candidate quotas by law, binding for all parties. RS: Reserved seat quotas, which reserve a number of seats, which in this case only women candidates can compete for (see www.quotaproject.org)

The second type in use in the MENA region is *reserved seat quotas*. Under this quota system, certain seats are reserved for women in advance, so that only female candidates can compete for them, such as the 60 seats in Morocco, elected on a special National List by both male and female voters (see Chapter 11). The Jordanian reserved seat quota system reserves 13 seats for women, selected among those women, who stood as candidates in the general election, the so-called best losers, i.e., candidates, who gained the highest share of the votes in their respective constituencies without being elected (see Chapter 9). Reserved seats is a well-known measure for securing the election of national minorities.

Electoral gender quotas has been named a *Fast-Track Model* in contrast to the *Incremental-Track Model*, i.e., the slow and gradual development in the old democracies (Dahlerup and Freidenvall 2005). Most post-conflict countries adhere to the Fast Track Model (see Chapter 8).

This book adds to the mounting research on gender quotas with new investigations on the implementation and reform of gender quotas in some political systems in the MENA region, see Chapters 8, 10 and 11. However, most chapters do relate to the adoption of gender quotas, since this measure has been a prominent part of the development of the public post-transition arena, and one of the key demands brought forward by the women's movements, even if not all feminists have agreed on the benefit of this strategy. In Egypt, for instance, the *National Council for Women* and *The Egyptian Center for Women's Rights* supported the adoption of a new gender quota system for the 2011–2012 election after the fall of President Mubarak, while the younger organization, *Nazra for Feminist Studies*, at first were skeptical to this measure, however changed following the result of the first free election with only 1.8% women elected.

The Effectiveness of Gender Quotas

Gender quotas in politics are controversial even within feminist circles (on arguments pro et con, see Dahlerup 2018: 71). It is, however, important to notice, that gender quotas per se do not target the *substantive representation*, i.e., changes in interest representation. Quotas regulate only access and numbers. However, women's organizations and feminist activists, who fight for adoption of gender quotas, want the elected women to make a difference, if not a whole revolution. Yet, the male political elites, who pass these rules in male-dominated parliaments, do it out of mixed motives, which implies as the quota chapters of this book show that a variety of different motives are involved.

Research has shown that the *effectiveness* of gender quotas in changing women's descriptive representation depends on how ambitious the quota rules are, to what extent they fit with the electoral system in place, and if the regulation includes rank-order rules and sanctions for non-compliance (Dahlerup and Freidenvall 2005; Dahlerup 2006; Krook 2009; Franceschet et al. 2013; Darhour and Dahlerup 2013). The *legitimacy* of electoral gender quotas depends on the quota design and on the prevailing discourses on why women are under-represented and men are over-represented—seen in relation to their share of the population (Al-Raida 2009; Dahlerup and Antic Gaber 2017; Dahlerup 2018).

In the literature, the concept of *effectiveness* is sometimes used in a broader meaning, connecting descriptive representation to substantive representation: Will more women in politics lead to changes in the male-dominated political culture and new policies? The importance of a 'critical mass' of women, e.g., 30% is brought forward; however, research has proved, that traditional, informal norms of the political institutions and the color of the government are of greater importance for the policy outcome than the sheer number of women (Krook and Childs 2008). Speaking of South Africa, Goetz and Hassim (2003) discuss the 'effectiveness' of women's political representation by assessing how far increasing numbers of women in politics will help to produce gender-sensitive policies and better public accountability to women. Even if an overview over the literature of the relation between descriptive and substantive representation finds the research results mixed, the picture that emerges shows "that women politicians contribute to strengthening the position of women's interests" (Wängnerud 2009). Especially in the Maghreb countries during the last decades, important constitutional changes and new laws have been passed (marriage laws, inheritance laws, laws on punishment of rape perpetrators, quota laws). Based on our analyses of women in Arab politics post-transition, this book discusses when, where and under what conditions such positive changes have been possible. But more research, including policy tracing, is necessary.

An Intersectional View on Representation

Multiple or changing identities is one issue of importance when studying women in politics from an intersectional perspective. Another important issue is the cumulative nature of disadvantages or, not to forget, advantages, which we also meet in public life. Recruitment patterns can be studied under this lens. Chapter 10 on youth quotas in Tunisian politics, demonstrates how in spite of many young women being elected, middle age politicians with higher seniority in parliament tend to benefit most. Chapter 11 on gender quotas in Morocco is able to show, how incumbent men in fact benefit the most from the gender quota law.

From an intersectional perspective, the election of women based on quota provisions is often met with the question: 'Which women are being elected?' Critics claim that most elected women are elite women in terms of class, education and family connections. Sarah Childs and Melanie Hughes (2018) suggest that from an intersectional perspective on men and masculinities we should instead ask: 'Which men?' How is the dominance of elite men, defined as men from the dominant ethnic, social and economic groups, possible all over the world? Based on an analysis of the accusation in the British Labor Party, that the election of many women in 1997 harmed the representation of working class men, and the Indian debate that a future adoption of quotas for women to parliament would harm the representation of casteless men, Childs and Hughes conclude:

> Elite men draw attention away from their political over-representation by scapegoating elite women, and they may find support from marginalized men, for whom blocking women's advances is easier than challenging elite men's rule. (2018: 285)

The newest Egyptian electoral law of 2015 speaks to this point. After the disastrous result for women of the first free election 2011–2012 after the fall of President Mubarak, the new electoral law of 2015 introduced a complex quota system for the 120 seats to be elected by List-PR (1/5 of all parliamentary seats). An almost 50% quota for female candidates were supplemented with specific quotas for youth, for Christian Cops, for workers, disabled and other groups. Together these quotas superseded the total of 120 seats, which implies that some of these minority candidates must cover several identities.[9]

Plan of the Book

In Chapter 2, Fatima Sadiqi gives a theoretical contribution, in which she presents the concept of the "Center" and traces its evolution from an antagonistic bipolar space in the pre-spring era to a more "diverse, protest-based and pragmatic" space in the post-spring era. The importance of this chapter springs from the fact that it explores the historical contexts which resulted in an initial Social/ideological competition between conservatives and modernists which developed in (1980s–2010) into a fiercer politicized ideological competition between the secularists and the Islamists and ended in the creation after 2011 of the center as an "ideological middle-ground" space with more versatile and diversified voices.

In Chapter 3, Ilyass Bouzghaia examines the different ways gender equality is perceived in CEDAW and in Islamic *Sharia* as two distinct paradigms that inform feminist activism in the MENA region, and how they shape trajectories of women's empowerment and/or marginalization. This chapter highlights the interactive nature of the different perspectives of gender equality conditioning areas of tension, negotiation and compliance. He also argues that many ideo-political, developmental, and legislative situations in the region overlap to constitute ambivalent states for women's rights. But on the other hand authors and theologians have managed to push the Islam and feminism. The chapter ends up suggesting that policy makers and feminist activists should invest in opportunities and face challenges in order to generate novel and effective solutions for increasingly changing and complex societies.

In Chapter 4, Ginger Feather makes use of World Values Survey data to assess variations in popular attitudes toward women's social, economic and political empowerment in North African countries, including variations over time, between the genders and among generations. The chapter maintains that cultural change among North African states toward women's empowerment informs and is informed by cultural change toward democratization, which, it is argued, in the MENA will likely be a feminized, social democracy—instead of the Western liberal model. That is, a state model with greater attention to a state's redistributive capacity, and thus to what is frequently termed women's issues.

In Chapter 5, Saskia Glas and Niels Spierings study why support for feminism was boosted by the uprisings in some Arab countries but not in others. Their analysis is based on Arabbarometer and World Values

Surveys from nine North African and Middle East countries. Within a comparative case study design, the context-dependent norm-diffusion frame help explain these differences and whether Muslim or secularist feminism have flourished. Most importantly, the results show that large-scale protests in countries that were already more gender equal are sufficient to further boost public support for feminism after the Arab Spring. It seems that mass protests need to take place in countries, where women are in a position to take the lead to foster feminist norm diffusion among publics at large.

In Chapter 6, Moha Ennaji analyses women's activism and its importance to the democratization process within a broader socio-political approach. He focuses on women's activism and its impact on public space and on women's civic and legal rights over the past three decades in the region. The chapter presents particularly trajectories of change and achievements in women's rights in three Maghreb countries, Morocco, Tunisia and Algeria before and after the post-spring. The historical trajectory of progress in women's rights is presented as an outcome of the vibrant and active mobilization of secular feminists.

Chapter 7, by Anwar Mhajene, explores the interactive relationship between women's organizing and shifting political opportunity structures (POS) and how POS openings or obstructions shaped Islamist women's political participation in Egypt's Muslim Brotherhood and Morocco's Justice and Development Party. It also explores how Islamist women's political organizing and framing strategies, in turn, reshape these political opportunities. This chapter applies a theoretical framework that views POS as both gendered and dynamic. The chapter finds that the choices, frames and strategies of Islamist women activists constantly change with the change of the political context and alliances and that women's organizing and strategizing considerably reshapes state structures.

In Chapter 8, Aili Mari Tripp analyzes how the Maghreb countries, Morocco, Algeria and Tunisia, have adopted significantly more women's rights provisions in their constitutions compared with the Middle East countries. Discussing the variations found within the MENA region, the chapter attributes these differences to the presence of unified legal systems in the Maghreb, strategies of the political elite in attempting to neutralize Islamic extremism in the Maghreb, political party strategies, especially among leading Islamist parties; and the role of women's movements in and across these countries. Constitutional reforms are seen here as an important measure of societal change, because it has implications for legislative changes, but also because they can be seen as normative statement about how a society sees itself and what it aspires to.

Chapter 9, by Marwa Shalaby and Laila Elimam, focuses one of the most understudied aspects in MENA's legislatures: female committee assignments. While research examining the dynamics of women's numerical presence has proliferated, studies examining the role of female legislators within these bodies remain scarce. With Jordan's lower chamber as the case, the chapter studies the dynamics of female deputies' committee leadership and membership. Variations in women's committee assignments since the introduction of the gender quota in 2003 are analyzed using original legislative data supplemented by qualitative interviews and legislator-level data. The study finds evidence for both horizontal (i.e., committee membership) and vertical (i.e., committees leadership) gender segregation in the Jordanian lower house.

In Chapter 10, Jana Belschner makes an in-depth study of the implementation and intersectional effects of the 'tandem quotas' for women and for youth, adopted for national elections in Tunisia in 2014. The findings suggest that both quotas have the potential to alter political recruitment and representation in Tunisian politics; however, they led to an overproportional share of young women MPs, as young female candidates could fulfill both quotas at a time. Based on an analysis of MPs' socio-economic background, their activity in parliament and their leadership positions, the study concludes that young women remain excluded from inner-party and parliamentarian power. The chapter concludes that, in the short-term, the way in which the political parties implement Tunisia's double quotas may negatively condition both women and youth's substantive and symbolic representation.

Finally, Chapter 11, by Darhour, provides a closer look at the very special reserved seats system adopted in the context of democratization and the strengthening of women's rights in Morocco from 2002 to 2016. It provides a critical analysis of the state's motives for the choice of the format of quota design and reform and the effects that the quota provision have on women's empowerment and democratic development. Despite being numerically effective in fielding 21% of women into the parliament in 2016, the National List provision, it is argued in the chapter, generated side effects on women's entitlement and legitimacy and thereby created the fallacy of a democratic and gender-inclusive parliament referred to as de-democratization. The chapter concludes that Morocco succeeded in institutionalizing various safety valves to include women in parliament but it failed in ruling out their marginalization and sidelining.

Notes

1. Further, the Economist includes fewer countries, 165 and 2 territories, while Freedom House includes 195 countries and 15 territories.
2. See also Paragraph 201 of the Beijing Platform for Action (1995), which states that, "The necessary conditions for an effective functioning of such national machineries include: (a) location at the highest possible level in the Government, falling under the responsibility of a Cabinet minister; (b) institutional mechanisms or processes that facilitates, as appropriate, decentralised planning, implementation and monitoring with a view to involving nongovernmental organisations and community organisations from the grass-roots upwards, (c) sufficient resources in terms of budget and professional capacity; (d) opportunity to influence development of all government policies." In addition, paragraph 203(b) recommends that national women's machineries "have clearly defined mandates and authority; critical elements would be adequate resources and the ability and competence to influence policy and formulate and review legislation."
3. https://www.oecd.org/mena/governance/women-in-public-life-mena-brochure.pdf.
4. See Mousawat program website http://www.moussawat.tn/sites/default/files/PV%20COPIL%20n°1.pdf.
5. In 2004, Egypt's nationality law was amended to include the right of citizenship to those born to either an Egyptian father or mother, in adoption of the principle of gender equality.
6. CRTD.A's Arab Women's Right to Nationality Campaign website, available at: http://crtda.org.lb/project/22.
7. UNHCR report Preventing and Reducing Statelessness: Good Practices in Promoting and Adopting Gender Equality in Nationality Laws. https://www.unhcr.org/531a001c9.pdf.
8. The reservations to the CEDAW conventions from some MENA countries, of which some were later withdrawn, see Chapter 3, did not include Art. 4.1.
9. As an international adviser for the Inter-Parliamentary Union, IPU to Egypt during the making of the new electoral law, Drude Dahlerup heard one of the generals exclaimed: "Can't we just demand that the women candidates have to represent at least one more category".

REFERENCES

Abou-Zeid, G. (2006). The Arab region: Women's access to the decision-making process across the Arab nation. In D. Dahlerup (Ed.), *Women, quotas and politics* (pp. 168–193). London and New York: Routledge.

Adler-Nissen, R. (2014). Stigma management in international relations: Transgressive identities, norms, and order in international society. *International Organization, 68*(1), 143–176.

Ahmed, L. (1982). Feminism and feminist movements in the Middle East, a preliminary exploration: Turkey, Egypt, Algeria, People's Democratic Republic of Yemen. *Women's Studies International Forum, 5*(2), 153–168.

Ahmed, L. (1992). *Women and gender in Islam: Historical roots of a modern debate*. New Haven: Yale University Press.

Al-Raida. (2009). Gender quotas and parliamentary representation. Special issue (Summer/Fall).

Baksh, R., & Harcourt, W. (Eds.). (2015). *The Oxford handbook of transnational feminist movements*. New York, NY: Oxford University Press.

Balaev, M. (2014). Improving models of democracy: The example of lagged effects of economic development, education, and gender equality. *Social Science Research, 46*, 169–183.

Bayat, A. (2013). *Life as politics: How ordinary people change the Middle East* (2nd ed.). Stanford: Stanford University Press.

Beckwith, K. (2014). Plotting the path from one to the other: Women's interests and political representation. In M. C. Escobar-Lemmon & M. M. Taylor-Robinson (Eds.), *Representation: The case of Women* (pp. 20–40). New York, NY: Oxford University Press.

Beer, B. (2009). Democracy and gender equality. *Studies in Comparative International Development, 44*(3), 212–227.

Bellin, E. R. (2011). Lessons from the Jasmine and Nile revolutions: Possibilities of political transformation in the Middle East. Crown Center: *Middle East Brief* 50. Brandeis University.

Bjarnegaard, E. (2013). *Gender, informal institutions and political recruitment: Explaining male dominance in parliamentary representation*. Basingstoke, UK: Palgrave Macmillan.

Bush, S. S., & Jamal, A. A. (2015). Anti-Americanism, authoritarian politics, and attitudes about women's representation: Evidence from a survey experiment in Jordan. *International Studies Quarterly, 59*(1), 34–45.

Butler, J. (1990, 1999). *Gender trouble: Feminism and the subversion of identity*. New York: Routledge.

Caldwell, J. (1982). *Theory of fertility decline*. London: Academic Press.

CAWTAR/OECD. (2014). *The report on women in public life: Gender, law and policy in the Middle East and North Africa*. Paris: OECD Publishing.

Childs, S., & Hughes, M. (2018). "Which men?" How an intersectional perspective on men and masculinities helps explain women's political underrepresentation. *Politics & Gender, 14*(2), 282–287.
Colombo, S., Campelli, E., Caruso, F., & Del Sarto, R. A. (2018, October). *New trends in identity politics in the Middle East and North Africa and their impact on state-society Relations* (Working Paper No. 14). Middle East and North Africa Regional Architecture. https://www.iai.it/sites/default/files/menara_wp_14.pdf.
Dabashi, H. (2012). *The Arab Spring: The end of postcolonialism*. London: Zed Books.
Dahlerup, D. (2006). *Women, quotas and politics*. London and New York: Routledge.
Dahlerup, D. (2014). Representing women: Defining substantive representation of women. In M. C. Escobar-Lemmon & M. M. Taylor-Robinson (Eds.), *Representation: The case of women* (pp. 58–745). New York, NY: Oxford University Press.
Dahlerup, D. (2018). *Has democracy failed women?* Cambridge: Polity Press.
Dahlerup, D. & Antić Gaber, M. (Eds.). (2017). Gender quotas in politics in Central East Europe. Special section of *Teorija in Praksa, 54*(2), 307–412.
Dahlerup, D., & Freidenvall, L. (2005). Quotas as a fast track to equal representation for women: Why Scandinavia is no longer the model. *International Feminist Journal of Politics, 7*(1), 26–48.
Darhour, H., & Dahlerup D. (2013). Sustainable representation of women through gender quotas: A decade's experience in Morocco. *Women's Studies International Forum, 41*(2), 132–142.
Dahlerup, D. & Leyenaar, M. (Eds.). (2013). *Breaking male dominance in old democracies*. Oxford: Oxford University Press.
Escobar-Lemmon, M. C., & Taylor-Robinson, M. M. (Eds.). (2014). *Representation: The case of women*. New York, NY: Oxford University Press.
ESCWA, United Nations Economic and Social Commission for Western Asia. (2015). *Report on National Women's Machineries*.
Ferree, M. M., & Tripp, A. M. (2006). Transnational feminist NGOs on the web: Networks and identities in the global north and south. In M. M. Ferree & A. M. Tripp (Eds.), *Global feminism: Transnational women's activism, organizing, and human rights* (pp. 247–272). New York and London: New York University Press.
Franceschet, S., Krook, M. L., & Piscopo, J. M. (Eds.). (2013). *The impact of gender quotas*. New York, NY: Oxford University Press.
Gamson, W. A. (1990). *The Strategy of Social Protest* (2nd ed.). Wadsworth Publ. Company.
Gandhi, J. (2008). *Political institutions under dictatorship*. Cambridge: Cambridge University Press.

Goetz, A. M. (2003). National women's machinery: State-based institutions to advocate gender equality. In S. Rai (Ed.), *Mainstreaming gender, democratizing the state?* (pp. 69–95). Manchester: Manchester University Press.

Goetz, A. M., & Hassim, S. (2003). *No shortcuts to power: African women in politics and policy making.* Cape Town: Zed Books.

Heydemann, S. (2016). Explaining the Arab uprisings: Transformations in comparative perspective. *Mediterranean Politics, 21*(1), 192–204.

Htun, M. N., & Jones, M. P. (2002). Engendering the right to participate in decision-making: Electoral quotas and women's leadership in Latin America. In N. Craske & M. Molyneux (Eds.), *Gender and the politics of rights and democracy in Latin America* (pp. 32–56). New York: Palgrave.

Inglehart, R., Norris, P., & Welzel, C. (2002). Gender equality and democracy. *Comparative Sociology, 1*(3), 321–345.

Jain, D. (2005). *Women, development, and the UN: A sixty-year quest for equality and justice.* Bloomington and Indianapolis: Indiana University Press.

Jost, J. T., Federico, C. M., & Napier, J. L. (2009). Political ideology: Its structure, functions, and elective affinities. *Annual Review of Psychology, 60,* 307–337.

Kandiyoti, D. (1988). Bargaining with patriarchy. *Gender & Society, 2*(3), 274–290.

Karshenas, M., Moghadam, V. M., & Chamlou, N. (2016). Women, work and welfare in the Middle East and North Africa: Introduction and overview. In N. Chamlou & M. Karshenas (Eds.), *Women, work and welfare in the Middle East and North Africa* (pp. 1–30). London: Imperial College Press.

Krook, M. L. (2009). *Quotas for women in politics: Gender and candidate selection reform worldwide.* New York: Oxford University Press.

Krook, M. L., & Childs, S. (2008). Critical mass theory and women's political representation. *Political Studies, 56*(3), 725–736.

Lister, R. (1997). *Citizenship: Feminist perspectives* (2nd ed.). New York: NYU Press.

Lycklama, G. N., Vargas, V., & Wieringa, S. (1998). *Women's movements and public policy in Europe, Latin America, and the Caribbean* (PhilPapers). Western University.

Maddison, S., & Sawer, M., (Eds.) (2013). *The Women's movement in protest, institutions and the internet: Australia in transnational perspective.* London and New York: Routledge.

McBride, D. E., & Mazur, A. G. (2010). *The politics of state feminism.* Philadelphia: Temple University Press.

O'Donnell, G., & Schmitter, P. C. (1986). *Tentative conclusions about uncertain democracies: Transitions from authoritarian rule.* Baltimore: Johns Hopkins University Press.

OECD. (2014). MENA government tools for gender equality. In *Women in public life: Gender, law and policy in the Middle East and North Africa* (pp. 59–90). Paris: OECD Publishing.

Paxton, P. (1997). Women in national legislatures: A cross-national analysis. *Social Science Research, 26*(4), 442–464.

Pitkin, H. (1967). *The Concept of Representation.* Berkeley, Los Angeles, and London: University of California Press.

Pratt, N., & Richter-Devroe, S. (Eds.). (2013). *Gender, governance and international security.* London: Routledge.

Rai, S., Farzana, B., Nazmunnessa, M., & Bidyut, M. (2006). South Asia: Gender quotas and the politics of empowerment—A comparative study. In D. Dahlerup (Ed.), *Women, quotas and politics* (pp. 222–245). London and New York: Routledge.

Sadiki, L., Wimmen, H., & Al Zubaidi, L. (2013). *Democratic transition in the middle east: Unmaking power.* London: Routledge.

Salime, Z. (2015). I vote I sing: The rise of aesthetic citizenship in Morocco. *International Journal of Middle East Studies, 47*(1), 136–139. https://doi.org/10.1017/S0020743814001494.

Shalaby, M., & Moghadam, V. M. (Eds.). (2016). *Empowering women after the Arab Spring.* New York: Palgrave Macmillan.

Sharabi, H. (1988). *Neopatriarchy: A theory of distorted change in Arab society.* New York: Oxford University Press.

Stepan, A. (2012). Tunisia's transition and the twin tolerations. *Journal of Democracy, 23*(2), 89–103.

Tripp, A. M. (2015). *Women and power in postconflict Africa.* Cambridge: Cambridge University Press.

Tripp, A. M., Casimiro, I., Kwesiga, J., & Mungwa, A. (2009). *African women's movements: Transforming the political landscapes.* Cambridge: Cambridge University Press.

UNDP. (2002). *Arab Human Development Report.* http://arab-hdr.org/. Accessed 11 April 2019.

Wängnerud, L. (2009). Women in parliaments: Descriptive and substantive representation. *Annual Review of Political Science, 12,* 51–69.

Young, I. M. (2000). *Inclusion and democracy.* Oxford: Oxford University Press.

Zubaida, S. (1989). *Islam, the people and the state: Essays on political ideas and movements in the Middle East.* London and New York: Routledge.

NATIONAL GENDER EQUALITY STRATEGY PLANS

Ministry of Family, Solidarity, Equality and Social Development. (2018). The Government Plan for Equality. ICRAM 2. Imprimerie AZ-Editions, Agdal Rabat.

Ministry of National Solidarity, Family and Women's Status. (2013). Mise en place dune base de données sexo-spécifiques: AL INSAF. Algeria.

National Council for Women. (2015). National Strategy for the Empowerment of Egyptian Women 2017–2020.

Programme de promotion de l'égalité centre les femmes et les hommes en Tunisie MOUSSAWAT (Program for the Promotion of Equality between Women and Men) (MOUSSAWAT).

Index

The Economist Intelligence Unit's Democracy Index (2015, 2018).
Freedom House. *Freedom in the World 2018.*
Gender Inequality Index by UNDP.
The Global Gender Gap Report by World Economic Forum.

Websites

Gender Quotas Database. Shows different types of gender quotas in use, country by country. Published by International IDEA, Stockholm University and The Inter-parliamentary Union, IPU: www.quotaproject.org.

The Global Database on Violence Against Women. *Reunite International.* http://www.reunite.org.

Women in National Parliaments. The world rank order of countries and regions. Published by The Inter-parliamentary Union, IPU: www.ipu.org.

PART I

Women's Rights, Feminism and Islamism

CHAPTER 2

The Center: A Theoretical Framework for Understanding Women's Rights in Pre- and Post-Arab Spring North Africa

Fatima Sadiqi

INTRODUCTION

A substantial portion of the literature on the post-Arab Spring youth in North Africa (and the Middle East) underlined that the youth in the region is facing uncertainty (Hale 2011; Lynch 2013; Mulderig 2013; Herb 2014; Langhor 2014; Schäfer 2015; Abbott et al. 2017; Gertel and Hexel 2018, among others). While these studies generally associate this uncertainty with factors like economic hardship and overall marginalization, they lack three perspectives: they do not contextualize facts historically, they do not highlight the pivotal role of women's rights and gender issues in the ebb and flow of uncertainty, and they do not provide a theoretical framework that may explain the facts on the ground. This chapter is an attempt to fill this gap; it starts from where these studies ended, namely that the post-Arab Spring youth face uncertainty and posits what I call "the Center"[1] as an overarching theoretical framework

F. Sadiqi (✉)
Sidi Mohamed Ben Abdellah University, Fez, Morocco

© The Author(s) 2020
H. Darhour and D. Dahlerup (eds.), *Double-Edged Politics on Women's Rights in the MENA Region*, Gender and Politics,
https://doi.org/10.1007/978-3-030-27735-2_2

that contextualizes facts within a historical continuum where women's rights and gender issues are salient in directing and redirecting ideological debates in major transitional and uncertainty-bound phases. I start from the assumption that women's rights and gender issues are the historical motors of change in the MENA region because they are located in Muslim Family Laws and their reform necessitates a transcendence of the sociocultural and economic realms to the legal and political realms where power and authority reside.[2]

In the bigger picture, reflection on the relationship between gender, religion, and the state in the region is not new. Back in the 1920s in Egypt and the 1940s in the Maghreb, women's struggle came at the intersection between colonialism and nationalism (Daoud 1993; Badran 1996) and after the independence of these countries the intersection shifted to modernization, postcolonialism, decolonization, political Islam and increasing demands for democratization (Moghadam 1993; Abu-Lughod 1998; Ennaji 2013; Sadiqi 2014). During these eras, ideologies shifted and reshifted between conservative, modernist, secular, and Islamist trends often creating intense antagonisms and uncertainty and at times subsidizing under political violence or pragmatism. Globalization, technology and generational gaps impacted the more recent shiftings in transformative ways. But inherent in the shiftings and reshiftings is a persistence of women's rights. I posit the Center and its pre-Spring background as a conceptual framework for understanding these shiftings and reshiftings and the central place of women's rights in the continuous ideological ebb and flow.

I define the "Center" as an ideological middle-ground space between antagonistic ideological paradigms that create change amidst uncertainty. As a concept, the Center is about the public sphere and the public discourses it generates. It may be seen as what Bourdieu and Wacquant (1992: 111) call a space that "does not restrict the political field to the political professionals involved in the production of political ideas, programs, and concepts" and hence is not about political discourse per se. In other words, the inclusion of political trends and parties in the Center does not mean that there is a center in these trends or parties; rather, while it includes various versions of these trends, the Center stretches the conceptual space to allow more diversity. The Center is basically created by women's rights and gender issues as these have been consistently used as the bone of contention between the antagonistic trends and paradigms. It is a physical (and virtual) site for demands of social justice and democracy at the heart of which are women's rights. To pull the threads of these themes and contextualize them, this chapter is organized into two main sections: (i) the pre-Spring ideological background of the Center where I first present the gendered history of the conservatives and the modernists, then the gendered history of the secularists and the Islamists, and (ii) the post-Spring center as a space of diversity and transformative evolution which is neither exclusively conservative or modernist, nor exclusively secular or Islamist, but diverse, protest-based, and pragmatic.

THE PRE-SPRING IDEOLOGICAL BACKGROUND OF THE CENTER

Four main ideological trends constitute the pre-Spring background of the Center: the conservative, modernist, secular, and Islamist. These trends have been impacted by specific historical contexts which resulted in an initial ideological competition between the conservatives and the modernists which developed into a fiercer ideological competition between the secularists and the Islamists. Interestingly, both competitions revolved around women's rights and gender issues. These facts are chronologically debunked in this section.

The Gendered History of the Conservative/Modernist Dichotomy (1930s–1970s)

The conservative/modernist dichotomy in Morocco has roots that go back to the 1940s when the French colonizers promulgated the 1930 Berber Dahir (Decree), which required Berbers to come under the jurisdiction of French courts.[3] This promulgation transformed the country in an unexpected and unprecedented way by instigating three things: nationalism, the birth of a "Moroccan identity", and the marginalization of Berber as an "element of discord".[4] These mighty transformations were reacted to by the emergence of two ideological trends: a conservative one, which highlights Islam and tradition as a central component of the Moroccan identity, and a modernist one, which highlights Islam and modernity as a central component of this identity. While both trends were fervent supporters of nationalism and resistance to colonialism, and a Moroccan identity that marginalizes Berber and considers it as a dividing element, they significantly differed in their reaction to the West.

Conservatives did not oppose Western modernity in politics, the military, and economy, but they opposed it in family and social matters. As for modernists, they viewed the West as a potential carrier of progress as long as it did not deny the Arab–Muslim identity of the country. The then dichotomy was "conservatives vs modernists" within a colonized Morocco. It was important in this period to construct Moroccan identity as primarily Arab and Muslim. This materialized clearly in the type of schools that conservative and modernist nationalists built at that time and the type of school curricular contents they strived to implement. While conservatives built schools that would basically teach Arabic and Islamic studies to Moroccan children, modernists built schools that included translation and French in addition to Arabic and Islamic studies.

The conservatives and modernists of the time were urban and upper class, but while they shared nationalistic fervor, both were gendered and male-biased and the notions of women's rights and gender issues were not on their agendas. However women within each camp organized beyond ideological lines and managed to historically inscribe themselves as the first feminist voices in modern Morocco.

The Conservatives

The conservative trend was heavily gendered. For example, while the conservative nationalists allowed women to participate in massive protests against the French colonizers and to smuggle arms during colonization, they tended to favor boys when it came to education on the assumption that boys would be the future leaders of independent Morocco. As for women, they were assigned the duty of safeguarding tradition and Islamic precepts and transmitting them to their children. It is true that some of these conservative nationalists, such as Mohamed al-Hajoui and Allal al-Fassi, who both gained prominence in the independent Morocco, supported girls' education but only as far as it served the nation. Mohamed al-Hajoui, for example, wrote:

> I believe that [women] must be educated in a way that fits our religion and serves the future of our children as useful members of our society. We need to help them [women] raise the future men of our country.[5]

In spite of this, a small number of older conservative women managed to engage in charity activism. An example here is Lalla Radia who, although uneducated, used some of her wealth to help poor girls in Fez enter school.[6] This type of charity activism gave early conservative women a sense of being useful and a sense of self-empowerment.

The Modernists
Like the conservatives, the modernists were male-biased, but unlike them, they were more open-minded as far as girls' education is concerned. For example, Mohamed Belhassan Al-Ouazzani, a prominent modernist of the time, supported the demand of the female members of his party *al-Shura wa al-Istiqlal* (Consultation and Independence) to constitute an association called *Akhawat al-Safa* (Sisters of Purity) in 1946. This association came to be the first feminist all-women association in the modern history of Morocco. Interestingly, this association drew members from the then conservative Istiqlal Party (Independence Party). *Akhawat al-Safa* held their first public meeting on 23 May, 1947 in Fez and invited women from other Moroccan cities to attend. Other public meetings followed, the first one, also a national gathering on December 12–13, 1948 and the second one, an international gathering in June 1951 which was attended by women's delegations from Egypt and Algeria. *Akhawat al-Safa* wrote reports about their activities that included literacy courses, outreach actions on the occasion of religious feasts or at the beginning of the school year, fundraising to offer schoolbags, books and copybooks to young girls from poor families. In terms of print, *Akhawat al-Safa* left one document which they called "*al-Wathiqa*" (the document) where they demanded the abolition of polygamy and dignity in and outside home.[7] By writing this document, *Akhawat al-Safa* expressed a feminist voice that was independent from the political party the association was affiliated to, a remarkable move given the overall historical context of Morocco. The document also used "*karamah*" (dignity), a term that will be later used in the post-Spring period protests.

Modernist women used their education to empower themselves as women. While early conservative women expressed their feminist perspective through charity activism, early modernist women capitalized on journalistic writing. An example here is Malika al-Fassi who, before joining *Akhawat al-Safa*, wrote an article she titled "The Sun Has Risen over Moroccan Women", which she signed as "*al-Fatat*" (The Young Girl) and where she underlined the necessity to educate girls. Malika was also interested in politics and was active in the Istiqlal Party. She was the only woman in the first cells of this party since its creation in 1946 and a militant leader of the women's section in it. Prior to that, she was the only woman in the list of 59 Moroccan nationalists who signed the Manifesto of Independence on January 11, 1944 and sent it to the French authorities demanding the independence of Morocco. Another woman, Alia al-Khsasia, wrote a journalistic article titled "Women's Emancipation" in 1950 where she reports a discussion between two young women about the emancipation of Moroccan women. In this article, Alia addresses issues like Middle-Eastern women and their activist work as well as their success in spreading girls' education as a tool for emancipation. Another example of conservative feminist women is Fatima Kabbaj who wrote a journalistic article under the title "Removal of the Veil and Decency" where she states that Islam does not forbid the removal of the veil on the condition that this removal be accompanied by decency and virtue. In sum, early women activists and journalists/writers dealt with women's issues and dilemmas from a feminist perspective and rallied across conservative and modernist party lines while using whatever means they had to support nationalism such as participating in protests and smuggling arms.

With the advent of independence and state-building in 1956, the Arab–Muslim identity became Morocco's official identity and Standard (written) Arabic, the lingua franca of the Arab world but not a mother tongue that women would use in everyday life, was made the official language and Sunni Maliki Islam was the official religion. King Mohamed V, the first king of independent Morocco, stated in his 1958 Throne Speech:

> We need an education that is Moroccan in its thinking, Arabic in its language, and Muslim in its spirit.

These words set the tone for the 1960s and 1970s ideological debates. However, the need and desire to keep a window open on the West were irresistible for both conservatives and modernists and French was made a second language in the Moroccan educational system, as well as in the administration, the military, and the formal media. In parallel, the state appointed itself as the guarantor of the co-existence of both conservatism and modernity by promulgating the first Personal Status Code (Family Law) between November 1957 and February 1958 with laws that institutionalized the husband's supremacy and the wife's obedience to accommodate the conservatives, and by supporting the massive education of girls in urban areas to accommodate the modernists.

Political conservative and modernist political parties followed suit.[8] This development allowed urban elite women to enter university (first created in 1958). The first cohorts of women with a university degree yielded the pioneer academic feminists who were caught between the two pulling forces of tradition and modernity. Hence, without highlighting religion, these feminists sought to address and fight patriarchy and saw in modernity a path to emancipation, salaried work and self-esteem, and without rejecting the French language and lifestyle, they sought to address and fight alienation. These feminists expressed their views through scholarship, political engagement, and activism. Although the use of Arabic was maintained, the general tendency leaned toward the use of French as the latter facilitated the expression of taboo topics. Academic scholarship and journalistic writings were the most popular expressions of these women's feminist ideas as reflected in the writings of Fatima Mernissi, Leila Abouzeid, Khnata Bennouna, Zakya Daoud and others. From the 1980s onward, and with rampant political Islam[9] in the background, the conservative-modernist dichotomy gradually developed into a secularist–Islamist one.[10]

The Gendered History of the Secularist/Islamist Dichotomy (1980s–2010)

The secularists advocated a separation of religion and politics in public spaces such as education and the media, and in lifestyle such as the dress code and behavior, while the Islamists advocated an Islamization of social life. However, both the secularists and the Islamists recognized monarchy as the embodiment of both trends given the position of the king as the supreme executive authority and arbiter in both politics and religion. Significantly, this new development did not supplant the initial conservative–modernist dichotomy but it politicized it. Islamists, de facto conservative, claimed a new view of Islam that discarded traditional customs and mores but highlighted nostalgia to the political past; and the secularists, de facto modernists, valued some aspects of tradition such as family cohesiveness but targeted the future. On the ground, while the conservative–modernist dichotomy was more attested at the social level, the secularist–Islamist dichotomy was more attested in politics and ideology. Consequently, while the conservative/modernist dichotomy was generally accommodated in Moroccans' behaviour and way of life, the secularist– Islamist dichotomy exhibited clear divergences among Moroccans.

The main divergences revolved around women's rights, behavior and the dress code as tokens of an either secular or Islamist social project.

As a result, the modernists/secularists, on the one hand, and the conservatives/Islamists, on the other hand, capitalized on women's issues in their campaigns and debates. The main goal of both camps was to create a modern society, not modern women. "We want our women to speak French (because a woman can then teach it to her children) but not to act French" one of my male secular interviewees told me (Sadiqi 2014). However, while modernists and secularists share many commonalities, central among which is modernity and women's rights, there are clear differences between conservatives and Islamists, central among which is attitude toward tradition, viewed by conservatives as a value system that spans the private and public spaces and viewed by Islamists (who were seeking a new homogenizing version of living, practicing and ruling in the name of Islam) as wrong interpretations of the Qur'an and Hadith. In politics, modernists tend to support secularists and conservatives tend to support Islamists. From the perspective of this chapter, focus is on the dichotomy secularists–Islamist as it is this dichotomy that both bears on women's rights and gender issues and stirs most tension and debates in the post-Arab Spring Center. The best way to appreciate this and the larger ramifications it entails is to compare the secularists and the Islamists.

The Secularists
The secularist ideology in Morocco has roots in the leftist ideology of the 1970s and 1980s, itself a reaction to what was conceived as a class-based hegemony of the state. With its goals of egalitarianism, the leftist ideology opened the door to the Moroccan secular feminist movement.[11] This movement had to adapt to the then new realities on the ground: a mixture of nascent democratization, political Islam and globalization. A combination of these realities shaped the trajectory and strategies of the movement. For example, the same modernist women who saw in the 1950s–1970s state a symbol of oppression and rallied to the left started to strategize with the state in the face of political Islam which was then considered a threat to both the state and women's rights. Consequently, secular feminists placed their discourse within the universal human rights framework and avoided grounding it in the realm of religion. For example, they did not attack Islam as a source of oppression but attacked patriarchy as such a source.

More importantly, secular feminists reacted to the leftist political parties' inertia in matters of women's rights and started to organize in independent non-governmental organizations (NGO) within their own leftist parties. Some of these NGOs were feminine-feminist extensions of their political parties with a considerable added value: autonomy from the parties. The first independent feminist NGO in Morocco was *L'Association Démocratique des Femmes Marocaines*—ADFM (Democratic Association of Moroccan Women) which developed from the communist *Parti du Progrès et du Socialisme* (Progress and Socialism Party—PPS) in 1985. In 1987, *L'Union de l'Action Féminine*—UAF (Union of Feminine Action) developed from *L'Organisation de l'Action Démocratique et Populaire*—OADP (Organization of Democratic and Popular Action). These two NGOs share similar broad principles and complement each other with the second being more prone to action as its name indicates. Both NGOs are still strong today. The creation of these two NGOs was hailed as a ground-breaking event in the life of Moroccan secular feminism. It not only marked the birth of women's activism in the public sphere of power and the subsequent feminization of this sphere, but it opened the door to the creation of more such NGOs, a turning point indeed.

The two NGOs played a major role in the process of democratization in Morocco. While independent, they did not oppose the broad lines of their original parties and skilfully used the support of these parties to advance their feminist project. When the Socialist Union for Popular Forces Party took power in 1998, secular feminists gained considerable visibility in decision-making not only in numbers (more than five women were promoted to the executive body of the party) but also qualitatively in pushing women's issues to the forefront of national politics. Further, in their strategies, they both criticized and supported the governments of their time. They criticized them for backgrounding women's rights and supported them in the face of ramping political Islam. They also put pressure on the state to reform the family law along CEDAW principles. They did not ask for total secularization, but they underlined the insufficiency of Islamic rights and the need to reform the Family Law using *Ijtihad* (fresh interpretation of *Sharia* law). Thus, in 1992, secular feminists, especially the UAF NGOs championed the One Million Signatures to Reform the Family Law Campaign. The success of this campaign was also a success of secular women mobilizing and protesting in the public spaces.

In sum, secular feminists scored substantial gains for women's rights that were politically translated into more seats in the parliament and more push for the quota system (Darhour 2008). Their efforts led to significant reforms like the 2004 Family Law, the 2008 Nationality Law to cite only these two. However, rising political Islam polarized public discourses and women's rights were the bone of contention. In the face of uncertainty, secular feminists started to reach out to feminist women in the Islamist parties seeking feminist unity across party lines, just like their predecessors in colonial Morocco. But first, who are the Moroccan Islamists and what do they want?

The Islamists
Political Islam appeared in Morocco in the 1980s as an Islamist trend with two faces: a moderate one, the Justice et Développement Party— PJD (Justice and Development Party) and an extremist one, the Justice and Benevolence (JP) Assocciation. While the former was ready to function within the Moroccan monarchical system, the latter did not acknowledge the supreme authority of the king. The advent of a new king in 1999, 9/11, and the ensuing War on Terror in 2001, and the Casablanca terrorist attacks in 2003 pushed the state to adopt a moderate Islamic stance. Thus a Sufi moderate scholar was appointed Minister of Religious Affairs in 2002, the first cohort of Murshidat (female spiritual guides) graduated in 2006 and the Rabita Muhammadia of Ulama was created in 2006. These dynamics were deeply based on women's rights and allowed some women's feminist voices to rise from within the party and the new state structures. These voices may be divided into two groups: those that are tied to the party, association or state lines and those that seek feminist expression as individuals. The PJD women and the murshidats are examples of the first group and individual scholars like Asma Lamrabet and Meryem Yafout are examples of the second group.

The main channels that early Islamic feminists used to disseminate their thoughts and ideas are: preaching, activism, and to a certain extent scholarship. The topics of preaching revolved mainly around how a believer should live and practice his/her religion. For example, "Islamic" feminists both advised women on how to practice their faith and by the same token disseminated the socio-political perspective that Islam had become misguided due to political interests and misogynistic readings. As for activism, it included the organization of religious gatherings and study groups to empower women and allow them to transform their roles in their families. The inspiration they could get from the lives of Prophet Muhammad and his Companions was perceived as very positive for most women. As for scholarship, it included a reading of the Qur'an from a feminist point of view. Gradually like secular feminists, Islamic feminists started to realize what unified women's quest for rights and the gap between the two started to narrow in the immediate years that preceded the Arab Spring (Sadiqi 2014, 2016; Elfatih 2015).

The PJD has been in power since 2011. Although Morocco was spared regime change given the political structure of the country and the reforms that had taken place in the 1990s and the 2000s, the PJD won a massive victory, partly due to the many modernists and secularists who gave it a pragmatic, not a religious, vote in the November 25, 2011 elections. The party then promised to implement secular legislative, administrative, and judicial principles, respect human rights and freedom of the press, and support women's rights.[12]

Although it does not forcefully impose Islamic law, the PJD encouraged common people to live a life guided by Islamic values, including wearing the veil for women. The fact that tradition is deep-seated and easily conflated with religion in Moroccan society enhanced the popularity of the PJD. However, after a couple of years in office, the PJD went back on its promises, especially in the domain of women's rights. It allowed only one woman Minister and assigned her the women's, children and the handicapped portfolio, openly encouraged the moralizing Islamist rhetoric in national debates and among intellectuals and the youth whether in the press, on TV or in virtual media, attempted to lower the age of marriage, and so on. The party was heavily criticized by secular and some Islamist electorate and was forced to "moderate" its statements in the second version of the government when it added four women as Deputy Ministers and only one more Minister. In its last year of the first phase, the PJD was no longer keeping its ideology out of politics, partly in preparation of the 2016 elections. On June 17, 2014 Abdelilah Benkirane, the Party's Secretary-General and Morocco's Prime Minister answered a parliament question–answer session on the status of women's rights in the following terms:

"Today, there is a problem with women's role in modern society; women don't even find time to get married, to be mothers, or to educate their children. Why don't we embrace this sacred status that God gave to women?"

This statement ignited a fierce reaction by women's rights secular NGOs and secular forces and the Prime Minister was attacked on various social platforms, press, and electronic media. Critics highlighted the government's failure to solve the country's economic problems and its recourse to offending women, hence revealing its true anti-women's rights agenda. Khadija Rouissi, an Opposition Member of the parliament qualified the Prime Minister's statement as a "a threat — an insult to all Moroccan women and all the fights waged for many years".[13]

Related to their clash on women's rights, the secularists' and Islamists' views also clashed on democracy: whereas the former viewed it as individual freedom and liberalism and do not make room for the Islamists, the latter viewed it as illiberalism. Women's rights organizations and the feminist camp in general (women academics in particular) reacted against the Islamists' views on their rights and on democracy and widely expressed their views that the use of Islam in politics was a real danger and constituted a backlash on what women and secular forces managed to achieve.[14] Virtual and non-virtual debates ensued and increasingly grew in intensity. The initial secularist/Islamist dichotomy started to give way to more versatile and diversified voices which were creating the Center.

The Post-Spring Center: A Space for Diversity, Protest, and Change Amidst Uncertainty

The mouthpiece of the Moroccan Spring is the 20-February Movement, which gave shape to the pre-Spring polarizations and antagonisms on women's rights mainly between the secularists and the Islamists, themselves having grown from but without dislodging the conservative/modernist polarization and antagonisms.

The 20-February Movement

Founded in late January 2011, the 20-February Movement appeared for the first time on the web in the shape of a Facebook page and a Youtube campaign video. The latter spread quickly and on 20 February, thousands of Moroccans rallied in the capital Rabat. The demonstrations quickly spread to other cities like Casablanca, Marrakesh, Fez, Tangiers, as well as towns like al-Hoceima, Safi, etc. and adjacent villages. Initially, the demonstrators were men and women, young and old, urban and rural, educated and non-educated, politicians and academics, intellectuals and laymen, activists and non-activists, conservative and modernist, and secularists and Islamists. They presented a diverse profile with no leadership and communicated mainly through social media and virtual campaigns/networking. The demonstrations were peaceful and the demands diverse, ranging from reducing the powers of the monarch, more democracy, a change in government, a new constitution, ending corruption, more economic opportunities, Berber rights, reform of education and better health services.

The reaction of the king was swift. On March 9, 2011, and just over a couple of weeks after the massive demonstrations, King Mohammed VI announced in a live televized address comprehensive constitutional reforms that would improve democracy and strengthen the rule of law. He also announced the formation of a special commission with the mission of crafting the constitutional reforms to be proposed to him not later than the following June, after which a referendum would decide on the contents of the draft constitution. On 17 June, and in another live address aired on the national TV channels, the king announced that the referendum was to take place on July 1, 2011. The referendum sanctioned the constitution almost unanimously.[15]

The 2011 constitution came with unprecedented reforms in the history of Morocco, such as more executive power and authority to the prime minister and the parliament, more independence of the judiciary and increased power to some independent commissions. The title "Prime Minister", was changed to 'Head of the Government' in the new constitution, and this function was endowed with three powers that had been prerogatives of the king: presiding over the Government Council, appointing the members of the government, and dissolving the parliament.[16] As for the parliament, it was vested with the power to pass laws on most issues. On the other hand, by recognizing the centuries-old marginalized Berber as an official language, the constitution asserted the Arab-Berber bilingual identity of the Moroccan state, a major break from the hitherto monolingual (Arabic only) official identity of the country.[17]

In a sense, these new reforms instigated divisions in the 20-February Movement and revealed the huge gap that separates secularists from Islamists. Struggle over leadership, the withdrawal of the al-Adl wa l-'ihsan (Justice and Benevolence), and the historical rise of the PDJ in the 2011 elections, resulted in a sharp decrease in the frequency of the protests.[18] However, notwithstanding the gradual decrease in the momentum of the 20-February Movement, the latter created a space where diverse groups met without having to converge; a space with two platforms: physical and virtual. This space was seen by many as a way of bringing back a lost vibrancy and dynamic interactions to public debates. Virtually, some media platforms that were instrumental in promoting the 20-February Movement on the web created their own social media mouthpieces. An example is the bilingual (Arabic and French) collaborative website "*Mamfakinsh*" (No Concession) which was created by a group of young Moroccans of both sexes who were inspired by the 20-February Movement. *Mamfakinsh* seeks to entrench the democratic values of individual freedoms and human rights in society, calls for radical social, economic, and political reform, and claims diverse political persuasions. Seen by many critics as a "citizen" media, it promotes free speech and the right to criticize the decicion makers, especially the government. As such, *Mamfakinsh* is a valuable source of information that the mainstream conventional media does not supply, misinterpret, or simply discard. *Mamfakinsh* inspired a growing number of Facebook groups and blogs that continue the spirit of the 20-February Movement. Some platforms have been created and owned by young women's rights advocates beyond ideology as the following section shows.

The Birth of the Center

The post-Moroccan Spring Center exhibits the following characteristics: it does not have a clear leadership, it is protest-based, it transcends the boundaries of the conservative–modernist and secularist–Islamist dichotomies, it uses conventional and social media and it is porous (i.e., with open boundaries that are not clearly delimited). Hence, seemingly incompatible standpoints (conservative, modernist, secularist and Islamist) may coexist and converse without converging in this space. Subsequently, the Center is bound to be complex and multifaceteous because it addresses different important facets of complex and quickly changing realities. In practical terms, the Center expands beyond the reform movements of the 1990s–2000s and as such, does not easily fall in the Anglo-American or Western European frameworks of what constitutes a "political center" because the base of social reform is expanded and the relations with politics are not direct. Finally, while protest was used in the pre-Center periods, it was more versatile and articulated in the Center as it capitalized on social media for mobilization (Dahlerup

2013). The inter- and intra-debates between various competing ideologies nourished the Center by neutralizing leadership, allowing diversity, and opening the space to evolutive and transformative dynamics as continuously new actors are being heard in the Center: Berber activists, radical secularists, radical Islamists, and so on, and allowing networking (now enhanced by social media) to make room for transversal alliances relatively quick. These dynamics are bound to create uncertainty because the base constantly moves.

In the Center, questions are addressed in a pragmatic way and answers are sought in a quick way: the heavy weight of patriarchy, corruption, the need for a secular space as a pre-condition for the advancement of women's rights as human rights, the inclusion of cultural and language rights, and so on. It is important to note that within the Center, secularism is not seen as the absence of religion; rather, both freedom of expression and freedom of religion or belief are seen positively. Religious freedom also includes the right to challenge dominant religious interpretations of the Qur'an, to change one's religion, and to leave it altogether. Being crucial not only for women, but also for religious minorities, these rights need a secular state that would implement and reinforce them. In fact, only a secular state is seen as capable of allowing religious fundamentalists to have a voice that is capable of limiting the inevitable harm they may cause. In sum, the divide is not inherently between the categories "religious" and "secular", but between the categories "anti-secular" and "promoters of secular values". The Center is also a way of protecting democracy by obliging all ideological hues to respect democratic rule. Given the complexities involved, it would perhaps be more meaningful to speak of a plurality of Centers in the field between the secularists and Islamists—or perhaps middle grounds (in the plural). This makes sense because of the numerous "types" of secularists and Islamists in the Center. Within this context, "inbetweeness" could be a recognizable experience for many Moroccans, North Africans and Middle Easterners (male or female).[19]

Physically, the Center is characterized by spectacular networking between diverse forces. For example, with the recognition of the Berber language, Berber NGOs, including a few feminist ones, entered the public field and weaved relations with various other networks and NGOs, especially human rights and women's rights associations. This culture of networking, which has always constituted a powerful strategy of the feminist movement, asserts the role and significance of the latter in the Center.

Women's Rights in the Center

Although the 20-February Movement did not specifically target women's issues, it is thanks to decades of women's struggle for their rights that issues like education and health care were prominent on the agenda of the movement. Further, it was the protest culture that secular women's activists instilled in the public sphere that opened the door to large-scale demonstrations either to oppose women's rights as in the 2000 Casablanca march[20] or to support them as in the 20-February Movement. Indeed the physical/virtual networking between civil society associations (including the feminine and feminist ones) greatly facilitated the recent protests in Morocco and beyond.

A number of women-related issues are raised in the Center: Islamist rhetoric that aims at rolling back women's achievements in terms of rights, the escalation of gender-based violence pursuant to the escalation of extremism in the region, domestic violence,[21] rape, ignited by the case of Amina Filali, a 16-year-old rape victim who committed suicide after being forced to marry her rapist, sexual harassment, etc. In addressing these issues, secular feminist forces are trying to gain initiative. For example, it was thanks to their endeavors that Article 475 of the Penal Code was modified so that the rapist faces heavy charges even if he marries his victim and sexual harassment is criminalized. In addition, women's rights are at the heart of the new political settlements in Morocco. These rights are increasingly included in "mutual accountability frameworks" between donors and aid recipients in governmental institutions with the aim of regulating political dialogue, aid, trade, gender aspects and wider economic relations. In parallel, initiatives to transform development programs to embed gender equality, women's participation and youth empowerment are on the agenda (Ennaji 2013).

On the other hand, a number of new women's rights platforms have materialized in the post-Spring period and have addressed three main topics: identity, legal Islam, and body issues. The identity issues that are emerging in the female youth's conversations are very much associated with the rural areas (as opposed to the urban ones) and are filling a gap in the pre-Center feminist movement. Thus, a number of Berber (Amazigh) feminist NGOs appeared. It is true that the first such NGO appeared at the beginning of this century, but more and more such NGOs followed the institutionalization of Berber as an official language in 2011, and more and more of them are making their voice heard. Nine such NGOs are now established organizations: Association Tinhinan Khemisset, Voix de la Femme Amazighe, Association Anaruz, Association Tinhinan Tiznit, Association Thaziri, Association Tamghart, Association Tayri, Observatoire Amazighe des Droits et Libertés and Forum des Femmes Amazighes de Tamazgha. These NGOs address issues that were sidelined by the mainstream Moroccan feminist movement, namely gender in relation to language, identity and geographical origin (whether it is urban or rural). When asked, the coordinator of one of these organizations deplored the fact that Moroccan secular feminists target elite urban women to the detriment of rural women, and Islamic feminists focus on religion and fail to capture the "Berber" element which, for her organization, constitutes the historical basis of the Moroccan social fabric that differentiates it from the Middle Eastern social fabric.

Similarly, more and more voices of the younger female generation are expressing support for transnational movements that call for equality in family laws such as Musawah (literally "Equality"), WISE (Women's Islamic Initiative in Spirituality and Equality), WLUML (Women Living Under Muslim Laws), the Oslo Coalition on Freedom of Religion and Belief, Karamah (lit. "Dignity"), etc. Islamic feminists in these transnational networks have been carving out non-patriarchal interpretation of key verses in the Qur'an that are generally justified by the patriarchal schools of jurisprudence. They are showing through a careful interpretation and weighing of texts that things can be seen differently. It seems that while the previous generations saw a tight relationship between legal Islam and the nation-state, the new voices are conscious of the centrality of legal Islam in family laws but seek to eschew this association altogether. Instead, many of them underline the importance of transnational interactions and consultations in matters of legal Islam. For them, transnational legal Islam is more conducive to equality and social justice. Interestingly, these young women do not equate transnational interaction/solidarity with globalization; on the contrary, they express resistance to globalization and underline the importance of local contexts and inclusion in matters of law. When asked to explain this "conundrum", they provided reasons like the "tedious slowness" of the state in implementing reforms and the "attested power" of international pressure on states.

In addition to Berber identity issues and transnational virtual legal Islam, body issues fare high in the topics addressed by emerging female feminists. Although these women recognize that body issues are not absent in the rhetoric of older women's movements, they often deplore that this rhetoric was "too timid" and "rather indirect". Other young women's platforms seek to express themselves freely and to share their ideas. One of these women, Fadwa Misk, created a blog with twenty other young women and called it *Qandisha* (from *Aisha Qandisha*, the name of a cannibal female *djin* in Moroccan folklore) and stated "The difference of opinion does not scare us, it can only be our strength" and added that she and her group chose *Qandisha* because in Morocco, "a woman is treated as Qandisha as soon as she claims her rights".[22] Of the various taboos that attracted this group's attention, the most salient is sexual harassment (*al-taharrush al-jinsi*).

In sum, it seems that theoretically, in the long run the Center will allow a broadening of the support base for women's rights movements, through engaging new youth activists and women in rural and urban slum areas. However, there is a growing feeling that the chief obstacle to these goals is the rise of extremist movements in the region.

Conclusion

The analysis presented in this chapter is meant to center women's rights and gender issues as pivotal in the pre-Center and the Center periods. These rights both create and result from uncertainty and they both create and result from diversity, change and evolution, hence their unique position in the North African historical, sociocultural, economic, legal and political landscapes. Women's rights and issues in Morocco (also in North Africa and maybe beyond) have historically nourished the "uncertain" middle grounds between varying degrees of conservatism, modernism, secularism and Islamism (including political Islam as I argue in Sadiqi Forthcoming). Although Women's rights and gender issues are also increasingly influenced by other strong belief systems (which may be seen by many as 'scientific'—such as the economy and economists in the West) and hegemonic globalization, they remain the real engine of the Center.

In the bigger picture, the use of gender as a lens through which emerging politicized identification processes within the public field are analyzed is a promising field of inquiry which brings together various feminist voices in the region and across the globe. From the perspective of this chapter, this approach brings to light a plurality of identity configurations at play in post-Spring Morocco—ethno-linguistic and non-ethno-linguistic, Islamist and secular, that were marginalized or elided in the process of decolonization. This in turn allows a contextualization of the dominant post-Spring narratives in Morocco and the region—the public role of Islam, women's roles; recent reforms regarding women's legal status, etc. In the midst of continuities and discontinuities, gender politics has indeed always been behind forging constantly new narratives and, thus, constitutes the hope that eternally springs from the cracks of uncertainty.

Notes

1. I first developed the concept of the Center in my book, *Women's Movements in Post-"Arab Spring"* (2016).
2. In my upcoming book *Daesh (ISIS) Ideology and the Gender Challenge: An Insider Perspective* I argue that women's rights and gender issues have been instrumentalized in the history of political thought and that they are central in any counter extremist ideology in the region.
3. The Berber (Amazigh) language and culture predated Islam and are still vibrant in Morocco although Berber has been acknowledged as an official language only in the 2011 constitution (see Sadiqi 2014 for an extensive account of the history of the Berber and its culture and its relationship to Moroccan women's rights).
4. Prior to the Berber Dahir, the populations of Morocco had an "Islamic" identity, which explains the rallying of Berbers and Arabs in the face of colonization.
5. The quote was originally in Arabic, I translated it from al-Hajoui (reprinted in 1995: 219).
6. More information about Lalla Radia and the modernist women cited below is found in Fatima Sadiqi, Amira Nouaira, Azza El Khouly and Moha Ennaji (2009).
7. In Sadiqi et al. (2009), I translated this document into English and presented it as the first printed public female feminist voice in Modern Morocco.
8. The marginalization of rural areas during the state-building period explains Morocco's current paradoxical situation where women have significant legal rights while illiteracy is still very high (Sadiqi 2014).
9. I use "political Islam" to refer to the 1970s onward type of political activity that uses Islam to gain power in the political arena. Political Islam is different from colonial conservatism which used Islamic identity as part of resistance to colonization.
10. The words "secular" and "secularism" derive from the Latin word "saecularis" (meaning "of a generation, belonging to an age") and have a

Catholic origin: the Christian idea that God exists outside time led medieval Western cultures to use secular to involve only temporal affairs and put aside specifically religious matters. However, like most concepts, when linked to "lived experiences," secularism adapts to the overall socio-cultural and political contexts.

11. See Sadiqi (2014) for a detailed analysis of the genesis of the secular feminist movement in Morocco.
12. Given Morocco's multi-party system where no single party can have an absolute majority in the parliament, the PJD has been sharing power with other parties but held the majority of seats (30% in its first phase of government 2011–2016 and 125 seats out 395 in the second phase 2016–2021).
13. See http://www.nytimes.com/2014/06/19/world/middleeast/prime-minister-told-parliament-women-better-off-at-home-than-in-workplace.html?_r=0. Accessed 16 July 2014. Broadly speaking, the tension between the Islamists and the secularists escalated in the recent years and the war of words is sometimes translated into physical violence as the April 24 killing of an Islamist student by a left-wing extremist attests to. Indeed clashes between Islamist and leftist students in Moroccan Universities are frequent.
14. For details, see Sadiqi (2014).
15. However, the 20-February Movement criticized the commission in charge of preparing the draft of the constitution on the grounds that its members were appointed and not elected. Although invited to participate in the work of the commission, members of the the 20-February Movement refused the invitation to participate in the government. Even when King Mohammed VI pardoned and in some cases reduced the sentences of 190 prisoners on April 14, 2011, including Islamists, some protesters wanted to keep up the pressure so that more reforms would come about. Further, the leaders of the movement rejected the constitutional reforms as insufficient and called for continuing protests and boycotting the referendum.
16. The king remains the military Commander-In-Chief and retains his position as the Chair of the Council of Ministers, the Supreme Security Council, as well as the primary bodies responsible for the security policy. A new constitutional provision also confirms the king's role as the highest political and religious authority in the country with the right to preside over the Cabinet in serious matters such as those involving religion, security or strategic policies.
17. As stated previously in the chapter, the monolingual identity of Morocco was decided in the 1930s after the Berber Dahir (decree) was promulgated by the French colonizers to divide Morocco along ethnic lines

"Arabs" and "Berbers," which in fact rallied Moroccans together in the name of Islam, initiated nationalism and conflated the Moroccan identity into "Arab Muslim."
18. The poor performance of the PJD in the government after two years pushed some 20-February Movement members to continue protesting and others to give the government more time.
19. Hanne Petersen (personal communication).
20. Secular and Islamist marches were organized in Rabat and Casablanca, respectively, on March 12, 2000, the first to promote reform of the Family Law and the second to oppose it. See Sadiqi (2014) for more details on the background and consequences of these two marches.
21. Progressive as it is, the Mudawwana does not address gender violence in a clear way.
22. See http://jinn.wikia.com/wiki/Aisha_Qandisha.

References

Abbott, P., Teti, A., & Sapsford, R. (2017). *Youth and the Arab uprisings: The story of the rising tide. The Arab transformations*. Aberdeen: The University of Aberdeen Press. https://doi.org/10.13140/rg.2.2.34963.17445.

Abu-Lughod, L. (Ed.). (1998). *Remaking women: Feminism and modernity in the Middle East*. Princeton: Princeton University Press.

Al-Hajoui, M. (Reprinted in 1995). *al-Fikr al-Sami fi tarikh al-Fiqh al-Islami* (Noble thinking in the history of Islamic thought). Beirut: Dar al-Kutun al'ilmiyyah.

Badran, M. (1996). *Feminists, Islam, and the nation*. Princeton: Princeton University Press.

Bourdieu, P., & Wacquant, L. (1992). *An invitation to reflexive sociology*. Chicago: University of Chicago Press.

Dahlerup, D. (2013). Disruption, continuity and waves in the feminist movement. In S. Maddison & M. Sawer (Eds.), *The women's movement in protest, institutions and the internet* (pp. 20–36). London: Routledge.

Daoud, Z. (1993). *Féminisme et politique au Maghreb. Soixante ans de lutte*. Paris: Maisonneuve et Larose.

Darhour, H. (2008). *Women's political empowerment: Implications of the use of a gender quota in the Moroccan parliament* (PhD dissertation), Morocco.

Elfatih, A. (2015). The Arab Spring: Its origins, evolution and consequences ... four years on. *Intellectual Discourse, 23*(1), 119–139.

Ennaji, M. (2013). Arab women's unfinished revolution. In *The project syndicate*. http://www.project-syndicate.org/commentary/women-in-politics-after-the-arab-spring-by-moha-ennaji. Accessed 21 November 2018.

Gertel, J., & Hexel, R. (Eds.). (2018). *Coping with uncertainty: Youth in the Middle East and North Africa*. London: Saqi Books.

Hale, H. (2011). Regime change cascades: What we have learned from the 1848 revolutions to the 2011 Arab uprisings. *Annual Review of Political Science, 16*, 331–353.

Herb, M. (2014). *The people want to fall of the regime ... or not: Explaining the diffusion of the Arab Spring*. Georgia State University.

Langhor, V. (2014). Labor movements and organizations. In M. Lynch (Ed.), *The Arab uprisings explained*. New York: Columbia University Press.

Lynch, M. (2013). *The Arab uprising: The unfinished revolutions of the New Middle East*. New York: Public Affairs.

Moghadam, V. (1993). *Modernizing women: Gender and social change in the Middle East* (Women and change in the developing world). Boulder: Lynne Rienner Publishers.

Mulderig, C. (2013). *An uncertain future: Youth frustration and the Arab Spring* (The Pardee Papers No. 16). Boston University.

Sadiqi, F. (2014). *Moroccan feminist discourses*. New York: Palgrave Macmillan.

Sadiqi, F. (Ed.). (2016). *Women's movements in the post-"Arab Spring" North Africa*. New York: Palgrave Macmillan.

Sadiqi, F. (Forthcoming). Daesh ideology and the gender challenge. An Insider Perspective (Under review).

Sadiqi, F., Nouaira, A., El Khouly, A., & Ennaji, M. (2009). *Women writing Africa: The Northern region*. New York: The Feminist Press.

Schäfer, I. (Ed.). (2015). *Youth, revolt, recognition: The young generation during and after the "Arab Spring"*. Berlin: Mittelmeer Institute Berlin.

CHAPTER 3

Whose Gender Equality? On the Boundaries of Islam and Feminism in the MENA Region

Ilyass Bouzghaia

Introduction

Gender equality is a term that features as an abstract appealing principle for policy makers to promote in their societies. This is a term that rarely goes under scrutiny in what it would imply for different cultures, societies and individuals. Since its inception, the United Nations managed to advocate gender equality as enshrined in its western-centered paradigm (Bielefeldt 2000). Islamic and Arab societies thus were demanded to ratify these UN conventions from the position of "third world societies" where women are more subject to gender subordination than the women of the west. Such cultural inequality between the East and West has generated multiple problematics in the course of trying to answer the question: whose gender equality are we trying to implement in the MENA region?

I. Bouzghaia (✉)
Center for Women's Studies in Islam,
Rabita Mohammadia of Ulema, Rabat, Morocco

Sidi Mohamed ben Abdellah University, Fes, Morocco

© The Author(s) 2020
H. Darhour and D. Dahlerup (eds.), *Double-Edged Politics on Women's Rights in the MENA Region*, Gender and Politics,
https://doi.org/10.1007/978-3-030-27735-2_3

Several feminist movements have been trying to answer this question from different perspectives insofar as they are affected by numerous socio-political conditions. However, the bottom line remains that Islam and secularism kept characterizing the most dominant disputes about gender equality in Muslim societies. This chapter then attempts to highlight the role of cultural paradigmatic differences in shaping different perceptions of gender equality in their interactive nature in the modern globalized world.

The first section then will provide a glimpse on the MENA region in terms of its shared political, developmental and legislative situations, and the second section will discuss the discursive nature of the boundaries between Islam and feminism, and the ideological complexities that characterize the tension, negotiation and compatibility between the two systems of reference. The third section addresses the controversy over the concept of gender equality as shaped by the local understandings of *Shari'a* law and "universal" CEDAW convention of women's rights. Eventually, this chapter shall reveal some elements of strengths and weaknesses of both feminist trends, and how this poses the question of investing in their opportunities and facing their challenges.

CONTEXTUALIZING POLITICS OF WOMEN'S RIGHTS IN THE MENA REGION

For the sake of mapping out the MENA region in regard to the subject of gender equality and women's rights, it is necessary to start with pointing out to elements MENA region countries share in their history, present and future. I draw here on three situations that are determinant in the way MENA countries deal with internal and external demands of promoting women's rights: First, the postcolonial political situation, second, the developmental situation, third, the legislative situation. Arguably, these are three interconnected situations that greatly affect and are affected by the continuous struggle of contemporary feminist activism.

The Postcolonial Political Situation

Several authors have pointed out to the impact of the colonialism on Arab Muslim countries at different levels. However, the main overarching impact might be the emergence of a weak political elites that got engaged in building the nation-state without completely breaking up with the colonial legacy and without a clear vision for development and women's rights. More, precisely, after the colonizer departed, there was a vacuum in political power that was later occupied mostly by authoritarian leaders who did not pay much attention to the woman's question; rather, they either marginalized and suppressed women's rights and feminist activism, or took complete control over the political scene to pragmatically instrumentalize Islam and modernity in their favor to suppress all political adversaries. Aili Tripp (Chapter 8) argues in this regard that "authoritarian leaders in the Maghreb used women's rights to neutralize Salafi and other religious conservative tendencies". Likewise, we can argue that many rulers have equally used Islam to neutralize and weaken secular feminist tendencies.

The Developmental Situation

Subsequent to the postcolonial political situation, regimes in the MENA region slowly and in variant degrees started to change toward more open forms of governing. However, the remaining fact has always been the weak developmental reforms for society and women in particular. National and international indexes of development annually indicate the extent to which corruption and lack of good governance still impact people's conditions and evidently women's quality of life (Djavad 2016). Although it is hard to homogenize the MENA region's situation in terms of human development indicators (HDI), there is still enough proof that the majority of MENA countries continue to score low in comparison with developed countries when it comes to enhancing people's health care services, access to education (especially among women) and the income per capita. This is a situation that was aggravated by the fact that the prevailing cultural set in the MENA region continues to be male dominated and leads to "the feminization of poverty" (Chant 2006), which indicates that women are doubly oppressed by their socio-political conditions and their cultural surrounding.

The Legislative Situation

According to Fatima Sadiqi (Chapter 2), during the first half of the twentieth century, women's struggle came at the intersection between colonialism and nationalism, and after the independence, this intersection shifted to modernization, postcolonialism, decolonization, political Islam and increasing demands for democratization. Indeed, throughout the last decades, drafting laws that organize gender relations have extensively drawn on the contest between conservative, modernist, secular and Islamist trends that negotiate the reference system that should inform the legislations for women's rights. Noteworthy, while the laws that regulate political, financial and punitive matters in most MENA region are usually positivistic, the laws that regulate family issues remain a dead set against attempts of secularization. Hence, there has only been space of amendment and adaptation in light of each country's capacity to use *Ijtihad* in order to highlight egalitarian potentials of Islam in accordance with international conventions (as will be discussed later).

In sum, the overall contextualization of the MENA region leads to the conclusion that women's rights issues have considerably been affected by the colonial aftermaths which have influenced the political, developmental and legislative situations in different ways and in varied degrees. Arguably, it is the continuum or the break with these situations which creates new atmospheres for women's rights to flourish or to decline. Therefore, women's rights in the MENA region continue to be largely conditioned by political and ideological factors which go side by side with increasing attempts of many authors and theologians to push the boundaries of Islam and feminism for more compatible views in a postcolonial globalized world.

Feminism and Islam: The Cross-Cutting Paths

This section aims to provide an insight into the characteristics of the feminist work in the MENA region in order to highlight the question of gender equality as the core contested concept. This section will firstly invoke the problematic of how feminism, as a term usually loaded with western values, would be adopted or adapted in Arab Muslim contexts, and then what might constitute a middle ground for the two paradigms.

The Newly Born Feminism in the MENA Region

Historically speaking, before the creation of the United Nations and its women's rights conventions (notably CEDAW), the terms 'women's rights' and 'gender equality' did not have an institutional compelling affect on the MENA region countries. That is to say, struggles for women's right were manifested through local, charitable and unorganized work, and without reference to the emblem "feminism" with its underpinning "universal" declarations of human rights. It was until the start of the 80s, when the "international" feminist movement and the CEDAW convention got momentum recognition, that countries were obliged to seriously think of what, why and how to conciliate their cultural local specificities with global standardized requirements of feminism and gender equality.

Feminism in the MENA region, as both a field based movement and an academic discourse, was initially hosted by leftist and secular political parties and followed their agendas. During the 80s until today, the political openness which coincided with the rise of political Islam and the Islamists' gradual integration in the political scene, constituted the impetus of what can be called today "Islamic feminism". This domain _Islamic feminism_ became at the center of an increasing number of studies during the last few decades both at the political and the intellectual levels. Authors like Margot Badran (2009), Miriam Cooke (2001), Valentine Moghadam (2000), Fatima Seedat (2016), Huma Ahmed Ghosh (2008), Amina Wadud (2000), Asma Lamrabet (2016), Asma Barlas (2002), Ziba Mir-Hosseini (2000) and Aysha Hidayatullah (2014) have written extensively on the Islamic phenomenon within feminism.

Margot Badran (2009) points out that the term "Islamic feminism" began to surface in the 1990s in various global locations echoing a discourse that critiques both patriarchal Islam(ism) and secular feminism. Islamic feminism appeared at the time of celebrating the Iranian Islamic revolution which considered secularism an anti-Islamic style of life that threatens the Muslim identity. For Badran, political Islam evacuated Islam from secularism and created a polarization between Islam and feminism in a time Muslims were asking the question: How to be modern and Muslim at the same time. Miriam Cooke (2001) goes in the same line arguing that Islamic feminism came to "invites people to consider what it means to have difficult double commitment: on the one hand, to a faith position, and on the other hand, to women's rights inside the home and outside".

Boundaries of the Islamic and the Feminist

Such double commitment is seen for some authors as an oxymoron, and for some others as a legitimate feminist pathway. Secular feminists like Haideh Moghissi (1999), see that women's rights can only stem from secular, cross-cultural and universal premises that should not be undermined by the specific socio-religious context of a society. While Moghissi mixes in this argument between Islam and fundamentalism considering them as inseparable, Fatima Seedat (2016) views that Islam and feminism are incompatible on the ground that there should be a critical space maintained between two intellectual paradigms that inform Muslim women's anti-colonial equality struggles in the neocolonial present. Holding the same view but from another perspective, Asma Barlas (2002) argues that because the Qur'an's epistemology is inherently anti-patriarchal, it does not need an external paradigm to be labeled feminist. In another regard, Barlas further explains that she would agree to be called an Islamic feminist only if we consider Islamic feminism as a discourse on gender equality and social justice that derives its understanding and mandate from the Qur'an. Here, Barlas finds it critical whether or not to consider the Qur'an as a "discourse" because not all Muslims are Islamic, and not all Muslims read the Qur'an in the same way. Therefore, she argues that "treating the Qur'an as a discourse is a rather obvious attempt to secularize (desacralize) it" (quoted in Hidayatullah 2014: 116).

Through other different argumentations, Islam and feminism would be compatible for other authors. Margot Badran (2009), for example, sees that secular feminism is Islamic and Islamic feminism is secular because Islam is *din wa dunya*, to translate the phrase, Islam combines 'the religion and the everyday life'. Moreover, Feminism for Badran needed a new edge, and Islamic feminism provided it through a new thinking and new tools taken from secular feminism to generate a progressive religious discourse that should not be excluded from the general body of feminism. Moroccan Islamic feminist Asma Lamrabet (2016) in the same line contends that it is both possible and legitimate for Muslims to be a believer and a feminist at the same time, since Islam enshrines great potentials of egalitarianism and in opposition to those who monopolize the feminist discourse within the secular endeavor. Leonard Grob et al. (1991) enumerate the general rights and ethics embedded in Islam which make of it a female friendly religion far from Islamophibic stereotypes and local patriarchal practices, usually attributed to Islam. For both Riffat Hassan (2008) and Huma Ahmed Ghosh (2008), it is possible to discuss Human rights within a religious framework. Eventually, as for Fatima Mernissi's (1991: ix) thoughts "We Muslim women can walk into the modern world with pride, knowing that the quest for dignity, democracy, and human rights, for full participation in the political and social affairs of our country, stems from no imported Western values, but is a true part of the Muslim tradition".

Indeed, the debate about the inclusivity and/or exclusivity of Islam and feminism of one another has created a series of rhetorical battles where concepts became fluid in the process of categorizing and labeling, and this has fueled ideological battles more than it has served real interests of women. However, it remains plausible to conclude that if we define both feminism, as a movement, and Islam, as a religion, broadly as open-ended frameworks of women's rights that are accepting mutual influence, then yes, Islam and feminism would be compatible. Likewise, if we define feminism and Islam more narrowly as closed and dogmatic paradigms that are doomed to contend, then no, Islam and feminism would not be compatible. Hence, this implies that there is a need of an open and pragmatic dialogue to solve the complexities of women's realities in different contexts.

Feminist Movements and Discourses in the MENA Region

In the MENA region and even beyond, Valentine Moghadam (2003) differentiates between three types of feminist movements in Islam. The first one, 'Islamic feminism', grounds its arguments on Islam and its teachings and can include non-Muslims in the discourse and debate. The second one, 'Muslim feminism', is a movement that believes in Islam but might also use arguments outside Islam such as an international human rights agreement to combat gender inequality. The last type is 'Islamist feminism' which advocates the notion that the Qur'an can mandate an Islamic government that would defend women's rights in the public sphere but not challenge gender inequality in the personal, private sphere. While Moghadam makes reference to these terms, she asserts that the most dominant and popular movement is the Islamic feminist movement.

Moghadam's differentiation between feminist movements in Islam extends to classifying these movements' discourses into three types: Islamist (traditional), liberal/left in orientation (secular) and Islamic feminist (progressive). The Islamist (traditional) discourse is mainly characterized by the view that women are not equal to men due to their biological differences, and biology necessitates different gender roles in society. Such view does not imply that women are inferior to men; rather, it means that women are most suitable for "their" roles as wives and mothers and their primary place is in the household raising children, not in the workplace competing with men (Margaret 2005). Traditional and conservative Muslims usually see that gender equality is detaching women from their femininity and thus gender equality is a concept imposed by Western forces implying sameness between genders (this idea will be further discussed in the next section).

The second discourse about women's rights in the Muslim context, called secular, is widely advocated by many western and Muslim feminists as an approach that focuses on rights, liberation and agency. This secular viewpoint places Muslim women's rights within the global understanding of "universal" human rights. Secular feminists in the Arab world typically address the legislative domain as a key to change the gender biases of a law usually derived from the Islamic *Sharia*. The secular approach also appears to uphold many of the western prejudiced stereotypes on Muslim women. For example, many Muslim secularists regard the veil or *hijab* as a form of social control and patriarchal legacy. While this view is widely spread among secular feminists, Islamic feminists (the third discourse) reject or problematize this secular paradigm because it tends to disregard Muslim spirituality as an aspect of women's identities and source of liberation.

The third discourse, Islamic feminism (progressive), therefore, features as a position that stands neither in complete opposition nor alignment with both the traditional view and the secular view. The Islamic feminist discourse is rather a call to reinterpret the religious texts by women in order to reconstruct more freedoms for women. In other words, it is a discourse that bases its argument on the premise that men have interpreted the Quran to further their own power in relation to women. Therefore, they blame men's interpretations and male-dominated norms for the unequal treatment of women, not Islam (Fattah 2006). Progressive or Islamic feminists rely heavily on hermeneutics and "Qur'anic exegesis" in order to bring about egalitarian potentials of Islam based on feminist reading of Islam.[1] Such reading emphasizes both Islamic legitimacy and personal agency as Amina Wadud proclaims (Wadud 2000).

It is, therefore, a double fold mission for Islamic feminists, who find themeselves caught between the patriarchal readings and practices in the name of Islam on the one hand and the hegemonic western and secular model of feminism on the other hand. Interestingly, Islamic feminists have recently managed to coin a metaphorical label that summarizes this double commitment. "Third way feminism" was brought into light as a concept that expresses a way out of two extremes: The traditional misogynist understandings of Islam, and the dominant supremacist discourses claiming impossibility to defend women's rights from a religious perspective (Lamrabet 2016). The work of Third way Islamic feminists is located in opposition to the total endorsement or rejection of either Islam or feminism as closed and full-fledged paradigms. In her book *Beyond Feminism and Islamism: Gender and Equality in North Africa*, Doris Gray (2015) defines this term as an inevitable negotiation of internal tensions between what has been dubbed 'tradition' and 'modernity' Fatima Sadiqi (2016), in her book, *Women's Movements in Post-"Arab Spring" North Africa* and in Chapter 2 of this volume, calls this "in between" discourse the "center" as she describes it to be "*an ideological middle-ground space between the increasingly antagonistic paradigms of secularism and Islamism in post-revolution North Africa*".

In fact, it is equally interesting to track the evolution of feminist discourses within political parties and movements. *Ennahda* movement in Tunisia and the party of justice and development (PJD) in Morocco represent an ideal example of Islamists' recent tendency to yield into more flexible and pragmatic attitudes from the position of governance rather than opposition. For example, *Ennahda* party-movement was not able to curb the secularist impulse to approve the equal inheritance law in 2018, and the PJD in Morocco pacified its refusal of the plan to integrate women in development after Casablanca Bombings and the implementation of the new family code in 2004 (as illustrated in Chapter 7). Also, the PJD in 2015 was powerless to prevent the adoption of the optional protocol to CEDAW[2] which was long objected on the basis of infringing the kingdom's sovereignty. One reasonable explanation of Islamists' willingness to make concessions more than ever before is offered by Asef Bayat (2013) who coined the term "post-Islamism" which refers to the shift of rigid Islamists' discourses into a hybrid tendency to combine Islam and democracy under the pressure of new political atmospheres and the growing intellectual demands to employ *Ijtihad* and reform the religious discourse.

Overall, it is within this broad spectrum of these feminist movements and discourses that one can trace whose gender equality is sought to be implemented in the MENA region. Agendas of gender equality, as adopted by diverse policy makers and feminist actors, are based on a number of underpinning paradigms and epistemologies to promote gender equality, each from its perspective. The following section then will discuss the overarching paradigmatic views toward gender equality as enshrined in CEDAW and Shari'a law, and the debatable issues they generate and future prospects they suggest.

On CEDAW and *Shari'a*: Whose Gender Equality?

Initially, it is important to note that the historical and cultural background of any society plays a vital role in shaping most of the current perceptions on any given subject. Gender equality is not a mere idea without its cultural and philosophical loads; rather, it is a product of certain historical and cultural settings. This is why the connotation of the terms 'gender' and 'gender equality' generates different, sometimes contending attitudes among people. In the Arab Muslim context, these terms, along with others like liberty, democracy and women's empowerment trigger controversy about the way they should be advocated and implemented.

Many research and studies, among which the chapter presented by Ginger Feather (Chapter 4), have pointed to the idea that concepts and values are greatly determined by the cultural set where they are being used. Therefore, it is logical to assume that gender equality, as a sociological paradigm[3] and as a feminist motto, has proved to be not very welcomed among Arab and Muslim communities. Surveys and polls like Pew survey (2013), Gallup (2006) and the World Values Survey (Inglehart et al. 2014) have included questions on gender relations and systems of reference that generally show that the majority of respondents appear to express skepticism, if not rejection, of gender equality as embedded in western secular paradigms.

Based on this, it becomes legitimate and important to investigate the underlining philosophical, cultural and religious paradigms that govern the views to gender equality and what they would imply for the (re) organization of gender relations in Muslim majority contexts. Hence, juxtaposing the Islamic *Shari'a* with the CEDAW convention as two prototypes for gender equality that in the MENA region shall help in highlighting how they would converge and diverge. Arguably, it is this differentiation which outlines the contours of the debate on gender equality as a contested concept.

Secularism/Divinity

Above all issues, feminists and policy makers in the MENA region appear to disagree whether laws that regulate gender relations and gender equality should be derived from a divine source of reference or from humanistic and positivistic thoughts. While many Islamic feminists insist that Islam is the source of reference that should inform Muslim legislations because it was revealed as both a faith and a law (*Aqida wa Shari'a*), secular feminists argue that Islam should be limited to the personal and spiritual side while legislations and political affairs should be held by human reasoning and current societal requirements.

Basically, one should depart from acknowledging the great impact religions play in people's mindsets and values, especially in Muslim societies. Paul Michell and Mohammed Al-Mossawi (2002) state that "*Religion [within a society] has always helped to define what is proper and fitting, and that is not different in Islamic societies*". In this line, it was found in the world values survey (2014) that in Morocco for example 88.9% rated that religion is very important in their lives, and in the Pew Survey (2013) that a large number of them (83%) are in favor of making Islamic law the official law in their country. For Fazlur Rahman (1998), to be a Muslim stems from one connotation of the word "Islam" which implied the feeling of surrender to God's will which brings peace and safety.

This is a belief that, for Mohammd Kadkhodaei and Terife Aghamajidi (2017), is the core of all values for Muslims, while in the West, rights and laws are positivist and are formulated by people according to their own preferences leading to individualism and liberalism. A number of other authors further point out to a cultural bipolarization between the "Western" mind and the "Eastern" one. In his seminal work, "The Clash of Civilizations", Samuel Huntington (1993) envisions future conflict between the Christian West and the Muslim Orthodox East occurring not along nation-state territorial lines, but along cultural lines. Such dichotomization is similarly held by Islamic authors like Mohamed Talabi (2013) who summarizes aspects of the "Western" civilization and its values as follows: Secularism at the political level, materialism at the philosophical level, capitalism at the economic level, liberalism and individualism at the social level. These aspects for Talabi represent a package of "Western values" that are different from heavenly and non-material thoughts in Islam.

Essentially, one can broadly deduce that, at the philosophical and ideological levels, Islamic values contrast with the broad feminist cause insofar as the Islamic values stress more on the centrality of the family as a social unit bound to certain religious purposes, while feminism, by definition, stresses on the woman and gender equality as the unit of analysis within the positivistic vision celebrating liberty and individualism. It is in this context that western loaded values have collided with Islamic values and created a state of ambivalence how to be a Muslim and meanwhile believe in gender equality. Such belief in gender equality, for Islamic feminists, should primarily stem from local Islamic potentials to support this principle, not from a "Universal" western paradigm.

The Local or the "Universal"

In her article "Islamic Women's Activism in the Arab World", Julie Elisabeth Pruzan-Jørgensen (2012) concludes that "many of these [Islamic Women] activists simply do not want the 'universal' women's rights as they are formulated in the UN conventions as they oppose their inherent secularism, individualism and aspiration toward equality (as opposed to equity) and they strongly oppose attempts to have it imposed on them". This is a statement that summarizes much about the dichotomy between Islamic/st and secularist feminist activism. Importantly, while each feminist trend insists that its source of reference should be the one that informs the country's legislations, almost none of them call for complete and absolute rejection of the other. Islamists and secularists usually don't mind if the rival source would support their own Islamic or "international" standards of women's rights. Thus, the debate is more about the primacy of sources of reference rather than establishing a one and only reference system in a country. Therefore, feminists in the Muslim context are generally divided into Islamic feminists who are skeptical toward the possible Western hegemonic implications of CEDAW, and secular feminists who fear that Islam is not sufficient or effective to account for gender equality requirements.

Within the scope of my Ph.D. thesis, which I submitted this year (Bouzghaia 2019), I conducted twelve interviews with famous Moroccan feminists who belong to different fields and ideologies. Among these feminists, many Islamist feminists denounced the calls to prioritize "international" conventions over national and religious laws. For example, Hanane Benchakroune (interview 2017), the director of *"Ish'ae"* center for family studies sees that "International conventions did not bring anything new and different from what the Islamic Shari'a already brought". Thus, she suggests that the problem is that "we just don't show pride of our own religious reference". Habiba Hamdaoui and Hafida Ferchachi (interview 2018), from Jama'at Al-Adl Wa Al-Ihsan (Justice and charity group) explain that "The international conventions came in the context of globalization that tries to erase the specificity of other cultures, while there are differences that should be respected, this is called a cultural invasion, so the question to be asked is whether these debates are imposed or they are coming from the heart of society". Accordingly, Aziza Bakkali (interview 2017), the head of *Azzahrae* forum criticizes those who "depart from these conventions to reject religion in order to call for equality in inheritance and abortion which come from another philosophical view".

Based on these arguments and others, the International Islamic Committee for Women & Child, affiliated to the Al-Azhar Islamic Research Academy in Egypt, issued a document against the CEDAW called "The Islamic Charter on Family". This charter was presented *"to the international conferences as an international Islamic declaration to rescue the family from the depravation that is being forced upon it by western globalization"*. The main argument in this charter is that, unlike Western societies, "the Muslim community is made up of families that are connected and cohesive like a single body, rather than being composed of detached individuals; and this cannot take place except through marriage".[4] Zainab Abdel-Aziz (2013) in a national seminar, highlights concepts like: Gender, empowerment, reproductive and sexual health, homo phobia, sexual orientation freedom, the family in all its forms, unremunerated work, maternity as a social function, stereotyped roles… etc. as terms that reflect aspects of the Western culture that are based on values of individualism, liberalism and permissiveness, in addition to a conflict and competition based orientation between the sexes.

To be more specific, it appears that the controversy over the local and the "Universal" is more centered around five main articles in CEDAW: (articles 2, 9[2], 15[4], 16, and 29).[5] These articles are usually subject of objection based on religious and nationalism argumentations which can be outlined in three main points. The first is the objection of the supremacy of an external system of reference. The second is the possibility that international conventions infringe the local cultural and religious specificities. The third is the claim that the cultural load of these conventions threaten the traditional configurations of the Muslim family. Noteworthy, such controversy does not always lead to rigid polarizations between distinct feminist trends. That is, many feminist activists, especially from the field of academia, manage to conciliate and bridge the gap between what is local and "Universal" for their contexts. For more in depth discussion, one needs to further inspect the gender related issues and how they constitute the dichotomy or the compliance between the secular and the Islamic.

Gender Differences and Gender Equality

Patterns of gender relations in issues like marriage, polygamy, divorce, custody and inheritance encompass a large space of understanding the cultural paradigms as enshrined in CEDAW and in Islam. In fact, the notion of gender equality in the MENA region is usually criticized based on the perception that it does not respect gender differences and calls for gender sameness. Such criticism implies the premise that gender equality undermines the role of women as mothers and wives, which threatens the structure and functions of the traditional family.

Article number 16 in CEDAW (1979) represents the most contested provision as it stipulates that "States Parties shall take all appropriate measures to eliminate discrimination against women in all matters relating to marriage and family relations and in particular shall ensure, on a basis of equality of men and women". This is a phrase that represents for many Islamic/sts a violation of many provisions in the Islamic Shari'a which does not treat men and women on the basis of equality, rather on justice, equity and complementarity. Soumia Benkhaldoun (2011), a leading female member in the justice and development party, condemns the way article 16 contradicts with Moroccan national and Islamic provisions. Benkhaldoun, along with many Islamists, suggests that Morocco should have kept its reservation on this article on the same basis that "An equality of this kind is considered incompatible with the Islamic Shari'a, which guarantees to each of the spouses rights and responsibilities within a framework of equilibrium and complementary in order to preserve the sacred bond of matrimony" (UN women's website reservations).

In opposition, secular feminists in the Democratic Association of Moroccan Women (ADFM) (2013) have always urged for a complete ratification of all the convention of CEDAW with the slogan "equality without reservations", claiming that "the extent and nature of reservations on the most important articles of CEDAW (articles 2-9-15-16) emptied the ratification of its purpose and its essence". Benkhaldoun sees that article 16 is obviously against the Islamic prescriptions which oblige the husband to pay the dowry for the wife and to support his family, while the woman is not obliged by law to support the family. Also, upon the dissolution of the marriage contract, the husband is obliged to pay the alimony, while the wife has full freedom to dispose of her property during marriage and at its dissolution without the husband's supervision. A reading of these Islamic prescriptions apparently gives the impression that they put more responsibilities on the husband and little, if no responsibilities on the wife, in an act of positive and protective discrimination. However, indeed, these prescriptions are socially and culturally the same that entail other inequalities, discrimination and violence against women in the name of protecting her, like the notion of Wilaya (tutorship) and Qiwama (Guardianship).

In the Moroccan legislation, the new family code stipulates shared responsibility between the husband and wife in article 4, for this reason, Raja Naji Mekkaoui (2011) argues that Morocco does not need to ratify the conventions because they are no more valid in the light of the progressive provisions of the new family law, which guarantees equality between spouses before, during and after marriage (…) it is even going beyond this equality by stipulating more privileges for the wife. Makkaoui further notes that interpretations of these reservations remain controversial because of ideological sensitivities.

Either because of ignorance or because of ideological dogmas, many Islamists hold the idea that gender equality in CEDAW entails treatment of men and women the same without considering their biological differences. In fact, this is a claim that is not pertinent and often reflects an ideologically instrumentalized strategy. By way of objective explanation, there are CEDAW articles that address the respect of biological differences between men and women in the provisions for maternity protection and reproductive rights for women (CEDAW articles 4[2], 5[b], 11[2]). This act of addressing these biological needs for women also points out that equality from this perspective does not requisitely mean identical treatment of the sexes. Katja Zvan Elliott (2015) explains in this regard that "Women do not have to be more like men to be equal because human rights are not androcentric, in which men would be made to be the standard of human experience. In other words, to demand to be treated like a human does not mean to be treated like a man. Equality, therefore, is not understood as the 'mechanical equality'".

Furthermore, the United Nations has issued some general recommendations (1999) where it explains three basic principles that outline its International agenda: (1) substantive equality, (2) non-discrimination and (3) state obligation. While the last principle deals with the issue of cases of interference in the national and religious sovereignties, the two first principles clarify the UN women's agenda in regard to gender equality. It explains that the principles of substantive equality are different from formal equality which translates into an identical treatment of women and men. Therefore, CEDAW upholds that it does not call for formal equality but rather for a type of equality where men and women cherish the same and equal rights and duties. CEDAW also rejects protective equality which means depriving women from their civilian rights based on traditional categorization and essentialization of their roles in society. The advocation of substantive equality thus stems from its definition as a sort of equality that seeks to guarantee not only equality of opportunities among men and women but also an equality of outcome through combating cultural and historical factors of marginalization and exclusion inflicted on women.[6]

Malika Benradi (interview 2017), a professor of law at Mohamed V University, explicates that "For us, the concept of equality we give it its legislative meaning, same rights and duties, and the complete equality does not exist in any country but in our research we specify it as same rights and duties in both the private and the public spheres. The problem is that people keep associating women with the private sphere while assuming that the man cannot wash the dishes and take care of his family". From a close perspective, Aicha El-Hajjami (interview 2017), a professor at Qadi Iyad University, further argues that equality lies in a sort of "complementarity that exists only in the biological roles where the man does not get pregnant nor can breast feed the babies, and even in Islam we see the role of each person is based on his/her own capacity and qualities".

Aicha El-Hajjami, who represents the type of feminists who seek to bridge gaps between Islam and feminism, presented justification of the legitimacy of withdrawing previous Moroccan reservations on CEDAW. For her, for example, the Moroccan woman was not equal to the man in terms of signing the marriage contract without her legal male tutor. El-Hajjami explains that eliminating the condition of the tutor is a legitimate Islamic act through questioning the authenticity of the *Hadith* and through invoking examples of women in the prophet's time who were not obliged to be married necessarily through their parents' supervision.

For the issue of equality, El-Hajjami sees that "Equality in CEDAW goes in line with Islam if we consider that Qiwama (male guardianship over the family) does not mean women's inferiority and men's superiority, rather it means that God has preferred men in some matters and women in some other matters", and "Bima Anfaqou" (for what men spend [for maintenance] from their wealth) means that "since men used to be supportive of women thus responsibility was given to him, but it definitely does not mean authority and oppression of women as some early interpreters like Ibn Katheer and Al-Qurtobi understood it".

Investing in the Opportunities and Challenges

Based on the above, it seems that Islamic and secular fundamentalisms exchange stigmatized perceptions on each other, and don't show readiness to cease skepticism toward the possibilities of compliance. Evidently, it is true that this perpetuates the traditional dichotomy between Islam and feminism, but this also gives cause to Islamic feminist to emerge and strongly seek to establish a female friendly reading of Islam from within. While this endeavor involves elements of strengths, it also involves points of weakness that overall need to be treated with the goal of investing in the opportunities and facing the challenges.

For Elizabeth Pruzan (2012), the main element of strength in the Islamic feminist movements is their shared source of reference _Islam_ as a guiding beacon to all interpretations and works. This creates a strong legitimacy and closeness to the people they are speaking on their behalf. Also, their attempts to perform in distance from political agendas, which creates possibilities of conciliation between the Islamic and the secular, especially that most of them are educated and belong to the intellectual elite. This is an asset that equally increases their openness and interaction with different worldwide experiences.

In contrast, Pruzan points out to other elements of weakness that put the Islamic feminist project under scrutiny. For example, they are critiqued for being a possible (re-)legitimization of repressive patriarchal traditions and practices, threatening individual freedoms and essentializing, monopolizing and politicizing interpretations of Islam and the ways of being a Muslim in a globalized world. Qudsia Mirza (2008) similarly outlines some methodological critiques to the Islamic feminist project. Mirza attacks the way interpretive techniques always lead to strong denial of the possibility that Quran might be a patriarchal text. Also, to avow that Islam is the only model within which reforming agendas can be executed. Another criticism is that Islamic feminism is being elitist and couched in the world of academic rhetoric rather than actually working on solving problems of women in their daily lives.

For this exact reason, which largely applies to both trends, we see that expectations from intellectual feminists are low when it comes to exerting a real impact on people's lives. To my mind, this requires them to bridge the gap between two missing links: between knowledge and policy makers on the one hand, and between knowledge and the public masses on the other hand. Otherwise, feminist agendas will remain a pool of struggle among ideological trends which eventually mobilize society with little or no well-grounded academic knowledge.

In my M.A. thesis (Bouzghaia 2012) titled *The Feminist Movement and Social Change in Morocco: Trends and Impacts*, I concluded that the Moroccan feminist movement in the whole _Islamist and secularist_ contributes equally and in a positive complementariness to the dynamics of social change in Morocco. The impact of the two distinct feminist trends on the social life of Moroccan people can be described from the perspective that since Islamist feminists inspire their work from Islam and utilize the social approach, they give more importance to the stability and cohesion of the family, and since secularist feminists derive their source of reference from the CEDAW and mostly utilize the legal approach, they emphasize more on the woman and gender equality. Such combination of the two agendas leads to a balanced work of sustaining and promoting both family solidarity and gender equality in a society that needs both values to be cherished in non-contradictive ways.

To sum up, it is true that the feminist work, both in separation and coordination, helps to forge the trajectories of change. However, the broad image indicates that such work should be intrinsically accompanied by a clear political will to promote women's conditions on the ground, and to administer the ideological alignments in discourse. With this, lot of challenges can be resolved and numerous opportunities can show up.

Conclusion

This chapter has shed light on the political, developmental and legislative situations that characterize the overall dynamics of the MENA region in regard to the question of women's rights and gender equality.

These situations are arguably fundamental in assessing the double-edged politics of empowering and sidelining women in Arab and Muslim contexts. These situations equally generate the atmosphere where feminist movements operate. The broad division of feminist movements into secularist and Islamists helps in tracing their underpinning paradigms and agendas and unveiling how they intersect in order to promote women's rights and gender equality. This chapter has focalized on the notion of gender equality as a central element in drawing the lines of convergence and divergence between the secular and the Islamic feminist endeavors.

Between the inclusive and the exclusive approaches to Islam and feminism, many authors, unlike ideo-political actors, have managed to push boundaries of the two paradigms into more possibilities of feminizing Islam and Islamizing feminism in the MENA region. However, the chapter suggests that there are still basic issues that are unresolved within the dualistic nature of policies, legislations and social values in the context of postcolonial globalized MENA region countries. The divinity or secularism of laws constitutes the main hindrance that creates ambivalence and fluctuation in advocating a clear paradigm for empowering women. Another subsequent issue is the local vs. the "Universal" dichotomy of systems of reference insofar as Islamic and secular feminist activists are not on one page when it comes to whether the CEDAW represents a "Universal" prototype for women's rights or a western hegemonic instrument that violates the cultural specificities of countries and threatens the Muslim family. Gender equality thus represents another controversial issue where many Islamists consider it as a western product that overlooks gender differences and the Islamic-based parameters of gender relations. The chapter thus has discussed different aspects of the issue showing that ideological sensitivities fuel and perpetuate this dichotomy based on false and erroneous premises. However, it remains very important that this debate should generate more objective understanding of gender dynamics in our transitioning societies.

Finally, it was shown that trajectories of change are largely characterized by the possibility of policy makers and feminist activists to invest in opportunities and face challenges in order to generate novel and effective solutions for increasingly changing and complex societies.

Notes

1. See more about Islamic feminists' hermeneutics and discursive debates in Hidayatullah (2014).
2. This protocol was added to article 2 in CEDAW in 2000 enforcing state parties to be subject of interrogation in case CEDAW committee receives communications submitted by individuals or groups of individuals claiming to be victims of a violation of their rights under the Convention.
3. With this term, I mean the way many sociologists have developed their views on the organization of society and family gender relations. Gender equality thus is understood as a sociological pattern of organizing gender relations in an equal manner where there is no hierarchy and discrimination in gender roles.
4. Check the Islamic Charter on Family in the website: http://www.iicwc.org/lagna/iicwc/iicwc.php?id=872. Accessed 24 March 2019.
5. For more information on these articles and their reservations, see UN Women. Declarations, Reservations and Objections to CEDAW.
6. See the document on these recommendations at: http://www.un.org/womenwatch/daw/cedaw/recommendations/General%20recommendation%2025%20(English).pdf. Accessed 24 March 2019.

References

Abdel-Aziz, Z. (2013). *Proceedings of the seminar: The intellectual background of family studies.* Organized by the Center of Family Studies and Research in Values and Laws. Casablanca: Annajah New Press.

Aghamajidi, T., & Kadkhodaei, M. (2017). The comparison of the Islamic and Western human rights. *Modern Journal of Language Teaching Methods, 7*(8), 360–371.

Badran, M. (2009). *Feminism in Islam: Secular and religious convergences.* Oxford: Oneworld Publications.

Barlas, A. (2002). *Believing women in Islam: Unreading patriarchal interpretations of the Qur'ān.* Austin: University of Texas Press.

Bayat, A. (2013). Post-Islamism at large. In *Post-Islamism: The changing faces of political Islam.* New York: Oxford University Press.

Benkhaldoun, S. (2011). *Hal taghayarat Ahkam Achari'a Al Islamiya Almota'aliqa bi Al-Osra* (Did prescriptions of Shari'a about the family change?). http://www.hespress.com/orbites/38846.html. Accessed 15 March 2019.

Bielefeldt, H. (2000). "Western" versus "Islamic" human rights conceptions? A critique of cultural essentialism in the discussion on human rights. *Political Theory, 28*(1), 90–121.

Bouzghaia, I. (2012). *The feminist movement and social change in Morocco: Trends and impacts.* Saarbrucken: Lap Lambert Academic Publishing.
Bouzghaia, I. (2019). *Gender equality and family solidarity in Morocco between Islamic values and feminist agendas: Rabat region as a case study* (Unpublished thesis). Sidi Mohamed Ben Abdellah University, Fes.
CEDAW. (1979). *Convention on the elimination of all forms of discrimination against women.* https://www.ohchr.org/documents/professionalinterest/cedaw.pdf.
Chant, C. (2006). Re-thinking the "feminization of poverty" in relation to aggregate gender indices. Special issue: Revisiting the gender-related development index. *Journal of Human Development and Capabilities, 7*(2), 201–220.
Cooke, M. (2001). *Women claim Islam: Creating Islamic feminism through literature.* NewYork: Routledge.
Democratic Association of the Moroccan Women. (2013). The withdrawal of the reservations to CEDAW by Morocco. Press release. http://www.adfm.ma/spip.php?article695&var_recherche=reservation&lang=en. Accessed 26 October 2018.
Djavad, S. I. (2016). Human development in the Middle East and North Africa. In S. N. Durlauf & L. E. Blume (Eds.), *The new Palgrave dictionary of economics.* London: Palgrave Macmillan.
Fattah, M. A. (2006). *Democratic values in the Muslim world.* Boulder and London: Lynne Rienner Publishers.
Gallup. (2006). Perspectives of women in the Muslim world. *Special report: Muslim world.* https://www.mostresource.org/wp-content/uploads/sites/146/2013/08/gallup_5_women_in_the_muslim_world.pdf. Accessed 3 March 2019.
Ghosh, H. A. (2008). Dilemmas of Islamic and secular feminists and feminism. *Journal of International Women's Studies, 9*(3), 99–116.
Gray, D. (2015). *Beyond feminism and Islamism: Gender and equality in North Africa.* International Library of African Studies. I.B. Tauris. Reprint edition.
Grob, L., Hassan, R., & Gordon, H. (1991). *Women's and men's liberation: Testimonies of spirit.* New York: Greenwood Press.
Hassan, R. (2008). *Are human rights compatible with Islam?* http://www.religiousconsultation.org.hassan2.html. Accessed 06 August 2019.
Hidayatullah, A. (2014). *Feminist edges of the Qur an.* Oxford: Oxford University Press.
Huntington, S. (1993). The clash of civilizations? *Foreign Affairs, 72*(3), 22–49.
Inglehart, R., Haerpfer, C., Moreno, A., Welzel, C., Kizilova, K., Diez-Medrano, J., et al. (Eds.). (2014). *World values survey: Round six: Country-pooled datafile version.* Madrid: JD Systems Institute. www.worldvaluessurvey.org/WVSDocumentationWV6.jsp.
Lamrabet, A. (2016). *Croyantes et féministes, un autre regard sur les religions.* Casablanca: Éditions La croisée des chemins.

Margaret, Y. S. (2005). *Women in Islam*. Detroit: Greenhaven Press.
Mernissi, F. (1991). Preface to the English edition. In *The veil and the male elite: A feminist interpretation of women's rights in Islam*. New York: Perseus Publishing.
Michell, P., & Al-Mossawi, M. (2002). The implications of Islam for advertising messages: The Middle Eastern context. *Journal of Euromarketing, 11*(3), 71–96.
Mir-Hosseini, Z. (2000). *Islam and gender: The religious debate in contemporary Iran*. London and New York: I.B. Tauris.
Mirza, Q. (2008). Islamic feminism and gender equality: Thoughts and perceptions. *ISIM Review, 21*, 30–31. https://openaccess.leidenuniv.nl.
Moghadam, V. (2000). Islamic feminism and the politics of naming. *Iran Bulletin*.
Moghadam, V. (2003). *Modernizing women: Gender and social change in the Middle East*. Boulder: Lynne Rienner Publishers.
Moghissi, H. (1999). *Feminism and Islamic fundamentalism: The limits of postmodern analysis*. London: Zed Books.
Naji Mekkaoui, R. (2011). Rajae Mekkaoui Taroddo ala Lkhaaifin min Tifakiyat Rafe Tamyiz dida Lmaraa [Rajae Mekkaoui answers those afraid of the CEDAW]. *Akhbar Alyawm Newspaper*, 16 November.
Pew Forum on Religion and Public Life. (2013). *The world's Muslims: Religion, politics and society*. http://www.pewforum.org/files/2013/04/worlds-muslims-religion-politics-society-full-report.pdf. Accessed 1 March 2019.
Pruzan-Jørgensen, J. E. (2012). *Islamic women's activism in the Arab world*. DIIS Report 2012:02. Copenhagen: Danish Institute for International Studies. www.diis.dk.
Rahman, F. (1998). *Health and medicine in the Islamic tradition*. Chicago: ABC International Group (Kazi Publications).
Sadiqi, F. (Ed.). (2016). The center: A post-revolution space for women's movements in North Africa: Morocco as an example. In *Women's movements in post-"Arab spring" North Africa* (pp. 15–30). New York: Palgrave Macmillan.
Seedat, F. (2016). Islam, feminism, and Islamic feminism: Between inadequacy and inevitability. *Journal of Feminist Studies in Religion, 32*(2), 138–142.
Talabi, M. (2013). *The conflict over values: A philosophical and historical view* [Assira' hawla Al-qiyam. Ro'ya falsafiya wa tarikhiya]. Rabat: Moroccan Center for Contemporary Research and Studies.
The Islamic Charter on Family. http://www.iicwc.org/lagna/iicwc/iicwc.php?id=872. Accessed 1 March 2019.
UN. (1999). General recommendation No. 25, on article 4, paragraph 1, of the convention on the elimination of all forms of discrimination against women, on temporary special measures. http://www.un.org/womenwatch/daw/cedaw/recommendations/General%20recommendation%2025%20(English).pdf. Accessed 4 March 2019.

UN Women. *Declarations, reservations and objections to CEDAW*. http://www.un.org/womenwatch/daw/cedaw/reservations-country.htm. Accessed 26 March 2019.

Wadud, W. (2000). Alternative Qur'anic interpretation. In G. Webb (Ed.), *Windows of faith: Muslim women scholar-activists in North America (Women and gender in North American religions)* (pp. 3–21). Syracuse: Syracuse University Press.

Zvan Elliott, K. (2015). *Modernizing patriarchy: The politics of women's rights in Morocco*. Austin: University of Texas Press.

INTERVIEWS

Aicha El-Hajjami, 16 November 2017.
Aziza Bakkali, 18 May 2017.
Habiba Hamdaoui and Hafida Ferchachi, 24 January 2018.
Hanane Benchakroune, 25 October 2017.
Malika Benradi, 20 July 2017.

PART II

Post-Spring Dynamics and Feminist Norm Diffusion

CHAPTER 4

Cultural Change in North Africa: The Interaction Effect of Women's Empowerment and Democratization

Ginger Feather

Introduction

The status of women in the Middle East and North Africa (MENA) has long been the focus of Western criticism. It is one of the purported motivations for European colonization and at least a partial justification for multiple US-led interventions in the region. These narratives of Muslim women's intrinsically subordinate position and its negative correlation with democratization emanate from Western studies (Fish 2002; Donno and Russett 2004) rather than from the insights of MENA citizens themselves. Moreover, these citizens are often themselves divided. A 2012 PEW report asserted "Most Muslims Want Democracy, Personal Freedoms, and Islam in Political Life,"[1] but the same survey also highlighted an obvious gender gap between men and women with regard to support for gender equality. Furthermore, this report was a snapshot in

G. Feather (✉)
Independent Researcher, Overland Park, KS, USA

time and could not speak to cultural shifts over time or attitudinal variation between genders or among generations.

This chapter seeks to fill these gaps by analyzing attitudinal shifts as a proxy for cultural change vis-à-vis women's empowerment and democratization in North Africa. Additionally, the chapter suggests that increases in women's empowerment at the personal-legal, socioeconomic, and political levels democratize the family and society simultaneously by dismantling normative male privilege and altering patriarchal power hierarchies. Thus, progressive or retrogressive cultural shifts toward women's empowerment and parallel shifts toward democratization inform each other. Notably, North Africa includes three of the most progressive MENA states with regard to women's empowerment—the Maghrebi states of Morocco, Tunisia, and Algeria, as well as Egypt and Libya—which makes studying cultural change in this MENA subset an informative exercise. In addition, I propose an alternative measure of democratization for the MENA region instead of the widely used combined Freedom House and Polity IV scores. Fourth wave MENA democratization is likely to be a feminized, social democracy—a maximalist definition—which includes social and economic rights (Held 2006). Likewise, due to gender quotas, high percentages of elected MENA parliaments are women. Consequently, MENA democratization is more accurately measured by the state's redistributive capacity, illustrated by its provision of social services, such as education and health care, which are often intrinsically cast as women's issues and associated with increased women's political empowerment.[2]

I explore one central research question: Do North African states demonstrate temporal and spatial cultural variation as well as variation between genders and across generations vis-à-vis women's empowerment and democratization? If so, does there appear to be an "interaction effect" or correlation between women's empowerment and democratization? My analysis proceeds as follows: First, I review the pertinent literature regarding culture, its initial treatment as static and deterministic and subsequent methodological and practical expansions of culture as both an independent and dependent variable and a site of contestation. Second, I develop my theory of the relationship between women's empowerment and social democratization, delineating how different aspects of women's empowerment alter existing power differentials within the family and society, in effect, democratizing both simultaneously. I suggest an expanded conceptualization of (wo)men's empowerment as neither a zero-sum game, nor a *pareto-optimal* outcome (i.e., not a loss for men and a win for women), but instead, through cooperation, a Nash Equilibrium in which all players—and by extension entire countries—increase their own payoffs. Third, I outline my methodological approach, including my choice of datasets, operationalization of variables, and working hypotheses. Fourth, I analyze the data, indicating temporal and spatial variation as well as variation between the genders and among generations. In conclusion, I outline the chapter's key findings, suggest preliminary policy implications, and specify the future direction of the research.

The Evolution of Culture as a Variable: Culture as Static, a Dummy Variable

The early academic literature on the relationship between culture and democratization identified certain cultural types as predictors of democratic development (Banfield 1958; Almond and Verba 1963; Putnam 1993). Although groundbreaking at the time, these studies were largely static, assessing attitudes at a fixed point in time across a small number of countries. Likewise, Huntington (1993, 1996) presented political culture as enduring and eternal and Geertz (1973) viewed the coherence of culture as a reified, stagnant system of meaning. Ironically, a key attribute of culture as defined by these scholars was its resilience against change. Nevertheless, the treatment of culture as static disregards the potential for cultural contestation and global norm diffusion. In alternative literature, Jackman and Miller (1996) found no evidence of the so-called durable cultural syndrome. In fact, when Jackman and Miller disaggregated Putnam's measures of political performance into individual indicators and ran them in separate regression models, they determined the effect of culture on democratization disappeared entirely (1996: 453). More importantly, from a methodological standpoint, viewing culture as static circumscribes the use of culture in statistical modeling. Viewed as static, culture can only function methodologically as a dummy variable, coded 0 or 1 in statistical modeling, dependent on whether or not a country exhibits a particular cultural tradition.

Culture as an Independent or Dependent Variable

In response to criticism regarding the use of culture as an explanatory value, Wedeen proposed a new notion of culture as semiotic meaning making practices, which operate at two distinct levels: At one level, culture defined as "semiotic practices refers to what language and symbols do—how they are inscribed in concrete actions and how they operate to produce observable political effects" (2002: 714). Thus, culture can be used as an explanatory variable (i.e., an independent variable) affecting some dependent variable. Simultaneously, culture as semiotic practices can be operationalized as the effects (i.e., a dependent variable) of institutional arrangements, structural hierarchies, and strategic interests (2002: 714). Jourde (2005) expands upon Wedeen's use of culture, demonstrating how the political elite may employ dramaturgical practices to script and stage cultural norms which reinforce authoritarian regimes (2005: 437). Despite these methodological advances, cultural usages remained largely snapshots in time.

Cultural Change: New Uses of and Approaches to Culture

With the development of the World Values Surveys (WVS), Inglehart (1977, 1988, 1990, 1997) overcame several shortcomings of the snapshot approach to examining the effects of culture. By adding time-series analysis, WVS researchers can study attitudinal shifts over time as well as attitudinal change based on specific demographic factors, such as gender, age, and education. Hence, the WVS data collection effort mitigates the static nature of previous cultural measures, enabling the systematic longitudinal examination of cultural change, envisioned by Hughes and Paxton (2007), vis-à-vis issues such as women's empowerment, gender equality, and democratization. Subsequently, cross-national studies pointed to the evolution of more progressive attitudes toward so-called post-modern values which deemphasize cost-benefit analysis in favor of more altruistic and egalitarian principles. Studies indicated that this attitudinal/culture shift positively affects gender roles, gender equality, and gender dynamics, emphasizing Muslim resistance to change due to patriarchal cultural norms (Inglehart 1999; Inglehart and Norris 2003a, b). Additional studies departed from modernization theory, which analyzed the impact of economic development on political change, to instead posit the effect of individual autonomy, gender equality, and democratization on cultural change (Inglehart and Welzel 2005, 2010). Nevertheless, little research explores cultural shifts among the North African states or MENA more generally with regard to women's empowerment and democratization, with the notable exception of Alexander and Welzel (2010, 2011). Furthermore, no studies, to my knowledge, analyze cultural change toward these issues, disaggregated by gender and generation. This chapter fills this gap to analyze both the spatial and temporal variation among North African states and the impact of gender and generation on this variation.

Culture Within the UN Human Rights Framework: An Area of Contestation

Although cultural relativists essentialize culture as homogenous and linked to tradition, religion, and national identity, feminists assert that culture in the MENA region is patriarchal and often bolstered by and conflated with conservative religious interpretations of Islam, which perpetuate traditional gender roles and undermine women's empowerment (Ahmed 1992; Mernissi 1975, 1987). I suggest that culture is contested. Kandiyoti depicts patriarchal cultural norms as "protection in exchange for submissiveness and propriety" (1988: 283), which systematically limits women's empowerment and at times treats women as perpetual minors, provided for by fathers or husbands. Joseph problematizes the portrayal of patriarchal cultural norms by feminists as strictly a case of power and violence, instead showing that love and nurturance are part of patriarchy (1994: 233). Nevertheless, patriarchal cultural norms privilege men and place women in a potentially protected, yet vulnerable position. In the MENA region, patriarchal norms represent multiple structures with causal effects upon each other (Walby 1990: 20), creating a system of mutually reinforcing constraints.[3] Such norms may serve to legitimize domestic violence as discipline. Patriarchal cultural norms suggest conjugal rape is an oxymoron, as marriage implies a husband's unrestricted sexual access to his wife. Unchecked, such cultural assumptions and practices allow predominantly male aggressors to act with impunity while often blaming primarily female victims. Consequently, cultural contestation and normative cultural evolution are clear to feminist activists and qualitative researchers analyzing the MENA region. Feminist activists and advocates juxtapose discriminatory national laws based on patriarchal cultural norms against the UN human rights framework, which represents a culture of consensus (Merry 2006). Feminist activists seek to harmonize national laws with international treaty commitments. In this way, feminists can inform and transform gendered cultural narratives.

Theoretical Framework

Problematizing the Causal Arrow of Democratization as Promoting Women's Empowerment

A gendered approach to the study of democratization is crucial (Waylen 1994: 327); yet, democratization in the MENA region which incorporates a gender lens is understudied. It has been widely documented that the nature and level of women's mobilization prior to democratic transition is pivotal in determining the type and quality of governance following a transition (Waylen 2007). Contrary to the literature which claims that democratization is good for women (Viterna and Fallon 2008), democratization in the MENA region may actually represent a conservative setback for feminist aspirations and progressive legal reform, unless coupled with women's empowerment. In short, premature democratization in the MENA region may simply facilitate the rise of conservative political parties within the political system, such as the Islamic Salvation Front in Algeria (1992), Ennahda in Tunisia (2011), the Muslim Brotherhood in Egypt 2011–2012, and the Justice and Development Party in Morocco (2011) and potentially undermine progressive reform agendas. Conversely, if women have reached a certain threshold of personal-legal, socioeconomic, and political empowerment, as in the case of Tunisia, during democratic transition, they can offer a counterweight to patriarchal and conservative backlash and promote progressive, inclusive reform agendas.

Consequently, MENA democratization, and more importantly the quality of democracy worldwide, will be tempered by the inclusion or exclusion of women as equal partners in the democratization process (Wejnert 2014; Wejnert and Rodriguez 2015; Moghadam 2012, 2013; Viterna and Fallon 2008; Waylen 1994, 1996). As UN Secretary General Kofi Annan (2002) stated: "When women are fully involved, the benefits can be seen immediately: families are healthier, they are better fed, their income, savings and investment go up. And what is true for families is true of communities and, eventually, of whole countries." As women strengthen their position within the family and move from private to public space, they desegregate positions of power and feminize formerly masculinized structures and institutions, simultaneously engendering and, in effect, democratizing those institutions through the inclusion of the underrepresented majority female population. National and international feminist activism and advocacy have been at the forefront of women's empowerment gains, especially in the Maghreb region. Consequently, whereas the majority of the early democratization literature focused on bargaining among political elites or top-down democratization (Linz 2000; O'Donnell et al. 1986), MENA democratization may be seen as occurring from the bottom-up, facilitated by feminist activism for gender equality and women's empowerment in tandem with youth mobilization demanding democratization, transparency, and inclusion as occurred in Algeria in the spring of 2019.

The Interaction Effect or Co-constitution of Women's Empowerment and Social Democracy

This chapter offers a new theoretical framework for understanding the interaction effect of women's empowerment with social democratization as facilitating cultural change in North Africa. For women's empowerment, I use Moghadam and Senftova's definition "as a multi-dimensional process of civil, political, social, economic, and cultural participation and rights" (2005: 390). This conceptualization assumes women's empowerment involves both the state's "due diligence" to protect all citizens equally and women's responsibility to exercise their rights. Ultimately, women's empowerment dictates the dismantlement of the patriarchal bargain and male privilege, but also requires women to own the increased responsibilities—which true equality implies and for which feminists advocate—including a shared notion of *qiwama* or joint provision for the family between spouses. This chapter explores the (d)evolving nature of cultural norms in North Africa as stemming from the interaction of four interlocking dimensions of women's empowerment with social democratization.

First, women's personal-legal empowerment is often limited by institutional and structural constraints imposed by the family as well as national legal structures, which may either impinge upon or reinforce a woman's autonomy and right to bodily integrity. Laws criminalizing domestic violence are indispensable to a woman's personal empowerment as they represent the state's recognition of the woman as an individual, separate from her husband and familial unit, with certain inalienable rights. Thus, the state's recognition of and enforcement of a woman's right to bodily integrity is the litmus test of a woman's personal-legal empowerment. The state's criminalization of domestic violence coupled with adequate sex education, access to birth control, and a woman's right to an abortion determine the degree to which a woman is empowered to exercise control over her own body (i.e., personal-legal empowerment). This measure, even more so than traditionally used measures such as age at first marriage, fertility rates, and life expectancy, sets the context and parameters under which a woman exerts her agency in other spheres.

Second, women's social empowerment through access to an education represents many girls' entry into public life, expands women's employment opportunities, and increases their political clout. The World Bank reports, the MENA region has "quadrupled the average level of schooling since 1960…and achieved almost complete gender parity for primary education."[4] Thus, cultural biases favoring sons for education are slowly changing. Nevertheless, illiteracy and lower levels of education among the poor are still largely gendered issues with decisions made within families. At the tertiary level, women in the MENA region, especially in the oil-rich Gulf States and Iran, have reversed the trend of favoring boys for primary and secondary education. In all six Gulf States, women have overtaken men in terms of tertiary education. In Iran, the ratio of female to male university students increased from 37.4% in 1990 to 110.5% in 2002 (Moghadam 2013: 180). Such educational advances dramatically increase a woman's status and voice within her family and society.

Third, women's economic empowerment has been affected by factors at the international and national levels, representing a mixed bag of opportunities and constraints. In the 1950s and 1960s decolonization, nationalism, and socialism led to the adoption of import-substitution industrialization (ISI) in Iran, Egypt, Turkey, and Algeria. With ISI, the national governments increased state ownership of industries and imposed high tariffs to protect inefficient state-run factories. Governments expanded public sector employment and invested in education and health care, fields historically dominated by women. Nevertheless, by 1975 the percentage of economically active females in the MENA region was less than half the economically active female population in non-Muslim states, while other Muslim-majority countries, such as Indonesia and Malaysia, began to develop large female labor forces due to woman-friendly industrialization strategies (Moghadam 2013: 79). In the 1980s and 1990s, multinational corporations (MNCs) relocated to countries where they could hire a less expensive labor force, representing a significant opportunity for MENA women. MNCs largely preferred to hire women to work in clothing, electronics, and textile assembly production for their nimbleness, attention to detail, and especially the lower salaries they were willing to accept. As wage earners, women gained greater leverage within their families. However, due to high male wages, labor migration from non-oil producers and remittances, low foreign direct investment, and only scattered export-oriented industrialization, the MENA region did not enjoy as high a concentration of MNCs as in Southeast Asia and Latin American countries (Mitter 1986; Moghadam 2013: 78, 96). Hence, the trend in the MENA region supports Ross' (2008) assertion that oil-producing states are characterized by structural and systemic constraints to women's participation in the labor force. Although only Algeria and Libya have large oil reserves, even non-oil producers, such as Morocco, Tunisia, and Egypt, experience similar constraints due to the migration of male labor to oil-rich states and remittances. At this same time, excessive government spending led to a debt crisis. Morocco, Tunisia, Jordan, and Egypt appealed to the IMF and World Bank and were forced to adopt structural-adjustment programs (SAPs) in exchange for debt rescheduling.[5] The SAPs compelled the governments to retract public sector employment and to reduce spending on social programs. Women in countries undergoing SAPs were affected disproportionately to men as the social programs most affected were education and health care, fields dominated by women (Waylen 1996: 42). Likewise, due to high levels of unemployment, MENA governments reverted back to a male wage earner mantra and traditional gender roles rhetoric, labor force participation in countries such as Egypt, Algeria, and Morocco. Likewise, at the national level, inadequate monetary and institutional support jeopardize women's ability to achieve their full economic citizenship. For example, the care burden for both the young and the elderly coupled with inadequate public policies and formal institutions, such as maternity leave and child care facilities, limit women's workforce participation (Moghadam 2010, 2018). Such constraints on women's economic empowerment are important, as women's labor force participation allows the public to gain confidence in women as political leaders (Moghadam 2013: 103).

The fourth and final type of empowerment, women's political empowerment, has become more salient as gender quotas jumpstarted MENA women's political participation practically overnight. Many North African countries have adopted proportional representational electoral systems and have implemented gender quotas with the percentage of women members of parliament (WMPs) increasing dramatically between 1990 and 2019: Algeria from 2 to 26%, Tunisia from 4 to 36%, Morocco from 0 to 21%, Libya from 0 to 16%, and Egypt from 4 to 15%.[6] Consequently, if the policy priorities are greatly impacted by whether an MP is male or female, then the issues more often promoted by women politicians, those issues which most affect women and children, are likely underrepresented in the majority of the world's executive, legislative, and judicial organizations. These issues include: women and children's health, sexual harassment, violence against women, the unequal division of paid and unpaid labor, and women's marginalization from economic and political power (Tripp 1994). The political sphere is a pivotal decision-making arena as politicians decide how to allocate state resources, necessarily favoring some constituents and issues to the detriment of others. Although questions remain about the critical mass necessary for women's representation to yield substantive benefits (Paxton et al. 2007: XIV-3) as well as the efficacy of affirmative action tactics to increase women's political representation (Darhour this volume), access to positions of political influence enables women to advocate from within the formerly masculine-state political system. In addition, the normative influence of women's presence in politics prompts changes in people's attitudes and expectations.

What's in Women's Empowerment for Men?

It is crucial to change the polemics of gender equality and women's empowerment from a *zero-sum game* where men must lose for women to win to a discourse on the mutual benefits of reducing power differentials within the family and society to optimize collective potential. At the personal level, the pressures on husbands as *qiwama* (provider) could be reduced if shared, which would also discredit assumptions of male privilege and entitlement and a wife's *taa'* (obedience), which leads to hypermasculinity and domestic violence (Feather 2019). Socially, at the micro-level, the probability of children continuing their education increases with their mother's educational advancement. Furthermore, at the macro-level, women's educational advancement directly impacts labor force productivity and output, with substantial increases in gross domestic product (GDP) as well as national growth rates (Cuberes and

Teignier 2016). Economically, when single-income families become two-income families, the average household earnings increase by 25%, allowing many families to move from poverty to middle class. Notably, the income earned by mothers has a more positive impact on household nutrition, health, and education of children than extra income earned by fathers as women reinvest 90% of their earnings back into the family compared to men's reinvestment of 35%.[7] At the macro-level, Moroccan feminist scholar, Mernissi, explained the importance of women's economic empowerment most convincingly, "Muslim economic weakness is attributable to the fact that only half the nation works, which in effect halves the country's creative potential and energy" (1975: 14). Finally, at the political level, larger numbers of women political leaders lead to healthier, more educated, and safer societies through increased spending on healthcare and education and reduced military spending (Koch and Fulton 2011; Volden et al. 2018). For these reasons, empowering women is not a loss for men, but instead a Nash Equilibrium in which both men and women improve their outcomes through cooperation. Although righting gendered power hierarchies initially takes affirmative action and gender quotas, these mechanisms are simply temporary measures to redress a legacy of gender-based discrimination.

Finally, privileging Western-style liberal democracy leaves scholars scrambling to describe the emergence of democratic institutions in the MENA region, such as parliaments and elections, which are often considered mere window dressing for authoritarian regimes. Thus, MENA states are deemed semi-democracies, neither fully democratic nor fully authoritarian; they are categorized as illiberal democracies (Zakaria 1997) or democratizing backwards (Rose and Shin 2001). Nevertheless, the percentages of women in Maghrebi parliaments are some of the highest in the world, surpassing many established democracies and even rivaling the percentages of several post-conflict African states.[8] Consequently, the type of democracy likely to develop in the MENA region will be flavored by the region's rich mixture of Islamic, collectivist, and socialist histories, but also *feminized* through gender quotas, which will ensure women's inclusion in sufficient numbers to inform the nature of democratic development and national priorities. Furthermore, as other scholars have suggested, the social democracy model is preferable to the hyper-masculinized neoliberal model as the redistributive aspect represents the state assuming some of the care burden from women through welfare policies (Walby 2004). These policies help ensure women's full *economic citizenship* and may include subsidized child and elder care, reduced work hours for parents of young children, and subsidies for in-home elder care (Moghadam 2010, 2018). Lastly, the Arab Spring demonstrations called for more than just democratization, an end to corruption, transparency, and human rights, protesters from Egypt, Tunisia, Morocco, and—more recently—Algeria called for economic rights and social justice, implying a type of democracy not connected to the neoliberal model, but instead to the breakdown of current patriarchal, and in the cases of Egypt and Algeria, militarized power hierarchies (Al-Ali 2012). For these reasons, I suggest, MENA democratization is likely to result in social democracy, characterized by the redistributive capacity of the state to rectify social inequalities.

Methodological Approach

In terms of operationalizing variables, the WVS has six waves covering 1981–2014, incorporating MENA countries in the last three waves. WVS uses representative national samples with a minimum sample size per country of 1000 respondents over age 18. The mode of data collection is face-to-face interviews. To operationalize each of the four types of women's empowerment, I have chosen one WVS question:

- **Women's personal-legal empowerment**: *Justifiable: For a man to beat his wife* (never) (higher = more progressive),
- **Women's social empowerment**: *A university education is more important for a boy than for a girl* (disagree or strongly disagree) (higher = more progressive),
- **Women's economic empowerment**: *When jobs are scarce, men should have more right to a job than women* (agree) (lower = more progressive),
- **Women's political empowerment**: *On the whole, men make better political leaders than women do* (agree strongly or agree) (lower = more progressive).

To operationalize social democracy, I use a measure of the government's ability to tax the rich and subsidize the poor:

- **Governments tax the rich and subsidize the poor is an essential element of democracy** (higher = more social democracy).

Additionally, this chapter assesses cultural change toward women's empowerment and democratization from four different perspectives: variance across countries, variance within a country over time, variance between genders, and generational variance. The following five hypotheses will be either confirmed or refuted based on the data:

H_1 (*Personal-Legal Empowerment*): Cultural shifts should demonstrate progressively *higher* rejection over time that a man is justified in beating his wife, with women more progressive than men in asserting a woman's right to bodily integrity and younger generations more progressive than previous generations.

H_2 (*Women's Social Empowerment*): Cultural shifts in favor of women's equal access to an education may vary by country, but should be progressively *higher* over time, are likely to be higher among women than men, and among younger generations than older generations.

H_3 (*Women's Economic Empowerment*): Cultural shifts *rejecting* that men have a greater right to scarce jobs will vary cross-nationally, but countries will become more progressive over time, with women more progressive than men and younger generations more progressive than older generations.

H_4 (*Women's Political Empowerment*): Cultural shifts will vary by country, but become increasingly progressive over time with a *lower* affirmation that men make better politicians than women do, with lower affirmation among women than among men and among younger generations than among older generations.

H_5 (*The Interaction Effect of Women's Empowerment with Social Democratization*): Women's empowerment and social democratization are occurring simultaneously in North Africa. Consequently, as cultural shifts occur toward women's empowerment, simultaneous cultural shifts should occur toward a *feminized* social democracy.

Data Analysis[9]

Women's Personal-Legal Empowerment

I operationalize women's personal-legal empowerment with the WVS question: "It is justifiable: For a man to beat his wife." Notably, this question is only included in Waves V and VI. My hypothesis is that societal expectations of women's bodily integrity is a strong indicator of women's personal-legal empowerment, i.e., their ability to exercise individual autonomy without fear of retribution. Thus, women's personal-legal empowerment is higher in countries which categorically reject domestic violence by indicating a man is "never" justified in beating his wife. In terms of cross-sectional time-series variation, clear attitudinal differences exist among countries concerning the rejection of domestic violence. Morocco is the only country included in two surveys on this question and ironically regresses in rejecting domestic violence (66.1% in 2007 to 59.2% in 2011). In the 2011–2014 survey, 67.8% of Libyans and Tunisians rejected domestic violence, while roughly only half as many Egyptians (38.9%) and Algerians (38.6%) rejected domestic violence (Table 4.1).

In all five countries, women more than men reject domestic violence. In Morocco in 2007 76.5% of women and 55.4% of men rejected domestic violence, but in 2011 the percentages dropped to only 68.4% of women and 50% of men rejecting domestic violence. Whereas Tunisia and Libya are the most progressive, Egypt and Algeria are the least progressive. In Libya 64.3% of men and 71.6% of women rejected domestic violence in 2014 and in Tunisia 57.6% of men and 79.2% of women rejected domestic violence in 2013. In Algeria and Egypt the rejection of domestic violence is roughly half that in Tunisia and Libya with only 28.9% of Algerian men and 48.5% of Algerian women rejecting domestic violence in 2014 and only 34.6% of Egyptian men and 43.3% of Egyptian women rejecting domestic violence in 2012.

With regard to generational variation, in 2007 in Morocco generational variation was negligible (64.8 and 66.9%), but by 2011 variation

Table 4.1 Cultural change toward women's personal-legal empowerment (i.e., rejecting domestic violence) cross-sectional, time-series, by gender, and generation

Rejects domestic violence	Total	Male	Female	Youngest	Middle	Oldest
Morocco 2007	66.1	55.4	76.5	65.9	66.9	64.8
Morocco 2011	59.2	50.0	68.4	65.6	57.2	50.6
Algeria 2014	38.6	28.9	48.5	38.7	40.7	34.1
Egypt 2012	38.9	34.6	43.3	40.4	41.1	33.4
Tunisia 2013	67.8	57.6	79.2	67.5	67.1	69.2
Libya 2014	67.8	64.3	71.6	68.2	65.5	75.4

Source World Value Surveys: Round-Six-Country-Pulled Data

by generation occurred, with 65% of the youngest generation, 57.2% of the middle generation, and 50.6% of the oldest generation rejecting domestic violence. Notably, the youngest generation showed the highest initial rejection of domestic violence in 2007, but demonstrated little variation over time. Conversely, between 2007 and 2011, the oldest Moroccan generation showed a 14% drop and the middle-age generation a 9% drop in the rejection of domestic violence, perhaps due to the destabilization of many families due to women's more equal access to divorce in the 2004 Family Law and the perception that gender relations had tilted too far in favor of women. Furthermore, in 2013 Tunisia demonstrated very little generational variation (67.1–69.2%), while in Libya the oldest generation was the most progressive (75.4%) in rejecting domestic violence, the youngest generation was the second most progressive (68.2%), and the middle generation the least progressive (65.5%) in 2014. Conversely, in Algeria and Egypt, the oldest generations were the least progressive (34.1 and 33.4%) in rejecting domestic violence, the middle generations the most progressive (40.7 and 41.1%), and the youngest generations falling somewhere between, but closely aligned with the oldest generation as less progressive (38.7 and 40.4%) in 2014 and 2012.

Cultural change toward a woman's personal-legal empowerment as proxied by the rejection of domestic violence is clear in Morocco, the only country which appears in two surveys. Unfortunately, however, Morocco demonstrates a regression or possible backlash in the rejection of domestic violence in the second survey. Likewise, Egypt and Algeria, the two highly militarized regimes show a strong conservativism in the rejection of domestic violence, which crosses genders and generations, and draws into question women's personal-legal empowerment.

Women's Social Empowerment

I operationalize women's social empowerment with the statement a university education is more important for a boy than for a girl and expect respondents who "disagree" or "strongly disagree" to be more progressive. For this question, North African states were only included in the last three WVS surveys: Morocco, Egypt, and Algeria in Wave IV, Morocco and Egypt in Wave V, and all five states in Wave VI. In terms of cross-national variation, in 2001–2002 almost twice the percentage of Egyptians (68.9%) and Algerians (69.4%) as Moroccans (38.4%) rejected the privileging of a boy over a girl for a university education. By 2007–2008, however, the percentage of Moroccans rejecting the privileging of boys over girls for a university education almost doubled (67.2%), perhaps due to feminist activism and the promulgation of the progressive 2004 Family Law. Egyptians, on the other hand, actually regressed slightly in rejecting the privileging of boys over girls for an education (60.5%). By the 2011–2014 surveys, Moroccan rejection of male privilege for a university education rose again to rival that of Tunisia (73.1%) with 70.6% of Moroccans rejecting the privileging of boys over girls for a university education. Libya (66.6%), Egypt (64.1%), and Algeria (59.3%) trailed behind. In terms of variation over time, Morocco demonstrated the lowest rejection of male privilege in education initially, but that percentage rose considerably in subsequent surveys. Egypt and Algeria, on the other hand, demonstrate a mixed response to male privilege in education, with Egypt actually starting out more egalitarian than Morocco in 2001 but fluctuating in later surveys, whereas Algeria was relatively progressive toward equal access to education in 2002, but regressed considerably by 2014 (Table 4.2).

In terms of variation between the genders with regard to women's social empowerment, women overwhelmingly more than men support a woman's equal access to education. Moroccan women rejected male privilege for an education much more than Moroccan men, nevertheless, while in each wave Moroccan men increasingly rejected favoring boys

Table 4.2 Cultural change toward women's social empowerment (i.e., rejecting a man's greater right to a university education) cross-sectional, time-series, by gender, and by generation

	Total	*Male*	*Female*	*Youngest*	*Middle*	*Oldest*
Algeria 2002	69.4	56.3	82.9	70.2	69.6	67.4
Algeria 2014	59.3	50.0	68.0	61.1	60.4	54.2
Egypt 2001	68.9	60.8	77.5	74.7	66.3	66.7
Egypt 2008	60.5	53.1	68.1	63.1	60.9	57.8
Egypt 2012	64.1	61.0	67.4	73.4	62.1	55.4
Morocco 2001	38.4	31.2	45.4	43.6	38.6	28.1
Morocco 2007	67.2	57.1	77.0	73.7	67.3	54.0
Morocco 2011	70.6	68.1	73.0	78.0	68.4	60.1
Libya 2014	66.6	53.5	81.0	75.1	76.9	64.8
Tunisia 2013	73.1	67.3	79.4	66.7	66.3	67.5

Source World Value Surveys: Round-Six-Country-Pulled Data

over girls for a university education, Moroccan women's rejection of male privilege for a university education started much higher, but dropped slightly in the 2011 survey. In Algeria the rejection of male privilege for a university education was extremely high among women (82.9%) but more modest among men (56.3%) in 2002, but in 2014 this support dropped dramatically among both women (68%) and men (50%). Likewise, in Egypt, women's rejection of male privilege in education waned with each wave, while men's attitudes fluctuated between waves. Libyan (81%) and Tunisian (79.4%) women rivaled Algeria's high rejection of privileging boys over girls for a university education in 2013–2014; with Tunisian men (67.3%) also demonstrating strong support for women's social empowerment, but Libyan men (53%) showing greater reticence.

In terms of generational variation with regard to women's social empowerment, in Morocco and Algeria, the generational trends are as hypothesized with younger generations more progressive than prior generations and with each generation growing more progressive over time. Likewise, in Egypt younger generations are consistently more supportive of equal access to education than prior generations, but the middle-age generation demonstrates a slight regression in egalitarian spirit between 2001 and 2008. In Libya and Tunisia, on the other hand, the middle Libyan generation and oldest Tunisian generation are the most progressive in 2013–2014, but with all three Tunisian generations in close alignment.

Therefore, my hypothesis of a country demonstrating consistently more progressive attitudes toward a girl's equal access to a university education is true for Morocco, but not for Egypt and Algeria. Women more than men are consistently more progressive in asserting women's equal right to an education across all five states, likewise the youngest generation is the most progressive in Morocco, Algeria, and Egypt while in Libya and Tunisia generational variation is less apparent.

Women's Economic Empowerment

I operationalize women's economic empowerment using the statement when jobs are scarce, men should have more right to a job than women and assume respondents who "agree" are demonstrating a less progressive attitude toward women's economic empowerment. In 2001–2002 Egypt (89.6%) and Morocco (86.9%) showed extremely conservative attitudes privileging men for employment when jobs are scarce; while in Algeria (66.3%) a much smaller proportion of respondents hold this view. In 2007–2008 Egyptians (89%) remained extremely conservative with regard to women's economic empowerment, which is surprising given Egypt's long history of feminist activism beginning with the Egyptian Feminist Union of Hoda Shaarawi in the 1920s and 1930s, Doria Shaafik in the 1950s and 1960s, and Nawal El Saadawi's writings since the 1970s. In addition, Egyptian women benefitted from state feminism, with equal access to education and employment in the 1950s, culminating in the formation of the National Council of Women in 2000 with Family Law reform that same year. In Morocco, on the other hand, the conservative trend favoring men for jobs dropped dramatically by almost 40% from 2001 to 2007 with only 50% of Moroccans privileging men for jobs. In the 2012–2014 surveys, varying percentages of respondents privileged men over women for scarce jobs with Algeria (58.0%) and Egypt (83.4%) increasingly progressive, Morocco (60.6%) showing a conservative regression, and Libya (68.7%) and Tunisia (71.1%) closely matched and more progressive than their Egyptian and Algerian counterparts. Given its socialist development model following Independence, it is not surprising that Algeria initially showed the most egalitarian attitudes toward women's economic empowerment, but Morocco demonstrated the greatest cultural change over time (86.9% in 2001 to 50% in 2007), following the passage of the 2004 Family Law, albeit with a marked conservative reversal (60%) in 2011. Egypt consistently shows much greater conservatism in privileging men over women for scarce jobs with 89.6% in 2001, 89% in 2008 and 83.4% in 2012. Algeria, on the other hand, showed increasingly progressive gender sensitivity with 66.3% in 2002 and 58.0% in 2014 favoring men over women for scarce jobs (Table 4.3).

When the respondents were disaggregated by gender, the distinctions between men and women were more apparent and consistent with the hypothesis that women more than men would favor women's economic empowerment. For men, *qiwama* and the sole provider *mantra* make employment akin to a religious duty and legal mandate, where a husband is legally responsible for providing for his wife and children. Consequently, in 2001 in Morocco 90.3% of men and 83.6% of women favored men for scarce employment opportunities, with these percentages dropping dramatically to 64.4% of men and 36% of women in 2007, following the 2004 Family Law and greater national attention to women's empowerment. Following the 2011 the Arab Spring and

Table 4.3 Cultural change toward women's economic empowerment (i.e., agreeing men have a greater right to employment) cross-sectional, time-series, by gender, and by generation

	Total	Male	Female	Youngest	Middle	Oldest
Algeria 2002	66.3	79.1	53.2	67.1	64.6	67.8
Algeria 2014	58.0	69.1	46.6	53.0	58.3	65.9
Egypt 2001	89.6	92.9	86.1	86.4	90.9	92.1
Egypt 2008	89.0	93.1	84.8	86.9	89.7	89.5
Egypt 2012	83.4	85.4	81.3	82.6	84.2	83.0
Morocco 2001	86.9	90.3	83.6	87.0	85.6	89.9
Morocco 2007	50.0	64.4	36.0	45.1	47.2	64.8
Morocco 2011	60.6	74.7	46.7	56.4	61.6	66.8
Libya 2014	68.7	80.1	56.2	65.7	70.6	71.9
Tunisia 2013	71.1	82.5	58.5	69.0	70.4	75.2

Source World Value Surveys: Round-Six-Country-Pulled Data

complaints of high unemployment, the discourse privileging men over women for jobs rose again in Morocco to 74.7% of men and 46.7% of women. Egyptian women, like Egyptian men, were surprisingly the least supportive of women's economic empowerment, but Egyptian women became slightly more egalitarian over time (86.1, 84.8, and 81.3%); while Egyptian men fluctuated slightly in their privileging of men for scarce jobs (92.9, 93.1, and 85.4%). In 2002 Algerian women (53.2%) were the most progressive, dropping further to 46.6% in 2014, agreeing that men should be privileged for scarce jobs, with Algerian men dropping from 79.1% to 69.1% by comparison. By the 2013–2014 surveys, women demonstrated a 25% higher affirmation of women's equal right to employment with 80.1% of Libyan men but only 56.2% of Libyan women and 82.5% of Tunisian men but only 58.5% of Tunisian women agreeing that men have a greater right to employment when jobs are scarce.

Unsurprisingly, when the respondents are disaggregated into generations, the youngest generation appears to be the most progressive in not supporting men's greater right to scarce jobs, except in Algeria (2002) and Morocco (2001), when the middle generation showed the lowest support privileging men over women for jobs, although variation between generations was slight. In subsequent waves, the younger generations demonstrated a stronger gender sensitivity than prior generations who supported more traditional gender roles. Algeria with its socialist legacy showed the greatest support for women's equal access to jobs in both the 2002 and 2014 surveys, while Egypt in all three surveys demonstrated the least support for women's equal access to jobs and traditional gender roles, rivaled only by Morocco in 2001. Between 2001 and 2007 Moroccan attitudes dramatically shifted in favor of women's equal access to employment, declining only slightly in the 2011 survey. Libya and Tunisia, who are only polled in 2014 and 2013, respectively, further support my hypothesis that generational change begins with more progressive attitudes among the younger generation.

In terms of cultural change toward women's economic empowerment, perhaps the consistently conservative attitudes among Egyptians of both genders across time is the most surprising. When disaggregated by gender, women's higher support for women's equal rights to employment is more clear. Overall, by disaggregating by generations, it is possible to see the gradual change happening through the more progressive and inclusive attitudes of younger generations. Likewise, by analyzing all generations over time it is possible to discern that even the older generations are adopting more progressive attitudes.

Women's Political Empowerment

I operationalize women's political empowerment with the statement: Men make better political leaders than women do, focusing on those who "agree strongly" or "agree" as less progressive, so the lower the scores the better. Confidence in women as political leaders on par with men varies from country to country and across time. In 2001–2002 61% of Moroccans, 66% of Algerians, and 84% of Egyptians agreed or strongly agreed that men make better political leaders than women. By 2007, only 54% of Moroccans subscribed to this gendered stereotype, while in 2008 even more Egyptians (92%) viewed men as better political leaders. As of 2012–2014, Morocco continued to be the most progressive in terms of political empowerment with only 57.4% agreeing men make better political leaders, while Egypt continued to be the least progressive (86.4%) with Algeria (71.6%), Tunisia (72.5%), and Libya (74.6%) polling in between (Table 4.4).[10]

When disaggregated by gender, the trend is clear that women in greater numbers than their male counterparts do not agree that men make better politicians. In Morocco in 2001 only 69.8% of men and 51.7% of women supported this statement, which were some of the most

Table 4.4 Cultural change toward women's political empowerment (i.e., agreeing men make better political leaders) cross-sectional, time-series, by gender, and by generation

	Total	Male	Female	Youngest	Middle	Oldest
Algeria 2002	66.0	77.0	51.7	68.9	61.6	66.7
Algeria 2014	71.6	83.4	59.5	71.2	70.3	74.8
Egypt 2001	84.0	89.7	78.1	79.5	85.8	87.5
Egypt 2008	92.0	94.7	89.9	89.7	93.0	93.4
Egypt 2012	86.4	91.0	81.9	85.5	85.1	89.7
Morocco 2001	61.0	69.8	51.7	60.5	62.3	55.7
Morocco 2007	54.0	69.7	39.8	47.9	57.3	62.8
Morocco 2011	57.4	69.7	45.4	59.6	56.4	55.0
Libya 2014	74.6	85.6	62.4	73.9	74.4	67.0
Tunisia 2013	72.5	82.7	61.2	73.4	70.7	73.6

Source World Value Surveys: Round-Six-Country-Pulled Data

progressive attitudes across the region. In subsequent waves, men's support for women as political leaders did not change, but women's support fluctuated with increasing support in 2007 (39.8%) and then a slight regression in 2011 (45.4%), indicating a relatively high level of support for women as politicians compared to other North African countries. After Morocco, Algeria is the most progressive with 77% of men and 51.7% of women, affirming that men make better political leaders in 2002, with a slight regression in 2014 with both more men (83.4%) and women (59.5%) affirmed that men make better political leaders. Egyptians are the least supportive of women as political leaders in all three waves with 89.7% of men and 78.1% of women in 2001, 94.7% of men and 89.9% of women in 2008, and 91% of men and 81.9% of women favoring men as political leaders. In 2013–2014, Libya and Tunisia, on the other hand, demonstrated greater variation between men and women with regard to women's political leadership capabilities with 85.6% of Libyan men and 82.7% of Tunisian men favoring men over women as politicians, but only 62.4% of Libyan women and 61.2% of Tunisian women felt likewise.

When disaggregated by generation, the hypothesized generational variation of younger generations being more progressive does not appear on the question of whether or not men make better political leaders. In addition, across North Africa, the anticipated progressive cultural change across time toward women as political leaders is also not present. In fact, the younger generation actually appears less progressive toward women's political empowerment than the middle age generation and generations fluctuate over time in their support for women as politicians.

Over time, Morocco and Egypt fluctuated in their attitudes toward women as political leaders, but with Moroccans considerably more progressive than Egyptians with regard to women's political empowerment. Algeria, on the other hand, grew increasingly supportive of women as political leaders. Likewise, women more than men do not agree that men make better political leaders. Ultimately, attitudes vary erratically across space and time with regard to women's abilities as political leaders without exhibiting the hypothesized pattern. More than any other type of empowerment, attitudes towards women's political leadership/empowerment remains erratic cross-nationally, spatially, and across generations.

Social Democracy

To assess attitudinal change toward social democracy, I use the statement: Governments tax the rich and subsidize the poor, as an essential characteristic of democracy. This statement encompasses not only the social aspects of democracy in terms of a state's redistributive capacity, but also the feminized aspect of a democracy as including women's issues and concerns.

With a history of the "social contract" between the state and citizens, Egyptians and Algerians acquiesced to authoritarian rule in exchange for implicit promises of free public education, healthcare, and food and gas subsidies. Consequently, with regard to social democracy, in the 2001–2002 survey, Egypt (57.7%) almost doubled the score of Morocco (30.9%) in agreeing that taxing the rich and subsidizing the poor is an essential characteristic of democracy. Following the 2011 overthrow of the Mubarak regime, largely by the urban middle class, amid widescale claims of corruption and the dismantlement of welfare protections due to the SAPs (Beissinger et al. 2015), Egyptian support for social democracy dropped drastically by more than half to 25.3% in 2012, perhaps indicating their lack of confidence in their current government more than their lack of support for social democracy. Similarly, in 2014 Algeria (16.7%) showed the lowest support for social democracy in all age and gender categories, followed closely by Libya (19.1%), both oil states. As Layachi (2006) explains of the broken social contract in Algeria, in the 1960s and 1970s the Algerian government embraced a socialist development model with high levels of state spending on free education, health care, subsidized food, and services. The 1986 oil crisis, however, lead to a drop in state revenues and the retraction of state services, further exacerbated by the SAPs of the 1990s, which favored the neoliberal economic model with privatization and further retraction of state spending.[11] Ironically, despite the return of oil and gas revenues, Algerians pay the highest taxes across North Africa, far more than Libyans ever paid under Qaddafi or post-Qaddafi and far more than Moroccans and Tunisians pay (Fig. 4.1).[12]

As demonstrated by the March 2019 youth-led demonstrations in Algeria, which ended President Abdelaziz Bouteflika's two-decade rule and called for democracy, transparency, and improved public services, the excessive taxation did not translate into redistribution or social democracy. Consequently, Algerians simply do not trust their current government to use tax dollars equitably, in a manner conducive to social democracy. Conversely, Morocco and Tunisia, which lack Algeria and Libya's oil resources, still pay significantly less in taxes than their Algerian counterparts. Hence, perhaps instead of demonstrating support for social democracy, Morocco and Tunisia are showing a greater confidence in their current governments to act as a redistributive agent for the national

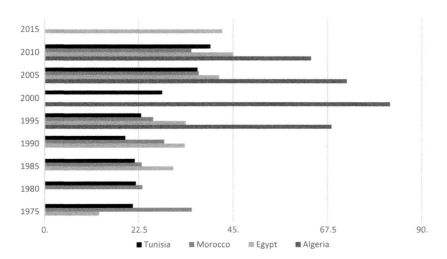

Fig. 4.1 Income tax rate across North Africa (*Source* 2018 World Bank Development Indicators)

wealth, with Morocco indicating a 36.2% expectation of government redistribution in 2011 and Tunisia a 30% expectation in 2013, roughly doubling Algeria's support for social democracy or, as suggested, possibly lack of confidence in the current government's redistributive capacity and will (Table 4.5).

When disaggregated by gender, in Morocco and Egypt, there was very little variation between men and women regarding the importance of a democracy's redistributive capacities. In 2007 30.6% of Moroccan men and 31.2% of Moroccan women viewed the government's ability to tax the rich and subsidize the poor as an essential characteristic of a democracy, while in 2011 the percentage rose significantly for men to 38.6% but only slightly for women to 33.8%. In 2008, Egypt, on the other hand, almost doubled the percentages of Moroccans for both men and women with 58.3% of men and 57.1% of women. Nevertheless, while Morocco's support for social democracy rose, Egypt's support fell dramatically to 26.1% of men and 24.5% of women affirming redistribution as an essential element of democracy. As expected, in 2014, percentages are lower in oil-rich Algeria and Libya with women showing slightly higher support for social democracy than men; likewise, Tunisia shows slightly greater support for social democracy with women slightly higher support than men.

When disaggregated by generation, support for social democracy demonstrates interesting trends. In 2007 and 2011, in Morocco the youngest generation indicates the highest support for social democracy at 32.3% and 40.5%, respectively. In Egypt, however, in 2008 and 2012, the middle generation demonstrates the highest support for social democracy.

Table 4.5 Cultural change toward social democracy (i.e., "agreeing" that a government's ability to tax the rich and subsidize the poor is an essential element of a democracy) cross-sectional, time-series, by gender, and by generation

	Total	Male	Female	Youngest	Middle	Oldest
Algeria 2014	16.7	16.0	17.4	16.4	17.5	15.5
Egypt 2008	57.7	58.3	57.1	54.3	59.1	58.1
Egypt 2012	25.3	26.1	24.5	23.1	27.9	23.8
Morocco 2007	30.9	30.6	31.2	32.3	30.7	28.4
Morocco 2011	36.2	38.6	33.8	40.5	36.6	26.9
Libya 2014	19.1	18.1	29.2	18.8	18.4	31.4
Tunisia 2013	30.0	29.2	31.0	31.4	30.5	27.4

Source World Value Surveys: Round-Six-Country-Pulled Data

Furthermore, while Egyptians of all generations demonstrate diminishing support for social democracy, Moroccans, excluding the oldest generation, showed increasing support for social democracy between 2007 and 2011. Algerians showed the least support for social democracy across generations with Libyans the second least supportive of social democracy across generations. Tunisians, like Moroccans, comply with my hypothesis that the younger generations, more than prior generations, will support social redistributive democracy; likewise, in Morocco, this support grows over time.

As for an obvious parallel or interaction effect between cultural change toward women's empowerment and social democratization, in Morocco (2007) the relationship is not apparent, but in Morocco (2011) the predicted correlation between women's empowerment and social democratization is more clear. Unfortunately, for the remaining countries, there were simply not enough data points for a definitive comparison. Furthermore, upheavals following the overthrow of Morsi in Egypt and Qaddafi in Libya may signal a retrenchment to more conservative discourses as occurs in poorer states, failed states, and populations facing personal survival risks (Inglehart and Norris 2004). Thus, WVS 7, which should be available in December 2019, as well as the Arab Barometer should be incorporated into future analysis to unequivocally determine whether indeed cultural change toward women's empowerment demonstrates an interaction effect with cultural change toward social democratization as hypothesized.

Conclusion: Progressive, Inclusive Policies and Discourses Inform Cultural Change Across North Africa, Facilitating Women's Empowerment and Social Democracy

Patriarchal culture is frequently blamed for women's subordinate position in MENA countries as well as for the slow pace of democratization. This chapter explores the contested and (d)evolving nature of culture across the five North African countries toward women's empowerment and social democratization. Based on this analysis, this chapter forms several tentative observations with regard to cultural change and the prospects of an *interaction effect* between women's empowerment and social democracy:

Similar to Walby's observations of the Western world, MENA women have experienced notable advances in education, paid employment, and political representation (Walby 2003). Nevertheless, women's personal bodily integrity remains inadequately protected across the MENA region. The 1993 Vienna Declaration and 1995 Beijing Platform for Action brought the issue of violence against women (VAW) to the forefront of international human rights attention. More recently, national-level studies into the prevalence of VAW generated advocacy campaigns to raise public awareness and pass VAW laws. In North Africa, Algeria (2016), Tunisia (2017), and Morocco (2018) have passed laws aimed at addressing VAW with varying degrees of institutional, financial, and administrative support to change public opinion which views domestic violence as a private matter. Consequently, with regard to women's personal-legal empowerment, progressive Tunisia and Libya nearly double the highly-militarized and arguably masculinized Egypt and Algeria in categorically rejecting domestic violence. Morocco's absolute rejection of domestic violence actually regressed between 2007 and 2011 for both men and women and across all generations. Women more than men in all countries upheld a woman's right to bodily integrity. Ironically, however, Algerian and Egyptian women were almost as conservative as their male counterparts in their widescale acceptance of domestic violence. As for generational variation, approximately two-thirds of all three Moroccan generations rejected domestic violence in 2007, but the rejection of domestic violence fell dramatically by 2011, especially among the middle and older generations, perhaps for the previously mentioned reasons. In Algeria and Egypt, the oldest generations were the most conservative with only one-third of respondents rejecting domestic violence. Conversely, in Tunisia and Libya, the oldest generations were the most progressive with more than two-thirds rejecting domestic violence.

Concerning women's social empowerment, similar trends continue. Morocco begins as the least progressive in rejecting male privilege for education, almost twenty percentage points lower than Algeria and Egypt. Nevertheless, Morocco demonstrates consistently increasingly progressive attitudes toward women's equal right to an education, likely due to the progressive legislation and public discourse surrounding gender equality in the late 1990s and 2000s. Egypt, however, fluctuates between surveys and Algeria regresses in rejecting male privilege. When disaggregated by gender, men and women demonstrate marked differences in their support for women's economic empowerment, with 20–30% more women rejecting male privilege for education in each country and across surveys. Algerian women (2002), Libyan women (2014), and Tunisian women (2013) showed the highest rejection of male privilege for education. Moroccan women's slight decline in the rejection of male privilege for education between 2007 and 2011 may be due to the problems educated Moroccan women are facing in finding suitable husbands (Zvan-Elliott 2015). In addition, educated Moroccan women are experiencing high unemployment rates, which may reduce their confidence in education as a pathway to financial autonomy. Moroccan men, on the other hand, demonstrate increasingly progressive attitudes toward women's social empowerment. As for Tunisian women, state investment in universal education across genders and greater success in securing employment commensurate with educational level translates into higher levels of support for education among Tunisian women and men. In terms of variation by generation, in Morocco each generation grew increasingly progressive over time in rejecting male privilege for education, with the youngest generation consistently more egalitarian than prior generations, highlighting the growing importance Moroccans of all ages place on education for both sons and daughters. In Algeria the youngest generation was consistently the most progressive, but all generations regressed dramatically between 2002 and 2014 in their rejection of male privilege in education, which may be explained by the citizens' disillusionment with the state's capacity to provide free education and public sector jobs, as previously mentioned. Tunisians, however, demonstrated very little variation among generations with consistently high percentages of men and women rejecting male privilege for education, consistent with the state's prioritization of universal education for men and women. In Libya, on the other hand, the oldest generation was noticeably more conservative in its support for girls' equal access to education.

With regard to women's economic empowerment, both Algeria and Egypt demonstrated increasingly progressive attitudinal changes toward women's economic empowerment, while Moroccans, though initially more progressive, fluctuated in their egalitarian attitudes. In terms of gendered trends, women showed higher levels of support than men for women's economic empowerment, but both men and women's support for male privilege in employment fluctuated. Likewise, although the youngest generation in each time period was the most progressive in refusing to privilege men over women for employment, each generation regressed between the final two surveys in their affirmation of gender equality, warranting in-depth case studies to determine what factors contributed to these fluctuations.

With regard to women's political empowerment, Morocco showed the greatest support for women as political leaders, while Egypt showed the least support with Libya, Algeria, and Tunisia falling between the two extremes. Nevertheless, no pattern of increasingly progressive support for women as politicians is apparent. By disaggregating by gender, it is clear that women more than men reject male privilege as political leaders, but neither gender demonstrates increasingly progressive egalitarian attitudes toward women's political leadership. In terms of generational variation, the younger generation is not the most egalitarian with regard to women's political empowerment and only the middle generation demonstrates increasingly progressive leanings over the three time periods.

Finally, with regard to attitudes toward social democracy, my findings are counterintuitive and require additional case study analysis. As mentioned previously, Egypt and Algeria's low scores likely do not imply a lack of support for redistribution, but rather a lack of confidence in their current government's capacity to redistribute, which skews the potential of clearly identifying an interaction effect between women's empowerment and social democracy. Morocco and Tunisia indicate a higher confidence in social democracy, probably correlating with greater confidence in their government's redistributive capacity. Disaggregated by gender, very little difference exists between men and women's attitudes toward social democracy. Furthermore, when disaggregated by generation, only Tunisian and Moroccan youth support social democracy more than prior generations, with growing support in Morocco over time. Again, these findings perhaps reflect a higher confidence among the younger generations of Moroccans and Tunisians in their government's capacity to redistribute, rather than support for or rejection of social democracy per se.

As demonstrated, viewing culture as contested and capable of change expands the use of cultural change as an explanatory variable in socioeconomic models and policy advocacy. The spatial and temporal cultural changes across North Africa toward women's empowerment and social democratization, as well as clear distinctions across genders and generations, problematize simplistic understandings of culture as static. Tunisia's state feminism and Morocco's 2004 Family Law reforms demonstrate that state support for women's empowerment and progressive laws and public policies coupled active feminist movements can promote dramatic, progressive cultural change. Democracy as an ideal type is, by nature, inclusive. Consequently, the inclusion and empowerment of women in socioeconomic and political spheres, in effect, feminizes and democratizes those spheres. Democracy is not a necessary condition for women's empowerment and may even represent a setback for gender equality if pursued prematurely in conservative countries which lack a certain threshold of women's empowerment. Nevertheless, women's empowerment does appear to be a necessary, but perhaps not sufficient condition for enduring democratic development in the MENA region.

Policy Implications

For national policymakers in North Africa, this study suggests that cultural change is underway in the MENA region which is strongly influenced by the feminist and UN human rights discourses as well as by the policies pursued by national governments. National trends suggest that progressive policies and discourses yield more inclusive societies. Consequently, money invested in women's education and access to paid employment will likely provide a solid return on investment for families as well as national economies. Likewise, the increase in WMPs in North African parliaments and consequent feminization of legislative agendas may lead to increased attention on women's issues, such as healthcare and education. In terms of the implications for US and European investment in the MENA region, instead of promoting democratization as the panacea to women's subordinate status and marginalization, perhaps incentivizing regional governments to promote gender equality and to empower women—personally-legally, socioeconomically, and politically—is a better approach to ensuring high-quality, stable, and enduring democracies develop in the MENA region.

Future Direction of Research

In terms of the future direction of this research, future WVS surveys as well as the Arab Barometer measures should be included to expand the data points in analyzing the hypothesized relationships. Furthermore, in-depth case studies are required to determine under what circumstances states and citizens assume a more progressive, egalitarian trope rather than resorting to traditional gender roles and patriarchal norms. Additionally, I would like to analyze the particular characteristics and contexts of fourth wave democratization across the MENA region by incorporating more countries into the analysis. Topics requiring further exploration include the impact of feminist activism on progressive policy change, the influence of the social contract, SAPs, and global economic trends on the nature of MENA democratic development, the priority given women's economic citizenship, and the policies WMPs promote as they feminize MENA parliaments, legal codes, and public policies.

Notes

1. The 2012 PEW Report is available on the Pew Research Center website at: pewresearch.org.
2. *Women and Children: The Double Dividend of Gender Equality* (New York: UNICEF, 2006) (http://news.bbc.co.uk/1/shared/bsp/hi/pdfs/11_12_06SOWC2007.pdf).
3. Walby determines patriarchy includes six structures: "the patriarchal mode of production, patriarchal relations in paid work, patriarchal relations in the state, male violence, patriarchal relations in sexuality, and patriarchal relations in cultural institutions." For greater detail on these structures, see Walby (1990).
4. For a synopsis of gains made in literacy and education in the MENA region, see www.worldbank.org/en/region/mena/brief/education-in-mena (last accessed 30 May 2019).
5. Morocco was the first Arab state to sign a SAP with the IMF in 1984, followed by Tunisia in 1986, Jordan in 1989, Egypt in 1991, and Algeria in 1994. For additional information regarding the impact of SAPs in the MENA region, see Mossallem (2015).
6. For current statistics on the number of WMPs in national parliaments, see the Inter-parliamentary Union's on-line compilation: http://archive.ipu.org/wmn-e/classif-arc.htm (retrieved 22 March 2019).
7. These statistics are from Global Vision International (https://www.gvi-usa.com/blog/why-is-gender-equality-important/) (last accessed 22 January 2019).
8. Rwanda following the 1994 genocide and South Africa following apartheid have among the highest percentages of women in parliament in the world at 61.3 and 42.7% respectively and Scandinavian countries historically rank among the highest in women's parliamentary representation: Sweden (47.3%), Finland (41.5%), and Norway (40.8%) (ipu.org) (last accessed March 21, 2019).
9. This chapter benefitted tremendously from the valued recommendations and analytic insight from Valentine Moghadam. Nevertheless, any errors or omissions are strictly those of the author.
10. One observation which is not readily apparent from the current scores is the large number of *don't know* responses among the Moroccan respondents (20% in 2001, none registered for 2007, and 14% in 2011), which may explain the erratic shifts in Morocco's 2007 data for all measures as it appears the researchers may have encouraged respondents to answer, pushing them to *agree* or *disagree*, rather than offering the *don't know* option as a valid response, which biases the results.

11. For an excellent analysis of the "social contract" in post-colonial Algeria, see Azzedine Layachi." Algeria: Crisis, Transition and Social Policy Outcomes," in Massoud Karshenas and Valentine Moghadam, eds., Soial Policy and Development: The Middle East and North Africa (New York: Palgrave, pp. 78–108.
12. See World Bank's Development indicators (wdi.worldbank.org) and UNDP's Human Development Report (2018).

References

Ahmed, L. (1992). *Women and gender in Islam: Historical roots of a modern debate*. New Haven, CT: Yale University Press.

Al-Ali, N. (2012). Gendering the Arab spring. *Middle East Journal of Culture and Communication, 5*(1), 26–31.

Alexander, A., & Welzel, C. (2010). Empowering women: The role of emancipative values. *European Sociological Review, 27*(3), 364–384.

Alexander, A., & Welzel, C. (2011). Islam and patriarchy: How robust is Muslim support? *World Values Research, 21*(12), 249–276.

Almond, G., & Verba, S. (1963). *The civic culture*. Princeton: Princeton University Press.

Annan, K. (2002). In Africa, AIDS has a woman's face. *The New York Times*. December 29, 2002 (Retrieved 3 August 2019).

Banfield, E. (1958). *The moral basis of a backward society*. New York: Free Press.

Beissinger, M., Jamal, A., & Mazur, K. (2015, October 19) What the Arab uprising protestors really wanted. *The Washington Post*. https://www.washingtonpost.com/news/monkey-cage/wp/2015/10/19/what-the-arab-uprising-protesters-really-wanted/?utm_term=.f303cc0f96a0. Last Accessed 2 April 2019.

Cuberes, D., & Teignier, M. (2016). Aggregate effects of gender gaps in the labor market: A quantitative estimate. *Journal of Human Capital, 10*(1), 1–32.

Donno, D., & Russett, B. (2004). Islam, authoritarianism, and female empowerment: What are the linkages? *World Politics, 56*(4), 582–607.

Feather, G. (2019). Moroccan women's movement: Navigating contested cultural norms and legal discrimination in the fight against gender-based violence. *The Journal of Applied Language and Culture*.

Fish, M. S. (2002). Islam and authoritarianism. *World Politics, 55*(1), 4–37.

Geertz, C. (1973). *The interpretation of cultures*. New York: Basic Books.

Held, D. (2006). *Models of democracy* (3rd ed.). Cambridge: Polity Press.

Hughes, M., & Paxton, P. (2007). Familiar theories from a new perspective: The implications of a longitudinal approach to women in politics research. *Politics & Gender, 3*(3), 370–378.

Huntington, S. (1993). The clash of civilizations? *Foreign Affairs, 72*(3), 22–49.
Huntington, S. (1996). *The clash of civilizations and the remaking of world order.* New York: Simon & Schuster.
Inglehart, R. (1977). *The silent revolution.* Princeton: Princeton University Press.
Inglehart, R. (1988). The renaissance of political culture. *American Political Science Review, 82*(4), 1203–1230.
Inglehart, R. (1990). *Culture shift in advanced industrial society.* Princeton: Princeton University Press.
Inglehart, R. (1997). *Modernization and postmodernization.* Princeton: Princeton University Press.
Inglehart, R. (1999). Postmodernization erodes respect for authority, but increases support for democracy. In P. Norris (Ed.), *Critical citizens: Global support for democratic government* (pp. 236–256). New York: Oxford University Press.
Inglehart, R., Haerpfer, C., Moreno, A., Welzel, C., Kizilova, K., Diez-Medrano, J., et al. (Eds.). (2014). *World values survey: Round six-country-pooled datafile version.* Madrid: JD Systems Institute. http://www.worldvaluessurvey.org/WVSDocumentationWV6.jsp.
Inglehart, R., & Norris, P. (2003a). *Rising tide: Gender equality and cultural change around the world.* Cambridge: Cambridge University Press.
Inglehart, R., & Norris, P. (2003b). The true clash of civilizations. *Foreign Policy, 135,* 63–70.
Inglehart, R., & Norris, P. (2004). *Sacred and secular: Religion and politics worldwide.* Cambridge: Cambridge University Press.
Inglehart, R., & Welzel, C. (2005). *Modernization, cultural change and democracy: The human development sequence.* New York: Cambridge University Press.
Inglehart, R., & Welzel, C. (2010). Changing mass priorities: The link between modernization and democracy. *Perspectives on Politics, 8*(2), 551–567.
Jackman, R., & Miller, R. (1996). A renaissance of political culture? *American Journal of Political Science, 40*(3), 632–659.
Joseph, S. (1994). Problematizing gender and relational rights: Experiences from Lebanon. *Social Politics: International Studies in Gender, State & Society, 1*(3), 271–285.
Jourde, C. (2005). "The president is coming to visit!" Dramas and the hijack of democratization in the Islamic Republic of Mauritania. *Comparative Politics, 37*(4), 421–440.
Kandiyoti, D. (1988). Bargaining with patriarchy. *Gender & Society, 2*(3), 274–290.
Koch, M., & Fulton, S. (2011). In the defense of women: Gender, office holding, and national security policy in established democracies. *The Journal of Politics, 73*(1), 1–16.

Layachi, A. (2006). Algerian: Crisis, transition and social policy outcomes. In M. Karshenas & V. Moghadam (Eds.), *Social policy and development in The Middle East and North Africa* (pp. 78–108). New York: Palgrave Macmillan.

Linz, J. (2000). *Totalitarian and authoritarian regimes*. Boulder: Lynne Rienner Publishers.

Mernissi, F. (1975). *Beyond the veil: Male-female dynamics in a modern Muslim society*. Cambridge: Schenkman.

Mernissi, F. (1987). *Beyond the veil: Male-female dynamics in modern Muslim society* (Vol. 423). Bloomington, IN: Indiana University Press.

Merry, S. E. (2006). Human rights and transnational culture: Regulating gender violence through global law. *Osgoode Hall Law Journal, 44*(1), 53–75.

Mitter, S. (1986). *Common fate, common bond: Women in global economy*. London: Pluto Press.

Moghadam, V. M. (2010). States and social rights: Women's economic citizenship in the Maghreb. *Middle East Law and Governance, 2*, 185–220.

Moghadam, V. M. (2012). *Globalization and social movements: Islamism, feminism, and the global justice movement*. Lanham, MD: Rowman & Littlefield.

Moghadam, V. M. (2013). *Modernizing women: Gender and social change in the Middle East*. Boulder: Lynne Rienner Publishers.

Moghadam, V. M. (2018). After the Arab Spring: Toward women's economic citizenship. In N. Butenschon & R. Meijer (Eds.), *The Middle East in transition: The centrality of citizenship*. Cheltenham, UK: Edward Elgar Publishing.

Moghadam, V. M., & Senftova, L. (2005). Measuring women's empowerment: Participation and rights in civil, political, social, economic, and cultural domains. *International Social Science Journal, 57*(184), 389–412.

Mossallem, M. (2015). *The IMF in the Arab world: Lessons Unlearnt*. https://eurodad.org/files/pdf/56b075f5395dd.pdf. Retrieved 22 March 2019.

O'Donnell, G., Schmitter, P., & Whitehead, L. (Eds.). (1986). *Transitions from authoritarian rule: Prospects for democracy*. Baltimore: Johns Hopkins University Press.

Paxton, P., Kunovich, S., & Hughes, M. M. (2007). Gender in politics. *Annual Review of Sociology, 33*, 263–284.

Pew Research Center. (2012, July 12). Mosts Muslims want democracy, personal freedoms, and Islam in political life. www.pewglobal.org/2012/.../most-muslims-want-democracy-personal-freedom.

Putnam, R. (1993). *Making democracy work: Civic traditions in modern Italy*. Princeton: Princeton University Press.

Rose, R., & Shin, D. C. (2001). Democratization backwards: The problem of third-wave democracies. *British Journal of Political Science, 31*(2), 331–354.

Ross, M. (2008). Oil, Islam, and women. *American Political Science Review, 102*(1), 107–123.

Tripp, A. (1994, January 7). *Gender, civil society and political participation in Africa* (Commissioned Paper). A Study of USAID's Capacity for Rapid Response in Support of African Civil Society Development.

Viterna, J., & Fallon, K. (2008). Democratization, women's movements, and gender-equitable states: A framework for comparison. *American Sociological Review, 73*(4), 668–689.

Volden, C., Wiseman, A., & Wittmer, D. (2018). Women's issues and their fates in the U.S. Congress. *Political Science Research and Methods, 6*(4), 679–696.

Walby, S. (1990). *Theorizing patriarchy*. Oxford: Basil Blackwell.

Walby, S. (2003). *Gender transformations*. London and New York: Routledge.

Walby, S. (2004). The European Union and gender equality: Emergent varieties of gender regime. *Social Politics: International Studies in Gender, State & Society, 11*(1), 4–29.

Waylen, G. (1994). Women and democratization: Conceptualizing gender relations in transition politics. *World Politics, 46*(3), 327–354.

Waylen, G. (1996). *Gender in third world politics*. Boulder: Lynne Rienner Publishers.

Waylen, G. (2007). *Engendering transitions: Women's mobilization, institutions and gender outcomes*. Oxford: Oxford University Press.

Wedeen, L. (2002). Conceptualizing culture: Possibilities for political science. *American Political Science Review, 96*(4), 713–728.

Wejnert, B. (2014). *Diffusion of democracy: The past and future of global democracy*. New York: Cambridge University Press.

Wejnert, B., & Rodriguez, E. (2015). Building a better world for future generations through implementation of global gender equality. In *Enabling gender equality: Future generations of the global world* (pp. 231–243). Bingley, UK: Emerald Publishing Group.

World Bank. (2018). *Income tax rate by country*. World Development Indicators, The World Bank Group.

Zakaria, F. (1997). The rise of illiberal democracy. *Foreign Affairs, 76*(6), 22–43.

Zvan-Elliott, K. (2015). *Modernizing patriarchy: The politics of women's rights in Morocco*. Austin: University of Texas Press.

CHAPTER 5

Changing Tides? On How Popular Support for Feminism Increased After the Arab Spring

Saskia Glas and Niels Spierings

INTRODUCTION

In 2010 and 2011, across the Arab region ordinary men and women took to the streets *en masse* to demand freedom, dignity, and social justice. Their demands were feminist too, including gender equality and women's empowerment (Bayat 2013; Moghadam 2013). Now, eight years after most protest signs have vanished, it has become clear that these demands have hardly been met in most Middle Eastern and North African (MENA) countries (Moghadam 2018; Szmolka 2017).

Electronic supplementary material The online version of this chapter (https://doi.org/10.1007/978-3-030-27735-2_5) contains supplementary material, which is available to authorized users.

S. Glas (✉) · N. Spierings
Radboud University, Nijmegen, The Netherlands

© The Author(s) 2020
H. Darhour and D. Dahlerup (eds.), *Double-Edged Politics on Women's Rights in the MENA Region*, Gender and Politics, https://doi.org/10.1007/978-3-030-27735-2_5

However, the Arab Uprisings may have succeeded in winning peoples' hearts for the feminist cause. If so, this is not without consequence, as public support is important for any social movement to advance its goals, even though it is given relatively little academic attention (Bayat 2005; Polletta and Jasper 2001). To our knowledge, no large-scale MENA-wide study exists assessing if the Arab Uprisings fueled feminism among wider publics (see Feather's chapter in this book for descriptive trends). Therefore, this chapter addresses to what extent MENA publics' support for feminism developed differently after the uprisings, and how this varies across MENA countries.

To that end, we develop and apply the lens of context-dependent norm diffusion, which acknowledges that the Arab MENA houses diverse societies that differ in factors that facilitate norm diffusion (see Abu-Rabia-Queder and Weiner-Levy 2013; Moghadam and Gheytanchi 2010). More specifically, we propose that and assess whether social movements garner wider public support when they (are perceived or imagined to) frame their issues so that they resonate with publics at large (Bayat 2005; Polletta and Jasper 2001). As the Arab Uprisings were grassroots movements and thus did not have clear leaders to present specific goals attractively (Charrad and Zarrugh 2014), we study whether the resonance of feminist norms with wider publics is dependent on (a) endogenous factors related to the particular forms the uprisings took highlighting feminist issues and (b) exogenic, pre-existing socio-political structures constructing feminism as inherently opposed to "an Islamic MENA identity" (see Abu-Lughod 1998; Ahmed 1992; Charrad 2011; Spierings 2015).

As our frame centers the dominant construct whereby feminism is depicted as anti-Islam, we also explore how feminism and religion are combined among publics at large. More specifically, we explore whether support for *Muslim* feminism and support for *secularist* feminism have increased to the same extent. The former refers to being both strongly attached to Islam and supporting gender equality and women's empowerment. The latter refers to being less religious (and feminist), but does not necessarily mean either supporting the division between religion and state or being an atheist; we use the term "secularist" to refer to being less strongly attached to Islam than is common in the MENA (see Glas and Spierings 2019).

The Diffusion of Feminism

Muslim and Secularist Feminism

Before turning to theories of norms diffusion and applying them to the Arab Spring, we shortly describe what we mean by people who "support feminism", and how this group is divided into "Muslim feminists" and "secularist feminists".

Based on Glas and Spierings (2019), we conceptualize "feminism" and "religion" broadly and inclusively, while still being demarcating. First, support for feminism refers to supporting women's control of resources (i.e., empowerment) and their equal political, economic, and social rights and opportunities (i.e., equality). So, MENA citizens who support feminism do not oppose gender equality and women's empowerment. At the same time, the *extent* of feminists' support for these issues may differ across issues and contexts, not in the least because feminist goals change depending on which goals have been reached and which issues are salient in certain contexts (see Celis et al. 2008; Walby 2011). This also leaves room for contradictory attitudes toward women's rights; for instance, Arab Muslims may support women's education without advocating for women's political rights (Glas et al. 2019). In our conceptualization, MENA citizens thus do not need to be advocates of complete equality and empowerment to be feminists, but rather support (certain issues concerning) *greater* women's empowerment and gender equality.

Second, while we acknowledge that religion also has multiple aspects such as practices, doctrinal beliefs, and feelings, this chapter focuses on the last. Feeling attached to religion ("affective religious beliefs") creates the most, or perhaps the only, clear-cut criterion to define who is religious and who is not, respecting people's own identification (Glas, Spierings and Scheepers 2018): one is more religious if s/he feels more attached to religion and vice versa. Contrarily, viewing people as religious only if they practice their religion a certain way or understand religious texts in a particular manner begs the (theological and normative) question who determines which expressions of religion are the proper ones. Therefore, we understand religious MENA citizens to be MENA citizens who feel (at least averagely) attached to Islam.

Vice versa, secularism thus does *not* refer to either (the Western notion of) being a non-religious atheist or wanting a division between religion and state, but rather as being *relatively* less attached to Islam compared to other citizens. Positioning oneself as strictly non-religious or non-Muslim in the MENA is a forceful political statement, and our focus is broader than this strongly activist group; we are interested in who supports feminism more generally among the larger public and whether this is the less religious section of society. Thus, "secularist citizens" are Muslims[1] who may still be pretty religious for Western standards, but who still tend to feel *relatively less* attached to Islam than many of their fellow citizens.

Altogether, our main focus is on Muslims who "support feminism", so those people who are relatively supportive of several forms of political, economic, and social equality between the sexes and women's empowerment. Additionally, when we talk about "support for Muslim feminism" this refers to combining support for feminism with "feeling highly religious", whereas "support for secularist feminism" concerning the same for feminism, but being "relatively less attached to religion in the MENA region".

Norm Diffusion

Now it is clear what meanings we attach to (Muslim and secularist) feminism, we turn to why the Arab Spring would impact them among publics at large. We start our argument by noting that feminist protests do not always immediately generate support among wider publics, as was the case for, for instance, feminists' fights in favor of criminalizing domestic violence. So, the question becomes: under what circumstances do protests do rally support? Applying and refining existing insights, we depart from the notion that it is pivotal whether protestors' demands resonate with publics. More specifically, public perceptions change because norms diffuse *if the issues protestors fight for resonate with the meanings larger publics attach to the world* (Bayat 2005; Polletta and Jasper 2001; Snow and Benford 1988).

Following this context-dependent norm-diffusion frame, various interconnected attributes of the Arab Uprisings can be expected to have the potential to fuel the diffusion of feminist norms. First, the protests often called for freedom, dignity, and social justice, including equality between women and men, thus highlighting feminist issues that could spread subsequently, either intentionally or unintentionally (Bayat 2013; Moghadam 2013, 2018). Second, women from all walks of life took to the streets beside men, and some women's movements even took a leading role in organizing the protests, further exemplifying feminist issues (Pedersen and Salib 2013). Third, the diffusion of feminism is likely considering the unprecedented scale of the protests in certain countries and the consequent media attention they garnered, which also increased the visibility of protestors' demands (Bellin 2012). Fourth, the uprisings have been characterized as bottom-up, grassroots movements. So, although the protests might not have had clear leaders to frame issues appealingly to publics, they mobilized support through (social media-based) interpersonal networks. The use of such networks implies shortened distances between sender and receiver and thus an increased likelihood of frame alignment and consequent norm diffusion (Charrad and Zarrugh 2014). Altogether, the Arab Uprisings thus carried the potential to resonate with publics at large and diffuse feminist norms more widely throughout MENA societies, because feminist demands were center-staged in large-scale, interpersonal protests.

Still, although feminist norm diffusion fits several characteristics of the protests, the potential of feminist norm diffusion was not equally present in all MENA countries. More specifically, (a) not all protests brought feminist issues to the fore and (b) feminism may not resonate with all publics to the same degree given their pre-existing meanings attached to the world, which are expected to be shaped by socio-political structures. We should thus focus on the different manifestations of protests in varying MENA countries and MENA countries' differing pre-existing socio-political structures (see Abu-Rabia-Queder and Weiner-Levy 2013; Moghadam and Gheytanchi 2010). Applying this focus, we deduce expectations concerning in which countries the uprisings did and did not impact support for (Muslim and secularist) feminism below.

Forms of Protests

How did the particular manifestation of protests impact public support? This subsection departs from the notion that the uprisings took rather different forms across the region (Moghadam 2014; Spierings 2017; Szmolka 2017). These factors endogenous to the uprisings are expected to shape the visibility of feminism and the resonance of feminist issues and consequently feminist norm diffusion.

First off, it seems unlikely that the Arab Spring shifted public opinion in favor of (Muslim or secularist) feminism in countries in which there were no mass uprisings (e.g., Algeria [Del Panta 2017]) or in which the protests had particular foci instead of broad calls for increased freedom and equality generally (e.g., Lebanon and Iraq [Wimmen 2014]). So, assuming that feminist demands need to be brought to the fore in a particular country to spread to that country's public, our first expectation is that *the presence of large-scale protests with calls for feminism is a* necessary *condition for support for feminism to be boosted following the Arab Uprisings.*

Here, it is important to note that two assumptions underlie this expectation, which we address empirically later. First, we assume that regional spill-overs in public opinion are far outweighed by the influence of the particular country MENA citizens inhabit. For instance, we expect that the broad-based, large-scale protests in Tunisia had far more effect on Tunisians' support for feminism than on neighboring Algerians'. This assumption also dovetails with our aim to not homogenize the region and take differences between Arab countries seriously. Second, we expect that the effect of the protests is not completely nullified by the subsequent rise to power of Islamist political parties. So, we for instance assume that when the uprisings increased Tunisians' support for feminism, this increase was not wholly quashed when Islamist Ennahda won the plurality of the votes in the parliamentary elections and formed the government. Both assumptions are tested empirically in the second part of this chapter.

Next, our frame proposes that feminist protests in and of themselves may not be *sufficient* to rally popular support; feminist issues have to resonate with publics, too. Considering the particularities of different protests in different countries may help to explain when protests including feminist calls resonate with publics at large. Specifically, in countries as Yemen, Libya, and Syria, the protests quickly evolved into large-scale violent civil conflicts (Spierings 2017), which tends to put feminism on the back burner in peoples' minds (Usta et al. 2008). Even though in these countries mass protests occurred, feminist issues will not resonate with publics' life worlds because publics are expected to be more preoccupied with the violence and on average view feminism as a secondary issue (Horn et al. 2014). So, we expect that *civil wars are sufficient to prohibit increases in publics' support for feminism after the uprisings.*

Moreover, we tentatively suggest, and will empirically explore, that *especially support for* Muslim *feminism tumbled in these countries*, as they saw resurges of Islamist radicals (i.e., Islamists who operate outside of institutionalized politics). As Islamist radicals generally denounce feminist interpretations of Islam, they are expected to reinforce notions that Islam is at odds with women's rights as human rights and thereby curb combinations of feminism and strong attachment to Islam among larger publics (Hall 2017).

Pre-existing Socio-Political Structures

The diffusion of feminist norms in countries that did see large-scale broad-based protests is also expected to be dependent on factors exogenous to the protests; pre-existing socio-political structures might facilitate publics' receptiveness to feminist norms. Particularly, we consider two elements: the pre-existing state of gender relations and public anti-Western sentiments.

To start with the latter, the Arab Uprisings' feminist norms are not expected to diffuse among strongly anti-Western publics, because feminist norms are not expected to resonate with the life worlds of these publics, in which feminism is often considered Western and thus wrong (see Abu-Lughod 1998; Ahmed 1992; Charrad 2011). Vice versa, in contexts in which anti-Western narratives are weaker, publics are expected to be more receptive to feminist norms because they view feminism less as a Western, neo-imperialist force (Ahmed 1992; Charrad 2011; Spierings 2014). Moreover, in the latter more pro-Western contexts, feminism is less likely to be depicted as a Western import antithetical to the Arab MENA, because the opposition to feminisms will realize that such delegitimizations resonate less with the pro-Western publics in their country. If feminism is less seen as anti-Arab this in turn ensures that protestors' feminist calls resonate more widely. Altogether, we thus expect that *among less anti-Western MENA publics the uprisings are more likely to increase support for feminism.*

Additionally, because in pro-Western climates feminism is framed less as opposed to Arab-Islamic identity, publics may more easily combine support for feminism with strong attachment to Islam (Glas and Spierings 2019). For these publics, it may be easier to adopt feminism without swearing off their religion which may be central to their identity or at least bring them strength and guidance in life. So, we also tentatively suggest that, following the uprisings, *the diffusion of feminist norms among more pro-Western publics may especially fuel their support for* Muslim *feminism.*

Second, feminist norms are expected to resonate more in MENA countries in which gender relations were already more equal prior to the uprisings. In these countries, societal frames had probably already been molded to be more receptive to feminist claims (Moghadam 2014), and, simply put, pre-sculpted publics' minds just needed a final push in the form of the uprisings. Moreover, more gender equal countries already signaled that feminism is not necessarily at odds with Arab identity. By having local women (and men) voice feminist demands, the narrative that feminism does not fit a MENA identity is undercut with real-life examples, increasing publics' receptiveness to feminist claims (El Haitami 2016).

Women's rights movements and female political representation are the aspects of equal gender relations expected to be particularly influential in shaping the impact of the uprisings. First, strong women's movements helped center-stage feminism in the uprisings, increasing their visibility during the protests and ensuring that protestors' feminist demands would not be forgotten thereafter. As Moghadam notes, "women's mobilizations before the Arab Spring helped shape the nature of the uprisings [...] and constitute a compelling explanatory factor for the divergent outcomes of the Arab Spring" (2018: 12). Similarly, female politicians probably increase attention paid to women in political debates, again ensuring that gender issues are not sidelined after the protests (Pedersen and Salib 2013). Although certain Arab female parliamentarians have been argued to have little real power and owe their positions to political gender quotas, it is important to not depreciate female parliamentarians writ large, as others do stand up for women's rights. Additionally, at the very least these female politicians show women can take up political positions, which is expected to increase the resonance of feminist norms among their constituents. Altogether, we expect that more gender equal relations thus fuel feminist norm diffusion and therefore we expect *the presence of strong pre-existing women's movements and prevalence of female parliamentarians to increase the resonance of the protests' feminist claims.*

Again, if strong women's movements and greater shares of female politicians undercut claims that feminism is opposed to Islam, they may also ease their combination. In more gender equal countries, publics may thus not only accept feminist norms more, but particularly combine adopted feminist norms with strong attachment to Islam (Badran 2005). Therefore, we expect that *especially support for* Muslim *feminism may increase in countries with more equal pre-existing gender relations following the Arab Spring.*

Data and Methods

Public Opinion Data

In order to assess how support for feminism has developed, we combine the large-scale quantitative surveys from Arab Barometer (AB, rounds 1 to 4) and the World Values Surveys (WVS, rounds 4–6—MENA countries were excluded in rounds 1–3). As we are interested in trends over time and the impact of the uprisings, we selected Arab countries surveyed at least twice between 2006 and 2014, including at least once after 2011, and within one survey type. Additionally, because we study Muslim feminism and secularist feminism among Muslims, we exclude non-Muslim respondents (about 5%). Consequently, the least religious respondents in our analyses still consider themselves Muslim, but they identify as far less religious than average ("secularist"—see "Muslim and secularist feminism" section above).

Our final sample consists of 46,701 respondents in 38 country-years in 10 Arab MENA countries: Algeria (AB), Egypt (AB), Iraq (AB, WVS), Jordan (AB, WVS), Lebanon (AB), Morocco (AB), Palestine (AB), Sudan (AB), Tunisia (AB), and Yemen (AB).

Measuring Support for (Muslim and Secularist) Feminism

To measure whether respondents support Muslim feminism or secularist feminism (or neither), we combine 7 questions concerning support for gender equality and women's empowerment with 4 items on attachment to religion (see Table 5.1). These items are widely used in previous works and have been argued to validly tap feminism and religiosity (e.g., Glas et al. 2018; Rizzo et al. 2007). All items are coded so that higher scores reflect greater support for feminism or religiosity.

To classify respondents as Muslim feminists, secularist feminists, or neither, we follow the approach introduced by Glas and Spierings (2019) and apply latent class analyses (LCAs), estimating an 8-class model.[2] Simply put, LCAs group respondents into "classes" based on their own answers on the feminism and religiosity questions. LCA can, for instance, demarcate a group of respondents that is both highly supportive of feminism and highly religious: supporters of Muslim feminism. Moreover, these analyses allow for contradictory attitudes concerning specific domains of women's rights by clustering multiple aspects of support for

Table 5.1 Items on feminism and religiosity

Item	Answer categories
Feminism	
Men are better political leaders than women	Strongly agree; agree; disagree; strongly disagree
Women can become presidents or prime ministers of Muslim states	Strongly disagree; disagree; agree; strongly agree
University education is more important for boys than for girls	Strongly agree; agree; disagree; strongly disagree
Married women can work outside the home	Strongly disagree; disagree; agree; strongly agree
Being a housewife is just as fulfilling as working for a pay	Strongly agree; agree; disagree; strongly disagree
Men and women should have equal work opportunities	Strongly disagree; disagree; agree; strongly agree
When jobs are scarce, men have more right to a job than women	Agree; neither; disagree
Religion	
How important is God in your life?	Ten categories from "not at all important" to "very important"
How important is religion in your life?	Not at all important; not very important; rather important; very important
Independently of religious service attendance, would you say you are …?	An atheist; not a religious person; a religious person
Generally speaking, would you describe yourself as …?	Not religious; somewhat religious; religious

Source AB and WVS

feminism. In our sample, 29.7% of respondents are considered feminists, and 15.4% could be clearly classified as Muslim feminists and 7.9% as secularist feminists.[3]

Classifying Countries' Forms of Protests

We firstly expect publics' support for feminism to be affected by whether their particular Arab country featured protests during the Spring. However, we argued that it is vital that these protests were (a) larger than usual and (b) broad-based, focusing on wide-spanning freedom and equality, including feminist claims. Relying on existing work (most notably Bellin 2012; Moghadam 2014; Spierings 2017; Szmolka 2017), of the countries included here we consider Egypt, Morocco, and

Tunisia to have seen such large protests that featured feminist claims. Another group of countries in our data had no protests that were larger in scale than usual (Algeria, Jordan, and Palestine) (see also Del Panta 2017). Others had sectarian protests without foci on feminism or freedom and equality at large (Iraq, Lebanon, Sudan, and Yemen) (see also Wimmen 2014). Finally, Yemen was the only country in our data that saw protests that descended into civil war (see Hall 2017; Moghadam 2014).

Classifying Countries' Pre-existing Socio-Political Structures

To measure cultural anti-Westernism, we rely on public opinion data and use two items asked in both AB waves 1 and 2, namely whether respondents agreed (0) or disagreed (1) that "American and Western culture have positive aspects" and "despite negative U.S. foreign policy, Americans are good people". We averaged respondents' answers and ranked the anti-Westernism of publics per country.[4] Countries that scored lower than the regional average on anti-Westernism are considered to be less anti-Western, and the others publics more. Note that, ideally, one would use the continuous anti-Westernism values, but the limited number of Arab countries (in our data and in the world) precludes such a method. Also, there does seem to be a relatively sizeable gap in anti-Westernism between our two cutoff countries (0.06 while most others are 0.03), indicating our dichotomy is not completely arbitrary. Still, at the extremes, Tunisia scores exceptionally low and Sudan exceptionally high on anti-Westernism, which we will take into account when we interpret our results.

Concerning gender relations, we take both women's movements and female political representation into account. For women's movements, we do not simply count the number of collectives, because it is vital whether collectives take the form of influential, *autonomous* feminist movements instead of state co-opted ones (Htun and Weldon 2012). For instance, Saudi Arabia does have women's organizations but these are charitable movements co-opted by the state, while Algeria has multiple feminist movements (e.g., SOS, Rachide, and Reseau Wassila) argued to be "effective [in] changing the lives of women" at the grassroots level (Salhi 2010: 123). Following regional experts (Moghadam 2014, 2018; United Nations Development Programme 2006), we consider Algeria, Tunisia, Morocco, and Egypt to have strong women's movements.

Women's political representation is measured using the percentage of women in national parliaments. Mainly, countries that scored below the regional average prior to the uprisings are considered to have lower female political participation, and the other countries more. Simultaneously, we do take into account that Algeria and Morocco saw big jumps in female political representation shortly after the uprisings.[5]

How Support for Feminism Changed After the Arab Spring

How did Arab publics' support for feminism develop? Figure 5.1 shows the percentage of publics per country that supports feminism during a particular year. First and foremost, our results show that there was no single country in which support for feminism decreased directly following the uprisings—although in most countries support dropped again after 2013, implying the effects of the uprisings may have been temporary rather than long-lasting. Still, the publics of almost all countries supported feminism more in 2013 or 2014 than before. These increases are statistically significant and hold regardless of demographic changes in sex, age, education, and marital states, as shown by additional logistic regressions.[6]

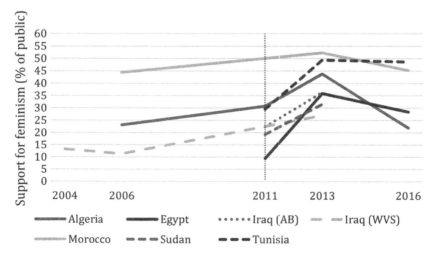

Fig. 5.1 Trends in support for feminism in countries with steeper increases after the Arab Spring

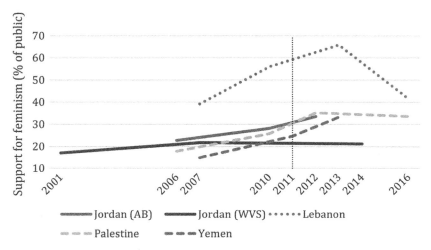

Fig. 5.2 Trends in support for feminism in countries without steeper increases after the Arab Spring

However, to attribute changes to the Arab Spring, it is not enough to show support for feminism increased after 2011. These increases may simply be part of an overall increasing trend and have little to do with the uprisings. We err on the side of caution and only consider the uprisings to have increased publics' support for feminism in countries where trends increased *more strongly* after the uprisings than before. These countries with steeper increases are in Fig. 5.1, others are in Fig. 5.2. Note that this "steeper increase" criterion means that countries in which feminism increased, but did not increase more strongly, are in Fig. 5.2.

More technically, for countries surveyed thrice (including once in 2010 or 2011), we used Paternoster tests to empirically check whether trends changed (Paternoster et al. 1998). For countries surveyed only twice, we assessed whether the changes in support for feminism were so strong they implied a change in trend. Finally, Morocco was surveyed thrice but not in 2010 or 2011, so our conclusions for Morocco especially remain tentative. Still, because the baseline support for feminism was so high in Morocco in 2006 already, we cautiously suggest that the 8-percentage point increase in 2013 does point to a significant change.

Making up the balance using the "steeper increase" criterion, the uprisings seem to have impacted support for feminism positively in some

Table 5.2 Per-country trends in support for feminism after Arab Spring

	Feminism	Muslim feminism	Secularist feminism
Egypt (AB)	Steeper increase	Steeper increase	Steeper increase
Iraq (WVS)	Steeper increase	Steeper increase	Steeper increase
Iraq (AB)	Steeper increase	Steeper increase	Steeper increase
Morocco (AB)[a]	Steeper increase	Steeper increase	Steeper increase
Sudan (AB)	Steeper increase	Steeper increase	No steeper increase
Algeria (AB)	Steeper increase	No steeper increase	Steeper increase
Tunisia (AB)	Steeper increase	[a]No steeper increase	No steeper increase
Yemen (AB)	No steeper increase	Steeper increase	No steeper increase
Lebanon (AB)	No steeper increase	No steeper increase	Steeper increase
Palestine (AB)	No steeper increase	No steeper increase	Steeper increase
Jordan (WVS)	No steeper increase	No steeper increase	Steeper increase
Jordan (AB)	No steeper increase	No steeper increase	Steeper increase

Note [a]Less certain conclusion. $N_{individual} = 46{,}701$

countries but not in others. In Algeria, Egypt, Iraq, Morocco, Sudan, and Tunisia, publics' support for feminism seems to have increased more strongly after the uprisings, but the same is not found for Jordan, Lebanon, Palestine, and Yemen (see also Table 5.2). This variation implies that region-wide spillovers were not present, and country-specific explanations are thus warranted, which is in line with our framework.

Explaining Increased Support for Feminism

Having established how public opinion trends changed after the Arab Uprisings, we get to the question of whether the different impact of the Arab Spring in varying countries can be explained by the forms the protests took and countries' socio-political structures. Based on their manifestations of protests and socio-political structures, our countries can be summarized in nine configurations (see Table 5.3), highlighting some important patterns concerning why publics' support feminism increased or did not.

Table 5.3 shows that, for instance, Morocco and Tunisia saw similar large-scale, broad-based protests, and had strongly equal gender relations and lower anti-Western sentiments; therefore, these two countries are in one row. Morocco and Tunisia fit all conditions explicated by our frame for the Arab Spring to feature feminist claims that resonate with larger publics, and consequently increase public support for feminism. The last column

Table 5.3 Overview of clusters of feminism results

	Forms of protests	Socio-political structures		Increased feminism
		Gender equal relations[a]	Anti-Westernism	
1. Morocco; Tunisia	Large, broad protests	Both	Lower	Yes; yes
2. Egypt	Large, broad protests	Movements	Higher	Yes
3. Algeria	No protests	Both	Higher	Yes
4. Palestine	No protests	Female politicians	Higher	No
5. Jordan	No protests	Neither	Higher	No
6. Iraq	Sectarian protests	Female politicians	Lower	Yes
7. Sudan	Sectarian protests	Female politicians	Higher	Yes
8. Lebanon	Sectarian protests	Neither	Lower	No
9. Yemen	Sectarian, civil war	Neither	Lower	No

Note [a]'Gender equal relations' indicates the prevalance of active women's movements and high level of women's political representation. $N_{individual} = 46,701$; $N_{survey} = 38$

in Table 5.3 shows that feminism did indeed increase more steeply after the uprisings in Morocco and Tunisia, providing initial support for our framework.

More broadly, first, our results imply that feminist norms diffused in countries that saw larger protests than usual which included broad claims for freedom and equality. Egypt, Morocco, and Tunisia imply that *having large-scale, broad-based protests is sufficient for feminism to be boosted after the Arab Spring* (outcome 1a). This finding also supports our assumption that the liberalizing effect of the Arab Spring is not negated by a consequent increase in political power of institutional Islamist parties. Tunisia's Ennahda, Morocco's PJD, and Egypt's Muslim Brotherhood have not annihilated the Arab Spring's advancement of public support for feminism.

However, all countries that saw large-scale, broad-based protests also have strong women's movements, which means that women's movements rather than protests may be decisive for boosts in feminism after the Arab Spring. In fact, all countries with strong women's movements— including Algeria—saw surges in feminism. Interestingly, Algeria did not see large protests, which implies that *having large-scale, broad-based protests is not necessary for feminism to be boosted after the Arab Spring* (outcome 1b). The Algerian, Egyptian, Moroccan, and Tunisian case however do exemplify that *having strong, autonomous women's movements is sufficient for feminism to jump after the Arab Spring* (outcome 2). Altogether, it thus seems that strong women's movements may be able to reverberate the feminist claims of protests from other countries to rally support in their own. Still, because Algeria borders countries that did see large protests—i.e., Morocco and Tunisia (and Libya)—we should be careful not to generalize the echoing power of women's movements across the entire region too quickly.

Third, our results imply that anti-Westernism does not seem to matter for the Arab Spring's impact on public support for feminism.[7] Indeed, comparing Iraq to Sudan (and Morocco and Tunisia to Egypt), we find similar outcomes for countries that differ (only) in anti-Westernism. This implies that the resonance of feminism is not blocked by anti-Western value climates per se. Simultaneously, our results do not disprove that anti-Westernism may have an impact if gender equality and protests were absent (see Jordan and Palestine versus Algeria). It may thus be the case that feminist norms do not resonate among anti-Western publics because they view feminism as Western imperialism, but this imperialist narrative is undercut in strongly gender equal countries where local men and women stand up for women's rights. As our countries cluster, we cannot rule out this option completely. However, the most parsimonious and obvious interpretation of our results for now is that *anti-Westernism is by itself not necessary or sufficient to block increases in feminism after the Arab Spring* (outcome 3).

When we consequently disregard changes in anti-Westernism between countries, we uncover additional patterns for countries that saw sectarian protests. In these countries, the Arab Spring boosted feminism if many female politicians were present, and it did not if female political representation was low. Indeed, comparing Iraq and Sudan to Lebanon and Yemen, our results show that *high levels of female political representation are sufficient for feminism to thrive in countries that saw sectarian protests* (outcome 4). Echoing the proposed power of women's movements in countries that did not see protests themselves, female politicians may thus be able to turn sectarian discontent toward feminist sentiment. So, female politicians may be able to use the political openings protests present, regardless of their particular foci, to voice feminist claims that seem to resonate with publics at large.

Last, comparing Yemen to the other countries in our data, we could conclude that the eruption of a civil war is a sufficient condition for feminism not to be boosted following the Arab Spring. Still, because this conclusion relies solely on one case that we can also explain (together with three others) with an alternative explanation, the impact of civil wars remains tentative.

Altogether, our main conclusion is that any type of large protests combined with any type of gender equality is sufficient for public support for feminism to be boosted after the Arab Spring (outcome 5, touching on outcomes 1, 2, and 4). It thus seems that female leaders voice feminist claims that resonate with the life worlds of publics in times of political upheavals. Vice versa, to block feminist boosts, anti-Western sentiments seem irrelevant while civil wars may be sufficient. Finally, our results do not rule out regional spill-overs into countries that saw no protests (Algeria), but imply that spill-overs were specific, perhaps limited to countries that bordered multiple countries that did see protests and already had strong women's movements (cf. Jordan and Palestine).

Exploring Muslim and Secularist Feminism

Now we have ascertained how the Arab Spring affected public support for feminism differently in varying countries, we turn to our additional question concerning what shape feminism takes. As seen in Table 5.2, in the vast majority of cases, Muslim feminism shows steep increases when feminism does, and, vice versa, Muslim feminism is not boosted when feminism is not boosted. The Arab Spring's effect on feminism seems closely tied to its effect on *Muslim* feminism.[8]

On the other hand, trends in secularist feminism seem less tied to general feminism's development. In fact, in most countries, secularist feminism was boosted after 2011 regardless of whether general feminism did so too. The effects of the uprisings thus seem to differ for secularist feminism versus general and Muslim feminism.[9] This may signal that the resonance of secularist feminist norms follows other mechanisms than general feminism and Muslim feminism, which warrants treating secularist feminism separately.

This brings us to our final question. What explains whether the uprisings spurred Muslim or secularist feminism? Do the particular manifestations of the protests and the socio-political structures of varying Arab countries also help explain whether publics combined feminism with religion? Presently, we do not (cl)aim to answer these questions completely, but we will outline our most notable findings.[10]

First, in all countries without large protests, Muslim feminism did not increase more steeply than before but secularist feminism did. Our results in Table 5.4 on Algeria, Palestine, and Jordan thus imply that *not having protests is a sufficient condition for Muslim feminism not to increase* (outcome 6a) *and for secularist feminism to increase* (outcome 6b). Although unexpected, this finding may imply that having local men and women voice their concerns is indeed needed to signal that feminism is not at odds with a Muslim identity. Protests in neighboring countries are not enough. If so, this again signals the limitations of spill-overs, which means that one should not expect feminism to thrive similarly in all Arab countries alike.

A non-exclusive alternative interpretation is that secularist feminism thrives when anti-Western sentiments run high. Although we find no discernible impact of gender equal relations, pre-existing socio-political structures thus do seem to matter as Egypt, Algeria, Palestine, and Jordan imply that *strong anti-Westernism is sufficient to increase secularist feminism* after the uprisings (outcome 7). Sudan is the exception, which means that either very high anti-Westernism has a different impact, or,

Table 5.4 Overview of clusters of Muslim and secularist feminism results

	Forms of protests	Socio-political structures		Increased feminism	
		Gender equal relations[a]	Anti-Westernism	Muslim	Secularist
1. Morocco; Tunisia	Large, broad protests	Both	Low	Yes; no	Yes; no
2. Egypt	Large, broad protests	Movements	High	Yes	Yes
3. Algeria	No protests	Both	High	No	Yes
4. Palestine	No protests	Female politicians	High	No	Yes
5. Jordan	No protests	No	High	No	Yes
6. Iraq	Sectarian protests	Female politicians	Low	Yes	Yes
7. Sudan	Sectarian protests	Female politicians	High	Yes	No
8. Lebanon	Sectarian protests	No	Low	No	Yes
9. Yemen	Sectarian, civil war	No	Low	Yes	No

Note [a]'Gender equal relations' indicates the prevalance of active women's movements and high level of women's political representation. $N_{individual} = 46{,}701$; $N_{survey} = 38$

more likely, that sectarian protests prohibit this outcome. So, it seems that the narrative that feminism is incompatible with Islam takes root in anti-Western societies, spurring secularist feminism, but that focusing on sectarian identity pulls religion back in. Although anti-Westernism did not seem to shape whether the uprisings would boost feminism, it thus may have a hand in how secularist feminism develops.

Similarly, while whether protests descended into civil wars could not be tied to feminism's development with substantial certainty, civil wars do seem to shape sub-forms of feminism. Comparing Yemen to Lebanon, *civil wars seem sufficient to prohibit secularist feminism from being boosted after the Spring* (outcome 8a) *and increase Muslim feminism* (outcome 8b). Although this rests on one case, sectarian civil wars may thus again reinforce religious identities, increasing their importance broadly, including under feminists.

Conclusion

Did the Arab Spring change MENA' support for feminism? This chapter set out to answer this question by applying a context-dependent norm-diffusion frame (see also Bayat 2005; Polletta and Jasper 2001; Snow and Benford 1988) to explain why the Arab Uprisings may have increased publics' support for feminism in some MENA countries but not in others. At its core, our frame links the impact of the Arab Spring on publics' support for feminism to whether the protests brought feminist norms to the fore and whether feminist norms resonated with the life worlds of publics (Abu-Rabia-Queder and Weiner-Levy 2013; Moghadam and Gheytanchi 2010; Spierings 2015). Infusing insights from the existing literature in our framework, we assessed whether (a) the specific forms the uprisings took and (b) countries' pre-existing socio-political structures, captured by anti-Western sentiments and equal gender relations, facilitated or hampered the visibility and resonance of feminist norms (Abu-Lughod 1998; Ahmed 1992; Charrad 2011; Moghadam 2014, 2018; Spierings 2014). In this endeavor, we also explored whether the Arab Spring may have differently impacted support for Muslim and secularist feminism.

We applied this frame to public opinion data from the AB and WVS on more than 46,000 MENA citizens, which we analyzed using LCAs and regression models. Assessing the public opinion trends, we firstly found that there was no country in our data in which public support for feminism was significantly lower after the uprisings than before. However, publics' support for feminism did not increase significantly more strongly in all countries. This implies, in line with our framework, that whether the Arab Uprisings impacted feminist norm diffusion was country-dependent; we cannot treat the region as a homogenous entity and no simple, region-wide spill-overs were present.

Using a comparative case study design, we subsequently found that several of the factors we focused on shed light on why feminism was boosted in some countries but not in others, and the framework helps to understand their interconnectedness. Most importantly, our results showed that mass protests in countries that were already more gender equal were sufficient to boost public support for feminism after the Arab Spring. It seems that, when protests call for political change, women's movements and female politicians are instrumental in echoing feminist norms and ensuring they resonate with Arab publics.

Additionally, our results implied that anti-Western sentiments and civil wars shape what type of feminism (Muslim or secularist) was boosted by the uprisings. Generally, in countries with strong anti-Western value climates, secularist feminism jumped after the uprisings. So, in strongly anti-Western societies, the narrative that feminism is incompatible with Islam may be more forceful and prompt feminists to opt for a secular route. Vice versa, Muslim feminism jumped in countries with sectarian protests that descended into civil wars. Sectarian civil wars may thus reinforce religious identities, increasing their importance under feminists. Still, this conclusion remains tentative as our data only include one of the countries in which the 2011 uprisings were characterized by sectarian protests leading to civil war (Yemen).

In fact, the problem of the limited number of MENA countries and the strong clustering of the factors we focused on underlay most of the challenges we faced. For instance, all countries (in the region and in our data) in which large-scale, broad-based protests took place also have strong women's movements, rendering it difficult to tease apart their effects. Of course, this observation may also show that the occurrence of mass protests is tied to the existence of strong women's movements (see Sadiqi's chapter in this book). At any rate, there remains some uncertainty regarding which particular characteristic or combination thereof facilitated or prohibited feminist norm diffusion after the Arab Spring. It is unlikely that this issue can be solved fully if additional quantitative data come available, so in-depth studies could zoom in on the mechanisms that this study brought to the fore. Still, comparable large-N data on more time points, especially between 2008 and 2010, within countries could help establish whether the trends our data show hold. Also, our conclusions on what factors matter could be scrutinized using additional quantitative data; for instance, data on Bahrain could further illuminate our results on sectarian protests, data on Saudi Arabia could deepen our insights into countries that saw no large-scale protests, and data on Syria would help to test our claims on civil war.

Keeping these limitations in mind, the context-dependent norm-diffusion framework has shown to be a valuable way to assess the divergent impacts of the Arab Spring on publics' support for feminism. Indeed, it seems that feminist norms did not unilaterally diffuse following the protests. Rather, mass protests need to take place in countries where women are in a position to take the lead to foster a public mindset more prone to support for feminism.

Notes

1. Because atheists or Christians may interpret religion and feminism differently than Muslims, we limit this chapter to Muslims.
2. Details are beyond the scope of this chapter. For more information on LCA, see Linzer and Lewis (2011). Online Appendix 4.A shows our LCA model. We follow Glas and Spierings' (2019) approach. Differences in our outcomes are due to our sub-sample—we find similar results to Glas and Spierings if we include all countries.
3. We found three feminist classes of which one (6.4%) could be classified neither as Muslim feminist nor as secular feminist.
4. Tunisia (0.222), Lebanon (0.291), Morocco (0.322), Yemen (0.356), Iraq (0.358), (average [0.419]), Egypt (0.420), Algeria (0.450), Palestine (0.483), Jordan (0.512), Sudan (0.575).
5. In November 2010: Tunisia (28%); Sudan (26%), Iraq (25%), Palestine (20%), (average [13%]), Jordan (11%), Morocco (11%), Algeria (8%), Lebanon (3%), Egypt (2%), Yemen (0%). http://archive.ipu.org/wmn-e/arc/classif310712.htm. Palestine's data was obtained from regional experts (e.g., Jad 2010). Algeria and Morocco jumped from 8 to 31% and from 11 to 17%, respectively.
6. Results are obtainable from authors. The only exception to our pattern is Jordan (WVS), where feminism did not significantly change compared to 2007, although this conclusion could have been different if the WVS provided a 2010 measurement, as the Jordanian AB data suggest.

7. We also find no discernible impact of anti-Westernism when we create four categories all marked by 0.06 cut-off points. In fact, Sudan, the most anti-Western country in our data, still shows steeper increases in feminism.
8. See trends in Muslim and secularist feminism in Figs. A4.1a through A4.2b in the online Appendix.
9. Interestingly, but beyond the scope of this chapter, after 2013, secularist feminism decreased in most countries, while Muslim feminism increased.
10. In Tunisia, the third, moderately religious feminist group especially grew after 2011, which explains why Tunisia saw boosts in feminism but not Muslim or secularist feminism. Still, as noted, the results on Muslim feminism remain uncertain. If Muslim feminism increased in Tunisia, outcome 5 also holds for Muslim feminism.

REFERENCES

Abu-Lughod, L. (1998). *Remaking women: Feminism and modernity in the Middle East.* Princeton: Princeton University Press.

Abu-Rabia-Queder, S., & Weiner-Levy, N. (2013). Between local and foreign structures: Exploring the agency of Palestinian women in Israel. *Social Politics, 20*(1), 88–108.

Ahmed, L. (1992). *Women and gender in Islam.* New Haven: Yale University Press.

Badran, M. (2005). Between secular and Islamic feminism/s: Reflections on the Middle East and beyond. *Journal of Middle East Women's Studies, 1*(1), 6–28.

Bayat, A. (2005). Islamism and social movement theory. *Third World Quarterly, 26*(6), 891–908.

Bayat, A. (2013). The Arab Spring and its surprises. *Development and Change, 44*(3), 587–601.

Bellin, E. (2012). Reconsidering the robustness of authoritarianism in the Middle East: Lessons from the Arab Spring. *Comparative Politics, 44*(2), 127–149.

Celis, K., Childs, S., Kantola, J., & Krook, M. (2008). Rethinking women's substantive representation. *Representation, 44*(2), 99–110.

Charrad, M. (2011). Gender in the Middle East: Islam, state, agency. *Annual Review of Sociology, 37,* 417–437.

Charrad, M., & Zarrugh, A. (2014). Equal or complementary? Women in the new Tunisian constitution after the Arab Spring. *The Journal of North African Studies, 19*(2), 230–243.

Del Panta, G. (2017). Weathering the storm: Why was there no Arab uprising in Algeria? *Democratization, 24*(6), 1085–1102.

El Haitami, M. (2016). Islamist feminism in Morocco: (Re)defining the political sphere. *Frontiers: A Journal of Women Studies, 37*(3), 74–91.

Glas, S., & Spierings, N. (2019). Support for feminism among highly religious Muslim citizens in the Arab region. *European Journal of Politics and Gender, 2*, 283–310.

Glas, S., Spierings, N., Lubbers, M., & Scheepers, P. (2019). 'How polities shape support for gender equality and religiosity's impact in Arab countries. *European Sociological Review, 35*, 299–315.

Glas, S., Spierings, N., & Scheepers, P. (2018). Re-understanding religion and support for gender equality in Arab countries. *Gender & Society, 32*(5), 686–712.

Hall, B. (2017). Yemen's failed transition: From peaceful protests to war of 'all against all'. In D. Della Porta, T. Donker, B. Hall, E. Poljarevic, & D. Ritter (Eds.), *Social movements and civil war* (pp. 104–135). Abingdon: Routledge.

Horn, R., Puffer, E., Roesch, E., & Lehmann, H. (2014). Women's perceptions of effects of war on intimate partner violence and gender roles in two post-conflict West African Countries: Consequences and unexpected opportunities. *Conflict and Health, 8*(1), 12.

Htun, M., & Weldon, S. (2012). The civic origins of progressive policy change: Combating violence against women in global perspective, 1975–2005. *American Political Science Review, 106*(3), 548–569.

Jad, I. (2010). Palestinian women contesting power in chaos. *IDS Bulletin, 41*(5), 81–88.

Linzer, D., & Lewis, J. (2011). PoLCA: An R package for polytomous variable latent class analysis. *Journal of Statistical Software, 42*(10), 1–29.

Moghadam, V. (2013). *Modernizing women: Gender and social change in the Middle East* (3rd ed.). Boulder: Lynne Rienner.

Moghadam, V. (2014). Modernising women and democratisation after the Arab Spring. *The Journal of North African Studies, 19*(2), 137–142.

Moghadam, V. (2018). Explaining divergent outcomes of the Arab Spring: The significance of gender and women's mobilizations. *Politics, Groups, and Identities, 6*(4), 666–681.

Moghadam, V., & Gheytanchi, E. (2010). Political opportunities and strategic choices: Comparing feminist campaigns in Morocco and Iran. *Mobilization: An International Quarterly, 15*(3), 267–288.

Paternoster, R., Brame, R., Mazerolle, P., & Piquero, A. (1998). Using the correct statistical test for the equality of regression coefficients. *Criminology, 36*(4), 859–866.

Pedersen, J., & Salib, M. (2013). Women of the Arab Spring. *International Feminist Journal of Politics, 15*(2), 256–266.

Polletta, F., & Jasper, J. (2001). Collective identity and social movements. *Annual Review of Sociology, 27*(1), 283–305.

Rizzo, H., Abdel-Latif, A., & Meyer, K. (2007). The relationship between gender equality and democracy: A comparison of Arab versus non-Arab Muslim societies. *Sociology, 41*(6), 1151–1170.

Salhi, Z. (2010). The Algerian feminist movement between nationalism, patriarchy and Islamism. *Women's Studies International Forum, 33*(2), 113–124.

Snow, D., & Benford, R. (1988). Ideology, frame resonance, and participant mobilization. *International Social Movement Research, 1*, 197–217.

Spierings, N. (2014). Islamic attitudes and the support for gender equality and democracy in seven Arab countries, and the role of anti-Western feelings. *Multidisciplinary Journal of Gender Studies, 3*(2), 423–456.

Spierings, N. (2015). *Women's Employment in Muslim Countries: Patterns of Diversity*. London: Palgrave Macmillan.

Spierings, N. (2017). Trust and tolerance across the Middle East and North Africa: A comparative perspective on the impact of the Arab uprisings. *Politics and Governance, 5*(2), 4–15.

Szmolka, I. (2017). *Political change in the Middle East and North Africa after the Arab Spring*. Edinburgh: Edinburgh University Press.

United Nations Development Programme. (2006). *The Arab human development report 2005: Towards the rise of women in the Arab World*. New York: United Nations Publications.

Usta, J., Farver, J., & Zein, L. (2008). Women, war, and violence: Surviving the experience. *Journal of Women's Health, 17*(5), 793–804.

Walby, S. (2011). *The Future of Feminism*. Cambridge: Polity Press.

Wimmen, H. (2014). *Divisive rule: Sectarianism and power maintenance in the Arab Spring: Bahrain, Iraq, Lebanon and Syria*. Berlin: Stichting Wissenschaft und Politik.

PART III

Women's Activism and the Reconfigured State

CHAPTER 6

Women's Activism in North Africa: A Historical and Socio-Political Approach

Moha Ennaji

INTRODUCTION

The major aim of this chapter is to highlight the agency of North African secular women since independence, with focus on Tunisia, Algeria, and Morocco. It deals with their activism for legal rights and political participation. Issues related to these domains are considered from a broad comparative perspective. The chapter reveals the positive role that women have been playing in the struggle for social change. It also shows that women's gains are irrevocable and that the future of the region is significantly linked to the fate of women's movements and women's emancipation from their oppressed positions.

Women's rights in North Africa as well as the wider social and development issues can be understood only within the complex political context of the region. Economic, social, and political development of the region has been constantly hindered by the stark gender gap, serious ongoing insecurity and conflict: civil war in Algeria (1991–2002), revolution in Tunisia (2010), uprisings in Morocco (2011), stagnating

M. Ennaji (✉)
International Institute for Languages and Cultures,
University of Fès, Fès, Morocco

economies, and increasing international pressure to conform to Western-based political and social models. As a result, the region has witnessed an increasing level of social marginalization and widespread poverty, a concentration of power and wealth in the hands of ruling political and financial elites; a general disillusionment with formal politics and absence of the rule of law, and a dramatic resurgence of religious extremism (Sadiqi 2003; Ennaji 2016b).

As pressure for democracy in North Africa continues to grow, the issue of women's rights is gaining prominence in policy debates. The region's progress depends on a larger role of women in the economy and politics (Sadiqi et al. 2009). In some parts of the region "the issue of women's rights" has been gaining prominence in policy debates for several generations (Moghadam and Roudi-Fahimi 2005).

Nowadays coalitions between feminist groups in North African countries are gathering momentum. By linking social and economic development to women's rights, these coalitions present women's demands as "society's demands". This is the case of *Collectif 95 Maghreb Egalité*, a network of over 80 feminine non-government organizations (NGOs) and individuals in the region.[1] In doing so, they are attracting the attention not only of human rights organizations but also of decision-makers.

On the one hand, significant challenges and prejudices impede the progress of North African women as agents of change, but on the other hand, the list of their accomplishments is remarkable and impressive. What is important from our perspective is that in spite of overwhelming challenges, progress is being achieved through women's determination and will to change themselves and their societies. The resources that women have are not uniform as women are heterogeneous, but they use whatever is available to them to achieve their goals (Nelson 1977).

North African feminists endeavor to promote women's empowerment through education, awareness, emancipation, and knowledge of new legal rights. They also propagate information about family law and the labor code through their NGOs and community-based groups. Women's activism has contributed considerably to democratization in the region, particularly in Tunisia, Morocco, and Algeria, because of its greater involvement in social and political affairs and because of the proliferation of women's associations and their access to the media. According to the 2018 Freedom House freedom status, Tunisia is a Free regime, Morocco is Partly free, and Algeria is Not free.[2]

This chapter deals with women's activism within a broader socio-political approach. Through participant observation, semi-structured interviews, and discourse analysis, this study focuses on secular women's activism and its relation with the State, and how it has impacted the political environment and gender relations over the past three decades in the region.

Women's Activism

To understand the significance of secular women's activism, it is essential to trace its history and underscore the role of feminist NGOs, taking into account women's own needs and views of gender and development. Women's activism has a major role in the struggle against gender inequalities and highlights their agency to achieve democracy and social justice and to challenge traditional thinking and practices of governance. It creates social dynamism through the mobilization and participation of women. Its modes of action raise new challenges for government development policies, and open up new ways of thinking about the issues of social justice and gender equality.

Women's issues have recently become an important political topic in the region attracting the attention of activists, journalists, researchers, and politicians. At the beginning of the twentieth century, women belonged to a generation where educated daughters had illiterate mothers (Sadiqi 2016). This was accompanied by a wave of enlightenment and awakening in the realms of philosophy and political thought. Historically, the most well-known feminist thinker in Morocco is Fatema Mernissi, whose work examines the impact of Islamic sexual ideology—the belief that a woman would 'wreak havoc' on male-dominated society if left uncontrolled—on the construction of gender and the organization of domestic and political life in Muslim society today (Ennaji 2016a).

Algerian Women's Activism

Algerian women's activism goes back to the war of independence (1954–1962). The anti-colonial struggle which entailed violence against women (arrest, torture, rape and murder by the French colonial power) certainly contributed to the recognition of women's participation in the fight for independence from the French. It showcased that a woman such as Nassiba Kebal, a young activist who was arrested and badly treated by the French army, could fight and suffer as much as any other male activist.

In 1947, the independence movement formed the Association of Algerian Muslim Women (AFMA) despite its patriarchal configuration. Led by Mamia Chentouf, the AFMA encouraged a form of feminism that was dedicated to altruistic activities, recognized and shielded the biological distinction between men and women, and acknowledged Arab-Muslim culture (Sidi Moussa 2016). Nevertheless, the French colonial power in the 1950s was unclear since it was both violent and oppressive toward Algerian women and reformists, voicing a number of liberal emancipatory steps,[3] mostly in relation to the reform of the family law, in 1959 (MacMaster 2007; Lazreg 1994: 142–150; Addi 2001: 78).[4]

Since independence in 1962, the government has recognized women's essential role in building the nation-state. However, gender equality was relegated to a secondary position in the 1960s and 1970s on the grounds that the construction of an independent State and development objectives were more urgent than the eradication of gender inequity.

Charrad (2001) has analyzed how Algeria after independence failed to establish a family law that would meet the needs of women in the new society. Comparing the three Maghrebi countries, she explains that the distinct results in the personal status law between the advanced Tunisian legislation of 1956, the conservative Moroccan law of 1958, and the weird blocked situation in Algeria that lasted until 1984, is due to the power of authoritarian States to apply political control over conservative family or tribal structures of power that followed the most traditional interpretations of Maliki school.[5] Charrad argues that the newly independent Algerian State displayed severe inconsistency in its endeavor to build the nation-state against regional interests, while allowing local or tribal civil society to have control over the private domestic sphere, which prevented measures to elaborate an adequate family law (2001: 179–182).

From 1962 until the cancelation of the code in July 1975, most Algerian judges simply overlooked the 1959 law which was strictly still in use, and based judgments on their ideology and the Islamic law *Sharia* (MacMaster 2007; Lazreg 1994: 150). It is important to underline that the conservative readings of the family law after 1962 did not imply that the Algerian woman was submissive or passive. Women's associations, including the official *Union nationale des femmes algériennes* (UNFA), as well as individual activists like Fadela M'Rabet, expressed their serious concern that the courts failed to enforce the family laws inherited from the French period. There are four major reasons behind this failure.

First, the Algerian nationalism was largely conservative. Second, there was a serious dichotomy between a minority secular and socialist political elite and a strong religious base. Third, the Algerian government delayed legislation on a new family code, since its political power was weak and it chose to avert politically threatening struggles. Fourth, the successive governments hesitated over the reform of the family law because they were well aware of the heavy weight of patriarchy, of the strong tribal system based on kinship structures and culture that would be hard to change without politically destabilizing the country (Vandevelde-Dailliere 1980; Addi 1999: 105–106, 115–116, 210–212).

Rai (2001)'s developmental theory of emancipation claims that women usually gain rights through their increased access to education and employment and through health care and economic development. But in the Algerian case, the potential for such progress was radically blocked by women's confinement. The political elites made the costly mistake of burying the question of women's reform and entrenching patriarchy, so setting the society on course for an eventual catastrophe, the resurrection of misogynous Islamic fundamentalism and a bloody civil war marked by a generalized violence against women (MacMaster 2007).

In 1981, a particularly traditionalist family code was discarded by the feminist movement. Demonstrations and petitions were organized to show women's refusal of such a conformist proposed legislation. As a result, the government had to abandon the 1981 project, but on June 9, 1984, a very comparable family code was enacted without public consultation.

Under this code, which was designed to appeal to Islamic fundamentalists by satisfying a few of their basic demands, women were mainly acknowledged as guardians of family and customs rather than as independent individuals. In 2005, the family code was finally amended by the government of President Abdelaziz Bouteflika in part under the pressure of women's associations, which have played an important role in imposing significant legal reforms.

Among other things, the new law grants women more rights in terms of marriage, divorce and housing, reduces the role of a woman's male guardian, and guarantees Algerian women the right to transmit citizenship to their offspring. However, most women's rights groups continue to regard the new family code as far too conservative to bring about true gender equality. This view is shared and commanded by Louisa

Hanoune, a secular feminist and the leader of the Party of Workers. Nevertheless, women's participation is also repressed by other issues, such as gender-based discrimination, the weak legal knowledge among women, and government restrictions on public freedoms and political rights. Despite these difficult conditions, the number of women's rights associations has increased since 2005. Their action and achievements have been hailed by observers all over the world. The large number of women's rights organizations illustrates the mounting activism and public participation among women (Iratni 2014).

While the amended 2005 family law constitutes the most important good development for women's rights over the last two decades, there were several other significant changes. The Algerian constitutional reform initiated in 2008 recognizes women's political participation (Article 31 bis). Likewise, a new article was introduced in the penal code (Article 341 bis) in 2004 to punish sexual harassment. Thus, women's safety in the public sphere has lately been enhanced, despite the risks of attacks by radical Islamist groups, which are reminiscent of the "Black Decade" of civil war.

Conversely, women's rights groups are more and more divided along class and ideology (between secular and religious), and feminist activists do not really concur on the best strategies and methods to accomplish more progress (Ennaji 2016a). Some activists advocate legal reforms, specifically within the family law, whereas others argue that instituting and implementing the rule of law and respect for civil public freedoms are more urgent goals. Yet, it seems that none of these stances can be indeed successful unless the State is serious about democratization and the rule of law, and women become more proactive and involved in the defense of their rights.

In addition, the government firmly controls civil society organizations, and women's rights associations lack access to funding. For example, an organization like the Wassila Network, which struggles against domestic violence, does not have the needed financial resources to undertake their mission. Despite the endeavors of organizations like the Children of Fadhman' Soumer to train women and inform them about their rights in the new family law, women are usually uninformed of their rights. Lastly, the discrepancy between rights guaranteed by the Constitution and the constraints imposed by the family law continues to be a major hurdle for women's empowerment (Marzouki 2010).

Algerian women's associations have continued the debate regarding the family code after 2005. Since then, the conversation on the family law has provoked an antagonistic pitch, characterized by a dispute between radical Islamic groups and the secular or Islamic progressive groups.[6]

Tunisian Women's Activism

Eight years after ousting Zine El Abidine Ben Ali, Tunisian women are slowly making progress in their legal rights, as they have recently accomplished equality of inheritance laws, as we shall see shortly. Habib Bourguiba, his predecessor and Tunisia's liberator from colonialism, was a staunch defender of women's rights who believed that a country could not grow without the involvement of women, hence his promulgation of the Code of Personal Status (CPS) in 1956. Bourguiba had pushed aside the main hurdles that stood in women's way of progress: ignorance, repudiation and polygamy. He also raised the marital age to 18, established legal divorce, fostered the creation of schools and encouraged women's employment outside the home. Although Benali privileged women's status and continued his predecessor's policy of State feminism as a significant factor in maintaining an image of a modern Tunisia, he muzzled freedom of expression and civil society organizations.[7]

Labidi (2016), among other Tunisian feminist researchers, raised questions about the situation of women and devoted particular attention to women's activism. Collective works were published by women's research centers such as "Le Centre de recherches, d'études, de documentation et d'information sur la femme" (CREDIF).[8] These studies and others brought forward the actions of secular women and the birth and development of women's activism since the first half of the twentieth century.[9]

They illustrate how women's involvement in the struggle against colonialism and after independence for their rights created a favorable environment for enacting a Personal Status Code in 1956 that promoted women's rights, making divorce follow a judicial process, establishing equality of salary for both sexes, barring stoning as a punishment for adultery, and prohibiting polygamy.

Abiding by the process of leading women to obtain full equality with men, Tunisia ratified the Convention on the Elimination of All Forms of Discrimination against Women (CEDAW) in 1985 but with some reservations.[10] In 2002, the citizenship law was amended allowing women married to Non-Tunisians to transmit their citizenship to their children. Ben Ali sustained this policy by conceding women more rights while disregarding women activists because they did not hold his rule.

Immediately after the revolution, the Islamists, who had won the elections of 23 October 2011, envisaged a total change in the status of women.[11] They alleged that Bourguiba had secularized Tunisia by encouraging women's emancipation and allowing girls and women not to wear the veil instead of training them to be good wives and mothers. To make a change, the Al Nahda Islamist party tried hard to introduce Sharia in the constitution to no avail.

Islamists claimed that the soaring divorce rate, the high unemployment rate, prostitution, and crime, were all the outcome of Bourguiba's secular regime (Mellakh and Kasdaghli 2013: 18). Women were the first targets of Islamist violence; they were ordered to wear the veil and wear long dresses. University campuses were invaded by radical Islamists called Salafists,[12] who insulted or even in some cases physically assaulted female professors, on the claim that they were secular or atheists because not "properly" dressed. Tunisian women resisted this violent Islamization of the society, which had a positive impact on the final draft of the new Constitution.

Tunisian women participated actively in the revolution and in the aftermath of the Arab Spring, voicing their rejection of poverty, oppression and authoritarianism. Before the Arab Spring, women activists were not many to protest in the streets for their rights, either because the State would not allow them to organize demonstrations, or out of fear of being arrested.[13] The Arab Spring took away the fear and made many women stand against oppression and dictatorship.

Before the Arab Spring, there were basically two secular women's NGOs that struggled for women's right and that worked hard to inform women about their legal rights: The Tunisian Association of Democratic Women (ATFD) and The Association of Tunisian Women for Research and Development (AFTURD).[14] Tunisians generally looked up at these organizations because they were brave enough to defy the State.

All of a sudden, there was an upsurge in the number of women's associations, and ATFD and AFTURD were no more the sole women's organizations. A recent study by Dorra Mahfoudh Draoui listed 784 associations, 244 of which running activities related to equality of opportunities for both genders.[15] This upsurge in women's organizations illustrates that, although at its burgeoning stage, civil society is doing much to empower women, and people are now free to create and run organizations. Under Ben Ali's regime, only government organizations existed, but they did not achieve much. That was one of the root causes of the revolution, which was sparked by young women and men (Arfaoui 2016).

Moroccan Women's Activism

Moroccan feminism has been developing since independence. After the end of the French colonial period, a reactionary family law was established in 1957, which denied women a number of basic rights. However, when women had more access to education and to the labor market, these basic rights became vital to their struggle. In such a context, women's rights are closely linked to democratization and political liberalization (Sadiqi 2014; Ennaji 2008).

Although Moroccan women are vital to the family structure on which society is based, the 1957 family law called the *Mudawana* gave them few rights. Based on Islamic law (*Shariâ*), it used to leave women in a vulnerable position within the family. Husbands could unilaterally divorce their wives and threw them out of their homes, while it was very difficult for women to get out of abusive relationships, as their right to divorce was highly restricted. Women could not marry without the legal consent of a guardian or tutor, and wives were forced by law to obey their husbands; while men could marry multiple women without their wives' approval.

The first Mudawana was established by an all-male committee of religious scholars, and thus was strongly based on Islamic law. It was a patriarchal code, with the man being described as the head of the family, and the woman as a dependent minor under the male responsibility; women were treated more like men's property than independent individuals. A woman, no matter how old, was under the guardianship of her father until she got married, and then she fell under her husband's authority.

A wife could be repudiated or divorced by the husband without any justification, and without providing any compensation for herself and her children. It was enough for the husband to disavow her. She could ask for divorce only under special restricted circumstances, like being abandoned without any financial support for a long period of time by the husband or only if she pays him a material compensation.

Children were not protected. The mother lost custody over her children if she re-married or if she behaved 'indecently' by taking a lover, for example. A child-born from relationships outside marriage was recognized neither by the State nor by society; he could neither have a family name nor a seat in school. He was basically an outcast, a burden to society (Ennaji 2012).

Since the early 1960s, secular women's NGOs have been fighting for reforming this family code to guarantee equal rights (Pittman and Naciri 2010). Two major women's rights NGOs, known as the *Association Démocratique des Femmes* (ADFM), and the *Union de l'Action Feminine* (UAF), and their allies campaigned to reform these excessive laws and ensure equal rights for women under the family code, thus giving momentum to the Mudawana reform movement (Ennaji 2010).

One of the most significant strategies and forms of activism at the time was the petition of 'one million signatures'. This campaign, which was national and massive in favor of the Mudawana reform, was initiated by UAF in 1992, using its newspaper called "8 Mars". The campaign was a vast victory and gained huge public support. Subsequently, the late King Hassan II ordered that a reformed code be drafted in consultation with some women's groups. The reform, which was enacted in 1993, included a few changes beneficial to women. For example, women were now allowed to designate the guardian or tutor who would give approval for their marriage; fathers were no longer allowed to compel their daughters into marriage, and polygamy became slightly restricted and subject to the agreement of the first wife (Ennaji and Sadiqi 2012).

Though the UAF, ADFM, and other secular women's groups were disappointed by the limited nature of the reforms, they considered them a victory, because they broke a taboo: once the Mudawana was amended, it could no longer be seen as an irreversible text, thus lifting the mask of sacredness around it, as we mentioned earlier. Women's NGOs continued to lobby the government by raising awareness about women's rights, gender-based discrimination, and domestic violence. They continued to strategize and campaign for broader legislative changes and altered their communication capacities to integrate a human rights agenda and democratization arguments together with the necessity to re-interpret Islamic laws (Pittman and Naciri 2010; Eddouada 2016).

King Mohamed VI, who accessed the throne in 1999, showed hints of being less repressive than his father and expressed his will to reform the family law. Advocacy campaigns intensified under the socialist-led government and after a heated debate with Islamist groups, a new Mudawana was passed in 2004. Unlike the previous reform, it advanced women's rights and eliminated many discriminatory provisions (Zoglin 2009). The minimum age for women to marry was raised from 15 to 18, the same as for men; women no longer needed to obtain permission from a guardian before marrying; men were forbidden from unilaterally divorcing their wives; women were given the right to file for divorce; and restrictions were imposed on polygamy such as the approval of both the first wife and the second would-be wife and only with the approval of a judge.

The secular feminist movement did not stop once it had achieved its original goals. Since the promulgation of these reforms, women's progressive groups in Morocco have been lobbying to change some discriminatory laws that survived the reforms, namely polygamy and unfair inheritance laws. They have also been organizing demonstrations and providing education to the public, aiming to ensure that the reforms are understood and are incorporated into daily life.

The Mudawana reform was opposed by *Salafists* (religious extremists), the *Ulama* (religious scholars), and many Islamic educators, who claimed that the new family code was against the Islamic values traditionally predominant in the country. Islamist groups campaigned robustly to hold back the impact of secular liberal women's NGOs (Borrillo 2016).

The greatest success of the Moroccan feminist movement (secular and Islamic) lies in the fact that it has brought a holy text (i.e., the Mudawana) to public debate. The movement's use of universal values and socially acceptable local strategies has succeeded in impacting the main political actors in the promulgation of the new family law enacted in 2004. The Moroccan feminist movement has managed to demystify the "holiness" of *Shariâ* (Islamic law), a fact that contributed to the democratization of the public sphere and to the respect of human rights.

The struggle to amend the family law occurred in a controversial socio-political context with a strong opposition, stemming from the organizing efforts of Islamist associations and factions. The conformist mentality and institutional environment were also favorable to lobbying for women's legal rights and reform of the family law. However, secular women's NGOs managed to draw the attention of decision-makers and civil society to the urgency of the reform. At the outset, liberal feminists used only secular arguments to advocate women's rights, but later on, under the pressure of Islamists, demanded reforms by appealing to

Islamic arguments in combination with universal human rights. Their struggle highlights the extent of their determination, capacity to mobilize the masses, which eventually bore fruit and brought the reform of the Mudawana.

In Morocco, for instance, women's organizations have a decisive role in the democratization and modernization of society. From the 1970s, women's NGOs have severely criticized the ways in which policymakers overlooked women's demands for emancipation and gender equity. Women's NGOs encourage women's empowerment and participation in decision-making and in public affairs. They have enabled women to assess their own situation critically and shape a transformation of society (Sadiqi and Ennaji 2006). They take part in diverse activities and have so far accumulated a great deal of experience in local development, showing that Morocco's women are dynamic and problem-solvers (Mernissi 1989). Unlike in many Arab countries, Moroccan women's NGOs are allowed by the government to receive financial aid from foreign organizations and donors.[16] The challenge facing these NGOs is to devise autonomous strategies and to establish themselves as independent forces in their partnership with the State and with political parties.

Moreover, over the past two decades, many Moroccan women's advocacy organizations have emerged to combat violence against women, gender-based legal and cultural discrimination, illiteracy and poverty among women and their under-representation in policymaking. They have made important steps forward: the ratification of CEDAW by Morocco on June 21, 1993; the revision of the work code and of the penal code (2003); it is no longer required for the husband to authorize the wife to practice a trade activity (1995); or for the signature of a work contract (1996); and the reform of the nationality code which now allows a Moroccan woman to transmit her citizenship to her children (2007).[17]

Since 1998, many national campaigns were organized to combat violence against women. They mobilized many government ministries, as well as civil society. As an outcome of these campaigns, Article 475 of the controversial rape marriage law was amended in 2014 for better protection of rape victims.[18] In 2018, the government initiated a new law to fight against street harassment.

However, the new family code has not eliminated polygamy and inequality concerning inheritance, whereby a woman inherits only half the share of a man. When there are no males among the inheritors, the females inherit only part of the legacy, and the rest goes to the family of the deceased male.[19]

THE STRUGGLE FOR POLITICAL POWER

All three countries have answered to the 2011 uprisings by passing gender quota laws in order to increase women's political representation, in all cases pushed by women's organizations and activists. As of 2012, women's share of the national assemblies has increased, reaching in Tunisia, 27%, in Algeria 21%, and in Morocco 17% (Darhour and Dahlerup 2013).

Despite many achievements, Algerian women are still under-represented in the government, parliament, and local municipalities. They were given the right to vote and run for office since independence in 1962. Since the establishment of a multiparty system in 1989, women have become relatively involved in politics.

In May 2007, female candidates won 30 of the 389 seats in the lower house of parliament. Most of them were active members of the ruling majority party *Front de Libération Nationale*. Louisa Hanoune's Workers' Party won 26 seats overall. These election results of just 7.7% were a slight progress over the elections in 2002, in which women won around 6%. In 2008, women held only 4 of the 144 seats in the upper house and had about 5% of the seats in the local municipalities (Marzouki 2010).

Women may participate in political parties at all levels, but they generally constitute no more than 10% of most parties' membership. In April 2009, the Ministry of Justice appointed a commission to consider a law that would mandate a quota of 30–40% for women in all political parties (Marzouki 2010).

Women's organizations that struggle for the social and cultural rights enjoy relatively more autonomy and liberty than those working for political and civil rights; the objectives of both types of organization are deeply related. However, even associations advocating women's social and cultural rights complain about the limited freedom of expression and poor funding, which hampers their action on the ground.

Likewise, in Morocco, women's NGOs struggle to be politically and financially autonomous from government, political parties and other institutions. However, they at times work hand in hand with democratic forces and government administrations on specific goals and projects like literacy, education, reproductive health, micro-credits, etc. The government usually devotes a budget to NGOs that work actively for achieving gender equity and sustainable development. The Ministry of Social Development, Family, and Solidarity, first led by Nouzha Skalli a well-known feminist and socialist and then by the moderate Islamist feminist Bassima Hakkaoui, sponsored these NGOs' development projects within the framework of the national campaign for human development (INDH).

This Ministry launched a vast national program for equality ICRAM (2012–2016) to help women integrate social and economic development through entrepreneurship. ICRAM is based on the founding principles of the 2011 Constitution and the Millennium Development Goals, which aspire to building new social relations between women and men, ensuring fair and equal participation in the design and implementation of the monitoring of development policies and programs in the different areas and the fair and equal sharing of the benefits and profits from this participation.

One of the remarkable achievements of the women's movement in Morocco has been the establishment of a 10% quota for representation of women in parliament and 20% of the political bureau of political parties. As a result, in 2007 there were 34 women in parliament and 7 ministers and deputy ministers; currently, there are 8 women in the government cabinet (one minister and seven secretaries of state).[20]

The new constitutional reform in Morocco increased the number of seats reserved to women from 30 out of 325 to 60 out of the 395 seats (15%) in 2011. Though still well below the 30% quota claimed by women's movements, it is an improvement from the initial quotas implemented in 2002. Electoral laws have also undergone significant changes to increase the political participation of women, starting with a reform of the ballot system and electoral code in 2002, through the introduction of a proportional list system, followed by the institution of positive discrimination in the form of a gender quota. In local councils, the participation of women exploded, as the rate of participation multiplied in a spectacular way, increasing from 0.56% in 2002 to 12% in 2009 to 22% in 2015, taking the number of elected women to local council from less than a hundred to 3465 in 2009 and to 6673 women in 2015.[21] According to the results of elections of May 20, 2016, women in parliament represent 21%—nearing the world average. They are present in decision-making positions although in insufficient numbers. In the

2011 elections, there were 67 elected women parliamentarians, 60 from the national list and 7 from direct local lists (Ennaji 2015; Tahri 2003; Darhour and Dahlerup 2013; see Chapter 11 in this book).

In Morocco and Algeria, women's activism was very strong between 2000 and 2010, while in Tunisia it became stronger after the Arab Spring because of the threat posed by Islamist parties and the non-conformist Salafi movements. The strength of the movement can be evaluated by the number of demonstrations, street protests, sit-ins, and petitions signed, and by the number of protestors and sympathizers that the movement has mobilized over these periods of time in the three countries. The use of social and standard media also proved successful as a strategy to reach out to the masses and to make women's voices heard by people and the State.

Thanks to women's activism, the Moroccan State responded by introducing legal and political reforms (amending the Constitution, reforming the family code, increasing women's representation, political reforms, etc.). Women's activism also led to the feminization of public space, women's participation in the democratization process, a gradual transformation of gender roles, as more and more women participate in public life (see Sadiqi and Ennaji 2006; see Chapters 4 and 5 in this book).

In Tunisia, feminist organizations, such as ATFD and AFTURD, had been struggling hard to minimize the intimidation by political Islam and to attain their objective of protecting women's rights and achieving gender equality with men. Although Islamists were in power since the revolution, feminist activists managed through their advocacy campaigns to convince first interim government formed after the Revolution to nullify their reservations against the CEDAW.[22] This goal was attained on August 16, 2011, recognizing equality in marriage, divorce, and custody.

This measure was followed by a gender parity law in Tunisia in April 2011 which established that no electoral list would be approved if it did not include an equal number of male and female candidates, alternating throughout the list, in the election of the National Constituent Assembly (NCA) on October 23, 2011. This law was central in the winning of 27% of the NCA's seats by women (see Chapter 10). Unfortunately, the percentage was not higher than in the last election under Ben Ali, because only very few women were put at the head of the lists. In the new constitution, Article 45 was passed, which stipulates that equality of representation between men and women in elected institutions of the State is guaranteed (Tchaïcha and Arfaoui 2017).

Another major achievement of the Tunisian feminist movement is the recent equal inheritance law that was approved by the government on November 23, 2018. This new law for gender equality in inheritance allows equal inheritance rights for those who follow a civil code, i.e., it is up to the family to follow either an Islamic or a civil code (Ennaji 2018).

Perhaps it is still too early to determine the impact of the Arab Spring. In general, the future of women's rights looks uncertain (Ennaji 2013). Hopefully, we will not have to wait long before women begin to actively participate in politics and become equal to men. Today, many women are considering ways to utilize the positive effects of the Arab Spring to benefit human rights and move away from discrimination.[23]

Conclusion

In North Africa, women's activism has a major role in sensitizing women, families, and social actors to the importance of integrating women in economic, social, and cultural development. It has impacted the struggle for women's rights, and made a vital contribution to the democratization and modernization of society (Sadiqi and Ennaji 2006). Secular women's groups rallied with the progressive and democratic forces, while most Islamist feminists joined the Islamist movement, and obtained important social and political gains in post-Arab Spring (new seats in parliament and decision-making positions in the government (Moghadam 2012; Jaquette 2001).

The effects of the legal and political reforms, for instance quota regulations and the new family laws were positive, as they led to women's empowerment and improved their political participations and representation, as mentioned above. Indeed, most research on gender and politics points to the difficulties in evaluating such effects, because so many other factors intervene. The success of the reforms is only relative because no country on earth (even in the developed world) has achieved full gender equality. According to the Gender Gap report of 2017, North African countries have managed to close the gender gap in education, health, and employment by 50%.[24]

In Morocco, female illiteracy has decreased from 78% in 1962 to 41.9% in 2014 (Ennaji 2018). The influence of women's activism on public policy is evident, especially in Morocco and Tunisia, and it can be evaluated in terms of the activists' influence on different steps in the political decision-making, such as agenda-building, actual legislation, pressure for the election of more women and support for elected women, and pressure for the proper implementation of reforms.[25]

Overall, the extensive social and political involvement of women has transformed gender roles in Morocco, Algeria, and Tunisia. Their activism has resulted in the relative improvement in their social status and gender roles with regard to institutional aspects. The political internal contexts, especially the political, religious or economic factors, have engendered a hot debate on gender issues. Women who enjoy the benefits of relative political participation and representation, still constitute a minority (Sadiqi 2014). Despite political rights—to use Moghadam's (2012: 35) terms— "the gap between formal equality (as written in laws) and substantive equality (as enjoyed in practice and expressed in participation and representation) has been large for certain segments of the population, and especially large for women." In North African countries, this gap in formal and substantive equality between men and women remains profound despite recent reforms. This is one of the reasons why many feminists demand mentality changes and further reforms to consolidate women's presence in public space. These include institutional and social reforms and expanded political representation (Sadiqi 2016; Moghadam 2012; Eschle 2000). Such reforms are urgently needed to make up for decades of discrimination and exclusion. Despite the unexpected backlash of the Arab Spring, women are actively working together and building coalitions to address their fundamental concerns. What is clear is that the uprisings have ignited the spirit of hope in women, who now believe that they have the collective power to demand change and can very well transform the region for a better future.

Notes

1. For more information on this network, see this report: https://www.youtube.com/watch?v=j6dcN4tFt2s. Accessed on December 9, 2018.
2. See the details on Freedom House website: https://freedomhouse.org/report/freedom-world/2018/algeria. Accessed December 3, 2018.
3. "Emancipation," was the term utilized by the French government to refer to reforms that would ensure equality of rights between Algerian Muslim women and women in metropolitan France with the goal of Westernizing them as individuals.
4. The legal reform of 1959 took place in two stages, first an Ordinance of 4 February provided a succinct summary of the legislation, followed by a

decree of 17 September which elaborated how the ordinance was to be implemented.
5. Marriage and family law in Algeria was based on an enormous regional variation from customary law among the Kabyle people, to the Ibadite code of the Mzab, and the minority Hanafi school of law, but the Maliki variant of Sunni law was predominant.
6. Limits on the political and legal rights of women reflect the general constraints on public life in Algeria. The freedoms of expression and the space allotted to civil society organizations are contained by a government that is strongly monitored by the army.
7. "State feminism" refers to a women-friendly policy adopted by the governments of Habib Bourguiba and Zinelabidine Ben Ali that granted women social and economic rights in order to benefit and build the State.
8. AFTURD (Collective). *Tunisiennes en devenir*. Vols. 1, 2. Tunis: Cérès Productions, 1992. CREDIF-ISHMN (Collective). *Mémoire de femmes. Tunisiennes dans la vie publique. 1920–1960.* Tunis: Edition Media COM, 1993.
9. Several women figures contributed to institutionalizing the urban women's movement. Nazli Fadil, daughter of Prime Minister Mustapha Fadil Bacha, who in 1896 and also founded a literary salon; Manoubia Wertani, the first woman to remove the veil in public, in 1924, and Habiba Menchari, who repeated this gesture in 1929; Wassila Ben Ammar and Nejiba Ben MRad, who founded the Association des Femmes Musulmanes in 1932.
10. Tunisia formulated reservations against the following 4 articles: 9, 15, 16 and 29, that recognized both parents equal rights in giving their nationality to their children. Reservations were made as to the dispositions relating to women's rights to choose their residence and home.
11. In 2012, 217 people were elected at the Constituent Assembly (including 49 women, 42 of them belonging to Al Nahda Party) to draft a new constitution. They came up with the text in January 2014.
12. However, the leader of Al Nahda Party had always pretended to be "moderate and democratic".
13. On 7 November 1789, Islamists had realized about 30% of valid votes. Ben Ali countered the Islamist threat by a merciless repression against Islamists.
14. The National Union of Tunisian Women represented state-feminism at its best.
15. For example, the Coalition for Women of Tunisia was founded in September 2012. "The coalition now includes more than 30 organizations that address women's problems in rural areas, where access to education and medical care is often scarce and quite poor.

16. The United Nations conferences held in the 1980s and 1990s enhanced feminist activism in North Africa and the Middle East. This was an outcome of the extension of the nation-state borders and of the endeavors to achieve gender equality at the global level.
17. Women today are considered full citizens, can transmit their citizenship to their offspring when they are married to a foreigner, and have equal rights in the workplace.
18. See this commentary: https://www.bbc.com/news/world-africa-25855025. Accessed April 3, 2019.
19. See my article on inheritance laws in Morocco: https://theconversation.com/moroccos-inheritance-laws-are-hurting-women-and-must-be-reformed-95446.
20. See the official website of the Moroccan government: http://www.maroc.ma/en/content/list-government. Accessed May 29, 2018.
21. This data is retrieved from this link: http://makeeverywomancount.org/index.php?option=com_content&view=article&id=2124:morocco-parliamentary-elections-2011&catid=69:political-participation-a-election-monitoring&Itemid=170. Accessed April 20, 2014.
22. The first government in the post-revolution period was led by Beji Caied Essebsi, currently the president of the party, Nidaa Tounis (The Call of Tunis).
23. For more on this point, see this link: http://www.al-monitor.com/pulse/ar/culture/2012/02/the-repercussions-of-the-arab-sp.html#ixzz4JZJcEe1R.
24. See the report online: http://www3.weforum.org/docs/WEF_GGGR_2017.pdf. Accessed December 2, 2018.
25. See this note on the support of women's NGOS in Morocco to a female member of parliament: https://www.medias24.com/MAROC/NATION/POLITIQUE/188430-Des-associations-feminines-qualifient-l-eviction-de-Neila-Tazi-de-violence-politique.html. Accessed December 11, 2018.

References

Addi, L. (1999). L'islam est-il soluble dans la démocratie? In *Mouvements*. Paris: La découverte.

Addi, L. (2001). *Army, state and nation in Algeria. The military and nation building in the age of democracy*. New York: Zed books.

Arfaoui, K. (2014). Women's empowerment: The case of Tunisia in the Arab Spring. In M. Ennaji (Ed.), *Multiculturalism and democracy in North Africa* (pp. 159–176). London: Routledge.

Arfaoui, K. (2016). What future for women in Tunisia. In M. Ennaji (Ed.), *Minorities, women and the state in North Africa* (pp. 151–166). Trenton: Red Sea Press.

Borrillo, S. (2016). Islamic feminism in Morocco: The discourse and the experience of Asma Lamrabet. In M. Ennaji, F. Sadiqi, & K. Vintges (Eds.), *Moroccan feminisms: New perspectives* (pp. 111–128). Trenton: Africa World Press.

Charrad, M. M. (2001). *States and women's rights: The making of postcolonial Tunisia, Algeria, and Morocco*. Berkeley and Los Angeles: University of California Press.

Darhour, H., & Dahlerup, D. (2013). Sustainable representation of women through gender quotas: A decade's experience in Morocco. *Women Studies International Forum, 43*(2), 132–142.

Eddouada, S. (2016). Women and the politics of reform in Morocco. In M. Ennaji, F. Sadiqi, & K. Vintges (Eds.), *Moroccan feminisms: New perspectives* (pp. 13–28). Trenton: Africa World Press.

Ennaji, M. (2008). Steps to the integration of Moroccan women in development. *The British Journal of Middle Eastern Studies, 35*(3), 339–348.

Ennaji, M. (2010). Women's NGOs and social change in Morocco. In Fatima Sadiqi & Moha Ennaji (Eds.), *Women in the Middle East and North Africa* (pp. 79–88). London: Routledge.

Ennaji, M. (2012). The new Muslim personal status law in Morocco: Context, proponents, adversaries, and arguments. In Graciela di Marco & Constaza Tabbush (Eds.), *Feminisms, democratization, and radical democracy* (pp.193–208). San Martin: UNSAM Edita.

Ennaji, M. (2013). Arab women's unfinished revolution. The Project Syndicate of February 23, 2013. http://www.project-syndicate.org/commentary/women-inpolitics-after-the-arab-spring-by-moha-ennaji. Accessed November 21, 2014.

Ennaji, M. (2015). Women and political participation in Morocco and North African States. In M. Vianello & M. Hawkesworth (Eds.), *Gender and power: Towards equality and democratic governance* (pp. 32–52). London: Routledge.

Ennaji, M. (2016a). Secular and Islamic feminist movements in Morocco: Contentions, achievements, and challenges. In M. Ennaji, F. Sadiqi, & K. Vintges (Eds.), *Moroccan feminisms: New perspectives* (pp. 29–50). Trenton: Africa World Press.

Ennaji, M. (2016b). The feminist movement and countermovement in Morocco. In S. Fadaee (Ed.), *Understanding southern social movements* (pp. 42–54). London: Routledge.

Ennaji, M. (2018). Morocco's experience in gender gap reduction in education. *Gender and Women's Studies, 2*(1), 5. http://riverapublications.com/assets/files/pdf_files/moroccos-experience-with-gender-gap-reduction-in-education.pdf.

Ennaji, M., & Sadiqi, F. (2012). Women's activism and the new family code reforms. *The IUP Journal of History and Culture, 6*(1), 1–19.

Eschle, C. (2000). *Global democracy, social movements, and feminism*. Boulder: Westview.

Iratni, B. (2014). Why no Arab spring in Algeria: Questioning multiculturalism and democracy experiments. In M. Ennaji (Ed.), *Multiculturalism and democracy in North Africa* (pp. 115–134). London/New York: Routledge.

Jaquette, J. (2001). Regional differences and contrasting views. *Journal of Democracy, 12*(3), 111–125.

Labidi, L. (2016). Historical women figures and women's daily struggles in Tunisia: Neglect and social responsibility. In M. Ennaji (Ed.), *Minorities, women and the state in North Africa* (pp. 121–149). Trenton: Red Sea Press.

Lazreg, M. (1994). *The eloquence of silence: Algerian women in question*. St Albas: Psychology Press.

MacMaster, N. (2007). The colonial "emancipation" of Algerian women: The marriage law of 1959 and the failure of legislation on women's rights in the post-independence era. Stichproben. Wiener Zeitschrift für kritische Afrikastudien, Nr. 12/2007, 7.

Marzouki, N. (2010). Algeria. In S. Kelly & J. Breslin (Eds.), *Women's rights in the Middle East and North Africa: Progress amid resistance*. New York: Freedom House.

Mellakh, H., & Kasdaghli, H. (2013). *Chroniques du Manoubistane*. Tunis: Cérès Editions.

Mernissi, F. (1989). *Doing daily battle*. New Brunswick, NJ: Rutgers University Press.

Moghadam, V. (2012). Democracy and women's rights: Reflections on the Middle East and North Africa. In G. Di Marco & C. Tabbush (Eds.), *Feminisms, democratization and radical democracy* (pp. 46–60). Buenos Aires: Universidad Nacional De San Martin Press.

Moghadam, V., & Roudi-Fahmi, F. (2005). *Reforming family laws to promote progress in the Middle East and North Africa*. Washington, DC: Population Reference Bureau.

Nelson, C. (1977). *Women, health and development*. Cairo Papers in Social Science. Cairo: American University in Cairo Press.

Pittman, A., & Naciri, R. (2010). Winning women's rights: Cultural adaptations and Islamic family law. In J. Gaventa & R. McGee (Eds.), *Citizen action and national policy reform: Making change happen*. London: Zed Books.

Rai, Shirin M. (2001). *Gender and the political economy of development: From nationalism to globalization*. Malden: Blackwell.

Sadiqi, F. (2003). *Women, gender, and language in Morocco*. Leiden: Brill Publishers.

Sadiqi, F. (2014). *Moroccan feminist discourses*. New York: Palgrave Macmillan.

Sadiqi, F. (2016). An assessment of today's Moroccan feminist movements (1946–2014). In M. Ennaji, F. Sadiqi, & K. Vintges (Eds.), *Moroccan feminisms: New perspectives* (pp. 51–76). Trenton: Africa World Press.

Sadiqi, F., & Ennaji, M. (2006). The feminization of public space: Women's activism, the family law, and social change in Morocco. *Journal of Middle East Women's Studies, 2*(2), 86–114.

Sadiqi, F., Nowaira, A., El Kholy, A., & Ennaji, M. (2009). *Women writing Africa: The northern region.* New York: The Feminist Press.

Sidi Moussa, N. (2016). *Algerian feminism and the long struggle for women's equality.* The Conversation, October 4, 2016. https://theconversation.com/algerian-feminism-and-the-long-struggle-for-womens-equality-65130. Accessed November 21, 2018.

Tahri, R. (2003). *Women's political participation: The case of Morocco.* Paper presented at the International Institute for Democracy and Electoral Assistance Conference on The Implementation of Quotas: African Experiences, Pretoria, South Africa, 11–13 November.

Tchaïcha, J., & Arfaoui, K. (2017). *The Tunisian women's rights movement: From nascent activism to influential power-broking.* London: Routledge.

Vandevelde-Dailliere, H. (1980). *Femmes algériennes à travers la condition féminine dans le constantinois depuis l'indépendance.* Algiers: Office des Publications Universitaires.

Zoglin, K. (2009). Morocco's family code: Improving equality for women. *Human Rights Quarterly, 31,* 964–984.

CHAPTER 7

Political Opportunities for Islamist Women in Morocco and Egypt: Structure or Agency?

Anwar Mhajne

Introduction

This chapter discusses the intersection of religion, gender, civil society, and the state in Egypt and Morocco and asks how do political opportunity structures (POS)—i.e., political openings for and obstructions against organizing—shape Islamist women's political participation in the Middle East and North Africa (MENA)? The chapter examines particularly how political dynamics shape Islamist women's political participation in Egypt's Muslim Brotherhood and Morocco's Justice and Development Party (JDP) and addresses the marginalization of Islamist women in the study of state-society politics.

After decades of being marginalized, the Arab Spring events empowered Islamists and gave them access to positions of power. From Morocco to Egypt, Islamist parties gained unprecedented success in the formal political sphere of governance through fair and free elections.

A. Mhajne (✉)
Visiting Assistant Professor, Stonehill College, Easton, MA, USA

© The Author(s) 2020
H. Darhour and D. Dahlerup (eds.), *Double-Edged Politics on Women's Rights in the MENA Region*, Gender and Politics, https://doi.org/10.1007/978-3-030-27735-2_7

In Morocco, the Islamist Party of Justice and Development (PJD) won the most votes and its front-runner, Mr. Benkiran, became the Prime Minister. In Egypt, the Muslim Brotherhood (MB) and the Salafi parties together seized 60% of the seats in the Parliament, and its leader Muhammad Morsi became the President (Bayat 2013). Their win in the elections has had consequences on their ideology, tactics, structure, and governance. Now Islamists must compromise, bargain and negotiate with other groups including leftist and liberal-secular organizations and parties to maintain their power. These negotiations will make Islamist parties more willing to change and transform their ideologies to achieve an agreement with the other parties. Islamists must show pragmatism in responding to domestic and international forces to be able to effectively govern their countries.

Various scholars have argued that Islamists are pragmatic actors whose actions are not entirely guided by ideology, but also by the socio-political context they are operating in domestically and internationally (Turam 2004). Due to the legacy of authoritarian regimes including unemployment, poverty, corruption, Islamists after the Arab Spring are under pressure to implement good governance policies and improve the economy. The electoral programs of Islamists such as the MB in Egypt are an example of the shift in their strategies. For instance, the MB's candidates in the post-uprisings parliamentary election refrained from using the movement's slogan "Islam is the solution." Their campaign focused instead on issues of poverty, corruption, and social justice as well as endorsed the free market economy and privatization policies. Similarly, the PJD in Morocco, which vowed to eliminate corruption and create transparency in state institutions.

Some scholars have examined the interactions and negotiations between Islamist parties and other parties, particularly the impact of alliances and coalitions on Islamist parties' ideologies and organizing strategies (Abdelrahman 2004, 2009; Wickham 2004; Cavatorta 2006; Schwedler 2006; Schwedler and Clark 2006; Browers 2007a, b). In the context of the Arab Spring, Islamist actors in Egypt and Morocco displayed similar behavior during the Arab Spring. They supported the protests by pressuring critical political actors in the country (i.e., the monarchy in Morocco and the military in Egypt) without antagonizing these actors. They formed strategic alliances with other opposition groups to evade seclusion. These alliances forced Islamist parties to be pragmatic and flexible in their ideology and positions on contested issues including women's rights.

This chapter contributes to the literature on Islamist parties' engagement in the democratic process by discussing how the political contexts influenced by alliances shaped women's issues and Islamist women's activism in two Islamist parties in Morocco and Egypt. In Egypt, members of the Muslim Sisterhood, a women's section of the MB, were active in the opposition. However, during the brief institutionalization of the Morsi regime, they became active in the formal political medium. Thus, their activism spanned the formal and/or informal political mediums depending on the openings or closures of the political system. In Morocco, women have been included on the PJD—the leading party following the Arab Uprisings—party list in elections. In addition to being influenced by the Muslim Brotherhood in Egypt, the PJD is also influenced by the AKP in Turkey, which to some extent promotes women's participation in various levels of electoral politics and society.

The POS literature on the region, as currently theorized, does not pay sufficient attention to how the gendered institutions of these structures and the shifts in these structures affect women's ability to act politically. This chapter contributes to the still minimal amount of gender-sensitive analysis of POS and its relationship to Islamist women's activism in the MENA. Further, this chapter applies a theoretical framework that views POS as both gendered and dynamic rather than fixed. It reveals how a lack of gender analysis of POS can mask specific important political processes in various countries in the Middle East and North Africa, such as Morocco and Egypt.

In short, this chapter addresses the organizing activities of Islamist women of PJD and MB. It examines how political opening and backlash influence Islamist women's framing of their demands and medium of organizing. It also sheds light on how Islamist women carve out more sustainable spaces for their participation within their respective organizations. Islamist women's decades of political consciousness and organizing experience during periods of political opening and backlash provided them with the necessary skills that allowed them to play a stronger role within their organizations.

METHODS

The data for Morocco comes from the abundant secondary literature of the PJD, while the data for Egypt comes from semi-structured interviews with sixteen members of the Egyptian Muslim Brotherhood and Muslim Sisterhood living in Turkey and in Egypt. Personal interviews were conducted with the Egyptian Muslim Sisterhood because little scholarly work has been written on the Muslim Sisterhood and its activities. The individuals interviewed and cited in this chapter have seen and accepted the citation used. They all agreed to be identified by their personal names. I use qualitative content analysis. Content analysis enables me to attain a condensed yet broad description of the Sisters' organizing strategies during the periods of regime transition described earlier. In the analysis of the texts, I focus on three categories: the medium of organizing (government or civil society), women's rights (any public mention or discussion of women's issues), and human rights (any mention of political freedom, poverty, or education).

Terminology

The term Islamists refers to individuals who call for governance that is compatible with, and derives its vision from, Sharia (Tadros 2016). This term is different from Muslim, which refers to people who follow Islam but do not particularly support an Islamist political project (Tadros 2016). It is also different from Islamic, which denotes daily practices, values, and social codes inspired by Islam.

The term *secular parties* in this chapter refers to a wide spectrum of political organizations that vary in their ideology from liberalism to socialism (Ottaway and Hamzawy 2007). Using the term "secular party" in the context of the Middle East and North Africa is relative because certain parties, which eschew political platforms inspired by religious values, reject being labeled as secular to avoid being accused of denouncing Islamic culture and values (Boduszyñski et al. 2015; see Chapter 2). These parties define themselves as the challengers of Islamists with extreme religious ideologies and agendas (Boduszyñski et al. 2015). Hamid (2014) states that by defining themselves in opposition to the Islamists, secular parties, in the case of Egypt, helped the regime label itself as the lesser of two evils, thus garnering the support of the international community and numerous secularists at home. In this chapter, I use the term *secular-liberal political parties* to describe non-Islamists.

Theoretical Model

To understand how Islamist women interacted with shifting POS in Egypt and Morocco before and after the Arab Spring, I rely on the dynamic approach to POS that considers the state and social movements at the same time. The dynamic approach, as explained by the work of Kriesi et al. (1995), refers to steady yet not permanent signals to social or political players, which prevents them from or incentivizes them to utilize their resources to start social movements. This dynamic concept of political opportunity emphasizes formal structures like state institutions as well as conflict and alliance structures, which offer resources and challenges restrictions exterior to the group (Tarrow 1996).

McAdam et al.'s approach holds that there are four dimensions that shape POS. The first is the comparative openness or closure of the political system. The second dimension is the stability of elite alliances (McAdam et al. 1996). The likelihood of new coalitions developing in the government inspires protestors to attempt exercising minimal power and may incite elites to pursue support external to the state (Tarrow 1996). The third is the presence of elite allies, who can play multiple supportive roles for social movements such as protectors against repression, or as legitimate advocates on behalf of citizenries (Tarrow 1996). Protesting groups create political opportunities for groups and elites within the system. Their actions can also provide the grounds for repression. Elites might take advantage of the opportunity generated by contenders to declare themselves as the representatives and protectors of the people (Tarrow 1996). The final dimension is the state's ability and tendency for repression (McAdam et al. 1996). A change in any of these four dimensions signals a shift in POS and in groups' organizing.

In the Egyptian and Moroccan case, I focus on the second dimension of POS. Shifts in elite alignments between players were one of the most noticeable and significant changes in these four elements. As Tarrow (1996) suggests, divisions among elites provide incentives for marginal groups to take the risk of collective action. Moreover, they encourage some elites to portray themselves as the advocates of the people and to expand their own political influence and legitimacy (Tarrow 1996). These unstable dimensions portray "movement outcomes as involving structures which shape and channel activity while, in turn, movements act as agents that help to shape the political space in which they operate" (Gamson and Meyer 1996: 289). The international context shapes the balance of power between the players and thus influences the alliances. Also, international agreements on human and women's rights affect the strategies and language activists in general and women activists in particular use to frame their demands.

In the case of Egypt, the model developed in this chapter shows this dynamism in the shifting alliances between three players who aspire to control the government: the military, the Islamists, and the secular-liberal political parties. These players aim to influence and eventually control the government and utilize civil society as a medium for organizing when the government is closed. The POS model for Morocco views politics in Morocco regarding alliances between the monarchy, leftist political parties, and Islamists. The connection between civil society groups and one of these players is essential for these groups to achieve their goals.

This chapter examines how the nature of and shift in alliances between the different players in Egyptian and Moroccan politics has resulted in a political opening for and/or backlash against the Islamist women's organizing. The nature of alliances between these various players and their relationship with the international system affects the POS as well. The players are not equal in power, but they all play a significant role in politics.

Women's issues are at the center of the negotiations for these alliances because they shape the support of domestic and international elements for the various players. The governments of Egypt and Morocco have been actively engaged in constructing gender through their policies and legal provisions. Two contradictory elements influenced these regimes' policies: (a) domestic confrontation with the Islamists, and (b) transnational pressure to adhere to global gendered regimes. The conflict with Islamists, in some instances, pressured these governments to legislate and implement more conservative laws and policies for women and the family. Moreover, international bodies increased influence, heightening the sense of obligation for Middle East and North Africa states to adhere to UN conventions concerning women's and human rights. These are the main factors shaping secular and religious women activists' relations to the state.

By examining the structure in terms of changing alliances between various groups, I reveal the role of agents, particularly leaders from each of the players, as an integral part of the structure. Civil society and the international context are important for shaping the alliances in the Egyptian and Moroccan government and in turn affecting the POS. Moreover, political power-sharing and political-alternation deals between Islamist and secular-liberal/leftist factions influenced women's rights. These deals also became catalysts for the collective mobilization of civil society groups against the regime.

POS and Gender

For women activists to utilize POS effectively, women's movements need to either employ gender frames positioning them more favorably within state contexts (Beckwith 1998), or employ discursive politics to shift/ to shape their political opportunities and their success. The interplay between women's rights, Islam, and democracy influences the framing of women's rights in the Middle East and North Africa. Women must negotiate with both religious and secular forces to design the most effective way to achieve their goals. These forces shape women activist's framing. At times, they strategically adopt Islamist frames of reference, but international institutions and agencies also influence their framing and goals (Al-Ali 2000).

In her study of Islamic women's rights activism in Iran and Turkey, Tajali finds that these activists frame their demands strategically "according to the discursive opportunity structure that best suits their contexts and furthers their aims" (2015: 566). Tajali also finds that Iranian and Turkish Islamic women's groups strategically choose to frame their demands depending on their socio-political contexts. Turkish Islamic and secular women's organizations articulate their demands for women's political participation through international agreements and human rights conventions of the United Nations such as the Convention on the Elimination of all Forms of Discrimination against Women (CEDAW), which Turkey has signed and ratified (Tajali 2015). Islamic activists in Turkey frame their demands for issues ranging from women's right to wear the head scarf to political representation in secular language to appeal to secular groups, while at the same time pressuring religious elites (Tajali 2015). In contrast, secular and religious women's rights groups in Iran, due to the religious nature of the government and its institutions, frame and validate their calls for increased women's participation in religious terms, while dissociating themselves from international human rights agreements (Tajali 2015). Tajali's work demonstrates how women's framing strategies shift according to the POS available at the time. When women activists are faced with a secular regime, they deploy a secular framework by leaning on international conventions such as CEDAW. However, when they are facing a religious regime, they deploy a religious framework by leaning on the more moderate interpretation of the Quran and Sharia Law.

The previous literature will help situate and analyze the organizing and framing strategies of Islamist women activists in Egypt and Morocco as well as look at the framing of parties of women's issues. We see that the different contexts for both countries shaped by alliances and the relationship of the countries to the international community shaped these strategies.

The Muslim Sisterhood in Egypt

The POS model for Egypt views politics in Egypt in terms of alliances between the military, the Islamists, and the secular-liberal political parties. Islamists, secular-liberal elites, and civil society groups have each modified their views regarding women's issues based on the political climate and cultural contexts. This domestic interaction between the players did not occur in isolation; rather it was influenced by the larger international context in which these players operated. For example, Hosni Mubarak attempted to project a secular image of his government to the international community and secular players in Egyptian politics by reforming domestic laws related to the family and women, as well as ratifying international agreements on gender.

The MB's participation in politics since Gamal Abdel Nasser's era (1950s) prompted them to act strategically in forging alliances with various opposition groups, including secular civil society organizations active in student and professional associations, in the political system (Wickham 2002). Modernizing their position on women's issues in society and politics was essential for the MB to ally with any of the other political players in Egypt (see Schwedler 2006; Wickham 2013; Tadros 2016). This shift in position regarding women enabled the MB to appeal to and collaborate with other ideological segments in Egyptian society. The MB issued its first statement on women as voters and candidates in 1994 declaring that women could run as candidates (El-Ghobashy 2005; Wickham 2013). However, this statement still excluded women from the structure of the movement. This did not drastically change until the military coup in July 2013. The door for more involvement of women in the internal structure of the movement in Egypt and in exile had been opened due to the unprecedented backlash by Abdel Fatah el-Sisi's government after the military coup in 2013 against the MB members as well as the expanding experience of the Sisters in the formal and informal mediums.

The period between 1980 until 2011 was marked by an alliance between the military and secular-liberal political parties. During this period of backlash against the MB, the Sisters joined the lines of civil society. They operated in the informal political medium, focusing on social welfare (Talhami 1996). When the government was blocked for the MB and MS, the Sisters organized mainly in domestic civil society institutions. Though the MS initially limited its activities to social work, such as sheltering poor families, they increasingly focused on mobilizing political and financial support for imprisoned Brothers deemed a "security threat" by the Hosni Mubarak regime (Talhami 1996). The Sisters also played an instrumental role in running media campaigns for the MB during national parliamentary elections in 2005 and 2010, building on women's access to people via mosques and welfare organizations (Tadros 2012). Twenty-one Sisters were nominated in 2005 in the initial list of candidates; however, only one woman received enough votes to become a member of the parliament. Fifteen Sisters also ran as independents in the 2010 parliamentary elections on behalf of the Brotherhood (Aboul Komsan 2010).

The position of women in the MB began to marginally evolve during this period due to ideological changes within the Brotherhood and the changing political context. International pressure, especially from the US to democratize, and internal pressure to Islamicize due to the rise of the Islamists and the popularity of their agenda shaped the political context in Egypt at the beginning of the twentieth century (Tadros 2016). To neutralize the influence of the Islamists who were gaining moral authority and shaping the discourse on morality in Egyptian society, Hosni Mubarak coopted women's issues to gain the support of secular groups and the international community. As a response to this strategy and an attempt to gain votes during parliamentary elections after 1995, the MB changed their position on women's political participation (El-Ghobashy 2005; Wickham 2013). However, this transformation restricted the Sisters' roles to the political activities of the MB and did not include them in the internal hierarchy of the MB, which remained male.

An interview I conducted with a prominent Sister, who referred to herself only as Mai, illustrated the role of the Sisters under the Hosni Mubarak regime until the uprisings:

> In relation to the movement inside Egypt, and the role of women under Mubarak's rule, the women participated in the activities and practices of

the movement, but they were banned organizationally due to the security situation under Mubarak. But they participated in all syndicates, activities and services without publicly declaring their ties to the movement because of the security grip. At the beginning of the revolution, the women went down to the squares and there were lots of martyrs in the January revolution. They participated in the protests and slept in the squares, all Egyptian squares and in Tahrir square. During the January revolution, women were the ones organizing and taking care of the needs of the squares and field hospitals. They were also present during the Battle of the Camels[1] challenging thuggery and supporting the men. And many women brought their kids to the squares and slept there. And they had an important role in educating the masses in the different streets on the importance of the revolution and importance of supporting it until it succeeds. (Interview, January 20, 2017)[2]

The period between February 2011 and June 2013 was marked by an alliance between the military and the MB. After the January 25 uprisings, the MB emerged as the only established alternative to the previous regime because they had a set agenda, financial resources, and widespread support due to their years of activism and social service provision (Laub 2014). Their political party, the Freedom and Justice Party (FJP) was formed by the MB after the uprising and consisted of members from the MS and MB. The party nominated 46 women on its lists in 2011 (Shehata 2011). Access to the political party allowed the Sisters to move between civil society and the Islamist political elites through membership. After joining the party, their work became more formally political as women ran for elections and held high positions in Morsi's government (Tadros 2017). This period was marked by an opening in the formal and informal medium for the Muslim Sisters, and their political activities increased compared to the Hosni Mubarak era. The FJP held training sessions for women to help them run for office and engage in politics, and the Sisterhood used the formal political medium, the government, to organize (Tadros 2017).

After the presidential elections in June 2012, the FJP leadership appointed Omayma Kamel to be a member of the Constituent Assembly delegated with drawing up the constitution, and a presidential aide to President Mohamed Morsi (Tadros 2017). Moreover, the FJP leadership appointed Dina Zakaria as the spokeswoman for the FJP. As of 2012, the MB allowed women to be elected as heads of the regional women's committees. These committees communicated directly with the Guidance Bureau, the highest decision-making body within the movement. Previously, only men held such positions. With the opening of political space, the Sisters' political engagement expanded even further, both publicly and within the MB structure. Sisters held positions in the FJP's secretariats across Egypt on women's political awareness and media relations committees as they began to achieve some more notable leadership positions (Tadros 2017). As of 2012, the MB allowed women to be elected as heads of their regional women's committees, which communicate directly with the Guidance Bureau (the movement's highest leadership and administration body) positions that were previously held only by men. However, women held no senior positions in the FJP or the MB. Women's rights became a central issue due to the concerns of the liberals and the international community about the national election of the FJP under the MB. Islamist women from the MB had to explain their position on women's rights as it relates to religion and international agreements.

Sabah Al-Sakkari, a member of the party's secretariat, stressed in an interview with Al Arabiya, "In my platform, I pay special attention to women and youths, whom I believe should get the chance to occupy the highest positions in the party. Women in particular are very important since the progress of any society is closely related to them" (Al Arabiya 2012). When she was asked about her opinion on allowing women to run for presidency, she responded "what [Muslim scholars] all agreed on is that a woman cannot be a Caliph, but there is nothing to prove that she cannot rule over one state within the Muslim nation" (Al Arabiya 2012). She stated that she would run for the presidency of Egypt if members of the Freedom and Justice party approved her nomination.

The period, which began in June 2013, has been marked by an alliance between the military and secular-liberal political parties. Between August and November 2012, Morsi started losing the support of some leftist and liberal factions within civil society, which eventually led to Morsi's ouster by the military on July 3, 2013 (Kingsley 2013). Leading up to this coup was the empowerment of the military as the primary guardian of Egyptian politics by secular parties headed by people such as Mohamed ElBaradei (Kingsley 2013). This was coupled with widespread demonstrations by various civil society groups calling for the ouster of President Mohammed Morsi (Kingsley 2013). During the presidential elections in May 2014, various secular-liberal political parties supported Abdel Fattah el-Sisi for president (Kingsley 2015). The 2013 military coup left civil society divided between groups who were for and against the coup.

Following the backlash, the Muslim Sisters joined civil society groups opposing the coup. The Sisterhood founded Women Against the Coup (WAC), the first of several women-only resistance movements established. This group remains the most active organization for women's mobilization across Egypt to this day (Interview, January 15, 2018).[3] The Sisters made violence against women a central issue for sustaining the support for their mobilization. They started providing data on cases of violence against women as early as November 2013 (Interview, January 15, 2018).[4] Their main work abroad focuses on communicating reports of human rights abuses in Egypt against the opposition to international human rights organizations such as Human Rights Watch (Interview, January 15, 2018).[5] After the military coup, human rights and women's rights, as described in international agreements, became the popular frame due largely to Abdel Fatah el-Sisi's government imprisoning and torturing members of the MB and the people with whom they associated (see the organization's Facebook group in Arabic: https://www.facebook.com/WomenAntiCoup/). The Sisters expanded their activism internationally to connect to international human rights NGOs and even considered registering their WAC organization with the United Nations. As Mai explains this period:

> And after the coup, the women had a major role in the squares by educating the crowds and rejecting the coup. The number of female martyrs a day before the evacuation of Raba'a is a great example of the important role they played. The number of women who were in Raba'a, Al Nahda, and Almanashiya is also a great example. And then after the coup, the work was mainly based on women due to the situation and the number of men detainees inside of detention centers. The women established various movements against the coup, such as women against the coup inside and outside of Egypt and there are others like it. And now the women are still fighting against the coup either by playing a role inside of detention centers, or by supporting their husband, or son, or brother in detention centers, or by spreading awareness among the different sectors of society, or by media, or by communication tools. After three years of the coup, women are still in the squares. (Interview, January 20, 2017)[6]

The Sisters' activism made it hard for the MB leaders to ignore the women's demands, prompting the Egyptian MB living in exile in Turkey to elect the first female member of its Shura Council during elections in 2017 (Mhajne 2018).

The progression in women's political activism and their role in the MB shows that different political contexts shaped Islamist women's organizing strategies. Similarly, these strategies have opened the space for Islamist women in the MB and made them visible as important political actors in Egyptian society. The political opening and closure influenced by the alliances shaped the Sisters' medium of organizing and the way they framed their demands. The Sisters' choices impacted the political trajectory of the Islamists and allowed them to play new roles in the Egyptian government (albeit briefly) and, eventually, in the MB's internal governance structures. Thus, their agency dynamically impacted the political opportunity structures they continue to contend with. As these results suggest, examining women's decisions about political framing and mediums of organizing is essential for achieving a more comprehensive understanding of their activism. Certain political processes, such as how the context interacts with women's activism, can be masked without considering the gendered and dynamic nature of POS. For instance, not examining civil society as a legitimate medium for political organizing by Islamists will mask how the efforts of Islamist women in civil society shape their strategic thinking and their perception of their role as activists. On how their activities in civil society helped the Muslim Sisters and the MB in the elections after the uprisings, Asma Shokr notes,

> It helped them get close to the people by forming multiple relationships. At the same time, we knew that our interaction with people will familiarize them with us and you can see its result in the love of people for us before the coup and before the demonization campaign by Sisi. (Interview, January 15, 2018)[7]

Some of the prominent activists in the MS, such as Asma Shokr and Dina Zakaria, noticed an increase in women's political roles in the movement and a change in women's political consciousness. There is a realization among the Sisters that their role in the MB is evolving and they anticipate a greater role in the future. The Sisters' decades of political consciousness and organizing experience during periods of opening and backlash against the MB provided them with the necessary skills that allowed them to play a stronger role within the organization and the resistance against the current Egyptian regime. Their involvement made various men affiliated with the MB realize that women are essential for any revival efforts of the movement after the coup. As Amar El-Beltagy, the son of leading Brotherhood figure Mohamed El-Beltagy, claimed in an interview I conducted with him in Istanbul, "Now Muslim Brotherhood women are participating in more than a half of their activities, if there is a revival of the movement or a new Brotherhood, women will have to be at the heart of it, much more than before" (Interview, January 11, 2017).[8]

PJD Women in Morocco

The POS model this chapter develops for Morocco views politics in Morocco in terms of alliances between the monarchy, leftist political parties, and Islamists. The connection between civil society groups and one of these players is essential for these groups to achieve their goals. The King holds the upper hand in decision-making, even after the constitutional changes in the aftermath of the Arab Spring, which transferred more power to the elected segment governing the state at both national and local levels (Berriane 2015). To be able to be in the government and to garner gains, the players in Morocco need to ally with or not offend the King. Morocco has prominent leftist parties and organizations, including several civil society groups who subscribe to leftist principles inspired by the French. Moreover, Islamists in the country and their narrative have been dominant since the 1980s (see Chapter 2).

Despite the political power, the monarch holds in Morocco, the attitude of the monarchy toward the opposition and power-sharing with other governing institutions is not set in stone; it changes depending on the vision of the monarch at the time. King Hassan II (1929–1999), who survived two coup attempts, ruled with an iron fist. The years after these attempts witnessed the imprisonment, torture, and disappearance of members of the opposition up until the early 1990s when a new constitution indicated the beginning of political opening for the opposition. This change was a result of an intensified international and domestic pressure of Hassan II's human rights record. This international pressure created a political opening for women's organizations to highlight to women the importance of claiming their political rights in state institutions (Darhour and Dahlerup 2013). The opening enabled domestic human and women's rights groups and associations to push Hassan II to accommodate international human rights standards (Tessler 1997; Waltz 1997; Clark and Young 2008; Salime 2012).

Also, during that time, leftist parties became strong allies and supporters of the women's and human rights movements. The leftist parties support for women's and human rights groups contributed to the success of civil society agendas around the Family Code (FC) reform (Clark and Young 2008). This made leftist groups major political players. The activism of women's and human rights groups and associations combined with the support they received from leftist parties and the King as well as the international pressure resulted in Morocco's ratification of the Convention on the Elimination of all Forms of Discrimination Against Women (CEDAW) in June 1993. However, it entered a few fundamental reservations to core articles in the convention because they were viewed as incompatible with Islam such as Article 9(2), which grants women equal rights with men regarding the nationality of their children and Article 16, which addresses gender equality within the domestic sphere of the family and spousal interactions. These reservations show the delicate balancing game the monarchy is playing between addressing international pressure, satisfying the demands of leftist groups, and not alienating Islamist parties and organizations. During this opening period, Islamists became a strong player in Moroccan politics, especially when the PJD was legalized as a political party and ran in the legislative election in 2002, which gave them 42 out of 325 seats in Parliament, positioning them to lead the opposition (Clark and Young 2008). Moreover, in 1998, the prime minister was selected from the leading opposition party, the Socialist Union of Popular Forces (USFP) (Khatibi 1998). These two political factions, the PJD and USFP, which Hassan II had consecutively revived and suppressed commencing in the 1970s to pit them against each other, became legitimate players in the political system (Clark and Young 2008; Lamchichi 1997).

A political opening for various groups followed King Mohamed VI's accession in 1999 after the death of his father King Hassan II. The new King released political prisoners, the press under him became freer, violations of human rights were diminished, and he initiated political reforms making the state more accountable to its citizens. Many of these newly released political prisoners were from the Islamist opposition. These changes resulted in the proliferation of civil society associations and organizations addressing issues ranging from human rights to sustainable development to cultural protection (Cavatorta 2006). It strengthened women's organizations which since 1992 have been pushing for reforming the FC. Finally, the efforts of these organizations were acknowledged through an announcement in 1999 of the Plan of Action for the Integration of Women in Development.

However, the political opening also strengthened the Islamists who opposed the Plan of Action. In response to the Plan, Islamists such as the PJD organized a larger march, which included many women, against the socialist government's Plan in 2000 (Clark and Young 2008). This incident marks the first-time Islamist groups in Morocco such as the PJD openly deal with the "woman question" (Eddouada and Pepicelli 2010). The participation of women in the march shed light on the complexity of Islamist parties' position on women's engagement and the perception of Islamist women of their agency regarding their socio-political roles. The rise of political Islam in post-independence Morocco helped Islamist movements attract significant followers including women who pushed Islamists to take women's demands for political participation more seriously (El Haitami 2016). The PJD did so by promoting women's political participation through the establishment of women's networks that are engaged in activism to improve women's roles within an Islamic framework, while at the same time attempting to accommodate global discourses on women's rights.

PJD women engaged in different activities from Da'wa and literacy programs to promoting women's socioeconomic rights within a religious framework (El Haitami 2016). They also were involved in national and international debates on women's rights and FC reforms (El Haitami 2016). In the mid-1990s, the PJD parliamentary group included several female members who launched two women's associations; Zahra's Forum and the Renewal of Woman's Awareness (Eddouada and Pepicelli 2010). Zahra's Forum is a cultural organization that addresses issues related to development, whereas The Renewal of Woman's Awareness aims to preserve Islamic identity as it refers to women and implements women's rights in accordance with Sharia law (Eddouada and Pepicelli 2010). These associations did not operate in a vacuum; they were a response to the strong feminist movement that emerged in the 1990s (Yassine 2003). The state's push in the early 2000s for appointing women in various religious leadership roles in theologians' constituencies and mosques controlled by the Moroccan state, marked a period of contention between liberal and Islamic feminisms in the country

(Moghadam 2003; Eddouada and Pepicelli 2010). They resulted in the big demonstrations of March 2000 in opposition to and support for the Plan of Action (Salime 2007).

The march protesting the Plan highlighted the strength of the Islamists and put the Plan on hold. The PJD and others claimed that they oppose the Plan due to the support it received from international institutions such as the World Bank as well as the reference of the document to international agreements such as CEDAW (Clark and Young 2008), which would result in "the unrestrained westernization of Moroccan society" (Clark and Young 2008: 345). They were against it because they believed that religious scholars had not been consulted and the dominance of the leftist parties and women's organizations in developing the Plan without input from other groups (Clark and Young 2008).

Even though the Action Plan was not implemented, women's organization with the help of leftist parties and the support of the King were able to implement the quota reforms in the parliamentary elections of 2002 to guarantee the representation of at least 10% women (Darhour and Dahlerup 2013). The quota was reformed in 2016 to increase the seats reserved for women to 15% (see Chapter 11). Due to the implementation of the quotas, the number and visibility of female political candidates has improved significantly. Their visibility since the implementation of the quotas highlighted to the society the importance of including women in politics. It also opened up new spaces bringing "candidates closer to female voters, attenuate tensions, at least momentarily, and enable women who have difficulty accessing public and male-dominated electoral spaces to gather information about the elections and express their concerns" (Berriane 2015: 445). The passage of the quota resulted in the elections of more women for office in 2002 and 2007, especially Islamist women from PJD, who had the biggest female candidates' representation for parliament. The format of the Moroccan gender quota for national parliament, which demands every party to present candidates for the National Women's lists, forced even reluctant political parties to come up with women candidates. For example, in the elections of 2002, six women PJD candidates won parliamentary seats (El Haitami 2016). PJD women parliamentarians maintained their six seats in the 2007 elections (El Haitami 2016). PJD women's role is not limited to participation in the political process as voters and party members; some of them serve as elected and appointed representatives. The

PJD requires that 15% of its internal seats be held by women. However, as Clark and Schwedler argue, even though Islamist women are incorporated within the formal party's structures, "the introduction of separate, 'parallel' women's sectors reflects the efforts of party leaders to ghettoize women's activities rather than envision meaningful gender equality within the party" (2003: 11).

Moreover, despite Islamist women's increased presence and visibility in the political sphere, they still have to negotiate their visibility in government and their position on women's issues with conservative male Islamist political leaders as well as with the hegemonic discourses of leftist political groups (El Haitami 2016). PJD candidates face unique political obstacles compared to their male colleagues and non-Islamist female candidates for being women (Rapp 2008). As Fatema Belhassen, a PJD candidate for the 2007 elections, notes, "With me, [voters] were experimenting with two things: electing a woman and an Islamist party" (Rapp 2008: 22).

In 2003, instead of implementing the Plan, King Mohammed IV opened the new parliament session with a statement affirming his commitment to reform the FC. Eventually, the Parliament approved the reform four months after this statement. Leaders of both Islamist groups, the PJD and JSO, supported the reform (Clark and Young 2008). Female PJD leaders displayed skepticism regarding the FC's potential to improve women's status (Clark and Young 2008). Initially, the PJD suggested modifications to some articles and refrained from voting on 21 of them (out of 400 total) (Clark and Young 2008). However, eventually, the party voted to approve the final version of the entire FC (Clark and Young 2008).

The reforms were possible due to the King's vision of improving the country's image internationally as well as the effect of the political situation that weakened the Islamist movement following the terrorist attacks of 2003 in Casablanca, which helped temporarily undermine the Islamists and facilitate the FC reform process. After the terrorist attacks in Casablanca, leftist leaning press and public opinion, albeit briefly, publicly opposed the Islamists and some of the PJD critics called for its dismantling (Clark and Young 2008). Consequently, even though the PJD had nothing to do with the attacks, it instantly started making voluntary concessions, such as openly condemning terrorism and emphasizing its support of the monarchy and democracy (Clark and Young 2008). The King was also able to advocate for reform with the support of secular political parties and women's associations and human rights activists (Clark and Young 2008). Moreover, King Mohammed VI framed the reforms by stressing that they were following the teaching of the Quran, thus making it more amenable to Islamists (Clark and Young 2008; Feliu 2012). For example, the King did not outlaw polygamy. Instead, he put in place bureaucratic obstacles making it difficult (Clark and Young 2008).

Mustapha El-Khalfi, a PJD leader, clarified the two reasons for the party's support of the 2004 reform as opposed to the 1999 Plan. The first reason was their belief that the 2004 reform was the result of a more democratic process and consultations than the 1999 Plan (Clark and Young 2008). The second reason is that the 2003 speech and 2004 reform were framed in a religious language without referring to CEDAW or other international rights agreement (Clark and Young 2008). PJD women approved these reforms and acknowledged that even though these reforms are based on Islamic teaching, they required a level of reinterpretation of the religious texts. For example, one of the founding members of The Renewal of Woman's Awareness, PJD deputy Bassima Hakkaoui, said that the reform was grounded in Islamic law through the interpretation of religious texts (Eddouada and Pepicelli 2010). By suggesting the compatibility of the reforms with the Quran and the ability to satisfy the demands of leftist groups, King Mohammed VI overcame opposition by Islamist groups and obtained the support of progressive movements. The compromise, even though it was not ideal, enabled significant gains for women such as the introduction in Article four of the principle of equality by which husband and wife are jointly responsible for the family. Moreover, Article 51 established equal rights and duties within marriage.

In 2011, the February 20th protests strengthened the PJD even further resulting in their election as the ruling party. This was possible due to the PJD's pragmatic decision to support the February 20th protest movement while not challenging the Monarchy. In response to the protests, King Mohammed VI responded by drafting a new constitution, which widened the political opening for opposition groups and emphasized women's and human rights, thus resulting in the elections of PJD in the November 2011 to the parliament (El Haitami 2016). Although the post protests constitution recognizes equal political representation for women, Prime Minister Abdelilah Benkirane's (PJD) ministerial cabinet included only one female minister (El Haitami 2016).

Bassima Hakkaoui, the minister of Solidarity, Women, Family and Social Development and a member of the PJD voiced her dissatisfaction with being the only woman in the post-uprisings government. She stated that she is "annoyed at the decreasing number of women in the Cabinet and wishes it were more," explaining that "political parties did not expend much effort to introduce new female faces who could take responsibility inside the new government" (Estito 2012). However, in 2016, the percentage of women in the House of Representatives increased to 21% compared to 17% in 2011, with the majority of women representatives being from the PJD (*The North Africa Post* 2016).

While the underrepresentation of women in the new government could indicate a lack of progress in women's political rights, the events of the Arab Spring in Morocco and subsequent elections increased the visibility of female Islamist participation in the public sphere and resulted in their election to the government as members of PJD. This visibility of female Islamist activists in the political sphere traditionally influenced by secular-liberal discourses in Morocco challenged previous perceptions of Islamist women and their role within their movements and the political system. However, it also put pressure on these women to clarify their position on women's rights and women's issues as it relates to their religious views. For example, Hakkaoui was accused of pretending to be tolerant when addressing her liberal opponents, while secretly planning on curtailing the progress secular-liberal women made toward achieving gender equality (El Haitami 2016). Even though, Hakkaoui and other PJD female members had reservations on international agreements, Hakkaoui's public criticism of the lack of female candidates employ the complexity of Islamist women's position on human rights. Instead of relying on international treaties and principals to promote women's rights, Islamist women, including PJD women engage in the reinterpretation of the religious text to enhance women's position in Morocco.

Conclusion

Women's issues have been at the center of the cooperation and contestation between Islamists and secular-liberal parties and civil society groups. The national context, which is influenced by the conflict between Islamists and non-Islamists, and the international context shaped the position of these players on women's issues. Both governments' appease to the international community and their portrayal of a secular image of their regimes resulted in the ratification of multiple international agreements such as CEDAW, reforming the PSL, as well as resulted in the passage of quota laws. The cooptation of women's issues came also as an attempt to neutralize the influence of the Islamists, who were gaining moral authority and shaping the discourse on morality in society by gaining the support of secular-liberal groups. Despite this cooptation of women's issues and Islamists' rejections of various top–down policies related to women, these policies resulted in an evolution in the Islamists' discourse on women's participation in politics. It also created an opening for Islamist women's participation. In the case of Morocco, the strength of leftist parties compared to Islamists has facilitated legal and social reforms to women's issues for both Islamist and nonIslamist women. Contrarily, in Egypt, the weakness of the left and its association with corrupt authoritarian regimes has slowed down the modernization process of the MB. The incorporation of the PJD in the democratic process forced them to negotiate with leftist groups leading to the amendment of their views on issues such as women's rights. However, in Egypt instead of containing Islamists through the democratic process, they have been forced to operate underground and in exile.

The political context has influenced the position of Islamist women in Islamist movements and their organizing strategies in Morocco and Egypt. The political opening and closure influenced by the varying political alliances shaped the medium of organizing and framing used by Islamist women. Some of the Islamist women utilized their organizing experience in civil society to gain access to and support for their candidacy in the formal medium. The opening gave the Islamist women more spaces for political participation and assumption of leadership roles in the formal medium as members of the political parties.

Notes

1. In February 2011, pro-Mubarak thugs on horses and camels attacked protesters in Tahrir Square (see http://english.ahram.org.eg/News/33470.aspx).
2. Author conducted the interview in Arabic over the phone and translated the interview to English, 2017.
3. Author conducted the interview in Arabic over the phone and translated the interview to English, 2018.
4. Author conducted the interview in Arabic over the phone and translated the interview to English, 2018.

5. Author conducted the interview in Arabic over the phone and translated the interview to English, 2018.
6. Author conducted the interview in Arabic over the phone and translated the interview to English, 2017.
7. Author conducted the interview in Arabic over the phone and translated the interview to English, 2018.
8. Author conducted the interview in Arabic and translated it to English, Istanbul, 2017.

REFERENCES

Abdelrahman, M. (2004). The leftists and Islamists in Egypt. *ISIM Newsletter*, *14*, 2.
Abdelrahman, M. (2009). "With the Islamists?—Sometimes. With the state?—Never!" Cooperation between the left and Islamists in Egypt. *British Journal of Middle Eastern Studies, 36*(1), 37–54.
Aboul Komsan, N. (2010). Egyptian women's status report 2010. *The Egyptian Center for Women's Rights*. March 10, 2011. http://ecwronline.org/?p=4569. Accessed 06 June 2017.
Agouchtim, A. (2016). Proportion of women in Moroccan Parliament rises to 21%. *The North Africa Post*. http://northafricapost.com/14582-proportion-women-moroccan-parliament-rises-21.html. Accessed 10 June 2019.
Al-Ali, N. (2000). *Secularism, gender and the state in the Middle East: The Egyptian women's movement*. Cambridge: Cambridge University Press.
Al Arabiya. (2012, October 03). Female member runs for chairmanship of Muslim brotherhood's party. https://www.alarabiya.net/articles/2012/10/03/241625.html. Accessed 07 August 2019.
Bayat, A. (2013). The Arab Spring and its surprises. *Development and Change, 44*(3), 587–601.
Beckwith, K. (1998). Collective identities of class and gender: Working-class women in the Pittston Coal Strike. *Political Psychology, 19*(1), 147–167.
Berriane, Y. (2015). The micropolitics of reform: Gender quota, grassroots associations and the renewal of local elites in Morocco. *The Journal of North African Studies, 20*(3), 432–449.
Boduszyński, M. P., Fabbe, K., & Lamont, C. (2015). Are secular parties the answer? *Journal of Democracy, 26*(4), 125–139.
Browers, M. (2007a). Origins and architects of Yemen's joint meeting parties. *International Journal of Middle East Studies, 39*(4), 565–586.
Browers, M. (2007b). The Egyptian movement for change: Intellectual antecedents and generational conflicts. *Contemporary Islam, 1*(1), 69–88.
Cavatorta, F. (2006). Civil society, Islamism and democratisation: The case of Morocco. *The Journal of Modern African Studies, 44*(2), 203–222.

Clark, J. A., & Schwedler, J. (2003). Who opened the window? Women's activism in Islamist parties. *Comparative Politics, 35*(3), 293–312.
Clark, J. A., & Young, A. E. (2008). Islamism and family law reform in Morocco and Jordan. *Mediterranean Politics, 13*(3), 333–352.
Darhour, H., & Dahlerup, D. (2013). Sustainable representation of women through gender quotas: A decade's experience in Morocco. *Women's Studies International Forum, 41*(2), 132–142.
Eddouada, S., & Pepicelli, R. (2010). Morocco: Towards an "Islamic state feminism". *Critique Internationale, 46*(1), 87–100.
El-Ghobashy, M. (2005). The metamorphosis of the Egyptian Muslim brothers. *International Journal of Middle East Studies, 37*(3), 373–395.
El Haitami, M. (2016). Islamist feminism in Morocco: (Re) defining the political sphere. *Frontiers: A Journal of Women Studies, 37*(3), 74–91.
Estito, I. (2012). Female minister in Morocco's new government: One too many? *Alakhbar English.* http://english.al-akhbar.com/node/3562.
Feliu, L. (2012). Feminism, gender inequality and the reform of the Mudawana in Morocco. *Scientific Journal of Humanistic Studies, 4*(6), 101–111.
Gamson, W. A., & Meyer, D. S. (1996). Framing political opportunity. In D. McAdam, J. D. McCarthy, M. N. Zald, & N. Z. Mayer (Eds.), *Comparative perspectives on social movements: Political opportunities, mobilizing structures, and cultural framings* (pp. 275–290). Cambridge: Cambridge University Press.
Hamid, S. (2014). Political party development before and after the Arab Spring. In M. Kamrava (Ed.), *Beyond the Arab Spring: The evolving ruling bargain in the Arab world* (pp. 131–150). London: Hurst Publishers.
Khatibi, A. (1998). *L'alternance et les partis politiques: essai.* Casablanca: Eddif.
Kingsley, P. (2013). Protesters across Egypt call for Mohamed Morsi to go. *The Guardian.* June 30, 2013. https://www.theguardian.com/world/2013/jun/30/mohamed-morsi-egypt-protests. Accessed 03 February 2017.
Kingsley, P. (2015). How Mohamed Morsi, Egypt's first elected President, ended up on death row. *The Guardian.* June 01, 2015. https://www.theguardian.com/world/2015/jun/01/mohamed-morsi-execution-death-sentence-egypt. Accessed 07 November 2016.
Kriesi, H., Koopmans, R., Duyvendak, J. W., & Giugni, M. (1995). *New social movements in Western Europe: A comparative analysis.* Minneapolis: University of Minnesota Press.
Lamchichi, A. (1997). *Le Maghreb face à l'islamisme.* Paris: L'Harmattan.
Laub, Z. (2014). *Egypt's Muslim Brotherhood.* Council on Foreign Relations. https://www.cfr.org/backgrounder/egypts-muslim-brotherhood. Accessed 10 June 2019.
McAdam, D., McCarthy, J. D., Zald, M. N., & Mayer, N. Z. (Eds.). (1996). *Comparative perspectives on social movements: Political opportunities, mobilizing structures, and cultural framings.* Cambridge: Cambridge University Press.

Mhajne, A. (2018). How the Muslim brotherhoods women activists stepped up in Egypt. *Middle East Eye*. January 2018. http://www.middleeasteye.net/fr/node/68295. Accessed 26 February 2018.

Moghadam, V. M. (2003). *Modernizing women: Gender and social change in the Middle East*. Boulder: Lynne Rienner.

Ottaway, M., & Hamzawy, A. (2007). *Fighting on two fronts: Secular parties in the Arab world*. Washington, DC: Carnegie Endowment.

Rapp, L. (2008). *The challenges and opportunities Moroccan Islamist movements pose to women's political participation*. Washington, DC: Center for the Study of Islam and Democracy.

Salime, Z. (2007). The war on terrorism: Appropriation and subversion by Moroccan women. *Signs: Journal of Women in Culture and Society, 33*(1), 1–24.

Salime, Z. (2012). A new feminism? Gender dynamics in Morocco's February 20th movement. *Journal of International Women's Studies, 13*(5), 101–114.

Schwedler, J. (2006). *Faith in moderation: Islamist parties in Yemen and Jordan*. Cambridge: Cambridge University Press.

Schwedler, J., & Clark, J. A. (2006). Islamist-leftist cooperation in the Arab world. *ISIM Review, 18*(1), 10–11.

Shehata, S. (2011). *Profile: Egypt's freedom and justice party*. BBC News. https://www.bbc.com/news/world-middle-east-15899548. Accessed 10 June 2019.

Tadros, M. (2012). *The Muslim brotherhood in contemporary Egypt: Democracy redefined or confined?* London: Routledge.

Tadros, M. (2016). *Resistance, revolt, and gender justice in Egypt*. Syracuse: Syracuse University Press.

Tadros, M. (2017). Does revolutionary politics reconfigure Islamist women's agency organizationally? The case of the Muslim sisters of the Muslim brotherhood in Egypt (1928–2013). *Feminist Dissent, 2*(2017), 85–114.

Tajali, M. (2015). Islamic women's groups and the quest for political representation in Turkey and Iran. *The Middle East Journal, 69*(4), 563–581.

Talhami, G. H. (1996). *The mobilization of Muslim women in Egypt*. Gainesville: University Press of Florida.

Tarrow, S. (1996). States and opportunities: The political structuring of social movements. In D. McAdam, J. D. McCarthy, M. N. Zald, & N. Z. Mayer (Eds.), *Comparative perspectives on social movements: Political opportunities, mobilizing structures, and cultural framings* (pp. 41–61). Cambridge: Cambridge University Press.

Tessler, M. (1997). The origins of popular support for Islamist movements. In J. P. Entelis (Ed.), *Islam, democracy, and the state in North Africa* (pp. 93–126). Bloomington: Indiana University Press.

Turam, B. (2004). The politics of engagement between Islam and the secular state: Ambivalences of "civil society". *The British Journal of Sociology, 55*(2), 259–281.

Waltz, S. (1997). The politics of human rights in the Maghreb. In J. P. Entelis (Ed.), *Islam, democracy, and the state in North Africa* (pp. 75–92). Bloomington and Indianapolis: Indiana University Press.

Wickham, C. R. (2002). *Mobilizing Islam: Religion, activism, and political change in Egypt*. New York: Columbia University Press.

Wickham, C. R. (2004). The path to moderation: Strategy and learning in the formation of Egypt's Wasat Party. *Comparative Politics, 36*(2), 205–228.

Wickham, C. R. (2013). *The Muslim brotherhood: Evolution of an Islamist movement*. Princeton: Princeton University Press.

Yassine, A. (2003). *The Muslim mind on trial*. Iowa City: Justice and Spirituality Publishing.

CHAPTER 8

Contrasting Women's Rights in the Maghreb and the Middle East Constitutions

Aili Mari Tripp

INTRODUCTION

Women's rights are being enshrined in African constitutions today in ways not seen in the past, especially in post-conflict countries (Tripp 2015). In all, 54 African countries have rewritten constitutions since 1990. There is a sharp increase in the proportion of women's rights provisions in these constitutions after the 1990s. The Maghreb countries (Morocco, Algeria and Tunisia) are among these African countries that have incorporated more women's rights provisions in their constitutions. These reforms are particularly evident in clauses pertaining to gender equality, gender discrimination, political participation, and labor. Only a handful of constitutions in the world use both male and female pronouns and three of these countries are in the Maghreb: Tunisia, Algeria, and Morocco.

A. M. Tripp (✉)
University of Wisconsin-Madison, Madison, WI, USA

© The Author(s) 2020
H. Darhour and D. Dahlerup (eds.), *Double-Edged Politics on Women's Rights in the MENA Region*, Gender and Politics,
https://doi.org/10.1007/978-3-030-27735-2_8

This chapter contrasts women's rights provisions in the Maghreb constitutions with those found in the Arab Middle East. It focuses particularly on the constitutional reforms in Algeria (2008, 2016), Morocco (2011), and Tunisia (2014).[1] These two regions share a common language of Arabic, religion (mostly Sunni Islam), and many centuries of external rule by Romans, Ottomans,[2] European colonialists and others. They also share some legal traditions of Islamic jurisprudence (Maliki in the Maghreb[3]) and various cultural practices like cousin marriage. Nevertheless, their legal regimes diverge significantly, with Maghreb constitutions going further in addressing women's rights than Middle East constitutions. This chapter explores why these large differences have emerged.

In general, the differences can be attributed to the fact that authoritarian leaders in the Maghreb used women's rights to neutralize Salafi and other religious conservative tendencies internally (see Chapters 7 and 9; Tripp 2019). They also used women's rights to serve other instrumental purposes such as creating a modernizing image of their societies in the international arena (Dahlerup 2017) and responding to pressures from the women's movement and other civil society actors. At certain critical junctures of changes in power or social upheaval, women's movements were able to push for reform or resist backsliding and were thus able to effect change. Most recently this occurred after the Arab Spring in Tunisia and after Morocco's version of the Arab Spring, the 2011 *vingt février* movement, and after the end of the civil war in Algeria in 2002. All three countries adopted women's rights provisions in their constitutions to a greater extent than Middle East countries (Tripp 2019).[4]

Constitutional reform is important to look at as a measure of societal change, not only because it has implications for the parameters of broader legislative change, but also because it can be taken to be a normative statement about how a society sees itself and what it aspires to. As such, constitutions are a reflection of these norms and the battles over wording and substance are a reflection of what we regard as changing norms.

It is still challenging for people to be able to realize their rights through legal means, especially for the most vulnerable in society who may have limited access to the legal system. Nevertheless, constitutional reform of women's rights opens the door to the possibility of accessing legal instruments to effect changes in behavior and signals expectations of what is acceptable behavior and what is sanctioned. It also gives activists a standard to which they can hold their leaders accountable. In authoritarian contexts, these provisions may be adopted in a top-down fashion, resulting in gender equality reforms being associated with autocracies. This puts women's rights activists in a catch-22 situation supporting such reforms, yet at the same time they may become associated with repressive regimes.

To explain the adoption of key provisions regarding women's rights in these constitutions, I built a database of women's rights constitutional provisions in the Arab countries in the Middle East and North Africa (MENA) from the time of independence starting in the 1950s until 2018. The database draws on constitutions obtained from the Constitute Project; Constitutionnet; Constitutions du Monde; Global Gender Equality Constitutional Database (United Nations) and Constitution Finder (now retired). Provisions with implications for women's rights were coded and compiled from the text of the constitutions searching on relevant key words. I sought to identify patterns of variance and changes over time. Extensive fieldwork in Morocco, Algeria and Tunisia provided a context for this database. The study draws on interviews conducted in Morocco between 2015 and 2016 (130 in all), in Algeria (40) in the fall of 2016, and Tunisia (35) in the spring of 2017. Interviews in all three countries were conducted with leaders and members of a variety of Islamist, feminist, and Amazigh women's rights organizations; human rights organizations, members of parliament; leaders of the women's legislative caucuses, women's ministry representatives; party leaders, lawyers, religious leaders; academics; journalists; and representatives of donor and UN agencies.

This chapter draws on this data to show how it is not enough to argue that religion or authoritarianism is an impediment to the adoption of women's rights in the Middle East and North Africa because there is considerable variance within the region, especially between the Maghreb and the Middle East. The Maghreb is predominantly Muslim and the religion is institutionalized and enshrined in the constitution. Most of the women's rights constitutional reforms were adopted in these countries during a period of authoritarian rule or semi-authoritarian rule in the case of Tunisia, which democratized with the adoption of the 2014 constitution. The chapter first lays out some counter-arguments and then shows empirically the differences between the Maghreb and Middle East constitutions with respect to women's rights, starting with the unified legal system that was uniformly adopted in the Maghreb after independence. The chapter then discusses briefly the process of change in the Maghreb constitutions.

Religion and Authoritarian Rule

Many of the explanations regarding women's rights in the region refer to the "Muslim world" as though it was one entity. Some have argued that Islam and autocracy work together to impede progress in women's rights or as a challenge to progress (Inglehart and Norris 2003). Steven Fish (2011) suggests that Islam is incompatible with democratization and finds evidence for this in the fact that women are subordinated in predominantly Muslim countries. He points to such data as female literacy rates, the sex ratio imbalance that favors men due to male migration to oil-rich countries, patriarchal dominance of the father in the family, sex segregation in schools, and extremist politics that is male oriented.

Others see the relationship between women's rights and authoritarianism differently. Cesari (2017) argues that religiously based legislation is the cause of the lack of women's rights in Muslim countries. Dawood I. Ahmed and Moamen Gouda (2015) similarly argue that the more constitutions in Muslim-majority countries are Islamicized, the less they advance women's rights, and the less democratic and politically stable they are.

Daniela Donno and Bruce Russett (2004), however, do not make such sweeping claims about Islam and women's rights. They agree that most Islamic countries are authoritarian, and they find that women's status is worse in Arab countries than in other predominantly Islamic countries. They argue that such connections are transitory and that at one time Catholic countries were more likely to be regarded as authoritarian than Islamic ones, yet this changed after 1990. Contrary to Fish, Donno and Russett do not argue that women's repression is key to maintaining authoritarian rule. When additional measures of gender equality are considered alongside Fish's variables, they find that Islamic countries are more likely to be autocratic, regardless of limitations on women's rights. They find that Arab countries do not repress women because they are autocratic and that neither Islamic nor Arab culture serve as an obstacle to achieving women's rights. Rather, other factors relating to the region need to be considered such as the role of religious groups, how secular the state is, and the role of international and civil conflict.

All Arab countries have a clause in their constitution stating that Islam is the state religion. A crossnational study carried out by Mala

Htun and Laurel Weldon (2018) argues that the institutionalization of religion as state doctrine influences the adoption of family law. However, the institutionalization of a state religion tells us little about the differences between countries within the MENA region and why some have adopted more progressive policies than others when it comes to family law.

Cesari suggests that the presence of a hegemonic religion in Muslim majority countries is what makes the crucial difference. This is where the state grants a certain dominant religious group exclusive legal, economic or political rights while simultaneously denying those rights to other religious groups. Thus, it is not separation of religion from the state nor state cooperation with religious entities that matters. Rather, according to Cesari, it is the privileging of one religious group at the expense of other religious groups that makes the difference. The hegemonic status of a religion includes the nationalization or regulation of religious institutions and schools, as well as restrictions on freedom of speech and women's rights. Most Muslim majority countries (with a few exceptions like Lebanon, Senegal and Indonesia) have two or three of the characteristics of religious hegemony.

Cesari has argued that secularization in Muslim majority countries in the post-independence period led to the advancement of political, economic and social rights of women, while the expansion of Salafi and Islamist movements led to the curtailment of women's rights in family law. Thus, women's rights generally expanded in education, employment, and political representation, but not in the area of family law. These advances in women's rights were made in authoritarian contexts, following a different path from the one taken in Europe, where women's rights expanded with democratization. The state itself became the most important agent in redefining Islamic law after the 1960s and in shaping Islamic norms. Women's bodies became a major site for politicizing Islam for both state and non-state actors.

Cesari is correct in arguing that hegemonic interpretation of religion matters in most Muslim-majority countries for women's rights, but one still has to explain why there is so much variance among Muslim countries across time and territory among these countries. One way of measuring this variance is by looking at constitutions, and one finds that there are significant differences between constitutions in the Maghreb and the Middle East. At the time gender reforms were made in Maghrebi constitutions, none of these countries were considered democracies. Tunisia subsequently has been deemed a fragile democracy. The countries have the same institutional relationship between religious institutions and the state as in the past. Islam retains a hegemonic status, and the state is the most important institution defining Islamic law and practice.

Unified Legal System

Most countries in the MENA region have dual legal systems in which "modern law" coexists with *Sharia* law. In countries like Jordan and Qatar, separate laws and courts are maintained for family law. Family law is generally adjudicated based on *Sharia* law, although these laws have evolved over time based on diverse principles. The laws are influenced not only by religion but also by the cultures of the Mediterranean region. Perhaps the main distinction between these two legal traditions is that *Sharia* law is unlegislated whereas modern law is legislated (Warrick 2009) (Table 8.1).

The three Maghreb countries are distinct from most Middle East countries (with a few exceptions) in that they adopted a unified legal system after independence. They had inherited from the French colonialists a pluralistic legal system that combined French, *Sharia* and Amazigh (Berber) courts. In Algeria, the French colonialists had replaced the Ottoman courts with secular courts when they introduced French law. The majority of Algerians were under *Sharia* or Amazigh law, but they could be reviewed by the French courts.

The French made no effort to unify the legal system, believing that this would further animate anticolonial sentiments. The French had set Islamic law against Amazigh codes in Algeria and Morocco. Thus, both countries combined customary, Islamic and French law at the time of independence. The French had tried to formalize Amazigh law in a 1930 decree and this generated enormous backlash, as it was seen as an attack on Islam and an attempt to divide the Imazighen (Berbers) and Arabs, even though in reality the Imazighen did not follow Islamic law at this time. Of the three countries, Algeria was most influenced by French law due to the long duration of colonial rule in the country.

With independence, all three countries adopted unified legal court systems and unified laws. They not only reformed the judicial and legal system, but they unified them, creating one set of courts and legal codes for all. In Tunisia, the French courts were eliminated in 1957. In Morocco, the Unification Law of 1965 integrated the *qadi* courts and

Table 8.1 Unified courts and laws in MENA Region, 2018

Country	Unified courts	Unified laws	Source of family law	Basis of family law/personal status law	Islamic inheritance mentioned in constitution	Laws for separate religious groups
Algeria	Yes	Yes	Personal status code (1984, amend. 2008)	Constitution	No	No
Morocco	Yes	Yes	Personal status code (1957, 2004)	Constitution	No	No
Tunisia	Yes	Yes	Personal status code (1957)	Constitution	No	No
Iraq	Yes	Yes	Personal status law (1959)	Constitution	No	Yes
Kuwait	Yes	Yes	Personal status law (1984)	*Sharia* law	Yes	No
Libya	Yes	No	Family law (1984)	*Sharia* law	No	No
Oman	Yes	No	Personal status law (1997)	*Sharia* law	Yes	Yes
Egypt	Yes	No	NA	*Sharia* law	No	Yes
Yemen	Yes	Na	Personal status law (1992)	*Sharia* law	Yes	No
Bahrain	No	No	Personal status code (2009)	*Sharia* law Uncodified	Yes	Yes
Jordan	No	No	Personal status law (2001, 2010)	*Sharia* law	Yes	Yes
Lebanon	No	No	15 different personal status laws (1936)	NA	No	Yes
Palestinian Authority	No	No	1976 Jordanian personal status law in the West Bank; 1954 Egyptian family law in Gaza	*Sharia* law	No	Yes
Qatar	No	No	Family law (2006)	*Sharia* law Uncodified	Yes	No
Syria	No	No	Personal status law (1953)	*Sharia* law	Yes	Yes
UAE	No	No	Personal status law (2005)	*Sharia* law	No	No
Saudi Arabia	No	No	No codified family law	*Sharia* law	No	No

Source Compiled from UN Women, Constitute. http://constitutions.unwomen.org; https://www.constituteproject.org; http://confinder.richmond.edu; http://www.constitutionnet.org/; http://mjp.univ-perp.fr/constit/constitintro.htm

the courts of the Jewish community into the national system as part of a nationalist impulse that allowed only Moroccans to be eligible for judgeships and integrated Islamic law into the statutory legislation. However, even though King Hassan II insisted that the unification of laws had been done in accordance with Islamic legal principles, the process, in fact, allowed for the secularization of legal institutions, of which women's rights was one aspect (Sharia Source 2016).

In Algeria, the judicial system was unified under the ordinance of 1965 and the system was streamlined, borrowing the Supreme Court model of Morocco. New civil, penal, and commercial codes were enacted, following German, Swiss and French templates (Liebesny 1975).

The adoption of unified legal systems and unified laws explains why it was somewhat easier to adopt women's rights policies in the Maghreb than in parts of Middle East where such a system did not exist (Engelcke 2014; Maktabi 2012). Unified laws were a necessary but not sufficient condition for later women's rights reforms. The centralized state control of the legal system applied all laws uniformly to all citizens and can be contrasted to the model of separate family laws for different confessional groups that one finds in some Middle Eastern countries like Lebanon (Mayer 1995) and the separation of family law under the jurisdiction of *Sharia* courts. Beyond the Maghreb, Iraq and Kuwait also have unified laws and a unified court system, while Libya, Yemen, Oman and Egypt have unified courts but not unified laws. None of these countries have gone as far as the Maghreb countries in reforming women's rights. Kuwait is far from being a panacea for women's rights. Shia religious leaders and some Islamic parties in Iraq are trying to repeal the country's 1959 personal status code, which provided a unified legal framework for family law. They want to replace it with *Sharia* law in a one of the few MENA countries that does not have *Sharia* law as the foundation of its legal system.

Contrasting Constitutions

Although Tunisia had advanced earliest in terms of women's rights legislation, Algeria first incorporated explicit women's rights provisions in its constitution in 1996 in the midst of the Black Decade. Most of the constitutional changes in Morocco and Tunisia were adopted after the Arab Spring and additional reforms regarding women and work were adopted in Algeria with its 2016 constitution (see Table 8.2). The three

Table 8.2 Convergence of gender-related provisions in Maghreb constitutions

Country	Year	Labor or work	Political representation	Gender equality	Non-discrimination clause	Mention of gender pronouns
Algeria	1963	0	0	1	0	0
Algeria	1996	0	1	1	1	0
Algeria	2008	0	1	1	1	1
Algeria	2016	1	1	1	1	1
Tunisia	1958	0	1	0	0	0
Tunisia	2014	1	1	1	1	1
Morocco	1962	0	0	1	0	0
Morocco	2011	1	1	1	1	1

Note Shaded areas 1 = adopted, 0 = not adopted
Source Compiled from UN Women, Constitute. http://constitutions.unwomen.org; https://www.constituteproject.org; http://confinder.richmond.edu; http://www.constitutionnet.org/; http://mjp.univ-perp.fr/constit/constitintro.htm

Maghreb countries have moved in a significantly different direction from other MENA countries when it comes to constitutional reforms. These differences between the two regions are also sharply evident in related legislation.

The women's rights provisions in Maghreb constitutions exceed what one sees in other MENA constitutions with the exception of Egypt and perhaps Iraq. However, it is necessary not only to account for the references to women's rights in the constitution, but also what is not mentioned, and what other provisions are referenced regarding the adjudication of family law, the depiction of motherhood and ultimately the extent to which the constitutional provisions are translated into law and applied. For example, although the 2014 constitution in Egypt gave women unprecedented rights (Table 8.3), there has been little follow-up in terms of legislative or other policy changes. Moreover, women's rights activism, as with other forms of civil society activity, is constrained and repressed. Egypt does not have unified family laws. The principles of Islamic *Sharia* law are the main source of family law legislation for Muslims (Article 2), while other faiths apply their own community's religious standards to family matters (Article 3).

In contrast to the Maghreb constitutions, there is no mention of women's rights in the constitutions of Kuwait, Lebanon, Saudi Arabia, United Arab Emirates, and Yemen (Table 8.3). Yemen's constitution refers to women as "sisters of men" and guarantees their rights and

Table 8.3 Constitutional provisions regarding women's rights (Maghreb countries highlighted)

Country	Year constitution passed or amended	Labor or work	Parity or quota in political representation	Equality of all citizens	Gender equality	Anti-discrimination clause with reference to gender	Gender-based violence
Algeria	2016	X	X	X	X	X	
Bahrain	2002	X		X	X	X	
Egypt	2014	X	X	X	X	X	X
Iraq	2005	X		X	X	X	X
Jordan	2011	X		X			
Kuwait	1962/1992			X			
Lebanon	2004			X			
Libya	2012			X			
Morocco	2011	X	X	X	X	X	
Oman	1996			X		X	
Palestine	2003			X	X	X	
Qatar	2003			X	X		
Saudi Arabia	2013				X	X	
Syria	2012			X	X	X	
Tunisia	2014	X	X	X	X	X	X
UAE	1971/1996			X			
Yemen	2001			X			

Source Compiled from UN Women, Constitute. http://constitutions.unwomen.org; https://www.constituteproject.org; http://confinder.richmond.edu; http://www.constitutionnet.org/; http://mjp.univ-perp.fr/constit/constitintro.htm

duties assigned by the *Sharia*. Jordan's constitution refers to women only by saying that the law will protect "motherhood." Bahrain, Jordan, Libya, Mauritania, Palestine, Qatar, and Syria have only one or two references to women while Egypt and Iraq have slightly more. But in all cases, they have considerably weaker provisions than what one finds, for example, in Tunisia's constitution (see Table 8.3).

A generic statement about gender equality and a clause opposing gender discrimination is found in most African constitutions today. Similarly, all three Maghreb constitutions contain these two clauses. However, only seven additional MENA constitutions contain a gender equality provision and another seven have an anti-discrimination clause (Table 8.3). Bahrain qualifies gender equality to say that women can have equality with men in political, social, cultural, and economic spheres as long as it does not breach "the provisions of Islamic canon law (*Sharia*)" (Article 5.b). Only Saudi Arabia does not have any form of such an equality provision, neither for all citizens nor in reference to gender. However, even though most MENA constitutions make reference to equality of citizens and half refer to gender equality explicitly, feminists point out that women are relegated to secondary or minor status when it comes to family law. The legal framework is divided in that it allows everyone education, the right to government employment, the right to work, and the right to vote. However, it simultaneously creates inequalities within the private sphere and within the home. The Maghreb countries are seeking to redress this imbalance through their constitutions and laws.

A few Arab constitutions mention women's right to political participation, but only in the Maghreb constitutions (and the Syrian constitution) do we find the promise that the state will proactively work to promote women's political rights by increasing their political representation. The term "gender parity" is used explicitly in the Moroccan and Tunisian constitutions, which is a much higher bar than one finds in most constitutions. The only other constitutions globally that mention gender parity are those of Ecuador (2008), Bolivia (2009), and DR Congo (2011). As for economic rights, Algeria, Morocco and Tunisia, all have provisions pertaining to women's right to equal access to work. The only other Arab countries with these provisions are Bahrain, Egypt, Iraq and Jordan.

In their constitutions, Egypt, Iraq and the Palestinian territories allow citizenship to be transferred from both the mother and father to the child as does. However, this is provided for in legislation in all three Maghreb countries: Algeria (2005), Morocco (2007) and Tunisia (1998), in addition to Bahrain.

The Maghreb countries are notable not only in what provisions they contain but also in what is absent from their constitutions when it comes to women. Most Arab constitutions that mention women focus on women's roles as mothers and on the protection either of mothers or motherhood, with the exception of the Maghrebi and Lebanese constitutions. As the Bahrain constitution states, the mother "tends the young and protects them from exploitation and safeguards them against moral, bodily and spiritual neglect."

Mothers and motherhood are often mentioned alongside children and childhood in the constitutions. The Egyptian constitution states: "The state ensures care and protection and care for motherhood and childhood, for breadwinning and elderly women, and women most in need" (Egyptian Constitution 2004, Chapter 2, Article 11).

Placing women's rights alongside children's rights has the tendency to infantilize them and reduces them to the same category of dependence that children and the elderly often fall under, regardless of their age. The equation of women with children is suggestive of the status of minors who are not accorded full citizenship, but rather, are in need of protection and special consideration. For example, the United Arab Emirates constitution says: "The community shall care for children and *mothers* and protect minors and others who are unable to look after themselves for any reason, such as illness or incapacity or old age or forced unemployment, assist and rehabilitate them for their own interest and for the interest of the community. Welfare and social security laws regulate these matters" (Part II, Article 16).

Relegating women to the category of vulnerable people in need of protection is not found in the three Maghreb constitutions. Although the Moroccan constitution mentions mothers, it specifies that *not all mothers* across the board require protection, only "certain categories of women and of *mothers*." This is an important recognition that not all women are the same: single mothers, widows, and very poor mothers face particular challenges in Moroccan society and bear additional burdens given gender inequality.

Another significant difference between the Maghreb and Middle East constitutions relates to religion. Only the Maghreb countries and Lebanon do not mention Islamic jurisprudence as a source of law (Table 8.1). This has implications for women's rights, particularly family law. Under pressure from the competing British and French consuls, Tunisia's constitution was written in 1861 at a time when there were the earliest debates over how to combine constitutionalism with Islam. It became one of the most "modern" constitutions among the Muslim-majority countries (Ahmed and Gouda 2015). Ever since then, a perennial struggle has ensued over the extent to which political authority should be accountable to Islamic law or to the constitution.

The problem for women's rights is not religiosity per se as some have argued, because Islam influences all law to one degree or another in these countries. Tunisia is the only country in the region where the *Sharia* plays little role in the legal system, and in Morocco and Algeria there are references to Islamic law but also to other more universal aspirations, which have been incorporated into the constitutions such as international treaties. Similarly, a measure like inheritance in the constitution provides little information about women's rights outcomes since five countries mention it in the constitution and six do not (including the Maghreb countries), yet all MENA countries have relied on Islamic jurisprudence to dictate inheritance laws for women. Tunisia became the first Arab country to adopt equal inheritance rights between men and women in 2018. A key component of Islamic jurisprudence regarding inheritance is the idea that women can inherit only half of what men can inherit.

The real question, then, becomes how is religion used to influence women's rights. Thus, the mention of *Sharia* law in the constitution as the basis of personal law (Table 8.1) is one of the most important measures necessary to understanding women's rights outcomes, but the struggle over its importance is a political one.

Women's Movements and State Agendas

Among the most important factors that explain the *changes* have to do with the interactions and agendas of three sets of actors: Women's rights activists, political elites and political parties. If one compares the constitutions of the Maghreb countries with those of other MENA countries with respect to women's rights, these countries have charted a significantly different path, representing a new set of political accommodations between Islamists and secularists, sometimes unpalatable to both groups (Salime 2011). How these accommodations are navigated lies at the crux of the future of women's rights in the region since ultimately women's rights have to be fought for through the political process. Moreover, these accommodations are critical to prospects for stability in the region.

Tunisia

After the Revolution of 2011 in Tunisia and the ouster of President Zine El Abidine Ben Ali from power, attention shifted to passing a new constitution. It highlighted the tensions between Islamists and secularists over the notion of complementarity and other concerns. At the time of the debate, the Islamist party, Ennahda, controlled the parliament and had formed a government. The assassination of a leftist leader in July 2013 threw the country into turmoil as the Ennahda party came under attack for giving political cover to extremists behind this and other politically motivated killings. The new constitution was passed in January 2014, after which Ennahda stepped down. New elections were held in October 2014 in which the secular Nidaa Tounes party won. The 2014 constitution, which includes gender sensitive language, ended up being the most progressive for women's rights in the region. But this outcome was not apparent at the outset of the deliberations over the constitution.

The Ennahda leader Meherziya Labidi was appointed first Vice-President of the assembly and three out of the seven members of the bureau supporting the President of the Assembly were also women. Another woman, Farida Labidi of Ennahda, was president of the committee in charge of sensitive rights and freedoms, which dealt with women's rights. In these debates, two issues related to gender became contentious. Ennahda numerically dominated the assembly and tensions between the Islamists and secularists ran deep, with the Islamists being put on the defensive around questions of the principle of equality.

The most controversial clause was advanced by Ennahda, stating that the "woman is the complement of man." This complementarity clause, in a country with a long history of gender equality and secularist influences, was regarded as a conservative Islamist influence. The secularists feared it would dramatically set back women's rights, as a female parliamentarian and another noted historian explained to me as did others (T18.3.29.17; T2.3.16.17). Ennahda's proposed change also stated: "The State guarantees the protection of women's rights and the promotion of their gains, as a real partner of men in the mission of the homeland building, and the roles of both should complement each other within the household." Women would be relegated to the domestic sphere and men to the public sphere, explained the historian (T2.3.16.17). Thousands of women protested this clause through demonstrations in the streets of Tunis in August 2012, with slogans "Equality all the way — no complementarity in the constitution." Ennahda felt that the idea of *mukammil* (لمكم, or complementarity) valued women's roles as wives and mothers, while the secularists and feminists felt that it threatened the achievements of women, reinforcing a patriarchal system that gave power to men and denied women their full citizenship and rights, making them dependents of men. As one feminist activist from *Association tunisienne des femmes démocrates* (ATFDT) (Tunisian Association of Democratic Women) put it, in the view of Ennahda, "The woman completes the man but is not equal to the man. The woman is not taken as an independent individual who has obligations and rights. The woman exists only through her family, through her children and her husband. Outside the family, she does not exist. There are no rights for single mothers, for example. The woman as such is neglected" (T2.23.15.17). In the end, the complementarity clause was removed.

In response to the pushback against complementarity, the Prime Minister Ali Laarayedh of the Ennahda party made a speech in which he announced that he was giving up on complementarity and that equality would remain in the constitution, according to another leader of ATFDT (T1.3.16.17). This clause was replaced with a strong commitment on the part of the state to protecting women's rights in Article 46 (see Table 8.4).

Feminist activists also won a major victory when they were able to introduce Article 21 to the Constitution, which states that "all male and female citizens are equal in rights and duties." They also were able to obtain a non-discrimination clause: "All citizens, male and female … are equal before the law without any discrimination" (Article 21).

The Islamists had wanted to include in the preamble of the constitution a reference to the "values of Islam" and the "respect for the sacred." Women's rights activists were concerned that without defining the term "sacred," they could be opening themselves up to a reversal of the Personal Status Code and laws that were quite advanced in Tunisia regarding adoption, abortion and polygamy. In place of these clauses, a compromise was reached so that the reference to "the sacred" was removed from the preamble. The constitution declares that the state is the guardian of religion, but it also protects freedom

Table 8.4 Gender equality provisions in Tunisia's 2014 constitution

Preamble
… the state guarantees the supremacy of the law and the respect for freedoms and human rights, the independence of the judiciary, the equality of rights and duties between all citizens, male and female, and equality between all regions
Article 21
All citizens, male and female, have equal rights and duties, and are equal before the law without any discrimination
Article 34
The rights to election, voting, and candidacy are guaranteed, in accordance with the law. The state seeks to guarantee women's representation in elected bodies
Article 46
The state commits to protect women's accrued rights and work to strengthen and develop those rights
The state guarantees the equality of opportunities between women and men to have access to all levels of responsibility in all domains
The state works to attain parity between women and men in elected Assemblies
The state shall take all necessary measures in order to eradicate violence against women
Article 40
Work is a right for every citizen, male and female. The state shall take the necessary measures to guarantee work on the basis of competence and fairness
All citizens, male and female, shall have the right to decent working conditions and to a fair wage
Article 74
Every male and female voter who holds Tunisian nationality since birth, whose religion is Islam shall have the right to stand for election to the position of President of the Republic
On the day of filing the application for candidacy, the candidate must be at least 35 years old
If the candidate has a nationality other than the Tunisian nationality, he or she must submit an application committing to abandon the other nationality if elected president

of religion. It says, "The state undertakes to disseminate the values of moderation and tolerance and the protection of the sacred, and the prohibition of all violations thereof. It undertakes equally to prohibit and fight against calls for *takfir* [declaring another Muslim as a non-believer] and the incitement of violence and hatred" (Article 6). The preamble references "our people's commitment to the teachings of Islam," but qualifies them as being "characterized by openness and moderation, and to the human values and the highest principles of universal human rights."

According to an expert who reviewed the constitution as part of a consensus committee, the notion of universality was also highly contested in their deliberations. Women's rights activists along with others argued against Ennahda's desire to talk about cultural specificity rather than the principle of universal rights of all peoples and all religions.

Yet another debate on the first article states that "Tunisia is a free, independent, sovereign state; its religion is Islam, its language is Arabic, and its system is republican." Ennahda had wanted to include the *Sharia* as the source of law but there was so much reaction in the streets and so much pressure from women, that they were obliged to withdraw this provision. Ennahda also wanted to say that "Tunisia is an independent and sovereign state whose religion is Islam. This article cannot be amended," according to the ATFDT leader. This was seen as a very important article because it would not be able to be amended. The secularist feminists argued that Islam belonged to Tunisia and therefore to the people and not to the state. The state should be neutral as the guarantor of freedom of belief, of worship and freedom of conscience (T1.3.16.17).

A final key debate was over the status of international treaties to which Tunisia was party. The Islamists wanted to make the treaties inferior to the constitution, which would mean that the Convention on the Elimination of All Forms of Discrimination against Women might no longer be fully respected, explained a woman parliamentarian who participated in the constitution making process (T18.3.29.17). The Islamists were unsuccessful in this pursuit. The end of the constitution making process marked a shift in Ennahda's position on women's rights as the constitution-making process no doubt crystalized the limits of how far they could push their agenda when it came to women's rights. Tunisia too had a long history with women's rights to relinquish them so easily. Whether the shift represented a change of heart among party leaders is debatable, but a change in rhetoric did occur. Tunisia's 2014 constitution ended up being of the most progressive in the world when it comes to women's rights (Table 8.4).

Morocco

In Morocco, the constitutional changes were precipitated by the 2011 *vingt février* (20th February) protests, which represented a coming together of feminist, Amazigh, Islamist, pro-economic rights advocates along with other secular and leftist concerns (Salime 2012). The protests took place in the context of the Arab Spring, although they were not as large as the protests in Tunisia or Egypt. The King responded quickly and sought to address some of the concerns of the protests through

Table 8.5 Gender equality provisions in Morocco's 2011 constitution

Preamble
… The Kingdom of Morocco, [a] united State, totally sovereign, belonging the Grand Maghreb, reaffirms that which follows and commits itself:
To ban and combat all discrimination whenever it encounters it, for reason of sex, or color, of beliefs, of culture, of social or regional origin, of language, of handicap or whatever personal circumstance that may be

Article 6
The public powers work for the creation of the conditions permitting the effectiveness of liberty and of the equality of citizens [feminine] and citizens [masculine] to be made general, as well as their participation in political, economic, cultural and social life

Article 7
The political parties work for the structuring and for the political instruction [formation] of the citizens [feminine] and citizens [masculine], for the promotion of their participation in the national life and the management of public affairs. They concur in the expression of the will of the electors and participate in the exercise of power, on the basis of pluralism and of alternation by democratic methods, within the framework of the constitutional institutions

Article 19
The man and the woman enjoy, in equality, the rights and freedoms of civil, political, economic, social, cultural and environmental character, enounced in this Title and in the other provisions of the Constitution, as well as in the international conventions and pacts duly ratified by Morocco and this, with respect for the provisions of the Constitution, of the constants of the Kingdom and of its laws
The State works for the realization of parity between men and women
An Authority for parity and the struggle against all forms of discrimination is created, to this effect

Article 30
All the citizens [feminine] and the citizens [masculine] of majority, enjoying their civil and political rights[,] are electors and eligible. The law provides the provisions of [a] nature encouraging the equal access of women and men to the elective functions
Foreigners under [Moroccan] jurisdiction enjoy the fundamental freedoms recognized to Moroccan citizens [feminine] and citizens [masculine], in accordance with the law

Article 34
The public powers enact and implement the policies designed [destinies] for persons and for categories of specific needs. To this effect, it sees notably:
to respond to and provide for the vulnerability of certain categories of women and of mothers, of children, and of elderly persons

Article 115
The Superior Council of the Judicial Power is presided over by the King. It is composed: a representation of [women] magistrates must be assured, from among the ten members elected, in proportion to their presence in the corps of the magistrature

Gender sensitive provisions: Articles 6, 7, 10, 11, 15, 16, 27, 31, 37, 38,42, 139, 146, 154, 161 constitutional reforms. The new 2011 constitution, which many felt did not go far enough in democratizing the political system, expanded the powers of the Prime Minister, made Tamazight the official state language along with Arabic. It also allowed for an increase in the number of reserved seats for women in parliament to 15%, thus increasing the proportion of women in the parliament. The new constitution was voted on in a referendum in July of 2011.

Over a dozen Moroccan women's associations, including the Moroccan Women's Democratic Association, were invited by the Advisory Commission to Revision of the Constitution (CCRC) to present their demands for the constitution. Most of these demands were incorporated into the new constitution. The gains that they made in the new constitution included

- a recognition of the diversity of Moroccan identities and the adoption of principles relating to universal rights of people to freedom, fundamental rights and obligations, and commitments to international treaties and conventions, which allow for effective citizenship for women.
- The constitution guaranteed women civil, political, economic, social, cultural and environmental equality with men.
- The state would work for parity between men and women. The constitution introduces the notion of the effectiveness of rights and freedoms. It advocates for affirmative action measures, as well as mechanisms, in particular the "Authority for Parity and the Fight Against All Forms of Discrimination", which will make it possible to move from constitutional recognition of rights to their promotion and implementation.
- One of the main demands of the human rights and feminist movement in Morocco demanded recognition of the supremacy of international conventions ratified by Morocco on national laws and the obligation to harmonize them accordingly. These are now incorporated into the constitution (Table 8.5).

Algeria

Of the three constitutions, the gender reforms were the most limited in the Algerian constitution. Up until 2008 there were no provisions in the Algerian Constitution specifically mentioning women's political rights.

This changed with the 2008 constitution. For example, Chapter 4, Article 31bis states, "The State shall work for the promotion of political rights of women by increasing their chances of access to representation in elected assemblies."

The 1976 constitution promised political rights for women. Women could be active in politics as long as it was in the service of the FLN, which was the only party. The 1976 constitution Article 81 stated that "Algerian women should be able to participate actively in political involvement and in social construction through the struggle within the party ranks and its national organizations" (Algerian Constitution 1976). By 1996 this had been removed, and men and women were to have equal rights and duties as citizens so as to ensure the "participation of all in the political, economic, social and cultural life."

Up until 2008 there were no provisions in the Algerian Constitution specifically mentioning women's political rights. This changed with the 2008 constitution when the following clause was added: "The State shall work for the promotion of political rights of women by increasing their chances of access to representation in elected assemblies." Additional amendments to the constitution in 2016 included several other key provisions, including the following: "The citizens shall be equal before the law without any discrimination on the basis of birth, race, gender, opinion or any other personal or social condition or circumstances." It required the state to take positive action to ensure equality of rights and duties of all citizens, men and women and an article was included, indicating that the "state works to attain parity between women and men in the job market," and "encourages the promotion of women to positions

Table 8.6 Gender equality provisions in Algeria's 2016 constitution

Article 32
The citizens shall be equal before the law without any discrimination on the basis of birth, race, gender, opinion or any other personal or social condition or circumstances
Article 35
The State shall work for the promotion of political rights of women by increasing their chances of access to representation in elected assemblies
The modalities of application of this Article shall be determined by an Institutional Act
Article 36
The State shall work to promote gender equity in the labor market
The State shall encourage the promotion of women in senior posts in public agencies and departments and at the level of institutions

of responsibility in public institutions and in businesses." As in Morocco and Tunisia, the impetus for expanding women's rights came from pressure from women's organizations but also from top-down initiatives allowing authorities to seek legitimacy as a modernizing state that was disassociating itself from the past of civil conflict involving Islamist jihadists (Table 8.6).

Conclusions

This chapter suggests that constitutional reforms in the Maghreb after 2000 were primarily tied to the impact of women's movements and the coalitions they built as well as to the political will of those in power, who influenced the adoption of quotas and increases in female legislative representation. National leaders sought constitutional reforms in order to blunt the political influence of Salafi and Islamist extremists and to pacify sectors of civil society demanding more democracy, women's rights and Amazigh rights. Political parties sought popular support in the face of threats to their influence. The developments are also tied to changes in opportunity structures such as modest political opening and the end of conflict (in the case of Algeria), both of which created renewed possibilities for women's mobilization.

The political equation had changed as civil society pressed for change in Morocco in 2011, resulting in constitutional reforms around women's rights, some changes in the role of the prime minister and an expansion of Amazigh rights. The ruling Party of Justice and Development (PJD) changed its rhetoric with respect to international treaties like the Convention on the Elimination of Discrimination of Women (CEDAW), the Personal Status Code and numerous other key reforms related to women's rights after coming to power in 2011. In Tunisia, the women's movement sought to defend women's rights during the constitution making process, resulting in acquiescence on the part of the Islamist party, Ennahda. In Algeria, the reforms were the result of state mediation between women's rights and Islamist influences. The shift in orientation on the part of dominant Islamist parties in Morocco and Tunisia after 2011, suggests that women's rights are malleable and are above gained through a political process of contestation. The lack of rights in Muslim-majority and authoritarian countries like Algeria, Morocco and Tunisia is not a permanent condition, but rather a changing landscape influenced by women's movements and political elites and parties.

This comparison of the Maghreb and the Middle East shows that arguments that suggest that authoritarianism and religiosity, especially Islam, are impediments to the adoption of women's rights reforms do not adequately account for the region, for change within Islamic and other deeply religious societies, for the need for political survival and legitimacy among parties and the elite, and for pressure from women's movements, particularly at critical junctures and during political crises. Institutional changes like the adoption of unified legal systems and the adoption of strategies to promote parity override cultural constraints.

Notes

1. This chapter draws extensively on research for my 2019 book *Seeking Legitimacy: Why Arab Autocracies Adopt Women's Rights*.
2. The Ottoman Empire did not reach to Morocco.
3. Maliki law is one of the four Sunni Islamic schools of jurisprudence (*fiqh*) prevalent in West Africa and North Africa and the southern part of Egypt.
4. A more detailed explanation of this process can be found in my book *Seeking Legitimacy: Why Arab Autocracies Adopt Women's Rights* (2019) on which this chapter draws.

References

Ahmed, D. I., & Gouda, M. (2015). Measuring constitutional Islamization: The Islamic constitutions index. *Hastings International and Comparative Law Review, 38*(1), 1–74.

Cesari, J. (2017). Introduction. In J. Cesari & J. Casanova (Eds.), *Islam, gender and democracy in comparative perspective*. Oxford: Oxford University Press.

Dahlerup, D. (2017). *Has democracy failed women?*. Cambridge: Polity Press.

Donno, D., & Russett, B. (2004). Islam, authoritarianism, and female empowerment: What are the linkages? *World Politics, 56*(4), 582–607.

Engelcke, D. (2014). *Processes of family law reform: Legal and societal change and continuity in Morocco and Jordan* (DPhil). St Antony's College, Oxford University.

Fish, S. (2011). *Are Muslims distinctive? A look at the evidence*. New York: Oxford University Press.

Htun, M., & Weldon, S. L. (2018). *The logics of gender justice: State action on women's rights around the world*. New York: Cambridge University Press.

Inglehart, R., & Norris, P. (2003). The true clash of civilizations. *Foreign Policy, 135*, 62–70.

Liebesny, H. J. (1975). *The law of the Near and Middle East: Readings, cases and materials*. Albany: State University of New York Press.

Maktabi, R. (2012). *The politicization of the demos in the Middle East: Citizenship between membership and participation in the state* (PhD thesis). University of Oslo.

Mayer, A. E. (1995). Reform of personal status laws in North Africa: A problem of Islamic or Mediterranean laws? *Middle East Journal, 49,* 432–446.

Salime, Z. (2011). *Between feminism and Islam: Human rights and Sharia law in Morocco*. Minneapolis: University of Minnesota Press.

Salime, Z. (2012). A new feminism? Gender dynamics in Morocco's february 20th movement. *Journal of International Women's Studies, 13*(5), 101–114.

Sharia Source. (2016). The dissolution of Sharīʿa in the 1965 Moroccan Court unification law. *Shariasourceblog*. Available from https://shariasource.blog/2016/12/16/the-dissolution-of-shari%CA%BFa-in-the-1965-moroccan-court-unification-law/.

Tripp, A. M. (2015). *Women and power in postconflict Africa*. New York: Cambridge University Press.

Tripp, A. M. (2019). *Seeking legitimacy: Why Arab autocracies adopt women's rights*. New York: Cambridge University Press.

Warrick, C. (2009). *Law in the service of legitimacy: Gender and politics in Jordan*. Abingdon-on-Thames: Routledge.

PART IV

Empowered or Sidelined? On Women's Political Representation and Influence

CHAPTER 9

Examining Female Membership and Leadership of Legislative Committees in Jordan

Marwa Shalaby and Laila Elimam

INTRODUCTION

For decades, Arab states continued to have one of the lowest proportions of female representatives worldwide. Women made up merely 6.6 and 10.5% of Arab legislatures in 2004 and 2010, respectively. Today, they constitute almost 19% of representatives in MENA's assemblies (IPU 2018). This significant increase can be mainly explained by the introduction of affirmative action policies in several Arab countries, such as Jordan, Algeria, Tunisia, Egypt and Morocco. In this chapter, we investigate whether women's numerical increase in MENA's legislatures has

---

Electronic supplementary material The online version of this chapter (https://doi.org/10.1007/978-3-030-27735-2_9) contains supplementary material, which is available to authorized users.

M. Shalaby (✉)
University of Wisconsin, Madison, WI, USA

L. Elimam
Rice University's Baker Institute for Public Policy, Houston, TX, USA

© The Author(s) 2020
H. Darhour and D. Dahlerup (eds.), *Double-Edged Politics on Women's Rights in the MENA Region*, Gender and Politics, https://doi.org/10.1007/978-3-030-27735-2_9

led to more power and influence for women by focusing on female deputies' membership and leadership of legislative committees in a case with a long period of sustainable female political representation: Jordan. While previous work has found that women are generally sidelined to committees that deal with social and/or women's issues (Shalaby and Elimam 2017, 2019), especially when they are newcomers to the decision-making process, no work has simultaneously explored women's leadership of legislative committees (i.e., vertical segregation) and membership in committees (i.e., horizontal segregation) in MENA. Our goal in this chapter is to bridge this important gap and explicate variations in women's membership and leadership of legislative committees in Jordan since the introduction of the gender quota in 2003.

On the one hand, extant literature on females' political representation in the MENA has mostly focused on the cultural, institutional, and structural impediments to women's access to power (Moghadam 2014; Dahlerup 2009; Amawi 2007; Sabbagh 2007; Abou-Zeid 1998); however, research has been scarce when it comes to their roles in the policy-making process. On the other hand, research on the inner dynamics of Arab parliaments and the role played by legislators within these legislative bodies has predominantly emphasized the "patronage" role of these institutions, with many scholars arguing that these legislatures exist to bolster the survival of the incumbent regimes (Sassoon 2016; Blaydes 2010; Sater 2009; Geddes 2005) and/or distribute rents to the regime's close allies.

Notwithstanding the contribution of this research, it falls short of exploring the compositional arrangements and power dynamics within legislative bodies in transitioning and authoritarian contexts. Scholars have shown that legislatures and parties can play an important monitoring role within dictatorships by questioning ministers (Malesky and Schuler 2010), and blocking the implementation of regime-backed policies and/or laws (Gandhi 2009: 109). Research has also shown that opposition parties can play an integral part in influencing the policymaking process under autocratic rule (Loidolt and Mecham 2016; Gandhi and Przeworski 2006); yet, we continue to know very little about the inner dynamics and the role of legislators within these bodies, especially women. Focusing on the lower chamber in Jordan between 2003 and 2018, we find that women tend to be horizontally segregated (i.e., concentrated in committees according to policy areas). Our data also demonstrate that women continue to be vertically segregated (i.e., less likely to assume committee leadership positions).

This study contributes to the literature on women's political representation in authoritarian regimes. It offers one of the first systematic insights on women's representation in Arab parliaments by examining women's committee assignments and leadership. (To our knowledge, no studies have addressed committee assignments—or female committee leadership—in the MENA region.) It also contributes to the literature on electoral institutions under authoritarianism by presenting analyses on the roles played by female legislators within these settings and paves the way for further scholarship on the topic.

WOMEN IN LEGISLATIVE COMMITTEES WORLDWIDE

Legislative committees have been studied extensively in developed and developing democracies due to their centrality to the decision-making process (Towns 2003). Committees are important because of the benefits accrued by legislators in terms of career advancement and access to resources (Schwindt-Bayer 2010; Heath et al. 2005; Cox and McCubbins 2005; Krehbiel et al. 1987; Fenno 1973). Committee assignments are also significant for gaining political expertise and closer access to high-level government officials.

Studies analyzing women's legislative committees' assignments and leadership positions in the US, Europe, and Latin America, have produced mixed results (Baekgaard and Kjaer 2012; Schwindt-Bayer 2010; Childs and Krook 2009; Carroll 2008; Beckwith 2007; Heath et al. 2005; Frisch and Kelly 2003; Towns 2003; Yule 2000; Darcy 1996; Kathlene 1994; Thomas and Welch 1991; Skjeie 1991). While some scholars have found evidence relating to gender differences, others assert that these variations are simply attributable to preferences as opposed to discrimination and/or supply versus demand.

For instance, Baekgaard and Kjaer (2012) consider the nature as well as source of gendered segregation in committee assignments in 98 Danish municipalities. The authors find that female legislators hold more seats in the children committees and fewer assignments in the finance and technical committees, but assert that this is driven by supply or preference as opposed to discrimination. Other scholars have also found that women are overrepresented on committees associated with welfare issues (Thomas and Welch 1991), health and education (Darcy 1996), and social affairs (Skjeie 1991), and make similar conclusions about female preferences over discrimination. Thomas and Welch (1991) find that women are more often represented on committees dealing with welfare matters compared to men in state legislative assemblies, but they attribute this to preferences. Their conclusions are echoed by Carroll's (2008) study on committee assignments in Congress, who likewise points to preferences or the supply-side of committee selection as opposed to demand. Skjeie (1991) also finds clear distinctions between the committee memberships of men and women in the Norwegian parliament but concludes that there is no evidence of marginalization. Rather, these patterns are a result of legislators' stated committee preferences, with significantly more women expressing interest in social affairs.

Another strand of research focuses on discrimination, with evidence pointing to the sidelining of women with committee assignments based on the horizontal division of labor (i.e., type of committee assignments), and in some cases, the vertical division of labor (i.e., leadership). For example, Towns (2003) finds that women are more frequently assigned to committees associated with social welfare in her study on the Swedish and Norwegian assemblies. Yule (2000) also analyzes vertical and horizontal segregation among the Conservative and Labor parties in two local authorities in the United Kingdom. Exploring vertical segregation, Yule (2000) finds that women in the Conservative party—despite facing greater backlash in comparison with those in the Labor party—hold a considerable number of leadership positions in one authority, which she attributes to the larger number of seats the party holds. When examining horizontal segregation, gendered stereotypes dictate women's (choice of and) assignments to committees in both parties, with women seen as experts in education and social services (Yule 2000).

These conclusions are largely consistent with findings on female marginalization in non-Western contexts (Schwindt-Bayer 2010; Heath et al. 2005). Heath et al. (2005) argue that female committee assignments tend to adhere to the vertical and horizontal divisions of labor in six Latin American legislatures. They find that women are excluded from "influential" committees and placed in social and women's issues committees. Their findings also demonstrate a positive relationship between increased proportion of women in the chamber, and vertical and horizontal discrimination. Likewise, Schwindt-Bayer (2010) finds that female legislators are more likely to be on committees associated with "compassion" issues and underrepresented in committees that yield the greatest power in Argentina, Colombia, and Costa Rica. Female leadership roles in legislatures is significantly low, particularly in the role of chamber president, with more females in the vice president and secretary positions. Meanwhile, Aparicio and Langston (2009) find that women or freshman legislators were more likely to serve on so-called burden committees in the Mexican Chamber of Deputies from 1997 until 2006.

In this chapter, we focus on exploring the membership and leadership of women in legislative committees (i.e., the horizontal and vertical segregation, respectively). Yule (2000) defines vertical division of labor/segregation in terms of the leadership roles acquired by female representatives, while the horizontal division of labor refers to committee membership that is defined by overrepresentation of men or women in certain policy areas, typically regarded as those associated with male or female domains. Explicating both the vertical and horizontal divisions of labor provides an excellent framework for assessing the nature and scope of female committee membership and leadership in the MENA region. It allows us to better understand not only the leadership roles women play in these contexts, but also the nature of legislative roles they assume.

Women in Legislative Committees in MENA

In contrast to the extensive literature on female committee assignments in the US, Europe, and Latin America, studies on the MENA are scarce. Our goal is to assess the presence and leadership of female legislators across different legislative committees. Extant literature emphasizes that once women are elected to higher echelons of power, they are often denied access to powerful positions by their male counterparts (Randall 1987) and/or sidelined to committees deemed by their male counterparts as more aligned with their feminine concerns and interests.

These findings are consistent with more recent feminist scholarship on the 'gendered' nature of political institutions and the call for a thorough analysis of the processes within these legislatures that produce and create a gender division of labor (Towns 2003). As maintained by Acker (1990, 1992), gendered norms can be institutionalized and reproduced in political organizations. Gendered institutions refer to the presence of gender in the processes, practices, images and ideologies, and distributions of power in the various sectors of social life. Furthermore, gender is continually produced in these contexts rather than being stable, static and fully formed prior to women's entry to the workplace and/or political institutions (Kenney 1996). As a result, women are more likely to face varying levels of discrimination and hostility once they enter these male-dominated realms (Yoder 1991); however, it remains unclear how and when these conditions change from one setting to another.

The dynamics of female appointments across different legislative committees shed an important light on the 'gendered' nature of political institutions. Work on committee assignments across different parts of the world has shown varying degrees of horizontal segregation along gender lines. More so, we are only aware of a handful of studies on women's vertical segregation in legislative committees. While the determinants of such segregation are still a bone of contention among gender and legislative politics scholars, work has consistently shown that women have limited access to some of the most-coveted committees and tend to be concentrated within narrow policy areas deemed by party and/or parliament leaders as most appropriate to their roles and interests. Furthermore, former studies, including our own research, have shown that a substantial increase in female descriptive representation—mostly because of quota adoption—may create a backlash effect (see Darhour, Chapter 11) that becomes evident in the way party and legislative leaders assign committee appointments. Focusing on the MENA region, our previous work on the determinants of female membership in legislative committees in five countries across two decades demonstrates that women are substantively marginalized from influential and other male-dominated committees (Shalaby and Elimam 2017, 2019). We find that while increasing the number of women in MENA's parliaments may produce a backlash effect, they tend to be less marginalized from influential committee positions over time—especially when there is a quota system in place. Our work also shows that female legislators' political expertise matters when it comes to access to important committee assignments.

This chapter builds on our work on the dynamics of women's membership in legislative committees as we are keen to investigate the composition and leadership of committees by gender, with a focus on whether female legislators are less likely to access leadership positions. We test *three main hypotheses* in this chapter:

H1: We expect to find systematic horizontal gender/sex segregation among the members of different committees according to policy issue area.
H2: We expect to find women to be under-represented in the top leadership positions in legislative committees.
H3: We expect to find systematic gender difference in leadership positions according to the policy issue areas (portfolio) of the committees.

Case Selection, Data and Methodology

The Case of Jordan: Political Context and Female Political Representation

Jordan is a hereditary monarchy currently rated as 'partly free' (Freedom House 2018). Legislative life in Jordan was revived in the early 1980s when the three-decade imposition of martial law was lifted. King Hussein recalled the Jordanian Parliament, which ushered in a brief period of political liberalization that also witnessed the proliferation of civil society organizations and the revival of electoral politics in Jordan where women could exercise their full political and legal rights in voting and running for office.

Since independence from British rule, the Jordanian legislative system has had two branches: the Chamber of Notables (Majlis al-Ayan) and the House of Representatives (Majlis al-Newab). In this study, we focus on the Lower House, whose members are directly elected, and which is considered as one of the region's influential legislatures. The parliament has played an important role since the re-introduction of parliamentary elections in 1989 (Lust-Okar 2006). Despite the limited legislative power of its members, it is the sole legislative body that has the authority to monitor the activities of the government and the implementation of laws and policies (Gandhi 2009). To achieve their monitoring role, MPs pose thousands of oral and written questions/queries to government officials, ministers and even the prime minister. While MPs tend to avoid issues that may destabilize or embarrass the King and the ruling family, MPs have been very active debating issues relating to the economy, Arab-Israeli relations, employment and minority rights.[1]

Political parties are considerably fragmented and play a meager role in the Jordanian electoral realm. The Islamists (mainly the Islamic Action Front), whose electoral participation has oscillated over the past two decades, represent the main opposition faction to the regime and are deemed the only structured party in the country. Parliamentary blocs are typically formed after the conclusion of the elections with little or no shared policy and ideological interests among members. Representatives frequently switch their bloc affiliations throughout the session, usually to gain a more advantageous position within the assembly. As a result, there is little consistency in MPs' political parties' affiliation and blocs membership (Detailed information is in the appendix).

Focusing on female political representation, Jordanian women have had the right to vote and run for elections since 1974; however, it was not until 1993 that three women competed in elections, and only one woman succeeded. In 1997, 17 women ran for elections, but none won. In response to the inability of female candidates to get elected—coupled with mounting pressure from international donors, women's movements,[2] and activists—a 16-member committee was tasked with studying the applicability of the quota system in the Jordanian context. A few months later, the recommendations of the committee led to the formulation of the 2003 Election Law Number 11.[3] According to the amended law, six seats were reserved for women regardless of the geographical distribution or electoral district (Abu Rumman 2003). Five of the six female parliamentarians ran as independents and were mainly backed by their tribes and local communities, while one female candidate, Hayat Musaymi, was a member of the Islamic Action Front (IAF) (Al-Attiyat 2005).

During the 2007 elections, women retained the six quota seats acquired in 2003 and one female MP[4] managed to win a district seat through competition (Table 9.1). Most of the female candidates running in the 2007 elections were also independents. Six of the seven elected women won quota seats, while Falak Jamani won a seat for the district of Madaba for the first time in Jordanian parliamentary elections since 1993.

The 2010 parliamentary elections took place under the new temporary election law of 2010. This election witnessed the introduction of six additional quota seats for women (increasing the quota from 6 to 12 seats) for an increase in total seats from 110 to 120 seats. Likewise, most of the female candidates were independents (IPU 2018). The election was boycotted by the IAF in response to Law No. 9 passed by the monarchy in 2009 which resulted in the absence of female candidates from the Islamist front. Despite this, Wafaa Bani Mustafa, an Islamist, ran as an independent and successfully secured a quota seat (Ryan 2010). Meanwhile, Abla Abu Elbah of the leftist Jordanian People's Democratic Party (Hashed) won a quota seat for Amman, and Nariman al-Rusan, who was re-elected in both the 2007 and 2010 assemblies, joined the centrist National Current party in 2010 (Jordan Politics 2019). Most notable about this election were the gains of Salma al-Rabdi and Maysar al-Sardiyah. Salma won a gender quota seat in Ajloun, becoming the first Christian woman to ever serve in the parliament, while Maysar was

Table 9.1 Female representation in Jordan (2003–2018)

Legislative session and number of terms	Size of chamber	Percentage and number of female MPs	Quota provisions
14th Legislature 2003–2007 (four terms)	110	5.5 (6)	Amendment to Article 11 of the 2001 Electoral Law introducing Female Quota; +6 seats
15th Legislature 2007–2010 (two terms)	110	6.4 (7)	No change
16th Legislature 2010–2013 (two terms)	120	10.8 (13)	Temporary Electoral Law No. 9; +6 seats (12 seats)
17th Legislature 2013–2016 (three terms)	150	12.0 (18)	New Election Law; +3 seats (15 seats)
18th Legislature 2016–present (three terms)	130	15.4 (20)	Election Law maintains women's quota at 15 seats

Source Jordan (2016), Inter-parliamentary Union. http://archive.ipu.org/parline/reports/2163_A.htm. Accessed 10 November 2018

elected as a quota candidate in the Northern Badia district, becoming the first Bedouin woman in the assembly (Ryan 2010). One female, Reem Badran, successfully won a general district seat for the third time in Jordan.

In 2012, King Abdullah dissolved the parliament and a new election law was introduced in response to the Arab Uprisings. The IAF once again boycotted the elections in opposition to the modified electoral law. Notably, the electoral changes[5] increased the women's quota, from 12 to 15 seats, to include three Bedouin districts.[6] Fifteen females acquired the reserved quota seats, and three women succeeded in winning district seats. Following the implementation of the mixed electoral system in the 2013 elections, two women won their seats under the single nontransferable vote (SNTV) system,[7] while Rula Al Hurub, won a seat under PR, the national party-list election, and was the only female candidate affiliated with a political party to win a district seat (the Stronger Jordan Party). Maryam al-Lawzi and Wafaa Bani Mustafa also managed to win two district seats running as independents. Insaf al-Khawaldah, from the district of Tafileh, joined the Islamic Centrist Party (ICP) and won a quota seat. In addition, Na'yim al-'Ayadat, from Amman, and Najah al-Azzah, from Jerash, who were members of the National Current party and Jordanian National Union party, respectively, won two gender quota seats.

The 2016 elections took place under a new electoral law and witnessed the participation of the Islamic Action Front. Women's political representation continued to surge with 20 female deputies holding seats in the Jordanian Lower House. Five women managed to win district seats in addition to the fifteen quota seats (Table 9.1). The parliament currently includes three female legislators who are members of the Islamist party (IAF). The three Islamist MPs are Dima Tahboub, Huda al-'Atum, and Hayat Musaymi, who was in the 2003 legislature. Al-'Atum won her seat through competition while Tahboub and Musaymi won gender quota seats. Four additional females managed to win district seats, including Faddiya Abu Qaddura (ICP), Randa al-Sha'ar, Sabah al-Sha'ar, and Safaa al-Mumni. Other women who had party affiliations were Insaf al-Khawaldah (formerly a member of the Islamist Centrist Party in 2013) and Shaha al-'Ammarin, both members of the Jordanian National Union Party.

Data and Methodology

The original dataset on legislators' individual characteristics, committee membership, and leadership was collected, translated and coded by the authors. We relied on primary materials obtained from the Jordanian Lower House as well as the committees' documentation available in Arabic on the parliament's website. Our dataset has five legislative sessions for Jordan, each of which ranges between two and four terms (see Table 9.1). It is important to note that committee membership and leadership change from one legislative term to the next. Because of the committee changes, we have included each legislator's committee assignment for each legislative term as an individual observation. As aforementioned, the number of legislative committees in the assemblies under study vary across time. In the 2007 and 2010 legislatures, there were a total of 16 standing and temporary committees, while in 2013 and 2016, that number went up to 20 standing committees. We have included only standing committees in our analysis (see note 13 for more information).

We manually coded the committee membership and leadership positions of individual legislators. Membership is coded as a dummy variable for membership in specific committee. For committee leadership, we coded them to include positions of the committee president, vice president (did not exist for Jordan's 2003, 2007 and 2010 legislatures), and secretary.[8] There were about 28 committee leadership positions in each of the legislative terms[9] for Jordan's 2003, 2007 and 2010 legislatures (14 committees with presidents and secretaries only).

In 2013 and 2016, there were about 60 committee leadership positions in each legislative round (20 committees with presidents, VPs and secretaries). Quantitative data were supplemented by one of the author's (Shalaby) extensive fieldwork and visits to the Jordanian Parliament. The author has also conducted numerous face-to-face interviews with female legislators, current and former MPs, parliamentary staff, and top officials. During these interviews, the author asked specific questions regarding the role of committees, the most-coveted committees, appointment procedures and whether women get the committee assignments they request. In the following section, we analyze the procedures relating to committees as well as the types of women's committee membership and leadership in the Jordanian Lower House.

Procedures of the Legislative Committees in Jordan
When it comes to the procedures for committee assignments, the rules regulating committee appointments are not publicly available, and in most cases, the by-laws are not institutionalized. MPs in Jordan typically state their committee preferences at the beginning of the legislative term, committee assignments are then determined by secret voting. Committee assignments do not strictly follow party and/or bloc affiliation given the absence of party systems and the fluidity of bloc membership in Jordan. Members' secret voting can be problematic for female MPs since males constitute the vast majority of the assembly without coherent party systems[10] to support equitable female representation on committee assignments and leadership.

Over the past decades, legislative committees within the lower chamber[11] have played an important role in formulating and discussing bills and policy proposals from the House and the King. The Financial committee, for instance, is responsible for setting the fiscal budget, government and ministries' spending and monitoring the implementation of the budget. The Palestine committee regulates relations with Israel and Palestinian refugees in Jordan. The Legal committee deals with studying legislation relating to issues such as election laws, constitutional amendments and laws regulating the internal rules of the legislature. There were 14 standing (permanent) committees in 2003, 2007 and 2010 with 11 members each.[12] In 2013—following the Arab Uprisings—the number of committees increased to 20, with the addition of committees on Integrity, Transparency and Fact Checking; Women and Family; Youth and Sports; and Structure and Behavior (see Table 9.1A for more details). Multiple committee memberships are allowed in Jordan; however, MPs are not allowed to join more than two permanent committees. Interestingly, almost 90% of females hold committee memberships. About 80% of female legislators have held two committee memberships in 2010, 2013, 2016. However, less than 10% hold more than two committee assignments (both permanent and temporary). From 2003 to 2016, there were 64 total women in the five parliamentary sessions.

Analysis

Women constituted about 5, 4 and 11% of all committees in 2003, 2007 and 2010, respectively (Table 9.2). In 2013, there were about 13% females across legislative committees, while in 2016 women constituted about 18% of committee memberships and leadership. The figures in Table 9.2 may signal that women's representation on committees in Jordan is proportional to their overall descriptive representation; however, these aggregated figures can be deceiving as they mask important variations relating to the type and role of females across committees. An issue that we will investigate in further detail in the following sections.

Female Committee Membership in Jordan: Horizontal Segregation?

We aim in this section to test our *first hypothesis* regarding the presence of horizontal gender/sex segregation among the members of different committees according to policy issue area. Table 9.3 displays the numbers of female executives and members from 2003 to 2018 in seven committees: Legal; Financial and Economic; Education, General Freedoms and Human Rights; Culture and Youth; Health and Environment; Labor and Social Development; and Women and Family. However, the committee on Women and the Family did not exist until 2013. Importantly, the overall percentage of females in the assembly is subtracted from the committee proportions to determine whether female members are over or underrepresented vis-à-vis their total representation in the assembly (Murray and Sénac 2018). This is displayed in the "over/under" row, where a negative number means that female members' representation is below their total proportion in the assembly, and a

Table 9.2 Women in committees in Jordan (2003–2018)

Legislative session	Number of committees (permanent)	Percent females in assembly	Women as share of all committee memberships and leadership (average across terms)	Average number of women in all committees (average across terms; rounded up)
2003	14	5.5 (6)	4.8	7
2007	14	6.4 (7)	4.0	6
2010	14	10.8 (13)	10.9	17
2013	20	12.0 (18)	13.5	28
2016	20	15.4 (20)	18.0	38

Source Based on authors' calculations. Data acquired from the Jordan Parliament (2017), *The Hashemite Kingdom of Jordan: The Parliament*. http://parliament.jo/. Accessed December 2018

positive number means that women are overrepresented on this committee (Murray and Sénac 2018).

A closer look at female committee membership lends evidence to our *first hypothesis*. Female legislators are underrepresented in committees dealing with Legal; General Freedoms and Human Rights; Investment (not shown in Table 9.3); and Financial and Economic issues. For instance, only four women (out of 120 available committee slots for members) managed to acquire membership in the Financial and Economic committee over the past 15 years (Table 9.3). However, it is important to note that over time, women are able to gain more access to some of the most-coveted committees, such as the Legal and General Freedoms committees. This is consistent with our previous work explicating the effect of quota duration—as well as female legislators' political expertise—on women's access to male-dominated committees in Arab legislatures (Shalaby and Elimam, Forthcoming). Table 9.3 also shows that female legislators are noticeably concentrated across committees dealing with social issues, such as Education, Culture and Youth; Labor and Social Development; and Women and Family. Interestingly, female legislators have been significantly overrepresented in the Education, Culture and Youth committee, where they held 30 seats (out of the 120 available committee slots for members) or 25% of committee seats, since the introduction of the quota in 2003. While looking at aggregate data in Table 9.2 may denote that women are equally represented in legislative committees, a more detailed analysis of the nature of their membership does not seem to support this assumption.

Table 9.3 Female committee memberships in Jordan House of Representatives (2003–2018)

Year and percentage of women in assembly	Level	Legal	Financial and economic	General freedoms and rights	Education, culture and youth	Health and environment	Labor and social development	Women and family (2013, 2016)
2003 5.5% (4 terms)	Executives[a]	0/8	0/8	0/8	0/8	2/8	0/8	NA
	Members[b]	2/36	0/36	3/36	5/36	4/35	2/36	
	Total[c] (%)	4.5	0	6.8	11.4	14.0	4.5	
	Over/Under (%)	−0.95	−5.45	1.35	5.95	8.55	−0.95	
2007 6.4% (2 terms)	Executives	0/4	0/4	0/4	0/4	0/4	1/4	NA
	Members	0/18	0/18	0/18	2/18	0/18	3/16	
	Total (%)	0	0	0	9.1	0	20.0	
	Over/Under (%)	−6.36	−6.36	−6.36	2.74	−6.36	13.64	
2010 10.8% (2 terms)	Executives	1/4	0/4	1/4	2/4	0/4	2/4	NA
	Members	1/18	3/18	1/17	2/18	0/18	3/18	
	Total (%)	9.1	13.64	9.5	18.2	0	22.7	
	Over/Under (%)	−1.73	2.81	−1.33	7.37	−10.83	11.87	
2013 12.0% (3 terms)	Executives	1/9	3/9	2/8	4/9	0/8	1/9	8/8
	Members	2/24	1/24	1/24	8/24	2/23	3/21	14/18
	Total (%)	9.1	12.1	9.4	36.4	9.7	13.3	84.6
	Over/Under (%)	−2.9	0.1	−2.6	24.4	−2.3	1.3	72.6
2016 15.4% (3 terms)	Executives	2/9	0/9	2/9	3/9	1/9	0/9	9/9
	Members	3/24	0/24	3/24	13/23	3/24	4/22	17/23
	Total (%)	15.2	0	15.2	50.0	12.1	12.9	81.3
	Over/Under	−0.18	−15.38	−0.18	34.62	−3.28	−2.48	65.92

[a]Female executives/leadership include presidents, vice presidents, and secretaries
[b]Membership is calculated based on the number of female members out of total number of members. For instance, women assumed two out of the eight available leadership positions in the Legal committee in 2003. Female and total membership are averaged across terms since each legislative session in our data contains two, three, or four terms
[c]The percentage of total female executives and members in each committee is a proportion of the total—both male and female—members in the committee
Source Based on authors' calculations. Data acquired from the Jordan Parliament (2017), *The Hashemite Kingdom of Jordan: The Parliament*. http://parliament.jo/. Accessed December 2018

Female Committee Leadership in Jordan: Vertical Segregation?

Focusing on women's vertical division of labor in Jordan and to test our *second hypothesis*, an aggregate analysis of women's committee leadership assignments shows that few women assume top leadership positions. Since the introduction of the quota system in 2003, only 13 women assumed the presidential role of six different committees (Table 9.4). In contrast, the vice-president (VP) and secretary positions were considerably more open and accessible to female deputies. Since the introduction of the VP position in 2013, 16 women acquired 25 positions, 12 of which were in 2013 and 13 in 2016. Similarly, women gained easier access to secretary positions. Over the past three legislative sessions (2010, 2013, 2016), 27 women acquired about 38 secretary positions (Table 9.4). As maintained by a prominent female legislator who served in the lower chamber for three consecutive terms: "they [male legislators] give us vice president positions very easily. You can see that they give away the vice presidencies or secretaries [of committees] as exit rewards. Even though in many situations, it's not really about the qualifications [of the female MPs]."

Figure 9.1 presents the distribution of female committee presidents, VPs, and secretaries across the five legislative sessions. The figure shows

Table 9.4 Summary of female committee leadership positions in Jordan's House of Representatives

Year	1st term	2nd term	3rd term	4th term
2003	6 MPs (none)	6 MPs (2 Secretaries)	6 MPs (1 Secretary, 1 President)	6 MPs (2 Secretaries)
2007	7 MPs (1 Secretary)	7 MPs (none)	NA	NA
2010	13 MPs (4 Secretaries)	13 MPs (3 Secretaries, 1 President)	NA	NA
2013	18 MPs (7 Secretaries, 2 VPs, 3 Presidents)	18 MPs (3 Secretaries, 6 VPs, 2 Presidents)	18 MPs (4 Secretaries, 4 VPs, 3 Presidents)	NA
2016	20 MPs (7 Secretaries, 4 VPs, 1 President)	20 MPs (5 Secretaries, 4 VPs, 1 President)	20 MPs (5 Secretaries, 5 VPs, 1 President)	NA

Note For details regarding names of MPs, district, committee leadership details, and education, please see Table 9.2A in the Appendix
Source Based on authors' calculations. Data acquired from the Jordan Parliament (2017), *The Hashemite Kingdom of Jordan: The Parliament.* http://parliament.jo/. Accessed December 2018

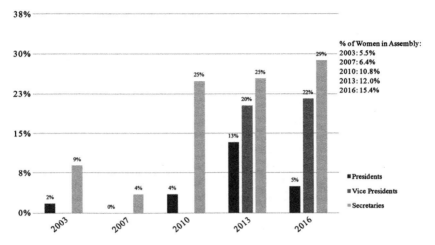

Source Data acquired from the Jordan Parliament (2017). *The Hashemite Kingdom of Jordan: The Parliament.* http://parliament.jo/. Accessed December 2018

Fig. 9.1 Percent female committee leadership positions compared to total leadership (average across terms)

the percentage of female committee leaders relative to the total number of leaders averaged across the legislative terms in each session. As aforementioned, most leadership positions held by women are in secretary and VP positions, while fewer women hold presidential positions. There was only one female president in 2003 compared to five women in secretary positions. In 2007, there were no female presidents and only one female secretary during the entire session.

In 2010, female leadership increased slightly during the second term, where females made up 4% of committee presidents in the assembly. This figure translates to one female president out of 28 total presidential positions during this session, which is significantly lower than their overall representation of 10.83%. The percentage of female presidents increased significantly during the 2013 assembly, where women held 13% of presidential positions, during the three terms. This surge is partly driven by the addition of six new committees. During that session, the number of standing committees increased from 14 to 20, along with the addition of the committee on Women and Family, which has been consistently presided over by a female legislator. What is also remarkable about the

2013 legislature is that it was the first session after the onset of the Arab Uprisings and sweeping protests throughout the region. The 2013 session was summoned amidst promises from the ruling regime of genuine reforms, social justice, and the protection of personal and public freedoms, which led to the establishment of committees dealing with transparency, integrity, human rights and women's issues. This session also witnessed the victory of powerful progressive female legislators, such as Rula al-Hurub and Hind al-Fayez, and the Islamist party (IAF) boycott of the elections. Unfortunately, these figures drop once again in 2016, where women make up only 5% of total committee presidents; which translates to one female president out of 20 presidential positions per term. A percentage that is much below their current representation in the assembly, which is 15%.

In contrast, the proportion of female VP and secretary positions has increased over time (Fig. 9.1). Female deputies are significantly overrepresented in these positions compared to their overall representation in the parliament. Women made up 25% of secretary positions in the 2010 legislature. In 2013, though women hold more presidential positions, their representation in secretary positions is still greater at 25%. In 2016, despite being underrepresented in presidential positions, women are significantly overrepresented in the VP and secretary positions, where they hold 22 and 29% of positions, respectively. These results lend support to our second hypothesis regarding vertical segregation of female legislators in Jordan's lower chamber over the past decades. We end our discussion by focusing on the gender-related difference in leadership positions according to the policy issue areas of the committees.

Female Committee Leadership Across Policy Areas

Particularly, we aim in this section to test our *third hypothesis* and assess the relationship between the portfolio of the committee and female leadership positions. Relying on data from Tables 9.3 and 9.2A (see Supplementary material) and our interview data, we find similar patterns concerning women's horizontal segregation across committees in the Jordanian context. For instance, six out of the thirteen female presidents held leadership over the Women and Family committees. Since their establishment in 2013, these committees consistently had female presidents, VPs and secretaries (Table 9.2A). As stated by one female MP referring to the current parliament: "So, for example, in the current parliament, this is the second parliamentary term where no woman holds the presidency of a committee except of the women's committee. That's it, nothing else. And of course, the women's committee does not have any male members except for one man, and he's the one who repeatedly insisted on entering it and he comes from a leftist background. This is really a problem!".

Furthermore, although women have been in the Parliament since 2003, only one woman—Falak Jamani—held the presidential role in the Health and Environment committee in 2003, while two other women were secretaries for the National Direction and Health and Environment committees. In 2007, there was not a single female committee president and only one female MP was a secretary for the Labor and Social Development committee out of the seven women elected to Parliament (see Executives' row in Table 9.3). Remarkably, Abla Abu Elbah managed to become the president of the Freedom and Citizens' Rights committee in 2010, which is considered an influential committee in the Lower House. Nevertheless, despite Elbah's distinguished career as the first ever Secretary General of the leftist party—Hashed—and one of the founders of the Jordanian Women's Union, she was only able to retain her role as committee president for one legislative term (Table 9.2A). Since the positions of committee VP as well as the women's issues committees were not introduced until 2013, five women were secretaries for the Labor and Social Development; Education, Culture and Youth; National Direction; and the Countryside and the Desert committees. For the first time ever, a female MP—Wafaa Bani Mustafa—managed to assume the secretary role for the Legal committee, which is deemed as one of the most coveted committees.

In 2013, there was a substantial increase in female political representation as well as in their committee leadership positions as previously explained. Sixteen out of the 18 MPs in Jordan's 2013 legislature assumed one leadership role, either president, VP or Secretary. For the first time ever, women managed to secure eight top leadership positions. Three women were the presidents of the newly established Youth and Sports; Women and Family Affairs, and National Direction the Media committees. Wafaa Bani Mustafa, a well-established lawyer who was re-elected in 2013, was the president of the newly established committee on Structure and Behavior for two legislative terms. Rula al-Hurub, the only female in the 2013 legislature running on a party ticket, was the president of the committee of Freedoms and Citizens' Rights for the second time in the Parliament's history. There were also 12 VP positions assumed by female MPs over the three legislative terms. Hind al-Fayez was the VP for the newly established committee on Integrity, Transparency and Fact-checking for two legislative terms. The other VP positions were predominantly for the Women and Family committee and other social issues committees, such as Youth and Sports; Tourism and Monuments, and Education and Culture (Table 9.2A). Women leaders were more evenly distributed across different types of committees. As shown in Table 9.2A, women were assigned the secretary positions in the Agriculture and Irrigation; Finance; Tourism and Monuments; Economy and Investment; Palestine; Education and Culture; and Women and Family committees.

Unfortunately, the upward trend observed in 2013 did not continue in the 2016 legislature. Out of the twenty women elected to the Parliament, only one MP—Reem Abu Dalbuh—a prominent lawyer with a long history of public service, managed to maintain her leadership of the Women and Family committee for three consecutive legislative terms. Nine female MPs assumed 13 VP positions, most of which were dealing with women (3x), and social issues, such as, Education and Culture (2x); National Direction and the Media (2x); Transportation; and the Countryside and the Desert (2x). Only two females were VPs for two technical committees: Foreign Affairs; and Integrity, Transparency, and Fact-checking. Like the 2013 legislature, we observe more women in secretary positions (17 positions total) and greater access to a wider array of committees. For instance, there were female committee secretaries for Women and Family (3x), and Education and Culture; Health and Environment; Tourism and Monuments; and National Direction and the Media. There were also female secretaries for other committees, such as the Administrative (2x); Freedoms and Citizens' Rights (2x); Integrity, Transparency, and Fact-checking; Legal; Foreign Affairs; Economy and Investment; and the Countryside and the Desert (2x).

These findings lend partial evidence to our third hypothesis relating to women's committee leadership positions. We observe significant gender differences between the portfolio of the committee and female leadership positions; however, these differences are conditional on the level of women's committee leadership. Female deputies manage to access a wide array of committee leadership positions, mostly as secretaries and vice presidents. However, there is a clear division of labor when it comes to women's top leadership of committees. Not only do they have fewer committee presidential positions compared to their overall representation in the legislature (Fig. 9.1), but female legislators also tend to preside over Women and Family and other social issues committees, such as Health and Environment, National Direction and the Media, and Youth and Sports.

Finally, another interesting finding in this section, clearly evident in 2013 with the introduction of six new legislative committees, is that male legislators are more likely to give away leadership roles in newly established committees to female legislators. While the spike in female committee leadership in 2013 can be partly attributed to the Arab Uprisings effect, it is important to note that seventeen out of the total 34 female leadership positions (50%) were within newly established committees. By 2016, when male legislators became more familiar with these committees and their roles, they are not as easily accessible to women deputies; hence, the noticeable decline in their committee leadership in 2016 compared to 2013 (Fig. 9.1). This is an interesting phenomenon worthy of further research.

Conclusion

This chapter offers one of the first systematic analyses of female committee membership and leadership under authoritarianism. The analysis delves deeper into female representation beyond simply examining their increasing numbers in MENA parliaments and uncovers important patterns of female vertical and horizontal segregation in the Jordanian parliament. Assessing women's vertical (i.e., leadership), and horizontal (i.e., membership in committees dealing with specific policy areas) divisions in the Jordanian parliament from 2003 to 2018, this study sheds an important light on the dynamics of female representation under authoritarianism and speaks directly to existing literature on women's roles within legislatures across different parts of the world.

To summarize, we find evidence for horizontal gender segregation across policy issues. Women deputies are concentrated across women, family and other social issues committees. Furthermore, women are consistently underrepresented in the Legal, General Freedoms and Human Rights, Financial and Economic committees. Likewise, there is clear vertical segregation, where women are underrepresented in top leadership positions. Indeed, female representatives most commonly hold VP and secretary positions as opposed to presidential positions, where they make up a modest proportion (with the exception to the 2013 legislature). Finally, our data demonstrates partial evidence regarding female vertical segregation relating to policy area. Female committee presidents are increasingly concentrated in committees dealing with women, family and other social issues. Only few female deputies managed to secure leadership positions of highly coveted committees since the introduction of gender quota, such as the Public Freedoms and Citizens' Rights and Legal committees.

In conclusion, this study contributes to the comparative politics of gender and institutions literature and paves the way for future research on women's legislative roles in non-democratic contexts. Most importantly, this research speaks directly to the issue of gender imbalance in leadership positions as it highlights the ways power relations are structured, and even transformed, in autocratic settings. Further research is needed to examine whether the results found in Jordan are present in other contexts throughout the MENA, with particular attention paid to countries that similarly have a dynamic legislature and a long and sustainable history of female representation, such as Algeria, Morocco, and, more recently, Tunisia.

Notes

1. Based on author's parliamentary database.
2. The establishment of the Jordanian National Commission for Women (JNCW) in 1992—under the auspices of Princess Basma—marks one of the most significant milestones of women's success in the political arena. The JNCW's main goals were to promote women's issues and to integrate women into the decision-making arena.
3. Law No. 11 of 2003 on women's parliamentary quota law: The Jordanian Parliament's official website, http://parliament.jo/.
4. Falak Jamani, who won a quota seat in 2003, succeeded in garnering support and competing in the 2007 elections to win a non-quota seat for the district of Madaba.
5. The Jordanian Parliament's official website, http://parliament.jo/.
6. The election commission calculates the percentage of votes obtained by total number of votes cast in their constituency; women with the highest percentage of votes are declared elected as long as no governorate obtains more than one reserved seat for women.
7. The first woman was Mariam Lozi (Amman, 5th District) who won 3631 votes, acquiring the most votes in a three-member district. The second

female who won under the SNTV system was Wafaa Bani Mustafa (Jarash North, 1st District), who won 3989 or 7.66% of the votes. Bani Mustafa occupied a quota seat in the 16th parliament.
8. The President of the committee is responsible for leading and scheduling the sessions, coordinating and running their proceedings, and representing and defending the decisions of the committee to the House. The Vice President is expected to do the same tasks if the committee president is absent. Finally, the secretaries are responsible for preparing and explaining the committee's reports as well as defending the committees' decisions to the House if asked to.
9. Note that because the number of terms in each session varies, the total number of leadership positions also varies. In 2003, the total number of terms were four, so there was a total of 56 presidential positions and 56 secretarial positions. Whereas in 2007, that number decreased to 28 presidential positions and 28 secretarial positions across two terms.
10. With exception to the Islamist party (Islamic Action Front), political parties play a meager role in the Jordanian electoral landscape, although they are permitted and have competed in elections for decades. Thus, the vast majority of candidates run as independents with no party affiliation. Legislators join a bloc after being elected to the assembly, and tend to change their affiliation several times throughout the session. Jordanian legislators do not join blocs based on shared ideology; rather, they join them to consolidate their positions within the assembly.
11. There are committees within the Upper House in Jordan (Senate), but we are only focusing on the Lower House in this chapter.
12. We excluded several cases of temporary and investigatory committees from our analysis for consistency and to ensure comparability of our results across sessions.

REFERENCES

Abou-Zeid, G. (1998). In search of political power: Women in parliament in Egypt, Jordan, and Lebanon. In A. Karam (Ed.), *Women in Parliament: Beyond numbers* (pp. 43–54). International Institute for Democracy and Electoral Assistance: Stockholm.

Abu Rumman, H. (2003). Qirra'a Awaliyya fil-Intikhabat al-Niyabiyya al-Urduniyya (A preliminary reading of Jordan's Parliamentary Elections). *Civil Society Issues*. Amman: New Jordan Center for Studies.

Acker, J. (1990). Hierarchies, jobs, bodies: A theory of gendered organizations. *Gender Society*, 4(2), 139–158.

Acker, J. (1992). The future of women and work: Ending the twentieth century. *Sociological Perspectives*, 35(1), 53–68.

Al-Attiyat, I. (2005). Participation in public life and its impact on women in Jordan. In N. H. Zander (Ed.), *Building democracy in Jordan: Women's political participation, political party life, and democratic elections* (pp. 25–66). IDEA: Stockholm.

Amawi, A. (2007). Against all odds: Women candidates in Jordanian elections. In V. M. Moghadam (Ed.), *From patriarchy to empowerment* (pp. 40–57). Syracuse: Syracuse University Press.

Aparicio, F. J., & Langston, J. (2009). *Committee leadership selection without seniority: The Mexican case* (Documento de Trabajo No. 217). Mexico City: CIDE.

Baekgaard, M., & Kjaer, U. (2012). The gendered division of labor in assignments to political committees: Discrimination or self-selection in Danish local politics? *Politics and Gender, 8*(4), 465–482.

Beckwith, K. (2007). Numbers and newness: The descriptive and substantive representation of women. *Canadian Journal of Political Science, 40*(1), 27–49.

Blaydes, L. (2010). *Elections and distributive politics in Mubarak's Egypt*. Cambridge: Cambridge University Press.

Carroll, S. J. (2008). Committee assignments: Discrimination or choice? In B. Reingold (Ed.), *Legislative women: Getting elected, getting ahead* (pp. 135–156). Lynne Rienner: Boulder, CO.

Childs, S., & Krook, M. L. (2009). Analysing women's substantive representation: From critical mass to critical actors. *Government and Opposition, 44*(2), 125–145.

Cox, G., & McCubbins, M. (2005). *Setting the agenda: Responsible party government in the U.S. House of Representatives*. Cambridge: Cambridge University Press.

Dahlerup, D. (2009). Women in Arab parliaments: Can gender quotas contribute to democratization? *Al-Raida, 126*(27), 2–38.

Darcy, R. (1996). Women in the state legislative power structure: Committee chairs. *Social Science Quarterly, 77*(4), 888–898.

Fenno, R. (1973). *Congressmen in Committees*. Boston: Little, Brown.

Freedom House. (2018). *Jordan*. https://freedomhouse.org/country/jordan. Accessed 10 November 2018.

Frisch, S. A., & Kelly, S. Q. (2003). A place at the table. *Women & Politics, 25*(3), 1–26.

Gandhi, J. (2009). *Political institutions under dictatorship*. Cambridge: Cambridge University Press.

Gandhi, J., & Przeworski, A. (2006). Cooperation, cooptation, and rebellion under dictatorships. *Economics and Politics, 18*(1), 1–26.

Geddes, B. (2005). *Why parties and elections in authoritarian regimes?* Paper presented at the American Political Science Association, Washington, DC.

Heath, R. M., Schwindt-Bayer, L., & Taylor-Robinson, M. M. (2005). Women on the sidelines: Women's representation on committees in Latin American legislatures. *American Journal of Political Science, 49*(2), 420–436.

Inter-Parliamentary Union. (2018). *Women in National Parliaments.* http://archive.ipu.org/wmn-e/world.htm. Accessed 10 November 2018.

Jordan Parliament. (2017). *The Hashemite Kingdom of Jordan: The Parliament.* http://parliament.jo/. Accessed December 2018.

Jordan Politics. (2019). *Nariman Ahmad Zuhair al-Rusan.* http://jordanpolitics.org. Accessed 11 June 2019.

Kathlene, L. (1994). Power and influence in state legislative policymaking: Interaction of gender and position in committee hearing debates. *American Political Science Review, 88*(3), 560–576.

Kenney, S. J. (1996). New research on gendered political institutions. *Political Research Quarterly, 49*(2), 445–466.

Krehbiel, K., Shepsle, K. A., & Weingast, B. R. (1987). Why are congressional committees powerful? *American Political Science Association, 81*(3), 925–945.

Loidolt, B., & Mecham, Q. (2016). Parliamentary opposition under hybrid regimes: Evidence from Egypt. *Legislative Studies Quarterly, 41*(4), 997–1022.

Lust-Okar, E. (2006). Elections under authoritarianism: Preliminary lessons from Jordan. *Democratization, 3*, 456–471.

Malesky, E., & Schuler, P. (2010). Nodding or needling: Analyzing delegate responsiveness in an authoritarian parliament. *American Political Science Review, 104*(3), 482–502.

Moghadam, V. (2014). Democratization and women's political leadership in North Africa. *Journal of International Affairs, 68*(1), 59–78.

Murray, R., & Sénac, R. (2018). Explaining gender gaps in legislative committees. *Journal of Women, Politics, and Policy, 39*(3), 310–355.

Randall, V. (1987). *Women and politic: An international perspective.* Chicago: The University of Chicago Press.

Ryan, C. R. (2010). Déjà vu all over again? Jordan's 2010 elections. *Foreign Policy.* https://foreignpolicy.com/2010/11/15/deja-vu-all-over-again-jordans-2010-elections/. Accessed 11 June 2019.

Sabbagh, A. (2007). Overview of women's political representation in the Arab region: Opportunities and challenges. *The Arab quota report: Selected case studies* (pp. 7–18). IDEA: Stockholm.

Sassoon, J. (2016). *Anatomy of authoritarianism in the Arab republics.* Cambridge: Cambridge University Press.

Sater, J. N. (2009). Parliamentary elections and authoritarian rule in Morocco. *The Middle East Journal, 63*(3), 381–400.

Schwindt-Bayer, L. A. (2010). *Political power and women's representation in Latin America.* New York: Oxford University Press.

Shalaby, M., & Elimam, L. (2017). *Arab women in the legislative process.* Carnegie Endowment for International Peace. http://carnegieendowment.org/sada/68780. Accessed 10 November 2018.

Shalaby, M., & Elimam, L. (Forthcoming). Women in legislative committees in Arab parliaments. *Journal of Comparative Politics.*

Skjeie, H. (1991). Rhetoric of difference: On women's inclusion into political elites. *Politics and Society, 19*(2), 233–263.

The Hashemite Kingdom of Jordan: The Parliament. (2018). http://Secretary.parliament.jo/. Accessed November 2018.

Thomas, S., & Welch, S. (1991). Impact of gender on activities and priorities of state legislators. *Western Political Science Association, 44*(2), 445–456.

Towns, A. (2003). Understanding the effects of larger ratios of women in national legislatures: Proportions and gender differentiation in Sweden and Norway. *Women & Politics, 25*(1), 1–29.

Yoder, J. D. (1991). Rethinking tokenism: Looking beyond numbers. *Gender and Society, 5*(2), 178–192.

Yule, J. (2000). Women councillors and committee recruitment. *Local Government Studies, 26*(3), 31–54.

CHAPTER 10

Empowering Young Women? Gender and Youth Quotas in Tunisia

Jana Belschner

INTRODUCTION

The Tunisian revolution in 2011 has gathered worldwide fame both as the trigger of multiple uprisings in the Arab world and as a revolution of the youth. Indeed, youth played a crucial role in the 2010/2011 events when they demonstrated all over the country against the authoritarian ruler Zine el-Abidine Ben Ali and the regime's inability to meet rising numbers of unemployment, the increasing costs of living, and a generally deteriorating economic situation (Gana 2013). Those socio-economic grievances were joined by political frustration with an authoritarian regime that severely restricted freedoms of opinion, expression, and assembly, and, at the same time, excluded large parts of the population from any form of political participation and representation (Collins 2011).

Subsequently, political participation and representation became key concerns of the newly elected National Constitutional Assembly (NCA) that was to draft a constitution for the new Tunisian Republic. Promoted by a highly active women's movement and a strong presence of

J. Belschner (✉)
University of Bergen, Bergen, Norway

international actors and donors in post-revolution Tunisia, the political representation of women was a prominent issue on the agenda. When the NCA finally adopted the new constitution in 2014, it included a provision for the adoption of a 50% gender parity quota for national elections. The quota requires that women candidates are given half of the positions on electoral lists, following a zipper-system. Incompliant lists are excluded from election. At the same time, but with less public attention and to some extent 'under the radar', the deputies voted for the introduction of a youth quota in the electoral code (Belschner 2018). The youth quota regulates that there must be one (male or female) candidate under 35 years among the first four candidates on each electoral list. If lists do not meet that requirement, they are still allowed to compete for election, but are deprived of 50% of their state reimbursement.

This chapter focuses on the intersectional effects of those paired quotas, by emphasizing the quotas' impact on the representation of gender and age groups in the Tunisian parliament. How are the quotas designed and implemented? How did they affect the shares of gender and age groups in the Tunisian parliament? How do they condition youth and women's substantive and symbolic representation?

I answer those questions based on a mixed-methods approach, combining an exploratory analysis of statistical data on MPs' gender and age with a qualitative analysis of their socio-economic backgrounds, their parliamentary participation, and their presence in inner-party and inner-parliamentarian leadership positions. In the first place, the analysis shows that the tandem quotas did lead to considerable increases in the share of young women MPs. Based on previous studies' assumptions about the intersectional effects of so-called tandem quotas for women and minorities (Bird 2016; Hughes 2011), I argue that this effect is related to the quotas' nested design. This makes it attractive for the political parties to nominate comparatively many young female candidates who can fulfill both quotas at a time. Thus, middle-aged men continue to form a stable majority in the parliament despite the double quotas. Comparing gender and age groups' socio-economic backgrounds and their patterns of parliamentary activity (presence in plenary sessions and committees, participation in votes, membership in committees), I find few significant differences between young men, young women, middle-aged women, and middle-aged men. However, leadership positions in the parliament and in the political parties are largely occupied by middle-aged men and some middle-aged women. I therefore conclude that, in the short-term, the over-representation of young women compared to middle-aged women may harm women's substantive representation, as the first are easier to sideline from power than the latter. Furthermore, the near absence of young men from parliament, who are commonly understood as those who drove the revolution, may also harm youth's symbolic representation.

The first section describes when, how, and why gender and youth quotas have been adopted in post revolution Tunisia. I continue by briefly reviewing the literature on electoral quotas' adoption and feedback effects in contexts of democratization. The following sections empirically examine the descriptive representation of gender and age groups in the Tunisian parliaments of 2011 and 2014. It follows an analysis of their rates of presence in plenary sessions, voting, and committees, as well their presence in inner-party and parliamentarian leadership positions in the current parliament. The conclusion sums up the empirical findings and indicates their relevance in a national and regional context of democratization triggered by youth-led uprisings.

The Tunisian Tandem Quotas for Women and Youth

On 14 January 2011, after weeks of ever-growing protests and demonstrations all over Tunisia, the authoritarian leader Ben Ali fled the country and the revolution succeeded. While the uprisings themselves were driven by remarkable shares of rural, often unemployed youth (Beissinger et al. 2015; Hoffman and Jamal 2012), the post-revolution democratization process has been conducted by a well-organized group of legal experts, civil society actors, international donors, and influential figures from the former political opposition (Gana 2013; Lieckefett 2012). In order to prepare the election of a Constitutional Assembly, the High Authority for the realization of the objectives of the revolution, for political reforms and democratic transition (HIROR), an interim government, was created in March 2011 (Zemni 2015). Subsequently, HIROR adopted a provisional electoral law for the election of the NCA that was to draw a new constitution and electoral law subsequently. One of the core features of the electoral law, beside the decision for a closed proportional representation (PR) list system, was the introduction of a parity gender quota. It requested the electoral lists to contain 50% male and female candidates and to place them alternately on the list positions (République Tunisienne 2011, Article 16). Interestingly, the law also contained a provision for youth representation, stating that "every list ensures that [at least one of] their candidates [...] is younger than 30 years old" (Article 33). However, whereas the gender quota was enforced by a list-rejection mechanism, no enforcement mechanism was added to the youth quota. At this stage, this provision was thus a pure recommendation.

In December 2011, the Tunisians eventually elected the NCA. The Islamist party Ennahdha won the majority of seats and formed a so-called Troika government with the secular parties CPR (Congrès pour la République, liberal) and Ettakatol (social-democratic). It took the NCA three years and four constitutional drafts, before eventually adopting the fifth and final version of the new constitution in January 2014. One of the most controversial issues during the drafting process had been the equality of men and women and particularly the question to what extent the parity regulation should be kept, weakened, or reinforced (Belschner 2018; Gray 2012). In summer 2012, Tunisia witnessed large-scale mobilization of the women's movement against the idea of the genders' 'complementarity' in the first constitutional draft, which was perceived as an attempt of Ennahdha to cut down on women's rights and gender equality (Charrad and Zarrugh 2014). The government eventually gave into the domestic and international pressures: The final version of the constitution does not only guarantee the protection of women's accrued rights, but also explicitly favors the retention of the parity gender-quota in elections. Article 34 states that "[...] the state seeks to guarantee women's representation in elected bodies" and article 46 concretizes that "the state works to attain parity between women and men in elected assemblies" (République Tunisienne 2014a).

After the adoption of the Constitution, the NCA had to draft and vote on a new national electoral law. Since gender parity had been constitutionally codified, the main discussions in the NCA regarding parity rather concerned the question of how exactly the quota should be designed and sanctioned. In the end, the deputies decided to keep the parity gender quota in the form that it had existed in the 2011 elections.

The idea of also introducing a youth quota first appeared on the agenda during the compilation of the electoral code (Belschner 2018). The constitution, quite explicit on the issue of parity, had a weaker reference to youths' political representation. Article 133 states that "the electoral code shall guarantee the representation of youth in local councils" (République Tunisienne 2014a). However, several propositions about how to guarantee youths' inclusion into the national parliament were discussed in the NCA. They varied from the obligation to have at least one youth in the first half of the electoral list to the adoption of a reserved seats quota.[1] Among the propositions that were finally voted on, the deputies favored a legislated candidate quota for (male and female) youth under 35 years of age, which requested the parties to place at least one young candidate among the first four positions on the electoral lists.[2] In case of non-compliance with the youth quota, the party in question loses half of its public indemnity amount (République Tunisienne 2014b, Article 25). The electoral code for local elections, adopted in 2017, reinforced both quotas and added a third quota for persons with disabilities (République Tunisienne 2017). However, in the following, this chapter will exclusively focus on quotas' working and effects on the national level, in particular in the legislative elections of 2014.

ELECTORAL QUOTAS IN A CONTEXT OF DEMOCRATIZATION

The progressive adoption of electoral quotas in Tunisia and their extension to other groups beyond women speak to two interrelated strands of the literature. The first is concerned with the question to what extent democratization is conductive for the adoption of equality policies, while the second examines more closely electoral quotas' implementation and the subsequent feedback effects on democratization processes (see Fig. 10.1).

Fig. 10.1 The interrelation between electoral quotas and democratization

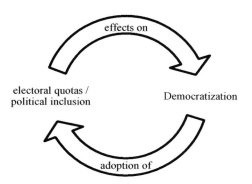

First, the adoption of (gender) equality policies, e.g., gender quotas, has frequently been attributed to dynamics of democratization and/or post-conflict reconstruction (Anderson and Swiss 2014; Bush 2011; Fallon et al. 2012; Hughes 2009; Hughes and Tripp 2015). Whereas conventional wisdom and early democratization research (Inglehart et al. 2002) tell us that transition toward or democracy per se should be conductive for (gender) equality, empirical evidence shows that this is not necessarily the case (Bauer and Burnet 2013; Jaquette and Wolchik 1998). In particular, women's groups and movements have been identified as critical actors for influencing the adoption of gender equality policies during transitional phases (Baldez 2003; Darhour and Dahlerup 2013; Horn 2010).

The adoption of youth quotas seems as well tightly related to those processes. Youth quotas reflect a trend to diversify quota policies progressively by extending them—from women—to other underrepresented groups defined by race, ethnicity, nationality, religion, caste, language, age, disability, profession, and/or location of residence (Krook and O'Brien 2010). Furthermore, to date, most governments introduced them in periods of democratization (Belschner 2018). Among them are three of the North African states that experienced constitutional and/or regime changes in the aftermath of the Arab Uprisings (Tunisia, Morocco, and Egypt; see Inter-Parliamentary Union 2016). However, a recent article that examines more closely the dynamics leading to youth quota adoption in Tunisia and Morocco finds that the youth quotas in Tunisia and Morocco were not part of the domestic youth movements' agendas. In contrast, the political elites initiated them top-down, with an interest in legitimization and stabilization of the post-uprising political orders (Belschner 2018). Although the broader youth movements therefore tend to be skeptical toward youth quotas (González and Desrues 2018), the quotas in the Tunisian case were explicitly framed with reference to the importance of including youth in the post-revolution democratic system.

This leads to the second process of interest, quotas' feedback effects on democratization. I here argue that those will be dependent on the ways electoral quotas are implemented, i.e., the extent to which the quotas deliver what they promised: The political inclusion of formerly excluded groups into politics. Until now, as is the case in Tunisia, all states that have adopted legislated youth quotas previously or simultaneously also adopted gender quotas (Belschner 2018). Therefore, the second strand of the literature this chapter relies on are studies investigating the intersectional implementation and effects of electoral quotas.

Comparing and theorizing the intersectional effects of electoral provisions for women and ethnic minorities in 81 countries, Hughes (2011: 605) firstly points to the importance of a quota's design when analyzing its implementation and effects. Placement rules and sanctioning mechanisms are thus the main determinants for political parties' room for maneuver when it comes to the enactment of the provisions. Hughes secondly shows that 'tandem quotas' for both women and minorities tend to privilege minority women: "In the presence of tandem quotas, adding minority women to the national legislature helps to satisfy both gender and minority quotas; *their election unseats fewer majority men*" (Hughes 2011: 605; italics added). Analyzing the effects of tandem quotas in 17 countries, Bird in contrast finds that "There are rarely representational gains for those located at the intersection of the two quota mechanisms. This is because quotas for women and minorities are rarely 'nested'. Rather they tend to operate independently, often through entirely separate contests to fill the parliamentary seats allotted to each group" (Bird 2016: 284).

The implementation and effects of tandem quotas are thus highly dependent on both quotas' designs and how these interact. To date, there is not much in-depth case research on the effects of tandem quotas for intersectional identity groups (but see Htun 2016), as studies have rather focused on the effects of single quotas (for gender OR minorities) on groups at the intersection of both (Celis et al. 2014; Lépinard 2013). As Jensenius for example shows for India, parties tend to enact minority quotas in a manner that fosters the nomination of women at the cost of the least powerful male politicians, that is, minority men (Jensenius 2016: 440). This practice, as Childs and Hughes point out, consequently contributes to upholding the power of majority or elite male politicians (Childs and Hughes 2018).

How then, do those logics condition quotas' intersectional effects on women's descriptive and substantive representation? A study by Fraga et al. (2005) finds that ethnic minority women can switch between group loyalties—strategically mobilizing intersectionality—and may thus have advantages in parliamentary negotiations and in achieving substantive policy goals. On the other hand, Celis et al. (2015: 769) hypothesize that "ethnic minority women's inclusion might well be about keeping the powerful in place rather than empowering the powerless" and that it might accordingly be difficult for them to represent potentially conflicting issues and interests. Indeed, Hawkesworth (2003) demonstrates how minority women in the US congress are excluded from power positions and substantive influence on policy formation by 'race-gendering' and Htun (2016) argues that gender and ethnic minority quotas in Latin America may have led to "inclusion without representation" for ethnic minority women.

This chapter aims to contribute to those bodies of the literature by shifting the focus toward age as a structuring element of political dynamics of in- and exclusion. I argue that the Tunisian tandem quotas for women and youth constitute an interesting case to explore the effect of paired gender and youth quotas on the representation of different gender and age groups. Considering the context of a youth-led revolution, the extent to which electoral quotas can achieve the political inclusion of young men and women and deliver descriptive, substantive, and symbolic representation will have considerable feedback effects on Tunisia's ambitious democratization process.

Quotas' Effects on the Representation of Gender and Age Groups in Tunisia

The following section analyzes the implementation of the Tunisian tandem quotas for women and youth. In a first step, I will conceptualize the gender and age groups by focussing on middle-aged men, middle-aged women, young men, and young women. Then a sub-section on the quotas' impact on descriptive representation follows, i.e., how they influenced the share of gender and age groups elected to the NCA in 2011 and the parliament, the People's Representatives Assembly (PRA), in 2014. The comparison of those two elections allows distinguishing between the effects of a single gender parity quota, which was in place in 2011, and a tandem gender and youth quota, which regulated the elections in 2014. The third part of this section traces the MPs' parliamentary participation and their presence in leadership positions in parliament and political parties by gender and age groups. Although it does not analyze substantive representation in the proper sense—i.e., exploring the rate of oral and written questions asked in plenary sessions, and on issues attracting specific gender and age groups in parliament—I argue that MPs' positioning in parties and the parliament does to an important extent condition subsequent substantive and also symbolic representation of groups. For example, an over-representation of young women MPs who appear to be sidelined from political power may not lead Tunisian youth to believe that they are adequately represented.

The analyses are based on data from different sources. Concerning the share of gender and age groups in the Tunisian parliaments, I rely on official election statistics published by the Superior Independent Instance for the Elections (Instance Supérieure Indépendante pour les elections, ISIE). However, these statistics do not indicate the age of candidates or elected MPs. Therefore, I complement the data by information collected in the *Marsad ANC* and *Marsad Majles* projects of the Tunisian NGO Al Bawsala.[3] The projects are accessible online (majles.marsad.tn)[4] and include continuously updated information on the elected representatives (biographical information, party affiliation, committee membership), proposals discussed in plenary sessions, outcomes of votes, as well as figures on MPs' presence in plenary sessions and their participation in votes. The high value of the 'Majles' project for research is the fact that it is, unlike a printed study, continuously updated and thus allows to trace developments over time even within a legislature—for example, the change of parties and parliamentary blocs that frequently occurs among Tunisian parliamentarians. Although this chapter relies on the data provided by Al Bawsala's project, the interpretations and conclusions I draw are exclusively my own.

Conceptualizing Age Groups

There are various ways to conceptualize age groups as a unit of analysis. In this chapter, I will rely on three complementary approaches: Age as a numerical span, age in the sociological sense, and age as related to distinctive generations. Although these approaches are sometimes portrayed as competing, I here understand them as complementary rather than exclusive.

The first approach is the most commonly used: to define age groups according to a span of years. This means speaking of young and middle-aged as categories related to a numerical age. For example, United Nation bodies commonly define youth in the age span of 15–24 years (UNDP 2013). However, some parliaments have relatively high minimum age requirements and in general, young people rarely gain office before the age of 35 (Inter-Parliamentary Union 2016: 5). In their studies on young parliamentarians, the Inter-Parliamentary Union therefore uses three different cutoff ages: 30 years, 40 years, and 45 years. In the

Tunisian case, the youth quota is defined as to apply to candidates under 35 years of age, determining this as an important threshold to study the quota's implementation.

Second, one may think of "youth" and "adulthood" as sociological categories that are highly dependent on specific cultural and historical contexts. Youth here involves a notion of inequality compared to the status of adulthood. For instance, someone may be considered youth as long as living in the parents' home, before being married, having own children, and/or the first permanent employment. As Harris (2016: 302) puts it, "The period of youth has been constructed as a time of citizenship training, during which young people are taught about political participation rather than facilitated to engage in it." Particularly political office then seems to be highly reserved for adults. This is reflected by the fact that most young MPs tend to be aged between 30 and 39 and often do already have a career, a family, and an adult life.

A third approach distinguishes youth after generations, claiming that the identities and challenges of each youth generation are unique and related to the political and cultural context they are young in. This seems highly relevant for the Tunisian context, where generational thinking is part of most Tunisians' identity. People who are today about 50 years or older count themselves as the 'Bourguiba' generation, with own memories of the first Tunisian president's rule (1957–1987), which is often portrayed as a glorious period in Tunisian history. Tunisians between the ages of 30 and 50 approximately are seen as a 'lost generation' who experienced in full fledge the more suppressive and more openly dictatorial rule of Bourguiba's successor Ben Ali (1987–2011) and were socialized into a political system where participation meant either exile or collaboration with the regime. Lastly, those under 30 are seen as the generation who did the revolution and who now carry the hope for a future democratic Tunisia.

I suggest combining those approaches when analyzing gender and age groups in Tunisian politics. In the sense of an age span, I will use the cutoff age set by the quota, 35 years, to distinguish young from middle-aged MPs. However, I will provide further differentiation of the middle-aged MPs (35–40 years, 41–50 years, 51–60 years, 61–70 years, and over 70 years), bearing in mind the generational differences outlined above. Furthermore, especially when analyzing MPs' socio-economic background, the sociological definitions of 'youth' and 'adulthood' will be taken into account when interpreting the results.

Descriptive Representation: Increasing the Shares of Young Women

This sub-section analyses the shares of elected MPs after gender and age groups in the Tunisian parliamentarian elections of 2011 and 2014. In 2011, the people elected 217 deputies to the NCA. The gender parity quota was already in place and led to the election of 58 female MPs (26.7%) female MPs.[5] This share rose to 31% (68 MPs) in the 2014 elections.[6] Figure 10.2 breaks down the shares of male and female MPs after age groups. As the bars to the left illustrate, middle-aged men have been majoritarian in both parliamentary bodies, with even a slight increase under tandem quotas for women and youth (59% in 2011 and 64% in 2014). The share of middle-aged female MPs is quite stable (20% in 2011 and 18% in 2014). The gender balance among the youngest parliamentarians under 35 has however most significantly changed from 2011 to 2014. Whereas there were 8% young male and 5% young female deputies in the NCA, the PRA has 9% young female, but only 2% young male MPs. This is surprising, since the overall share of youth under 35 years has remained about the same. However, the gender balance in the parliament is now more pronouncedly structured after age groups, as Fig. 10.3 shows. Whereas female MPs are concentrated in the younger age groups, and even provide the majority of MPs under 35 years, women are now outnumbered even more by male middle-aged and old MPs.

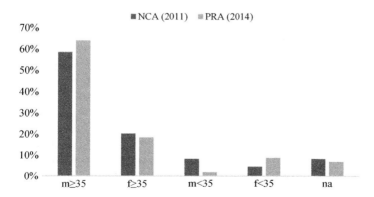

Fig. 10.2 Shares of gender and age groups of Tunisian elected MPs, 2011 and 2014 elections (%) (*Note* Counted at day of election; na-values indicate MPs for whom either age or gender were not available. *Source* ISIE; Marsad Majles)

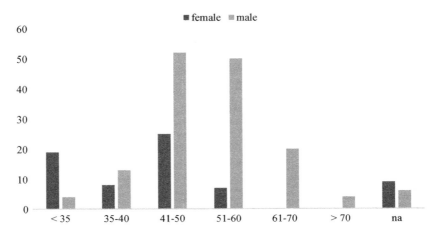

Fig. 10.3 Number of MPs after gender and age group in the PRA (2014) (*Note* Counted at day of election; na-values indicate MPs for whom either gender or age were not available. *Source* Marsad Majles)

In 2014, the parties had to comply with two legislated candidate quotas at a time. The parity regulation demanded them to fill every second spot on their lists with female candidates, whereas the youth quota requested that one person under 35 years must be placed within the first four positions. The quotas are thus "nested", that is they apply to the same electoral lists. As predicted by theories on tandem quotas' intersectional impact, the Tunisian parties mostly chose to kill two birds with one stone. They placed a young, female candidate on the second or fourth list position and a middle-aged male on the first and third position. Table 10.1 displays the share per gender and age group that has been elected on the 1st, 2nd, 3rd, or 4th (or more) position on the respective electoral lists. For example, 74% of middle-aged and still 25% of young male candidates have been elected as head of lists. Accordingly, due to the gender parity quota, most female MPs have been elected on second or forth position. Interestingly, the figures show that parties had a slight preference for middle-aged female candidates compared to young female candidates on the second position.

Table 10.2 exemplifies this logic by displaying the positioning of candidates on Ennahdha and Nidâa Tounès', the two biggest parties, electoral lists in the districts of Jendouba and Sfax 2. This example also

Table 10.1 Conditional probabilities for positioning on electoral lists after MPs' gender and age

	m ≥ 35	f ≥ 35	m < 35	f < 35
#1	0.74	0.13	0.25	0.13
#2	0.02	0.69	0.25	0.48
#3	0.20	0.02	0.25	0.09
#4 or behind	0.04	0.16	0.25	0.30
Total	1	1	1	1

Source Own calculations based on data from Marsad Majles

Table 10.2 Electoral lists of Nidâa Tounès and Ennahdha in the districts of Jendouba and Sfax 2 with placement, gender and age of candidates in 2014 elections

	Jendouba	Sfax 2
Nidâa Tounès	1. Belgacem Dkhili (male, 50) 2. Jihen Aouichi (female, 30) 3. Chaker Ayadi (male, 47)	1. Moncef Sellami (male, 76) 2. Heger Laaroussi (female, 46) 3. Ismail Ben Mahmoud (male, 48) 4. Fatma Mseddi (female, 34)
Ennahdha	1. Ahmed Mechergui (male, 45) 2. Sana Mersni (female, 29, incumbent)	1. Mohamed Frikha (male, 50) 2. Kalthoum Badreddine (female, 51, incumbent) 3. Badreddine Abdelkefi (male, 55, incumbent)

Source Own presentation based on data from Marsad Majles

shows that the Islamist party Ennahdha even preferred middle-aged male candidates as head of lists when there were female incumbents, who were then placed on the second position.

In summary, there are three main results concerning the effects of gender and youth quotas on the descriptive representation of gender and age groups in the NCA and the PRA. First, the introduction of the youth quota in 2014 has not led to an overall increase in young MPs compared to the elections in 2011. Second, it did change the gender balance among the young MPs, leading to a comparative over-representation of young women. Third, middle-aged men continue to provide a stable majority in parliament despite the double quotas. How then, does this descriptive representation of gender and age groups condition their substantive and symbolic representation?

Conditioning Substantive and Symbolic Representation: MPs in Parliament

Whereas research has convincingly shown that 'quota women' are not less qualified than their male counterparts (Franceschet and Piscopo 2012; Murray 2014) and that they are equally able to achieve gains in women's substantive representation (Clayton et al. 2017), this may be different if we specifically look at the intersection of gender and age groups. For example, young women may have less political and professional experience than elder female MPs and thus be confronted with (even more) difficulties in achieving influential posts of decision-making, i.e., being doubly disadvantaged. Therefore, the next sub-section takes a closer look on Tunisian MPs' socio-economic backgrounds, their activity in parliament, and the extent to which they have achieved inner-party and parliamentary power positions. Building on former research concerned with the link between descriptive and substantive representation, I contend that the question of *how* groups are present in parliament is an important condition for their ability to raise their voices (Childs and Krook 2008; Dahlerup 2006; Grey 2006: 493). This is especially important if there is such a clear age imbalance between the genders as in the Tunisian parliament. How does the fact that nearly half of the female legislators are under 40 years old whereas the great majority of male parliamentarians are middle-aged to old men constrain women's ability to become critical actors (Celis et al. 2008)? Are young women easier to exclude from political power than their middle-aged colleagues are?

In order to tackle these questions, I undertake a three-step analysis. First, I compare MPs' socio-economic profiles—their political experience, education, and professional background over gender and age groups. I then investigate which political parties the (young) women belong to and to what extent they are present in inner-party and parliamentarian power positions, as well as in the Tunisian government. In a third step, I analyze their presence in plenary sessions and committees, as well as their participation in votes, in order to check whether there are any substantial differences along gender and/or age lines.

The first noticeable characteristic of the young MPs is that they are actually not that young. Of the MPs who were not older than 35 in the 2014 election, over 60% were over 30 and will thus be too old to qualify for the youth quota requirement for the next parliamentary elections in 2019. That the young MPs are 'adults' in several regards becomes even clearer when employing a sociological definition of youth and taking a closer look on MPs' socio-economic backgrounds. Only three of the young MPs indicate that they are still students, whereas all others have completed a professional degree. The majority are lawyers, followed by education-related professions (professors, researchers, teachers) and some employees in the public and private sector. Interestingly, there is a nearly similar distribution of professions among the middle-aged MPs. The majority are lawyers, followed by a high number of teachers. A noticeable difference compared to the young women and men is that 18% of both middle-aged female and middle-aged male MPs indicate that they are managers or entrepreneurs and have thus occupied a leadership position. The majority of the Tunisian MPs are highly educated—over 60% of the middle-aged and 83% of the young MPs indicate that they have completed tertiary education, and 17% of the young even hold a Ph.D.

In summary, young MPs tend to have higher formal education than their middle-aged counterparts and have achieved roughly the same professional statuses, even if there are some more persons with leadership experience among the middle-aged MPs.

A second measurement for the degree to which gender and age may condition MPs' room for maneuver is their activity in parliament. In this chapter, I employ four indicators provided by the Marsad Majles project.[7] The first is MPs' presence in plenary sessions, where law projects are discussed and voted on. The second indicator, "participation in votes", captures the frequency with which an MP participates in those plenary votes. The third indicator, "presence in committees" measures the frequency with which an MP is present in the committees he or she is assigned to. As the Tunisian parliament is a part-time institution, and many MPs continue to work in their profession besides their mandate, some of them are more present than others both in plenary and in committee sessions. Lastly, the fourth indicator measures the number of committees an MP has been a member in since 2014. About half of committees are permanent, whereas the others are temporary (special) committees. Table 10.3 displays the median values of those indicators for the different gender and age groups. All data have been collected in autumn 2018 and therefore shows MPs' activity rates over a period of nearly 4 years. As the numbers show, there are few significant differences among the gender and age groups. Middle-aged female MPs seem to be slightly more present in committees and to participate a bit more frequently in votes than the other groups. Furthermore, middle-aged female and young male

Table 10.3 Median participation rates (in %) and median number of committee memberships of Tunisian MPs after gender and age groups

	m ≥ 35	f ≥ 35	m < 35	f < 35
Presence in plenary sessions	78	80	82	76
Participation in votes	53	64	56	63
Presence in committees	56	63	50	58
Membership in committees	5	6	7	5

Source Own calculations based on data provided by Marsad Majles

Table 10.4 Distribution of committee presidencies and vice-presidencies after gender and age groups

	Permanent committees		Special committees	
	Presidency	Vice-presidency	Presidency	Vice-presidency
m ≥ 35	9	6	5	4
f ≥ 35	0	1	2	2
m < 35	0	0	1	0
f < 35	0	2	0	2
Total	9	9	8	8

Source Own calculations based on data provided by Marsad Majles

MPs accumulate the highest number of membership in committees compared to middle-aged male and young female MPs.[8]

The picture becomes more nuanced, however, when looking at leadership positions within the committees (see Table 10.4). The Tunisian parliament works in nine permanent committees and eight special committees. All permanent committees and five out of eight special committees are headed by middle-aged male presidents, including the committee on youth.

Two special committees—the committee for martyrs and injured of the revolution, application of the general amnesty law, and transitional justice as well as the committee for the affairs of women, family, children, youth, and the elder—have middle-aged female presidents. In general, women MPs rather occupy the position of vice-presidents, a result also found in Morocco, see this chapter. Middle-aged female MPs are vice-presidents in one permanent (Health and social affairs) and two special committees (People with disabilities and precarious categories; Electoral Commission). Young female MPs hold two vice-presidencies in permanent (Industry, energy, natural resources, infrastructure, and environment; Youth, cultural affairs, education, research) and two in special committees (Regional development; Affairs of women, family, children, youth, and the elder). Note that there are only four young male MPs, of which one (i.e., 25%) holds a presidency in a special committee, whereas only four out of 23 young female MPs (i.e., 17%) hold a vice-presidency. Thus, middle-aged men occupy most leading positions in inner-parliamentarian committees, followed by middle-aged female, young male, and young female MPs (in this order). This hierarchy can also be observed in another body reflecting inner-parliamentarian positions of power. The 'assembly's office' (bureau de l'Assemblée) that is in charge for governing the administrative procedures for the functioning of the parliament[9] is composed as follows: Eleven middle-aged men (including the president and the first vice-president), one middle-aged women who is the second vice-president, one young man, and no young women. Finally, the Tunisian government consists of 25 ministers, only 6 of them female. Exactly one minister is aged under forty—Madame Majdouline Cherni, minister for youth affairs and sports.

A last indicator I suggest to look at is the gender and age composition in the two governing parties' leadership (recorded in summer 2018). Nidâa Tounès elects 10 members of their leading organ, the 'political office', from among MPs. 5 of them, i.e., 50%, are women, but all middle-aged. There are neither young male nor young female members. Ennahdha's most relevant leadership organ is the executive board. Its members are in charge of the implementation of the decisions of the general conference and the Shura Council, take and communicate positions on policies, and approve of candidate selection for national, regional, and local elections. The executive board has 27 members. Six of them (22%) are women, and they are all middle-aged. Again, there are neither young male nor young female members.

Conclusion

This chapter has taken a closer look on the adoption and the intersectional effects of paired gender and youth quotas in post-revolution Tunisia. It aimed to answer the following research questions: How were the quotas designed and implemented? How did they affect the shares of gender and age groups in the Tunisian parliament? How do they condition youth and women's substantive and symbolic representation?

In a first step, I showed that gender and youth quotas were core policies in Tunisia's democratization process, promising political inclusion to formerly excluded groups who had been important drivers of the revolution, that is, women and youth. The following analysis of the quotas' impact on descriptive representation of gender and age groups showed that parties in the 2014 elections under the closed PR-list system preferred to nominate young women over young men. This allowed them to kill two birds with one stone and fulfill both quotas at a time. In other words, the parties nominated as many as necessary, but as few as possible women and youth candidates, resulting in even higher rates of middle-aged male MPs than in the 2011 elections and high shares of young female MPs in the Tunisian parliament.

In order to investigate the consequences of this dynamic for women and youth's substantive and symbolic representation, I analyzed MPs' socio-economic backgrounds, their presence and activity in parliament, as well as their occupation of inner-parliamentarian and inner-party power positions after gender and age groups. Young female and male MPs have higher education and exhibit similar professional backgrounds as their middle-aged counterparts. Although there are few significant differences between MPs' activity and presence rates in plenary sessions and committees, young MPs of both genders are nearly absent from inner-parliamentarian as well as from inner-party leadership positions. Those are occupied predominantly by middle-aged to old men, complemented by some middle-aged women who often occupy vice-presidencies. I therefore argued that young MPs in general, and young women in particular, may be easier to side-line from power than their middle-aged colleagues.

Thus, the way in which the Tunisian parties have enacted the double quotas may, at least in the short run or until parliamentary and political experience outweigh the disadvantage of a young age, negatively condition both women and youth's substantive and symbolic representation. On the one hand, young women's absence from leadership positions in committees and inner-party decision-making may hinder them to push effectively for policy change. On the other hand, the near absence of young men may pose a problem for youth's symbolic representation, as young men are the group mostly considered to have conducted the Tunisian revolution. In this sense, the Tunisian double quotas are a clear example of the double-edged effects of a policy of political inclusion, adopted in a context of democratization, which may have negative feedback effects on this same democratization process by not leading to a substantive and symbolic change of politics.

It will be interesting to see how parties compose their electoral lists in the next legislative elections, scheduled for December 2019, and if they follow the same logics of acting as shown for the 2014 elections. Particularly the question to what extent the young female incumbents will be re-nominated and elected despite the fact that a good share of them will have 'outgrown' the youth quota by then is going to be a crucial test for the quotas' suitability to substantially change patterns of representation. This would be an important sign that the youth quota serves to empower a pool of potential political offspring and eventually to renew the Tunisian political elites, rather than to create a precarious caste of young quota candidates that is replaced every legislature.

Acknowledgements This work was supported by the Norwegian Research Council under grant number 250669/F10.

Notes

1. See http://majles.marsad.tn/fr/loi_electorale/page_loi_electorale_points_de_desaccord.
2. Note that the quota refers to youth ("jeunes") of both genders and only applies to the top four positions on each list.
3. More information on AlBawsala is accessible here: https://www.albawsala.com/en/.
4. The website is available in Arabic and French.
5. In the months following the election, several male deputies were replaced by females, which increased the women's share in the NCA to 67 deputies (31%).
6. Again, male deputies were replaced by females in the following months and female MPs number rose to 78 (36%) by 2018.
7. State as of September 2018.
8. In general, all MPs including backbenchers have been members in at least one permanent and one or more special committees.
9. See a list of the duties and prerogatives of the deputies belonging to this body on http://majles.marsad.tn/2014/fr/assemblee/bureau.

References

Anderson, M. J., & Swiss, L. (2014). Peace accords and the adoption of electoral quotas for women in the developing world, 1990–2006. *Politics & Gender, 10*(1), 33–61.

Baldez, L. (2003). Women's movements and democratic transition in Chile, Brazil, East Germany, and Poland. *Comparative Politics, 35*(3), 253–272.

Bauer, G., & Burnet, J. E. (2013). Gender quotas, democracy, and women's representation in Africa: Some insights from democratic Botswana and autocratic Rwanda. *Women's Studies International Forum, 41*(2), 103–112.

Beissinger, M. R., Jamal, A. A., & Mazur, K. (2015). Explaining divergent revolutionary coalitions: Regime strategies and the structuring of participation in the Tunisian and Egyptian revolutions. *Comparative Politics, 48*(1), 1–24.

Belschner, J. (2018). The adoption of youth quotas after the Arab uprisings. *Politics, Groups, and Identities.* https://doi.org/10.1080/21565503.2018.1528163.

Bird, K. (2016). Intersections of exclusion: The institutional dynamics of combined gender and ethnic quota systems. *Politics, Groups, and Identities, 4*(2), 284–306.

Bush, S. S. (2011). International politics and the spread of quotas for women in legislatures. *International Organization, 65*(1), 103–137.

Celis, K., Childs, S., Kantola, J., & Krook, M. L. (2008). Rethinking women's substantive representation. *Representation, 44*(2), 99–110.

Celis, K., Erzeel, S., & Mügge, L. (2015). Intersectional puzzles: Understanding inclusion and equality in political recruitment. *Politics & Gender, 11*(4), 765–770.

Celis, K., Erzeel, S., Mügge, L., & Damstra, A. (2014). Quotas and intersectionality: Ethnicity and gender in candidate selection. *International Political Science Review, 35*(1), 41–54.

Charrad, M. M., & Zarrugh, A. (2014). Equal or complementary? Women in the new Tunisian Constitution after the Arab Spring. *The Journal of North African Studies, 19*(2), 230–243.

Childs, S., & Hughes, M. (2018). "Which men?" How an intersectional perspective on men and masculinities helps explain women's political underrepresentation. *Politics & Gender, 14*(2), 282–287.

Childs, S., & Krook, M. L. (2008). Critical mass theory and women's political representation. *Political Studies, 56*(3), 725–736.

Clayton, A., Josefsson, C., & Wang, V. (2017). Quotas and women's substantive representation: Evidence from a content analysis of Ugandan plenary debates. *Politics & Gender, 13*(2), 276–304.

Collins, N. (2011). *Voices of a revolution: Conversations with Tunisia's youth* (1st ed.). Washington, DC: National Democratic Institute. http://iknowpolitics.org/sites/default/files/conversations-with-tunisia-youth-apr-2011.pdf. Accessed 18 March 2019.

Dahlerup, D. (2006). The story of the theory of critical mass. *Politics & Gender*, 2(4), 492–502.
Darhour, H., & Dahlerup, D. (2013). Sustainable representation of women through gender quotas: A decade's experience in Morocco. *Women's Studies International Forum, 41*(2), 132–142.
Fallon, K. M., Swiss, L., & Viterna, J. (2012). Resolving the democracy paradox: Democratization and women's legislative representation in developing nations, 1975 to 2009. *American Sociological Review, 77*(3), 380–408.
Fraga, L., Martinez-Ebers, V., Lopez, L., & Ramírez, R. (2005). *Strategic intersectionality: Gender, ethnicity, and political incorporation* (1st ed.). Berkeley: Institute of Governmental Studies. http://citeseerx.ist.psu.edu/viewdoc/download?doi=10.1.1.571.5343&rep=rep1&type=pdf. Accessed 18 March 2019.
Franceschet, S., & Piscopo, J. M. (2012). Gender and political backgrounds in Argentina. In S. Franceschet, M. L. Krook, & J. M. Piscopo (Eds.), *The impact of gender quotas* (1st ed., pp. 43–56). Oxford: Oxford University Press.
Gana, N. (2013). *The making of the Tunisian revolution: Contexts, architects, prospects*. Edinburgh: Edinburgh University Press.
González, M., & Desrues, T. (2018). *Youth representation under authoritarianism: the process of quota adoption in Morocco*. Unpublished paper presented at the Workshop on Youth, Inequality and Regime Response in the Global South, University of Bergen, Bergen.
Gray, D. H. (2012). Tunisia after the uprising: Islamist and secular quests for women's rights. *Mediterranean Politics, 17*(3), 285–302.
Grey, S. (2006). Numbers and beyond: The relevance of critical mass in gender research. *Politics & Gender, 2*(4), 492–502.
Harris, A. (2016). Young people, politics and citizenship. In A. Furlong (Ed.), *Handbook of youth and young adulthood* (2nd ed., pp. 301–306). London and New York: Routledge.
Hawkesworth, M. (2003). Congressional enactments of race-gender: Toward a theory of raced-gendered institutions. *American Political Science Review, 97*(4), 529–550.
Hoffman, M., & Jamal, A. (2012). The youth and the Arab Spring: Cohort differences and similarities. *Middle East Law and Governance, 4*(1), 168–188.
Horn, D. M. (2010). *Women, civil society and the geopolitics of democratization*. New York: Routledge.
Htun, M. (2016). *Inclusion without representation in Latin America: Gender quotas and ethnic reservations*. Cambridge: Cambridge University Press.
Hughes, M. M. (2009). Armed conflict, international linkages, and women's parliamentary representation in developing nations. *Social Problems, 56*(1), 174–204.
Hughes, M. M. (2011). Intersectionality, quotas, and minority women's political representation worldwide. *American Political Science Review, 105*(3), 604–620.

Hughes, M. M., & Tripp, A. M. (2015). Civil war and trajectories of change in women's political representation in Africa, 1985–2010. *Social Forces, 93*(4), 1513–1540.

Inglehart, R., Norris, P., & Welzel, C. (2002). Gender equality and democracy. *Comparative Sociology, 1*(3), 321–345.

Inter-Parliamentary Union. (2016). *Youth participation in national parliaments 2016* (1st ed.). Geneva: Inter-Parliamentary Union. https://www.ipu.org/resources/publications/reports/2016-07/youth-participation-in-national-parliaments. Accessed 18 March 2019.

Jaquette, J. S., & Wolchik, S. L. (1998). *Women and democracy: Latin America and Central and Eastern Europe*. Baltimore: Johns Hopkins University Press.

Jensenius, F. R. (2016). Competing inequalities? On the intersection of gender and ethnicity in candidate nominations in Indian elections. *Government and Opposition, 51*(3), 440–463.

Krook, M. L., & O'Brien, D. Z. (2010). The politics of group representation: Quotas for women and minorities worldwide. *Comparative Politics, 42*(3), 253–272.

Lépinard, É. (2013). For women only? Gender quotas and intersectionality in France. *Politics & Gender, 9*(3), 276–298.

Lieckefett, M. (2012). La Haute Instance et les élections en Tunisie: du consensus au "pacte politique"? *Confluences Méditerranée, 82*(3), 133–144.

Murray, R. (2014). Quotas for men: Reframing gender quotas as a means of improving representation for all. *American Political Science Review, 108*(3), 520–532.

République Tunisienne. (2011). *Décret-loi n° 2011-35*. http://constitutionnet.org/vl/item/2-decret-loi-ndeg-2011-35-du-10-mai-2011-relatif-lelection-de-lassemblee-nationale. Accessed 22 March 2019.

République Tunisienne. (2014a). *Constitution de la République Tunisienne*. http://www.legislation.tn/sites/default/files/news/constitution-b-a-t.pdf. Accessed 22 March 2019.

République Tunisienne. (2014b). *Loi électorale de la Tunisie*. http://www.isie.tn/wp-content/uploads/2018/01/Loi-Organique-n%C2%B02014-16.pdf. Accessed 22 March 2019.

République Tunisienne. (2017). *Loi électorale de la Tunisie*. http://www.legislation.tn/sites/default/files/fraction-journal-officiel/2017/2017F/014/Tf201771.pdf. Accessed 22 March 2018.

UNDP. (2013). *Enhancing youth political participation throughout the electoral cycle: A good practice guide* (1st ed.). New York: United Nations Development Programme. http://www.undp.org/content/dam/undp/library/Democratic%20Governance/Electoral%20Systems%20and%20Processes/ENG_UN-Youth_Guide-LR.pdf. Accessed 22 March 2019.

Zemni, S. (2015). The extraordinary politics of the Tunisian revolution: The process of constitution making. *Mediterranean Politics, 20*(1), 1–17.

CHAPTER 11

Whose Empowerment? Gender Quota Reform Mechanisms and De-democratization in Morocco

Hanane Darhour

INTRODUCTION

Today, an all-male parliament has in most parts of the world lost its democratic legitimacy (Sadiqi and Ennaji 2011; Dahlerup 2018b). Globally, the empowerment of women in politics has become a warranted legitimate goal, as well as a determinant of the level of a country's democracy (Kenny 2013; Krook 2009; Waylen 2009, 2012; Franceschet 2011). Women's empowerment gained momentum with the global economic changes, the national and international support for the country's social and political reforms, the changes in political priorities, the growing importance of democracy in the world, as well as with the increased role of women's movements worldwide (Daoud 1993; Ennaji 2007; Dalmasso and Cavatorta 2010; see Chapter 2 by Sadiqi).

The rapid expansion of electoral gender[1] quotas in the past decades has been met with considerable scholarly attention. Yet, there has been

H. Darhour (✉)
Faculty of Letters and Human Sciences, Ibn Zohr University, Ait Melloul, Morocco

little empirical work examining the mechanisms used to *reform* electoral gender quota over time and evaluate its outcomes on empowering quota elected women. A genuine political participation of women goes beyond the numerical aspect of representation to analyzing their capacity to be critical actors. Hence, this chapter provides a critical analysis of state's motives for the choice of the format of quota design and reform and the effects of quota provisions on women's empowerment and democratic development. Analysis of the use of mechanisms for extending women's presence in elected bodies allows us to discuss the ways in which the state and male political elites respond positively to calls for reform of gender policies without relinquishing any of their power.

I argue that a gender quota provision is not a trustworthy indicator of a country's level of democracy and that quota design might either lead to positive outcomes reinforcing a country's democratization or to negative outcomes resulting in de-democratization. I define de-democratization as any process where the state's policy choices reverse the desired results and create a rather democratic fallacy. The demarcation line between democratization and de-democratization is when gender quotas seize to be protective strategies for women and become instead protective of the status quo and when women turn to be democratic accessories scaffolding the democratization process.

This study applies a gender, institutionalist and critical approach (see Kulawik 2009; Lovenduski 1998) in order to understand the dynamics of gender, power, and change in the parliament across the last four legislative elections. Drawing on policy tracing and 12 in-depth formal interviews conducted from 2003 to 2017 with women and men members of parliament (MPs), women's rights activists, as well as a number of informal interviews with academics, this chapter argues that the quota reform by supplementation and extension is a win-win solution for the state and women which hides underneath a double-edged political strategy with both positive and negative effects on women and democratization. Firstly, the chapter asks: what institutional arrangements were used in Morocco to reform the reserved seats (henceforth RS) system? Secondly, in which context, how and why RS were reformed and extended? Thirdly, what effects those reforms had on female MPs' perceptions of their mandate and role as representatives and what do they reveal about Morocco's democratization process?

To reflect on these research questions, this chapter is divided into three main parts: (1) the theoretical issues of gender quotas, where I first present an overview of different types of gender quotas with a specific focus on RS and their impact on women's empowerment and democratization, (2) the RS system in Morocco section investigates the provisions adopted in the last four parliamentary elections and the motives of gender quota reforms, and (3) the counter-productive effects of RS in Morocco section, where I present four negative effects of reservation.

Theoretical Issues About Gender Quotas

In the debate on quotas, gender quotas are often referred to as temporary measures, or jump-start mechanisms, to be removed once the political playing field for women is levelled. Quotas have been recommended by the Committee for the Elimination of All Forms of Discrimination Against Women (CEDAW) which sought to clarify the importance of "temporary special measures," calling on States to have a preferential treatment for women and implement gender quotas to empower women in politics.[2] Gender Quotas have two fold objectives: (1) to come to terms with the persistent underrepresentation of women in parliament and change policy-making in a gender-equal way; (2) to permanently break the barriers that women are encountering in political recruitment processes (Bjarnegard and Zetterberg 2011; Freidenvall and Krook 2011).

Three main types of political quotas exist. First, *voluntary party quotas* have been adopted by political parties in a number of countries and involve a party committing itself to nominating a certain percentage of female candidates for electoral lists. Second, *legislated candidate quotas* by the law of a country and stipulate that a certain number of candidate positions must be reserved for women (Dahlerup 2006). They sometimes include conditions on the position of women on the electoral list, for instance by requiring that every second entry on the list must be a woman. Finally, *reserved seats* are positions set aside for women among representatives in a legislature, specified either in the Constitution or by legislation. Practices of using RS or electoral gender quotas, which guarantee access to political power by gender, have been institutionalized in different socio-political and cultural contexts. Arendt (2018) stressed the importance of the political context to measuring the outcomes of gender quotas. Gender quotas in the form of *RS* started in the 1930s. Through the 1970s, RS were the main type of quota used in developing countries as in Africa, Asia, and the Middle East through reforms to the constitution and the electoral law.

RS come in many different types, some by election and others by appointment. Most of the times, reservation policies are often established through the creation of *separate electoral rolls* for women (Nanivadekar 2006), *designation of separate districts for female candidates* (Norris 2006), or *post-election distribution of seats for women* based on each party's proportion of the popular vote (Goetz 2003; Goetz and Hassim 2003). For instance, in Uganda, Article 78(1) of the Constitution states that the parliament shall consist of 1 woman representative for every district. There are 112 districts in Uganda. 153 of 465 (33%) seats in the Ugandan Parliament are held by women as to the 2016 legislative elections. In Rwanda, 30% of the seats, elected by a special procedure, are reserved for women according to the Constitution. In addition, the normal District Seats (DS) are regulated by gender quota provisions. All in all, 49 of 80 (61%) seats in the Rwandan Chamber of Deputies are held by women as to the 2018 elections, which is a world record. In Tanzania 30% of the seats are reserved for women and allocated to the political parties in proportion to the number of parliamentary seats won in an election. 136 of 393 (35%) seats in the Tanzanian National Assembly are held by women (IDEA 2018). In Pakistan, RS are allocated to the political parties in proportion of the number of general seats they win in the direct contest. A political party gets one women's reserved seat for every 3.5 general seats. RS can also be filled by appointment, as in Kenya and some Arab states like Jordan.[3]

Reservation for a limited number of women in political institutions is no longer considered sufficient. The "acceptable minimum" of women has increased (Dahlerup 2018b) since 2000, when a number of countries have instituted much larger provisions targeting a critical minority of 30 or 40% of women as demanded in the global commitment for gender quotas reflected in CEDAW. The incremental track as in the Scandinavian experience, according to Dahlerup and Freidenvall (2005), is no longer considered a model today as it was achieved in a 70–80 years process. Today the women and states are not willing to wait that long (incremental track), they want a short cut to equal representation. However, equality of result measures, namely RS raised controversial debate and updated scholarship on why women are still underrepresented in Politics (Dahlerup 2018a; Daoud 1993). Research indicates that despite the positive effect of RS in the major breakthrough of women into politics, RS have far reaching counter-productive effects on the legitimacy of elected women and their capacity to make a difference. Women elected through quotas are often portrayed as token or proxy women with no real political power. No one takes them seriously (Lloren 2014).

In addition, RS are regarded as mechanisms serving patronage[4] politics and legitimizing authoritarian regimes (Franceschet and Piscopo 2008; Krook 2009; Burnet 2011). In several Arab countries, efforts in increasing women's presence in elected office has been part of state feminism.[5] State-led efforts have been associated with attempts to build support, consolidate power in reaction to imminent legitimacy crises as in Morocco in 2002, and Egypt in 2015 (Shalaby 2016), or as a reaction to international pressure (Bush 2015; Welborne 2010). While some studies have demonstrated that institutional mechanisms, such as quotas, can remedy descriptive gender inequalities in politics regardless of the country's level of democracy (Tripp and Kang 2008; see Chapter 4), other researchers, who focus on substantive representation, have shown that this is not necessarily the case in the Arab world and Morocco (Dalmasso and Cavatorta 2010; El Moussalli 2011; Sater 2017; Belarbi 2012). As maintained by Goulding (2009: 76) studying Tunisia, "the efficacy of gender quotas set forth to encourage women to become active participants in their government is hindered by the authoritarian structure in which they exist". Sater (2012: 73) found similar findings for the Moroccan case as he argues that quota mechanisms are indeed *embedded* in the fabric of existing authoritarian structures, with very limited impact on producing genuine change.

At the broader level, RS are common because they are perceived to fulfill states' numerous aims (Htun 2003). The first aim is to seek its own *survival* by strategically designing well-controlled representative institutions that make certain discriminated social groups break into power positions on the detriment of losing power in front of other real challengers of the state. The second aim is to secure the minimum sense of *justice by* adopting measures of compensatory discrimination so that the least privileged groups benefit from the distribution of primary goods as well as from an equal access to power positions. The third aim is to keep *order* through the creation of unified and adaptable political institutions that incorporate and reflect diverse social forces by directing their participation into official institutions. The last aim is to ensure its *legitimacy* by basing its political decisions on consensus-deliberation among free and equal citizens representing different views (Htun 2003). Kymlicka (1995: 53) states that "finding morally defensible and politically viable answers to minority rights' claims is the greatest challenge facing democracies today."

At the party level, RS failed to bring about long-term change in candidate recruitment procedures, as they "do not challenge male power within the political parties because the seats are not distributed in a selection process in which women compete against men" (Bjarnegard and Zetterberg 2011: 192). As a result, women elected through RS are stigmatized and perceived to have less legitimacy than women elected in open seats because of their election in what is considered as token seats (Longwe 2000: 27). Tokenism is the antonym of agency and authority (Karpowitz, Mendelberg and Shaker 2012). A recent study finds that the lack of substantive representation in the reserved seat quota system stems from a lower perceived legitimacy of women appointed through the RS system; the lower legitimacy, in turn, causes a lower effectiveness in directing policy agendas and making a difference in the lives of women (Grajzl and Obasanjo 2019: 24). Furthermore, RS increase gender discrimination, taking form in various overtones about the morality of elected women, and their claimed sexual relationship with prominent political leaders. Meier and Lombardo (2010) suggest, that women are perceived as perpetual outsiders in the political process because they start their careers late and hence have much shorter careers in politics.

The following section presents the historical evolution of the RS system with a specific focus on the institutional arrangements adopted during the 2011 and 2016 quota reform.

Reserved Seats System in Morocco

In a global perspective, the RS system in Morocco is a very special type of electoral gender quotas. To shed light on its specificity, we trace its evolution over the last four legislative elections. Three main stages can be discerned: (1) a fragile provision of creating a nation wide National List (NL) with 30 seats that the parties agreed to reserve voluntarily to women in 2002; (2) a legislated and expanded provision of 60 NL seats explicitly reserved for women in the electoral law of 2011; (3) a legislated provision that opened, in 2016, a new pathway for the participation of young women under the age of 40 in a 30 seats nationwide NL for youth, which was reserved in 2011 to young male candidates exclusively.

Levels of women's political representation began to change in 2002 to reach 35 women elected, when the new king Mohamed VI oversaw significant changes in the electoral system (Table 11.1). The changes involved switching to a closed list-voting system, in which votes are cast for the entire lists of political parties rather than for individual candidates. The 2002 election took place under a revised voting system in which 325 deputies were elected from 91 constituencies. The rules stated, in Article 1 of the organic law of the House of Representatives, that 10% of the House of Representatives is to be elected in a national list (NL) election. The law didn't state that the NL seats should be reserved for women—to avoid falling in the trap of being ruled unconstitutional. Political parties, in response to compelling national and international pressures made an "honorary agreement" to reserve the 30 NL seats for female candidates (Darhour and Dahlerup 2013).

In 2007, thirty-four women were elected. In 2011, the NL was legislated and extended in the electoral law. Article 23 (2) of the Organic Law No. 27-11 on the House of Representatives by stating that "305 of the 395 members of the lower house are elected by direct universal suffrage under a list system in 92 multi-member constituencies. An additional nationwide constituency with a tandem quota that reserves 60 seats for women and 30 seats for young men and women under the age of 40. RS for women are filled by winners elected through a proportional

Table 11.1 Women's representation in *Majliss-annouwab* (1997–2016)

Election years	1997	2002	2007	2011	2016
No of women elected via DSs	2	5	4	7	10
Total No of parliamentary seats	325	325	325	395	395
Proportion of women elected via DSs (%)	0.6	1.7	1.4	2.3	3.28
Women elected via youth NL	No quota	No quota	No quota	30 RS for male youth only	11 (30)
RS for women	No quota	30	30	60	60
Total number of women elected	2	35	34	67	81
% of elected women	0.6	10.7	10.5	17.0	21

Source Darhour and Dahlerup (2013), updated

representation system based on nation-wide closed party lists[6]". It also stated in article 24 (2) that lists of candidates that violate the provisions of Article 23, including the quota requirements, shall be rejected. On top of the quota, women made additional gains in 2016, including 10 women elected via local constituency seats and 11 other women elected to youth NL which was in 2011 exclusive to male youth.

Table 11.2 shows that 19 young males against 11 young females have been elected. It should be noted here that 7 out 11 seats were won by females from one single party (i.e., Party of Authenticity and Modernity, PAM) while the USFP, PJD and RNI have presented 5, 4 and 4 female candidates respectively to fill the other 23 seats. From the 19 participating parties in the 2016 elections, only the PAM presented a national youth list with 29 female young candidates and one male young candidate, which ranks it first in terms of women's representation, followed by the PJD and IP and RNI. In comparison with the total number of seats won by party, the PAM and socialist parties USFP and PPS rank with a rate of 25% each, followed by the PJD, IP; RNI, UC and MP with a rate of 16–18.5% respectively. As a result, state provisions for promoting women's political representation have been effective in bringing a substantial number of women into parliament, from 1% in 1997 to today's

Table 11.2 Women elected to the parliament via NLs and DLs across parties, 2016

Political parties	Women NL	DL	Youth NL		Total women elected/total of seats by party	FMPs by party (%)	FMPs in the parliament (%)
			Young women candidates	Women elected			
PJD	18	4	4	2	24/125	19	6
PAM	14	5	29	7	26/102	24.5	6.5
IP	7	–	1	–	7/46	15	2
RNI	6	1	4	–	7/37	19	2
MP	5	–	–	1	5/27	18.5	1.2
USFP	4	–	5	–	5/20	25	1.2
UC	3	–	–	–	3/19	16	0.7
PPS	3	–	15	1	3/12	25	0.7
Total N of women	60	10	58	11	81/395		21

Source Author's calculations based on data from the Space of Elections of Morocco on 2016, http://www.elections.ma/elections/legislatives/corps_electoral.aspx

21% in 2016. Morocco has thus passed the threshold which in old democracies was the most difficult to overcome, that of moving from zero to 20% of women.

Motives of the Adoption of a Specific Quota Provision

Investigations into the state motives behind the adoption of a specific quota provision are mostly speculative, and tend to forget, that the most normal situation in politics is, that there are different motives among the different stakeholders involved, and even mixed motives among the highest decision-makers. Morocco is a "partly-free" political system (Freedom House 2018) and consequently information about the decision-making processes is somewhat limited, and does not allow for regular policy tracing. But a short overview on the political context and culture in Morocco as well as information drawn from interviewed respondents would be a good frame to understand better how, when and why RS as a quota provision has been implemented.

Much of the evolution of women's political representation in Morocco has come as a response to increasing national and international pressure for greater transparency and democratic accountability. This can be clearly perceived in the King's speech of 2008 which recognizes women's political participation as a lever of democracy and development.

> We continue to strive so as to provide Moroccan women means that allow them to be part of the democratic institutional process … We also make sure that women can benefit from an increasing rate of fair representation in the Government, Parliament, local authorities and all decision making spheres …, we intend to strengthen the efficient contribution they provide, just like men, to both democratic construction and development process.[7]

In fact, the process of democratization, consolidation of the rule of law and the strengthening of human rights in Morocco started in 2002 with the reservation of 30 seats for women in the parliament. Many other gender reforms followed: the family code (Mudawanna)[8] in 2003; the nationality code in 2007; and the reform of the communal charter in 2008. The momentum for gendered legal reforms was consolidated after the Arab Uprisings of 2011 (Touhtou 2012) which led King Mohammed VI to adopt wide-ranging constitutional reforms. The 2011 Constitution placed equality at the highest level of the hierarchy of norms and at the heart of the Kingdom's societal project[9] (Article 19) and ordered the creation of a governmental authority to work toward parity and address all forms of discrimination.[10]

The question that remains, from the panoply of quota measures that exist, is why certain quota types are implemented rather than others? Can we judge a country's level of democracy by its design of a specific quota type and by the political arrangements it uses to promote women's political representation? Do RS as applied in Morocco create a democratic fallacy, which makes quotas mere democratic accessories not fundamental to statecraft democratization? Are RS beneficial only to women? Do RS reflect principled concerns to empower women or do they serve other strategic political functions?

How and Why Quotas Were Enlarged?

The political discontent during and after 2011 pushed for political reform. Promoting women's and youth political participation has been at the center of the reform. To accommodate social groups, the number of parliamentary seats was supplemented from 325 in 2007 to 395 in 2011 *with 70 additional parliamentary seats.* Out of 395 members, 305 (77%) were elected in multi-seat constituencies, while 60 (15%) seats of the remaining 90 were reserved for women and the 30 (8%) remnant seats were reserved to male candidates under the age of 40. Later in the 2016 elections and due to mounting demands of the women's movement in Morocco for gender equality as stipulated in the constitution, the revision of the organic law 16-20 stipulated that the youth NL should contain young male and female candidates under 40[11] rather than be limited to only young males under the age of 40, as previously stated in Organic Law No. 27-11.

The scrutiny of the last four elections reveals three political arrangements as shown in Table 11.3: (1) designing a NL of 30 seats in 2002 *exclusively* reserved for women, (2) *extending* the RS system from 30 to 60 seats for women in 2011, (3) *supplementing* the total number of parliamentary seats with 70 additional seats (from 325 in 2007 to 395 in 2011), (4) *opening* the youth NL (which was exclusive to males under the age of 40 in 2011) to young female candidates in 2016.

The striking truth is that this supplementation pattern in gender quota reform has been adopted, likewise, to increase women's presence in the Cabinet and local elections. In the Cabinet of 2013, of

Table 11.3 Gender quota design and reform mechanisms (2002–2016)

	2002	2007	2011	2016
RS for women	30	30	60	60
RS for youth	None	None	30 (for males only)	30 (for both)
Total number of parliamentary seats	325	325	395	395
Reform mechanisms	RS of 30 seats	RS of 30 seats	RS of 60 by supplementing 70 Seats to the total number of seats	RS 60 + opening the RS for youth to women

Source The author's based on data from the official website of Moroccan elections http://www.elections.ma/elections/legislatives/corps_electoral.aspx

30 portfolios, only one woman was appointed minister from 2011 to 2013 (compared with seven in the 2007 elections). In the government reshuffle that took place in October 10th 2013, 2 female ministers and 4 female minister delegates were nominated. The most surprising thing is that the number of portfolios in the government reshuffle of 2013 increased from 31 to 39. Eight *supplementary* portfolios were *added* to give access to *more* women in executive politics.

In similar ways, the reform of the Communal Charter in 2008 introduced a 12% quota for women at the communal elections through the creation of "*additional* electoral constituencies" exclusively reserved for women candidates. A further amendment in 2011 introduced provisions specific to the election by creating additional electoral constituencies created in municipalities and districts (Article 143).[12] Although, the law is not explicit in this regard, there is a political consensus that these additional constituencies can only be accessed by women. In 2015, a modification of the law in Article 76 and 77 of the organic law No. 34-15 stipulates that "It is *created* at the territorial level of each prefecture, province or district prefecture, a single electoral district. It is reserved for women, in each electoral district, at least one-third of the seats, without however being deprived of their right of candidacy under the seats reserved for the first part of the list of candidatures referred to in Article 85 of this organic law."[13]

In sum, this section discussed the choices made and ambiguities raised by the design and then the reform of the RS system. Now the question that follows is: Are there any counter-productive effects of the Quota provisions adopted in the last four elections on quota elected women and democratization?

Counter-Productive Effects of Reserved Seats

This section presents four counter-productive effects of gender quotas and shows how state mechanisms for quota implementation at first and then quota extension after indeed succeeded in increasing women's descriptive representation but with various side effects on the legitimacy and power of quota elected women and thereby on the quality of the country's democratization.

Institutionalizing Segregation

Quotas were adopted with the intention to find solutions to women's underrepresentation in politics. To larger extents, they have been successful in increasing the number of women, but in parallel, their implementation seems to have led to institutionalizing a new culture of segregation. Theoretically, Moroccan RS system maintained via a NL has in fact created a non-territorial form of representation, called in Mansbridge terms (2003) *surrogate* representation (i.e., representation of a perspective or a group). However, it has failed to institutionalize the representation of Moroccan women's concerns as a group by women MPs as it does not allow for a direct electoral relationship and a formal relation between the representative and the represented. Voters cast their votes for the women's list in connection with their party preferences (Darhour and Dahlerup 2013: 4).

Interviews have confirmed that the segregation against quota elected women remains a major obstacle. Women's perceptions about their *spatial disposition* are dictated by the type of quota that got them into the parliament. Both their status as newcomers and quota elected makes them inorganic to the mainstream structure. Their feelings of inferiority and stigma is the result of the politics of supplementation. On the contrary, the very few district elected women (see Tables 11.1 and 11.2) are much more proud and confident about their political legitimacy and competence. They consider themselves integral to the mainstream structure of the parliament since they have gained their access through an open competition with men. According to a female MP the low representation of women in open seats underlie the continuing discriminatory practices, institutional sexism and cultural stereotypes, which affects negatively the recruitment policies and candidate selection.[14]

Previous researchers confirm that the symbolic representation of the woman-politician-pretender as marginal to politics, or lacking legitimacy or effectiveness in contrast to the male-politician-norm affects negatively both their chances of being present in political institutions (descriptive representation), as well as their abilities to act for women (substantive representation) once there (Meier and Lombardo 2010). Dahlerup (2018a) also maintains that the problem of stigmatization of quota elected women remains one of the basic obstacles they suffer from once they are in the parliament. Although supportive of the use of gender quotas, Lovenduski (1998) noticed, likewise, that the entrance of a large new cohort of women MPS in 1997 to the UK house of Commons context was met with considerable institutional resistance manifested in the daily reassertion and repetition of inappropriate and sexist values.

Recruiting Token Women

Another side effect of the Moroccan RS system can be discerned from female MPs' perceptions of their *functional disposition* (i.e., how they view their parliamentary responsibilities and w*ho do they claim to represent?* The implementation of gender quotas in 2002 has considerably changed conceptions of representation and the roles of representatives. Before the implementation of the NL in 2002 that reserved 30 seats for women, representatives' role was dual: (1) to pursue the interests of their constituents based on a *geographical area*; (2) and/or to represent the ideology of their party. After the introduction of the NL, the legislative mandate of nationally elected representatives automatically changed. They became representatives elected beyond strict constituency delimitation and thereby supposed to represent (1) particular interest/social groups and/or (2) the interests of the whole nation.

Constituency elected MPs give primary concern to their local electorate because ultimately their re-election is based on their opinion. Quota elected women do not have this privilege and thereby have no choice other than to be loyal to party concerns and to cultivate relationships with party leaders and other political elites. "Quota and non-quota elected women are not the same. They come through different channels into the parliament," A PJD female MP Said.[15] Quota elected women were mandated because of their gender at the national level. Their political mandate is not based on a geographical representation or constituency. In contrast to DL candidates who are in direct contact with voters from the same constituency and campaign and compete with males to win their trust, NL candidates target the whole Moroccan society.

Krook (2009) states that the quota system places the burden of recruitment on the parties and political leaders who control the recruitment process. NL women bear direct accountancy and varying degrees of dependence on party leaders. The adoption of a separate NL for women has failed to secure an electoral base for women politicians, which is necessary to build long-term political influence within the party and society more broadly (Lloren 2014: 10). Female politicians are torn between conflicting expectations with regard to their political contribution. "While feminist movements have always wanted female politicians to be their representatives and have criticized elected women for not being feminist enough, the attitude of political parties toward women's substantive representation has always been ambivalent" (Dahlerup 2018b: 201).

Pitkin (1967: 220) acknowledges that most representatives act within "an elaborate network of pressures, demands and obligations". The main pressure is to be re-elected. The fact that they were elected raises many problems about the unorganized and diverse group of female constituents. The indirect relationship of quota women with the electorate makes it difficult for them to represent their electorate. This difficulty is maintained even with the presence of an independent and strong women's movement in Morocco that normally should be capable of mediating quota women relationships to women and people, providing realistic representational input, and assisting them to increase legislative output. The reason for the absence of collaboration between the women's movement groups and women in the parliament has been basically created by the design of an all-women NL. Civil society activists are potential aspirants and competitors. These problems are further heightened when we consider the abstinence, apathy and ignorance of voters in a country like Morocco where voter turnout is very low, estimated at 43% and at 29.5% if those not included on the electoral register are taken into account in 2011 elections.

Women are becoming reluctant to damage their reputation if they run for election in RS. Nationally elected women tend to derive their force from their relationships to male political figures; while district elected women derive their power from a larger network of support, including the voters who voted for them and the confidence of their own political parties which nominated them as candidates in winning positions.[16] Women winning DSs are positively perceived because DLs allow for a real competition with males not a woman-woman competition.[17] Fouzia Assouli, President of the Women's League Federation and a social activist explains the problem of quotas by saying that: "a quota is nothing more than a mechanism of access. Change should happen at the level of political parties and mentalities. If the numbers are there but their impact is low then we should look for a mechanism that is not perceived as a rent[18]".

Engendering Clientelism

The use and abuse of RS has led to nepotism and the taking of seats by elites. Party leaders are rewarded by nominating their blood relations, wives and relatives in NL seats. Many of these women have no background either in politics or in women's rights movements.[19] In addition, RS create a division among the constituents of the women's movement, mainly women members of women's sections in political parties, civil society activists who also aspire to be recruited in a specific political party. A leading member of Jossour stated clearly in an informal interview that "women MPs are disconnected from civil society activists. Even the most active feminists, once they get elected they start to bear allegiance only to male political elites. During their mandate, they seek building new relationships with male party elites so as to secure reelection to the parliament."[20] This implies that women MPs' political strength is measured by their social closeness to powerful political elites in the party or government.

The same result has been stressed by Lloren (2014: 7) who states that RS are seen as a mechanism serving patronage politics. They reinforce the importance of family ties and the influence of the leader. In line with this, Bennani (2008) finds that the selection of candidates for the women's NL does not reward activism but rather follows a clientelistic logic. In connection with its effect on engendering clientelism in the ranks of female political actors, an investigation of the evolution of women elected in DSs and the rate of their novice/experienced status shows the following (see Table 11.4): (1) RS constitute a glass ceiling for women as most parties put their women candidates in NLs rather than DLs, which

Table 11.4 Women elected and re-elected to district seats (2002–2016)

Election year	Number of FMPs elected on district lists	Rate of women elected/all MPs	Parliamentay experience[a]	NL or DL experience	Experienced FMPs (% rounded)
2002	5	1.2	0/5		0
2007	4	1.1	2/4	DL for all	50
2011	7	1.7	1/7	DL	14
2016	10	2.5	4/10	DL for all	40
Total	26	–	7/26	–	27

[a]Parliamentary experience indicates that the MP has been elected previously on a district or national list
Source Darhour and Dahlerup (2013) updated

are considered men's seats. The highest rate of women' representation in DLs is 2.5% in 2016. (2) The average rate of experienced constituency women in the last four legislative elections (2002–2021) is 27%. (3) None of the 27% of experienced FMPs was elected in a NL. Table 11.4 shows clearly that the NL did not become an entrance to DSs because 27% of District seats women were re-elected in district constituencies. Therefore, the NL does not provide a sustainable and long-term solution to the women's political underrepresentation. This stark distinction between district and NL affects negatively perceptions of quota women.

Leading to de-Democratization

Gender quota reform mechanisms provide an example of the contortions and paradoxes of the state's gender policies in Morocco.[21] No one can deny that today, Morocco has achieved a considerable change in the numerical political empowerment of women with a rate necessary for democratic practice and similar to so many democratic countries but this indicator does in no way consolidate the democratization process. On the contrary, it poses threats to democratization and creates a democratic fallacy of change that will vanish as soon as quotas are withdrawn.

Democratization happens when there is a substantial and institutionalized *redistribution of power* from an authoritarian entity toward elected and appointed institutions at the national and local levels (Benabdellah 2001). In Morocco, the need to soften control and open the political space to other social classes to include women and youth has definitely succeeded to change the composition of the political structure but it failed to redistribute power substantially and equally to all political actors and more importantly unsettle the patriarchal practices of regime support. The choice of a separate parallel NL to field women into the parliament reflects the efforts of political elites to ghettoise women's political participation. The patriarchal resistance of the political elite to real change (Kenny 2013) leads to a politics of bricolage. Not disrupting the political elites is considered here as a protection of the political system. As Sater maintained, "the presence of women itself does not change the structure of power in the political system" (Sater 2007: 737).

The interviewed female MPs confirmed that quotas make women visible but on the sideline of so many hard political issues. They also stressed that quota reform mechanisms refer directly to the principles of charity and in no way to the respect of the fundamental human rights of women. The same attitude is stressed in a recent study which states that "women MPs do not want to be elected because they are women. They want to compete on equal terms with men" (Jossour Forum des Femmes Marocaines 2017). Another local female politician expressed her dissatisfaction with gender quotas

> where are we from equality and parity? The attitudes of political parties and society are negative. We perceive the quota as a gift and we (women) are like a decor. We are not given any responsibility and we are confined to the social, the sport or the cultural commissions. Before I worked without quota and I was more comfortable. It is the clientelism that prevails (girl, sister, stepdaughter …) at this level. Everything has been divided. The way to equality is still very long.[22]

By designing exclusive lists for women, the discriminatory gender division of gender roles has been maintained in representative political institutions. A Human Right activist pointed that

> women's exclusive national lists show clearly how the political decision-makers are co-opting with changes, not genuinely seeking gender equality as prescribed by the Constitution.[23]

An exclusive national list strengthens that women's integration in politics is constructed around notions of their difference from men, rather than equality. Gender quota is accepted as long as it does not shake the political privileges of male elites. Specifically, the supplementation strategy used did not threaten at all men's MP's district seats. The multiplicity of mechanisms for promoting women's political participation, promulgated shortly on the eve of the four elections, reveals a politics of experimentation that is not grounded on a comprehensive and informed strategy for the political empowerment of women. The *politics of charity* used to include women at first, followed by a *politics of quota extension by supplementation* to include more of them later in response to the uncertain political context of post-spring revolutions are good examples of double-edged politics that fluctuates between integrating *and sidelining* women. More importantly, the Moroccan case indicates that openning new breakthroughts for women in politics coexists with consolidating the patriarchal and clientelist political structures.

Conclusion

Whose empowerment is being sought by the design and reform of the Moroccan version of RS, the state's empowerment or the women's empowerment? This chapter tried to answer this question by using an institutionalist critical approach of RS that traces their evolution and sees if they are being used as principled positive measures addressing the question of women's political underrepresentation or they serve well beyond that other political interests. This chapter made the case against the unique design and reform of RS in Morocco and showed that Morocco succeeded in institutionalizing various safety valves to include women in parliament but it failed in ruling out women's marginalization. In doing so, the Moroccan case stresses many findings of previous works (Htun 2003; Franceschet and Piscopo 2008; Krook 2009; Burnet 2011). We argued that these measures resulted in serious counter-productive outcomes: (1) institutionalizing segregation; (2) recruiting token women; (3) engendering clientelism; (4) and finally leading to de-democratization. We conclude that the most successful quota in numerical terms (i.e., RS) is unlikely to contribute to long-term change of political party dynamics related to recruitment practices and therefore probably not a sustainable change in case they are removed. The very modest increase of women's representation outside the national list in Morocco shows that men's control of the district seats have never been contested in the first place even after four elections of gender quota adoption and reform.

The Moroccan case, then, shows that RS do not reflect principled concerns to empower women, on the contrary quotas have many other strategic functions. First, they are convenient institutional mechanisms that do not primarily allow a substantial and equal redistribution of power among male and female MPs. Second, they can be easily adapted to the features of the political context and structure without challenging the status quo.

As it has been demonstrated, RS, which seem to be as a win-win solution for the state and women, hide underneath a double-edged political strategy with both positive and negative effects on women and democratization. This is a strong a proof for the non-linear aspect of democratization. Under the layers, de-democratization is likely to happen at the very moment we think there is a visible ceding and decentralization of power. The institutional perspective provides a proof that the political opening to women and youth alike, via quota mechanisms, serves the state before it serves women and youth alike. The Moroccan quota system with all the institutional mechanisms which started by using the logic of charity and experimentation, then moved to legislation and supplementation and lastly generated sidelining and segregation for quota women make a strong case for a dire need for changing the actual Moroccan quota provisions. Having said this, this does not mean that gender quotas lead only to unintended consequences. Many rather positive outcomes can be perceived as short and long-term outcomes of the implementation of quotas in Morocco. For instance, the surrogate representation of women empowers quota women to act as watch dogs of the appropriateness of the gender policies implemented. The rising pace of legal reforms, for instance, affecting women's rights enacted since the adoption of quotas in 2002 is a strong proof for the role of quota women beside many other socio-political activists.

However, voluntary political openings to youth and women to participate in politics and how this is being done should not be taken for granted as whole heartedly positive. There is a strong connection between quota designs and the entitlements (spatial and functional dispositions) they allow for women MPs. The Moroccan case in this respect speaks to universal patterns of how state responses to women's demands for more political representation reinforce the status quo and reproduce new dynamics that stabilize male dominance (Dahlerup 2018a; Norris 2006). Fast track change, when dragged from above, could be in fact a reinvention of male dominance that cedes power in a very deliberate and controlled way that pose limits for a genuine appropriation of power.

It remains that the best solution for the Moroccan version of RS is to diversify the paths of women's entry to the parliament by introducing new institutional mechanisms ensuring that women are not downgraded and stigmatized because of the quota that got them elected, i.e., for instance candidate quotas for district seats by law, including rank order rules as in Algeria and the zipper-systems as in Tunisia. All in all, triumph in one battle of inclusion in politics does in way mean that women have won the war against gender-based discrimination.

Notes

1. The social attributes associated with being male and female and the relationships between women, men, girls and boys. These attributes and relationships are socially constructed and are learned through socialization. Sex and gender do not mean the same thing. While sex refers to biological differences, gender refers to social differences, which can be modified since gender identity, roles and relations are determined by society.
2. General Recommendation No. 5 (seventh session, 1988) The Committee on the Elimination of Discrimination against Women, http://www.un.org/womenwatch/daw/cedaw/recommendations/recomm.htm#top.
3. See International IDEA project at https://www.idea.int/data-tools/data/gender-quotas/reserved-overview.
4. Patronage system is a mechanism of elite circulation and regime support—lacking significant opposition and comprised of a mixture of rural notables, tribal leaders, and urban elites and businessmen loyal to the regime.
5. Brand (1998: 10) defines state feminism as "policies directed from the state leadership level, which aim at mobilizing or channeling women's (re) productive capabilities and coopting them into support for the state through such programs as raising literacy, increasing access to the labor market, establishing state-sponsored women's organizations."
6. Loi organique no 27-11 relative à la Chambre des représentants [Organic Law No. 27-11 on the House of Representatives], http://www.adrare.net/XYIZNWSK2/elements/pdf/loi_chambredesrepresentants.pdf.
7. Extract from the Message addressed by HM King Mohamed VI on December 19, 2008, to the "1st meeting of Moroccans in the world" organized by the CCME (Council of the Moroccan Community Abroad) in Marrakech.
8. The Family Code (Moudawanna) was revised in 2004 with the participation of civil society, and expanded the rights of women in areas such as guardianship, marriage and child custody, and access to divorce.
9. European Parliament 2017 "Delegation to Morocco—17–20 July 2017: Briefing note for FEMM Members", http://www.europarl.europa.eu/RegData/etudes/BRIE/2017/596801/IPOL_BRI(2017)596801_EN.pdf.

10. This authority is known as Autorité pour la parité et la lutte contre les discriminations (Authority for Parity and the Fight Against discrimination: APALD).
11. Organic Law 16-20, 11 August 2016. http://www.chambredesrepresentants.ma/sites/default/files/loi-organique_20.16_ar.pdf.
12. Organic Law No. 59-11 (2011) relating to the election of the members of the councils of the local authorities, http://www.sgg.gov.ma/Portals/0/lois/Loi_59.11_Fr.pdf?ver=2015-12-15-115855-490.
13. Organic Law No. 34-15 (2015) relating to the election of the members of the councils of the local authorities, http://www.sgg.gov.ma/Portals/0/lois/Loi-organique_34.15_Fr.pdf?ver=2015-12-15-120034-117.
14. Interview, female MP for RNI, lawyer and president of NGO called *Union of Feminine Action* (UAF), April 2013.
15. Interview, female MP for the PJD, April 2013.
16. Interview, male MP, member in the executive committee at IP, April 2013.
17. Interview with a female activist, responsible for the political participation of women in the CNDH, April 2013.
18. Tanmia (2017) Evaluation des mécanismes de promotion de la représentation politique des femmes au Maroc, http://www.tanmia.ma/evaluation-des-mecanismes-de-promotion-de-la-representation-politique-des-femmes-au-maroc/. Interview, female MP for the PJD, April 2013; Interview, female MP for RNI, lawyer and president of NGO called *Union of Feminine Action* (UAF), April 2013; Interview, female MP, member of the political office of the political party of Union Constitutional (UC), April 2013.
19. Informal interview with feminist activists and civil society activists.
20. Informal interview, female member of a feminist association Jossour Forum of Moroccan Women, December 2017.
21. Interview with a male MP, member in the executive committee at IP, April 2013.
22. Interview with a female University professor and political activist elected at the communal elections for three mandates. Cited in Tanmia (2017) Cited in: http://www.leseco.ma/maroc/65222-les-limites-de-la-discrimination-positive.html
23. Interview with a female activist, responsible for the political participation of women in the CNDH, April 2013.

References

Arendt, C. M. (2018). From critical mass to critical leaders: Unpacking the political conditions behind gender quotas in Africa. *Politics & Gender, 14*(3), 295–322.

Belarbi, A. (2012). *Egalité-Parité: Histoire Inachevé*. Casablanca: Editions Le Fennec.
Benabdellah, M. A. (2001). *Propos sur l'évolution constitutionnelle au Maroc* [Considerations on the Constitutional Evolution of Morocco]. https://fr.scribd.com/document/348181509/Evolution-Constitutionnelle.
Bennani, C. M. (2008). Hommes d'affaires versus profs de fac. La notabilisation parlementaire d'un parti de militants au Maroc. *Revue internationale de politique comparée, 15*(2): 205–219.
Bjarnegard, E., & Zetterberg, P. (2011). Removing quotas, maintaining representation: Overcoming gender inequalities in political party recruitment. *Representation, 47*(2), 187–199.
Brand, L. (1998). *Women, the state, and political liberalization*. New York: Columbia University Press.
Burnet, J. E. (2011). *Women have found respect: Gender quotas, symbolic representation and female empowerment in Rwanda* (Paper 3). Anthropology Faculty Publications. http://scholarworks.gsu.edu/anthro_facpub/3.
Bush, S. (2015). *Forms of international pressure and the Middle East*. Project on Middle East Political Science. http://pomeps.org/2015/08/21/forms-of-international-pressure-and-the-middle-east/.
Dahlerup, D. (Ed.). (2006). *Women, quotas and politics*. London: Routledge.
Dahlerup, D. (2018a). *Has democracy failed women?* Cambridge: Polity Press.
Dahlerup, D. (2018b). Gender equality as a closed case: A survey among the members of the 2015 Danish parliament. *Scandinavian Political Studies, 41*(2), 188–209.
Dahlerup, D., & Freidenvall, L. (2005). Quotas as a "fast track" to equal representation for women: Why Scandinavia is no longer the model. *International Feminist Journal of Politics, 7*(1), 26–48. https://doi.org/10.1080/1461674042000324673.
Dalmasso, E., & Cavatorta, F. (2010). Reforming the family code in Tunisia and Morocco: The struggle between religion, globalisation and democracy. *Totalitarian Movements and Political Religions Journal, 11*(2), 213–228.
Daoud, Z. (1993). *Feminisme et Politique au Maghreb: Septs Décennies de Lutte*. Casablanca: Eddif.
Darhour, H., & Dahlerup, D. (2013). Sustainable representation of women through gender quotas: A decade's experience in Morocco. *Women's Studies International Forum, 41*(2), 132–142.
El Moussalli, J. (2011). *The feminist movement in modern Morocco: Directions and issues (in Arabic)*. Rabat: Publications of the Moroccan Centre for Studies and Modern Research and Top Press.
Ennaji, M. (Ed.). (2007). *Société Civile, Genre et Développement*. Fès: Publications de l'Université de Fès.

Franceschet, S. (2011). Gendered institutions and women's substantive representation: Female legislators in Argentina and Chile. In M. Krook & F. Mackay (Eds.), *Gender, politics and institutions*. London: Palgrave Macmillan.
Franceschet, S., & Piscopo, J. M. (2008). Gender quotas and women's substantive representation: Lessons from Argentina. *Politics and Gender, 4*(3), 393–425.
Freedom House. (2018). *Democracy in crisis: Freedom in the world 2018*. https://freedomhouse.org/sites/default/files/FH_FITW_Report_2018_Final_SinglePage.pdf.
Freidenvall, L., & Krook, M. L. (2011). Discursive strategies for institutional reform: Gender quotas in Sweden and France. In M. L. Krook & F. Mackay (Eds.), *Gender, politics and institutions*. London: Palgrave Macmillan.
Goetz, A. M. (2003). The problem with patronage: Constraints on women's political effectiveness in Uganda. In A. M. Goetz & S. Hassim (Eds.), *No shortcuts to power: African women in politics and policy making* (pp. 110–139). New York: Zed.
Goetz, A. M., & Hassim, S. (Eds.). (2003). *No shortcuts to power: African women in politics and policy making*. Cape Town: Zed Books.
Goulding, K. (2009). Unjustifiable means to unjustifiable ends: Delegitimizing parliamentary gender quotas in Tunisia. *Al-Raida, 126–127*, 71–77.
Grajzl, V. D. and Obasanjo, I. (2019). Do parliamentary gender quotas decrease gender inequality? The case of African countries. *Constitutional Political Economy*. https://doi.org/10.1007/s10602-018-09272-0.
Htun, M. (2003). *Sex and the State: Abortion, divorce, and the family under Latin American dictatorships and democracies*. Cambridge: Cambridge University Press.
Jossour Forum des Femmes Marocaines. (2017). *Evaluation des mécanismes de promotion de la représentation politique des femmes au Maroc*. Fondation Friedrich Ebert.
Karpowitz, C. F., Mendelberg, T., & Shaker, L. (2012). Gender inequality in deliberative participation. *American Political Science Review, 106*(3), 533–547.
Kenny, M. (2013). *Gender and political recruitment: Theorizing institutional change*. New York: Springer.
Krook, M. L. (2009). *Quotas for women in politics: Candidate selection reform worldwide*. Oxford: Oxford University Press.
Kulawik, T. (2009). Staking the frame of a feminist discursive institutionalism. *Politics and Gender, 5*(2), 262–271.
Kymlicka, W. (1995). *Multicultural citizenship: A liberal theory of minority right*. Oxford: Clarendon Press.
Lloren, A. (2014). Gender quotas in Morocco: Lessons for women's descriptive and symbolic representation. *Representation, 50*(4). https://doi.org/10.1080/00344893.2014.979224.

Longwe, S. H. (2000). Towards realistic strategies for women's political empowerment in Africa. *Gender and Development, 8*(3), 24–30.

Lovenduski, J. (1998). Gendering research in political science. *Annual Review of Political Science, 1,* 333–356.

Mansbridge, J. (2003). Rethinking representation. *American Political Science Review, 97*(4), 515–528.

Meier, P., & Lombardo, E. (2010). *Towards a new theory on the symbolic representation of women.* Paper presented to APSA Annual meeting, Washington, DC, September.

Nanivadekar, M. (2006). Are quotas a good idea? The Indian experience with reserved seats for women. *Politics and Gender, 2*(1), 119–128.

Norris, P. (2006). *Fast track strategies for women's representation in Iraq and Afghanistan: Choices and consequences.* 102nd American Political Science Association Annual Meeting APSA 2006.

Pitkin, H. F. (1967). *The concept of representation.* Berkeley and Los Angeles: University of California Press.

Sadiqi, F., & Ennaji, M. (2011). *Women in the Middle East and North Africa: Agents of change.* Abingdon: Routledge.

Sater, J. N. (2007). Changing politics from below? Women parliamentarians in Morocco. *Democratization, 14*(4), 723–742.

Sater, J. N. (2012). Reserved seats, patriarchy, and patronage in Morocco. In S. Franceschet, M. L. Krook, & J. M. Piscopo (Eds.), *Impact of gender quotas.* New York: Oxford University Press.

Sater, J. N. (2017). Patronage and democratic citizenship in Morocco. In R. Meijer & N. Butenschøn (Eds.), *The crisis of citizenship in the Arab world.* Brill: Leiden.

Shalaby, M. (2016). Women's political representation and authoritarianism in the Arab World. In *POMEPS women and gender in Middle East politics.* https://pomeps.org/wp-content/uploads/2016/05/POMEPS_Studies_19_Gender_Web.pdf.

Touhtou, R. (2012). *Debating civil society in Morocco: Dynamics of gender, development and social capital.* Germany: Lambert Academic Publishing.

Tripp, A. M., & Kang, A. (2008). The global impact of quotas: On the fast track to increased female legislative representation. *Faculty Publications: Political Science, 41.* http://digitalcommons.unl.edu/poliscifacpub/41.

Waylen, G. (2009). What can historical institutionalism offer feminist institutionalists? *Politics and Gender, 5*(2), 245–253.

Waylen, G. (2012). *Understanding institutional change: A gender perspective.* Paper presented to CPP Seminar, Manchester, November.

Welborne, B. C. (2010). *The strategic use of gender quotas in the Arab World.* Arlington: IFES. http://iknowpolitics.org/en/learn[.......]egic-use-gender-quotas-arab-world.

Index

A
African Union (AU), 13, 14, 33
age groups, 258, 259, 264–272, 274
Algeria, 15, 17–19, 23, 34, 39, 53, 98, 102–106, 108, 110–120, 122–124, 126, 127, 136, 139, 141, 142, 144–148, 151, 157, 158, 160, 169, 171, 173, 174, 205–207, 210–217, 224, 225, 231, 251, 298
Algerian women's activism, 159
Al Nahda, 164
ANC, 265
anti-Westernism, 141, 145, 146, 148, 149, 152
Arab Barometer (AB), 121, 125, 139, 141, 144, 149, 151
Arab Spring, 2, 3, 6, 10, 24, 39, 59, 108, 114, 133–135, 138, 143–147, 149–151, 164, 171–173, 179, 180, 182, 192, 198, 206, 212, 221. *See also* Arab Uprisings

Arab Uprisings, 2, 4, 6, 8, 10, 13, 29, 132, 134, 135, 137, 144, 149, 150, 181, 241, 247, 250, 262, 287. *See also* Arab Spring
Asia Pacific, 5
Association Démocratique des Femmes des Maroc (ADFM), 57, 166
Association of Algerian Muslim Women (AFMA), 160
Association of Tunisian Women for Research and Development (AFTURD), 164, 171, 174
authoritarian, authoritarianism, 8, 34, 73, 100, 107, 118, 160, 164, 180, 199, 206–209, 225, 226, 232, 233, 250, 257, 259, 283, 294

B
Badran, Margot, 50, 75, 76, 138, 239
Bahrain, 15, 151, 211, 214–216
Bangladesh, 32

Ben Ali, Zine El Abidine, 163–165, 171, 174, 218, 257, 259, 266
Berber, 51, 61, 63–65, 67, 69, 210
Bourguiba, Habib, 163, 164, 174, 266
Bouteflika, Abdelaziz, 119, 161

C

candidates, 26, 27, 31–35, 37, 40, 41, 169, 171, 180, 186, 187, 195, 196, 198, 220, 238, 239, 252, 258, 259, 261, 265, 266, 268, 269, 273, 274, 281, 284–286, 288, 289, 291–293, 298
CAWTAR, 20
CEDAW. *See* Committee on the Elimination of Discrimination against Women (CEDAW)
"Center", 38, 49–51, 60, 62–64, 66, 67, 75, 79, 83, 126, 132, 135, 138, 184, 190, 198
Christians, 68, 81, 151, 238
Christian cops, 37
Civil society organizations (CSOs), 7, 8, 19, 20, 162, 163, 174, 186, 237
civil war, 141, 145, 147, 149–151, 157, 161, 162, 206
clientelism, 293, 295, 296
Code of personal status (CPS), 163
Collectif 95 Maghreb Egalité, 158
colonisation, colonialism, 8, 50, 51, 72, 73, 163
committee assignments, 40, 233–236, 240–242
Committee on the Elimination of Discrimination against Women (CEDAW), 14, 15, 19, 21, 22, 32, 38, 41, 57, 72, 74, 75, 79, 80, 82–90, 163, 168, 171, 185, 193, 195, 197, 199, 225, 281, 282, 298
conservatives, 22, 38, 50–56, 60–62, 73, 74, 78, 101, 102, 113, 114, 116, 122–124, 160, 161, 184, 196, 206, 218, 234
constitutions, constitutional, 7, 14, 16, 17, 21, 24, 36, 39, 61, 68, 162, 170, 192, 205–209, 212–217, 221–223, 225, 241, 259, 260, 262, 287, 299
counter-productive effects, 281, 282, 290
CSO's. *See* Civil society organizations (CSOs)
culture, 5, 8, 29, 36, 63, 64, 67, 68, 71, 83, 98–101, 121, 124, 141, 160, 161, 182, 208, 210, 222, 242–244, 248, 249, 287, 290
  cultural change, 2, 38, 98, 100, 101, 103, 109–112, 114–117, 120, 121, 124, 125
  cultural shifts, 98, 101, 109

D

Dahir, Berber, 51, 67, 68
de-colonization, 50, 67, 74, 104
democracy, 1, 2, 4–6, 8, 13, 21, 31, 32, 51, 60, 61, 63, 77, 79, 80, 98, 102, 107, 108, 118–121, 124, 158, 159, 185, 196, 210, 225, 262, 279, 280, 283, 287, 288
  de-democratization, 41, 280, 296, 297
  democratic process, 181, 197, 199
  democratization, 1–4, 8, 38–40, 50, 56, 57, 74, 97–103, 108, 109, 121, 124, 125, 158, 162, 165–168, 171, 172, 208, 209, 259, 261, 262, 264, 274, 275,

280, 281, 287, 288, 290, 294, 297
Democratic Association of Moroccan Women, 57, 84
descriptive representation. *See* representation
development, 1–4, 6, 8, 9, 16, 18–21, 24, 25, 35, 40, 41, 55, 64, 73, 79, 84, 99, 100, 107, 114, 119, 125, 127, 147, 149, 157–163, 168, 170, 172, 194, 225, 242–244, 248, 265, 273, 280, 287
discrimination, 3, 15–17, 21, 28, 32, 84, 85, 90, 107, 162, 166, 168, 170, 172, 173, 205, 215, 220, 222, 224, 233–235, 283, 284, 288, 299
district seats (DS), 239, 240, 282, 294, 296, 298
divinity, 89

E

Economist Intelligence Unit's Democracy Index, 5
education, 3, 11, 18, 20, 28, 31, 37, 52–55, 61, 64, 73, 98, 100, 104–107, 109, 111–114, 118, 119, 122, 123, 125, 126, 133, 140, 142, 158, 161, 165, 167, 170, 172, 174, 182, 209, 215, 233, 234, 243–245, 248, 249, 270, 271, 273, 274
Egypt, 9, 12, 15, 17–20, 22–26, 32, 34, 35, 41, 50, 53, 83, 98, 102, 104–106, 108, 110–118, 120, 122–124, 126, 139–141, 144–146, 148, 151, 179–182, 184, 186, 187, 189, 190, 199, 212, 213, 215, 221, 226, 231, 262, 283
Egyptian Center for Women's Rights, 35

electoral systems, 26, 27, 33, 34, 36, 106, 239, 285
elites, 3, 7, 158, 183, 185, 186, 293, 298
emancipation, 8, 10, 54, 55, 157, 158, 161, 164, 168, 173
Eurasia, 5
Europe, 5, 209, 233, 235

F

Family law, 22, 23, 50, 54, 57, 58, 65, 69, 85, 112, 114, 124, 158, 160–163, 165–167, 172, 174, 209–213, 215, 216
20-February Movement, 60–62, 64, 68, 69
female legislators, 40, 233–236, 240–243, 247, 250, 270
feminism(s), 3, 7, 9, 10, 16, 38, 39, 57, 72, 74–77, 79, 82, 87, 89, 114, 124, 132–152, 160, 163, 165, 174, 283, 298. *See also* Islamic feminism
feminist movement, 9, 10, 13, 24, 27, 28, 56, 63–65, 68, 72, 75, 77, 79, 87–89, 124, 141, 161, 167, 172, 194, 223, 292. *See also* women's movement
Freedom House, 5, 6, 41, 98, 158, 173, 237, 287
Front de Libération Nationale, 169

G

gender
  gender differences, 84, 89, 233, 249
  gendered history, 51
  gender issues, 16, 49–52, 56, 66, 67, 138, 173
  gender policies, 7, 280, 294, 297
Gender Inequality Index, 46

Gender quotas, 2, 6, 11, 14, 24, 25, 31–37, 98, 105–107, 138, 262, 280–284, 290, 291, 295, 297. *See also* quotas
Gender Quotas Database, 46
Global Database on Violence Against Women, 23
Global gender gap report/Gender gap report, 172
global perspective, 3, 6, 24, 284
Green parties, 32

H
Hakkaoui, Bassima, 170, 197, 198
Hanoune, Louisa, 161, 169
Huntington, Samuel, 81, 99

I
ICRAM, 19, 21, 170
identity, 27, 28, 51, 52, 54, 61, 64–69, 75, 101, 137, 138, 148, 149, 194, 263, 266, 298
ideological positioning, 9. *See also* reference system
  conservative, 51
  ideological trends, 51, 88
  Islamist, 9, 51, 88
  secular, 10, 51
Ijtihad, 57, 74, 79
implementation, 20, 33, 35, 40, 41, 79, 170, 173, 195, 223, 232, 237, 239, 241, 261, 263, 264, 266, 273, 290, 291, 297
inclusion, 3–5, 12–14, 50, 63, 65, 102, 103, 107, 124, 261–264, 274, 275
Inglehart, R., 2, 80, 100, 208, 262
inheritance, 23, 24, 36, 79, 83, 84, 163, 167, 168, 172, 175, 211, 217
institutional mechanisms, 41, 283, 297, 298
institutions, 6–11, 16–20, 29, 30, 36, 64, 102, 105, 107, 169, 171, 180, 181, 183, 185, 187, 192, 195, 209, 210, 212, 222, 224, 225, 232, 233, 235, 236, 251, 282, 283, 291, 294, 295
international agreements, 183, 185, 186, 189, 190, 195, 198, 199
  international community, 182, 186, 187, 189, 198
  international conventions, 14, 20, 74, 83, 185, 222, 223
International norms, 16
Inter-Parliamentary Union (IPU), 41, 126, 231, 238, 262, 265
interpretations of the Qur'an, 56, 63
intersectional, 28, 37, 40, 258, 263, 268, 273
  intersectional view, 37
Iran, 104, 185
Iraq, 15, 18, 34, 136, 139, 141, 144–146, 148, 151, 211–215
Islam, 38
  Islamic jurisprudence, 206, 216, 217
  Islamism, 8–10, 66
  Islamization, 55, 164
  political Islam, 9, 50, 55–58, 66, 67, 74, 75, 171, 194
Islamic extremism, 39
  Islamic fundamentalists, 161
Islamic feminism, 2, 75–78, 88, 194
Islamists, 5, 7, 9, 10, 28, 38, 39, 50, 51, 55, 56, 58–63, 66, 68, 74, 75, 77, 79, 82, 84, 85, 89, 136, 162, 164, 167, 171, 172, 174, 179–182, 184, 186, 187, 191–199, 207, 209, 217–219, 221, 225, 237, 238, 247, 260
Istiqlal Party (IP), 53, 286, 299

J
Jordan, 15, 34, 40, 105, 126, 139, 141, 144–148, 151, 210, 211, 214, 215, 231, 232, 237, 239–245, 247, 248, 251, 252, 282
Justice and Benevolence (JP), 58, 61

K
Kuwait, 15, 211–214

L
leadership, 4, 10, 12, 40, 61–63, 117, 118, 124, 188, 189, 194, 199, 232–236, 240–252, 258, 259, 264, 271–274, 298
Lebanon, 15, 33, 34, 136, 139, 141, 144–146, 148, 151, 209, 211–214, 216
Left parties, 32
legal reforms, 16, 22–24, 161, 162, 287, 297
  family law, 22
  legal system, 5, 22, 39, 206, 207, 210, 212, 217, 226
  nationality law, 22
legislative committees, 232, 233, 235, 236, 240–243, 250
legislative elections, 193, 261, 275, 280, 282, 284, 294
legitimacy, 12, 36, 40, 78, 86, 87, 183, 225, 226, 279, 282–284, 290, 291
liberal, 2, 22, 31, 38, 77, 107, 160, 167, 184, 189, 194, 198, 260
Libya, 34, 98, 105, 106, 110–120, 122–124, 136, 146, 211, 212, 214, 215

M
Maghreb, 5, 12, 17, 23–25, 36, 39, 50, 73, 103, 205–207, 209, 210, 212–217, 222, 225, 226
male dominance, 11, 29, 31, 297. *See also* patriarchy
  dimensions of, 30
Maliki law, 226
marginalization, 38, 41, 49, 51, 67, 86, 106, 125, 158, 179, 234, 296
Marsad Majles, 265, 271
members of parliament (MPs), 29, 40, 106, 207, 237–242, 245, 247–249, 258, 264–275, 280, 286, 290, 291, 293–297
MeToo, 30, 31
Middle East, 5, 39, 49, 206, 207, 209, 210, 212, 216, 226, 281
modernists, 38, 50–56, 59–62, 74
Moghadam, Valentina, 2, 4, 50, 75, 77, 102–105, 108, 126, 127, 131, 132, 134, 135, 138, 140, 141, 149, 158, 172, 173, 194, 232
monarchy, 55, 180, 184, 192, 193, 196, 197, 237, 238
Moroccan women's activism, 165, 171
Morocco, 9, 15, 17–19, 21, 23–25, 34, 35, 37, 39–41, 51–54, 56–59, 61, 64, 66–68, 79, 81, 84, 85, 88, 98, 102, 105, 106, 108, 110–124, 126, 139–146, 148, 151, 157–159, 167–173, 175, 179–182, 184, 186, 192–194, 198, 199, 205–207, 210–217, 221–223, 225, 231, 251, 262, 272, 280, 281, 283, 284, 287, 288, 292, 294, 296–298
MPs. *See* members of parliament (MPs)
Mudawana, 165–168. *See also* Family law

Multiparty system, 169
Muslim Brotherhood (MB), 39, 102, 145, 179–181, 186–192, 199

N

National Constituent Assembly (NCA), 171, 257–261, 264, 267, 269, 275
national strategies, 16, 18–20
National women machineries (NWMs), 17, 18, 20
Nazra for Feminist Studies, 12, 35
Nidåa Tounès Party, 268, 273
Non-Government organizations (NGO's), 12, 14, 17, 19, 20, 22, 41, 57, 60, 63, 64, 158, 159, 164, 166–170, 190, 299
Nordic countries, 24, 25, 32
norms diffusion, 39, 99, 132–135, 138, 149–151
North Africa, 49, 66, 98, 103, 109, 117, 119, 124, 125, 157, 158, 172, 226
NWMs. *See* National women machineries (NWMs)

O

OECD, 20
Oman, 15, 211, 212, 214
opportunity structures, 2, 9, 10, 185, 225
Organisation of Democratic and Popular Action (OADP), 57

P

Pakistan, 32, 282
parity, 13, 14, 33, 104, 171, 214, 220, 222–224, 226, 258–260, 264, 267, 268, 288, 295
parliamentary elections, 136, 180, 187, 195, 237, 238, 270, 281
Party of Justice and Development (PJD), 58, 59, 68, 69, 79, 145, 180, 181, 193–199, 225, 286, 291
patriarchy, 9, 29, 55, 56, 63, 101, 161. *See also* male dominance
patriarchal structures, 2
Penal Code, 23, 24, 64, 162, 168
People's Representatives Assembly (PRA), 264, 267–269
Personal status law, 24, 160, 211
Platform for Action, 13, 16, 17, 41
political context, 39, 68, 157, 181, 187, 191, 199, 281, 287, 297
political elites, 10, 36, 72, 103, 161, 188, 217, 225, 262, 275, 280, 291, 293, 295
political opportunity structures (POS), 39, 179, 191, 192
political participation, 5–7, 13, 17, 34, 39, 105, 142, 157, 162, 170, 172, 173, 179, 185, 187, 194, 199, 205, 215, 257, 266, 280, 287, 288, 295, 296, 299
political parties, 5, 7, 26, 27, 32, 33, 39, 40, 53, 55, 57, 75, 79, 102, 136, 168–170, 184, 186–190, 192, 193, 195, 197–199, 217, 222, 225, 237, 252, 258, 263, 264, 270, 281, 282, 284–286, 292, 293, 295, 296
political reforms, 62, 171, 172, 193, 259, 279, 288
Politics as a workplace, 30
positive measures, 296
Progress and Socialism Party (PPS), 57, 286
protests, 2, 6–8, 12, 39, 52, 54, 61, 64, 68, 134–138, 140, 141,

144–151, 171, 180, 188, 197,
    221, 247, 259
  large-scale protests, 39, 136, 151
public life, 2–4, 12, 21, 32, 37, 104,
    171, 174
public opinion, 5, 135, 136, 141, 144,
    149, 196
  public support, 39, 132, 135,
    144–147, 149, 150, 166

Q
Qatar, 15, 210, 211, 214, 215
quotas
  legislated quotas, 32
  quota candidates, 275
  quota design, 36, 40, 280, 289, 297
  quota elected women, 280, 290,
    291
  quota provision, 37, 40, 239, 280,
    282, 287, 290, 297
  quota reform mechanisms, 294, 295
  reserved seats, 32, 34, 35, 40, 223,
    261, 280, 281
  tandem quotas, 258, 263, 264, 267,
    268
  voluntary party quotas, 32, 281
Qur'an, 59, 65, 76, 77

R
reference system, 74, 82
regime change, 2, 59, 262
religion, 9, 50, 52, 54–56, 58, 59,
    63, 65, 68, 76, 77, 81, 83, 101,
    132–134, 137, 139, 140, 148,
    149, 151, 179, 189, 206–210,
    216, 217, 219–221, 262
religiosity, 139, 140, 217, 226
representation
  descriptive representation, 36, 236,
    242, 259, 264, 269, 274, 290,
    291

  substantive representation, 27, 28,
    35, 36, 259, 263, 264, 270,
    283, 284, 291, 292
  symbolic representation, 27, 40,
    258, 259, 264, 265, 269, 274,
    291
  underrepresentation, 30, 198, 281,
    290, 294, 296

S
Salafists, 164, 167
SDGs. *See* Sustainable Development
    Goals (SDGs)
sectarian protests, 141, 145, 146,
    148–151
secular, 2, 9, 18, 28, 39, 50, 51,
    55–60, 63–69, 73–76, 78, 80–82,
    84, 87, 89, 149–151, 157, 159,
    161–164, 166, 167, 172, 182,
    184–187, 189, 190, 196, 198,
    199, 208, 210, 218, 221, 260
secularists, 22, 38, 51, 55, 56,
    59–61, 63, 68, 78, 82, 182,
    217–219
secularization, 57, 74, 209, 212
Sharia, 210, 212, 213, 215, 217, 221
sidelining, sidelined, 2, 30, 65, 89,
    138, 232, 234, 235, 265, 297
Skalli, Nouzha, 170
social-democracy, 4, 38, 107–109,
    118–121, 124
socio-political structures, 132, 135,
    137, 144, 145, 147–149
state, 7–11, 16, 21, 27, 38–40, 50, 54,
    56–58, 61, 63, 65, 73, 81, 82,
    90, 98, 103, 104, 106–108, 118,
    119, 123, 126, 134, 137, 159,
    164, 166, 168, 170, 171, 174,
    180, 182–185, 189, 192, 193,
    208–210, 212, 215, 219–225,
    275, 296–298
Sub-Saharan Africa, 5, 24

Substantive representation, 27, 28, 36, 259, 263, 264, 270, 283, 284, 291, 292. *See also* representation
Sudan, 14, 15, 34, 139, 141, 144–146, 148, 151, 152
supplementation, 280, 288, 290, 295, 297
Sustainable Development Goals (SDGs), 12, 19, 21

T

tandem quotas, 40, 258, 263, 267, 268. *See also* quotas; youth quotas
token women, 291, 296
Tounès, Nidaa, 268, 269, 273
Tunisia, 9, 15–19, 21–25, 33, 34, 39, 40, 79, 98, 102, 105, 106, 108, 110–117, 119, 120, 122, 124, 126, 136, 139, 141, 144–146, 148, 151, 152, 157, 158, 163, 164, 169, 171–174, 205–207, 209, 210, 212–221, 225. 231, 251, 258–262, 264, 266. 273, 274, 283, 298
Tunisian Association of Democratic Women (ATFD), 164, 171, 219
Tunisian women's activism, 163
Turkey, 104, 181, 185, 191

U

uncertainty, 2, 3, 6, 7, 9, 10, 49, 50, 58, 63, 66, 67, 150
UNDP, 4, 19, 20, 127, 141, 265
unified legal system, 39, 207, 210, 212, 226
Union de l'Action Feminine (UAF), 57, 166, 299
Union nationale des femmes algériennes (UNFA), 160

United Arab Emirates (UAE), 211, 213, 214, 216
United Nation (UN), 3, 10, 12, 13, 20, 71, 74, 82, 86, 101, 102, 125, 175, 184, 185, 190, 207, 265
universal, 10, 56, 72, 75, 76, 78, 82–84, 89, 123, 167, 168, 217, 220, 221, 223, 285, 297
UN Women, 84, 86, 90
UN World Congress on Women, 32

V

VAW. *See* Violence against women (VAW)
Violence against women (VAW), 11, 18, 20, 23, 24, 28, 85, 106, 159, 161, 168, 190, 220

W

Wassila Network, 162
West, 4, 9, 31, 51, 54, 66, 71, 81, 211
women's activism, 1, 2, 9–12, 39, 57, 82, 158, 159, 163, 171, 172, 181, 191
women's empowerment, 1, 3, 4, 7, 9, 10, 17, 20, 22, 38, 40, 80, 98, 100–103, 106, 108, 109, 114, 121, 124, 125, 131–134, 139, 158, 162, 168, 172, 280, 281, 296
  economic empowerment, 104, 105, 107, 108, 113–116, 122, 123
  political empowerment, 10, 18, 21, 38, 98, 102, 105, 116–118, 123, 124, 294, 296
  social empowerment, 104, 108, 111–113, 122, 123
women's interests, 13, 27–29, 36
women's movements, 4, 5, 9–12, 16, 24, 33, 35, 39, 66, 135, 138,

141, 145–147, 150, 157, 170, 174, 185, 206, 225, 226, 238, 257, 260, 279, 288, 292, 293
women's political representation, 2, 6, 24, 27, 36, 106, 142, 169, 233, 240, 284, 286–288
women's rights, 2–5, 8, 10, 11, 14, 16, 17, 20, 22, 24, 38–40, 49–52, 56–60, 62–64, 66, 67, 72–79, 82, 89, 133, 137–139, 146, 157, 158, 161–163, 165–167, 171, 172, 174, 180, 182–185, 189, 190, 193, 194, 198, 199, 205–209, 212–214, 216–221, 225, 226, 260, 280, 293, 297
World Values Surveys (WVS), 38, 80, 81, 100, 108, 109, 111, 121, 125, 139, 144, 149, 151
WVS. *See* World Values Surveys (WVS)

Y
Yemen, 15, 136, 139, 141, 144–149, 151, 211–214
young women, 37, 40, 54, 62, 65, 66, 165, 258, 259, 264, 265, 269–271, 273, 274, 284, 286
youth, 21, 26, 37, 40, 49, 59, 64, 66, 103, 124, 242–244, 248–250, 257–262, 264–267, 271–273, 275, 288, 289, 297
youth quotas, 258–262, 264, 266, 268–270, 273–275. *See also* quotas

Z
zipper-system, 258, 298. *See also* quotas

Printed by Printforce, the Netherlands